Quranic Schools in Northern Nigeria

In a global context of widespread fears over Islamic radicalisation and militancy, poor Muslim youths, especially those socialised in religious seminaries, have attracted overwhelmingly negative attention. In northern Nigeria, male Qur'anic students have garnered a reputation for resorting to violence in order to claim their share of highly unequally distributed resources. Drawing on material from long-term ethnographic and 'participatory' fieldwork among Qur'anic students and their communities, this book offers an alternative perspective on youth, faith, and poverty.

Mobilising insights from scholarship on education, poverty research, and childhood and youth studies, Hannah Hoechner describes how religious discourses can moderate feelings of inadequacy triggered by experiences of exclusion, and how Qur'anic school enrolment offers a way forward in constrained circumstances, even though it is likely to reproduce poverty in the long run. A pioneering study of religious school students conducted through 'participatory' methods, this book presents vital insights into the concerns of this much-vilified group.

Hannah Hoechner is a postdoctoral researcher in anthropology and migration studies at the University of Antwerp and the Université libre de Bruxelles. She completed her doctorate at the University of Oxford and has conducted extensive ethnographic research in Nigeria, Senegal, and the US. Her work has been published in *Africa, Children's Geographies, Qualitative Research, International Journal for Social Research Methodology, European Journal of Development Research*, and *Afrique Contemporaine*. As part of her work in Nigeria, she has produced the 'participatory' docudrama *'Duniya Juyi Juyi – How life goes'*, which won the Africast 2012 Special Award for 'Participatory Video for Development'.

THE INTERNATIONAL AFRICAN LIBRARY

General Editors

LESLIE BANK, *Human Sciences Research Council, South Africa*
HARRI ENGLUND, *University of Cambridge*
ADELINE MASQUELIER, *Tulane University, Louisiana*
BENJAMIN SOARES, *University of Florida, Gainesville*

The International African Library is a major monograph series from the International African Institute. Theoretically informed ethnographies, and studies of social relations 'on the ground' which are sensitive to local cultural forms, have long been central to the Institute's publications programme. The IAL maintains this strength and extends it into new areas of contemporary concern, both practical and intellectual. It includes works focused on the linkages between local, national, and global levels of society; writings on political economy and power; studies at the interface of the socio-cultural and the environmental; analyses of the roles of religion, cosmology, and ritual in social organisation; and historical studies, especially those of a social, cultural, or interdisciplinary character.

For a list of titles published in the series, please see the end of the book.

Quranic Schools in Northern Nigeria

Everyday Experiences of Youth, Faith, and Poverty

Hannah Hoechner

International African Institute, London

and

CAMBRIDGE
UNIVERSITY PRESS

CAMBRIDGE
UNIVERSITY PRESS

University Printing House, Cambridge CB2 8BS, United Kingdom

One Liberty Plaza, 20th Floor, New York, NY 10006, USA

477 Williamstown Road, Port Melbourne, VIC 3207, Australia

314–321, 3rd Floor, Plot 3, Splendor Forum, Jasola District Centre,
New Delhi - 110025, India

79 Anson Road, #06-04/06, Singapore 079906

Cambridge University Press is part of the University of Cambridge.

It furthers the University's mission by disseminating knowledge in the pursuit of
education, learning, and research at the highest international levels of excellence.

www.cambridge.org
Information on this title: www.cambridge.org/9781108425292
DOI: 10.1017/9781108348270

© Hannah Hoechner 2018

First published 2018

Printed in the United Kingdom by Clays, St Ives plc

A catalogue record for this publication is available from the British Library

ISBN 978-1-108-42529-2 Hardback

To the *almajirai*

Contents

Figures

Maps

Tables

Acknowledgements

This book has benefited from many people and institutions. First and foremost, I give thanks to all the *almajirai* who participated in my research, who confided in me and who allowed me into their lives. Some of them shared with me aspects of their personal life stories that, out of shame or for other reasons, they otherwise kept to themselves. I sincerely hope that they will agree with my representation of their lives, and feel I was worthy of their trust. Special thanks are owed to the nine youths participating in our film project – Sadisu Salisu, Naziru Usman, Ikira Mukhtar, Kabiru Idris, Buhari Murtala, Anas Ali, Abdullahi Yahaya Sa'ad, Auwal Mahmud, and Isma'il Abdullahi – who have shared their time and insights generously with me. Sadisu, moreover, has been an excellent research assistant as I completed this book, updating me on the situation in Kano after my departure and complementing my knowledge of the *almajirai*'s lives. I would also like to express my deep gratitude to the *malamai* in Kano who welcomed me into their schools, especially Malam Ahmadu at Sabuwar Kofa, Malam Nasiru, Malam Usman, and Malam Ahmed in Albasu, Malam Dan Daho in Daho, Malam Maisittin at Kofar Famfo, and Malam Gali at Tashar Kasuwar Rimi. It was a great honour to learn from them.

Many people in Kano went out of their way to accommodate me and my research. Special thanks for this go to Bashir Albasu, the *Hakimi* of Albasu, and his family, especially Hajiya and Gwaggo, who generously hosted me; to Rahila Yakubu, Bashir Albasu, and Ishaq Abdallah for their valuable assistance; to Usman Aliyu for his careful transcriptions; and to Auwalu Indabawa and Nasiru Bappah Muhammad for the extra miles they walked during our film project. I am lucky that I had the chance to meet Hajiya Talatu at Sabuwar Kofa, 'Yar Wudil and Hauwa Ibrahim in Albasu, and Biba in Daho, to name just some of the many women who supported me openhandedly and whose wisdom and kindness were great sources of inspiration. I am grateful to the ESSPIN (Education Sector Support Programme in Nigeria) team in Kano, especially Yardada Maikano and Lola Alao, to the Child *Almajiri* Empowerment and Support Initiative (CAESI), especially Hajiya Rakiya and Samuel Enaboakpe, and to Fiona Lovatt and the boys at *Gidan*

Almajirai for offering me their time and insights. I thank the people at the Department of Mass Communication, Bayero University Kano, especially Umar Faruk Jibril, at Mambayya House, at the Centre for Research and Documentation, and at the Development Research and Projects Centre, as well as Malam Kiyawa, Aminu Sharif Bappa, and Uba Abdalla Adamu for generously sharing knowledge and contacts. Muhammad Sarki and the people at the Centre for the Study of Nigerian Languages endeared their language to me and had patience with me even when I had lost mine. Finally, I am grateful to Abbe Katerega, Susan Elden, Frank Roger, Victoria Crawford, and Haidar Sulaiman for their hospitality and friendship.

Numerous people have provided feedback on pieces of this book or its arguments in various forms. I am grateful to Abdul Raufu Mustapha, who was a wise and gentle mentor during my DPhil and afterwards. His untimely passing is a great loss to me. Heartfelt thanks go to Laura Camfield for her inspiration, guidance, and encouragement ever since I started my MPhil. I am deeply grateful to Murray Last for the thorough scrutiny and sympathetic advice he generously offered me over the years. Thanks also go to the wider ODID (Oxford Department of International Development) community for many engaging discussions, intellectual inspiration, and moral support. In Oxford, I am grateful to Masooda Bano, Gina Crivello, and Jan-Georg Deutsch, who sadly passed away before this book was completed, for providing feedback at different stages of my MPhil and DPhil. In Belgium, the LAMC (Laboratoire d'Anthropologie des Mondes Contemporains) at the Université libre de Bruxelles and CeMIS (Centre for Migration and Intercultural Studies) at the University of Antwerp provided accommodating and stimulating working environments as I completed this manuscript. I thank my colleagues at these institutions for their ideas, care, and encouragement. Various fellow researchers I met along the way have also provided precious support. I thank Olly Owen, Andrew Walker, Carmen McCain, and Pete Kingsley for sharing their insights, contacts, and time with me. I thank Adam Higazi for numerous exchanges and careful feedback on several parts of the manuscript. Phil Ostien provided me with newspaper articles on *almajirai*. I am grateful to Joel Noret, Anneke Newman, Insa Koch, Ina Zharkevich, Colm Massey, and Aurélien Baroiller, who provided thoughtful comments on earlier versions of several chapters.

Special thanks are owed to Robert Launay and Elsbeth Robson for their insightful and constructive feedback on the manuscript, which helped me much improve my work. As this book drew towards completion, Stephanie Kitchen at the International African Institute provided excellent editorial support. I thank Miles Irving for his diligent work on the maps, Rohan Bolton for compiling the index, and Judith Forshaw for careful copy-editing. I am grateful to Fiona Lovatt and Susan Elden for permission to use their photographs, and to Claire Allard for help designing the cover page.

Financial support from the German Academic Exchange Foundation, the German Academic Scholarship Foundation, the Wiener-Anspach Foundation, and the Fonds Wetenschappelijk Onderzoek – Vlaanderen is gratefully acknowledged. I also give thanks to the Goethe Institute Kano for making our film project possible through its generous funding and support, and for giving permission for our film *'Duniya Juyi Juyi – How Life Goes'* to be displayed on the Cambridge University Press website.

Finally, I would like to thank my family and friends for their patience, trust, and encouragement, from which I drew the necessary confidence to complete this book. While many more deserve mention, Katharina Rall, Insa Koch, Julian Bank, Maria Mancilla Garcia, Nora Khayi, and Julien Beghain were particularly important for me on this journey, and I thank them with all my heart.

Earlier versions of the chapters in this book have appeared in the articles '"Nous voulons les professeurs de hadiths!" Almajirai, éducation islamique "moderne" et exclusion dans le nord du Nigeria' (*Afrique Contemporaine* 257, 2016, pp. 91–104); 'Porridge, piety, and patience: young Qur'anic students' experiences of poverty in Kano, Nigeria' (*Africa* 85(2), 2005, pp. 269–88); 'Mobility as a contradictory resource: peripatetic Qur'anic students in Kano, Nigeria' (*Children's Geographies* 13(1), 2015, pp. 59–72); 'Participatory filmmaking with Qur'anic students in Kano, Nigeria: "speak good about us or keep quiet!"' (*International Journal of Social Research Methodology* 18(6), 2015, pp. 635–49); 'Islamic Education in Nigeria' (*Oxford Islamic Studies Online*, 2013); 'Striving for knowledge and dignity: how Qur'anic students in Kano, Nigeria, learn to live with rejection and educational disadvantage' (*European Journal of Development Research* 23(5), 2011, pp. 712–28); the book chapters '"People will think you are nobody": how Qur'anic students in Nigeria struggle for respect and knowledge' in Anna Strhan, Stephen G. Parker, and Susan Ridgely (eds), *Bloomsbury Reader in Religion and Childhood* (Bloomsbury Academic, 2017, pp. 165–72); 'Growing close where inequalities grow large? A patron for Qur'anic students in Nigeria' in Catherine Allerton (ed.), *Children: ethnographic encounters* (Bloomsbury Academic, 2016, pp. 127–30); 'Experiencing inequality at close range: almajiri students and Qur'anic schools in Kano' in Abdul Raufu Mustapha (ed.), *Sects and Social Disorder: Muslim identities and conflict in northern Nigeria* (James Currey, 2014, pp. 98–125); 'Traditional Qur'anic students (*almajirai*) in Nigeria: fair game for unfair accusations?' in Marc-Antoine Pérouse de Montclos (ed.), *Boko Haram: Islamism, politics, security and the state in Nigeria* (African Studies Centre Leiden, 2014, pp. 63–84); 'Striving for knowledge and dignity:

young Qur'anic students in Kano, Nigeria' in Marisa O. Ensor (ed.), *African Childhoods: education, development, peacebuilding, and the youngest continent* (Palgrave Macmillan, 2012, pp. 157–72); and as part of the book *Searching for Knowledge and Respect. Traditional Qur'anic students (almajirai) in Kano, Nigeria* (IFRA-Nigeria, 2012). Permission to publish this material here is gratefully acknowledged.

Note on translation and anonymisation

Translations from Hausa are mine. Where I feel that a Hausa term carries additional meaning not covered by the English term, I include the original Hausa term in brackets. When I did not tape-record conversations, I noted down informants' statements from memory as soon as possible. While I saved particularly noteworthy words and expressions in my mobile phone immediately, I may not always have retained the exact wording of longer exchanges.

I have anonymised participants who did not want to be mentioned by name, or where I felt that it was necessary to protect their identity, for example because they talked to me in confidence or off guard, or about issues that are sensitive. In some instances I have changed not only the names of informants but also other information that would make it possible to identify them.

Map 1 Kano State

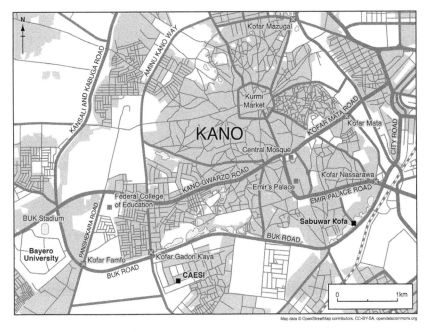

Map 2 Kano City

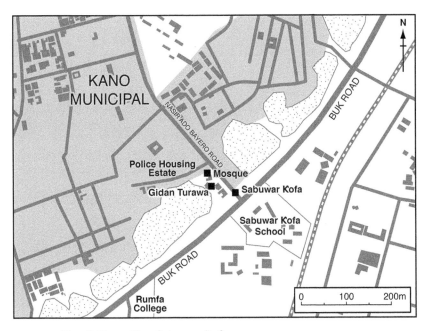

Map 3 Kano City, Sabuwar Kofa

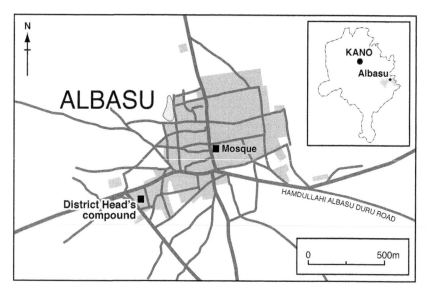

Map 4 Albasu

1 Porridge, piety, and patience
Qur'anic schooling in northern Nigeria

'Your family eats their porridge without stew!' proposed Abdulmalik, a seven-year-old boy in a football jersey several sizes too big. This sentence was a good example of an insult, I was told. Jokingly I had complained to the children in Albasu, a village in eastern Kano State in northern Nigeria where I lived for four months, that nobody had gone to the trouble yet of teaching me swear words in Hausa, the region's lingua franca. Surely, I would do well to fill this gap in my language skills! I had come to northern Nigeria to research Qur'anic schools there,[1] and the boys and young men who study in them experience a vast amount of abuse in their daily lives. By asking about the insults they hear from the people who consider them nuisances, I was hoping to learn more about such experiences of abuse.

Most Hausa dishes consist of cereal porridge (*tuwo*) eaten with a stew (*miya*) that is made, for example, from baobab tree leaves, okra, or pumpkin and spinach. Having to eat the sticky *tuwo* on its own indicates dire food deprivation. I was surprised to learn that labelling someone as being food-deprived was abusive, especially as this came from a boy who himself, by most definitions, would be considered poor. Poverty is both deep and widespread in Kano, particularly in rural areas. This is evidenced, for instance, by high malnutrition rates. An estimated 46.3 per cent of children under five years of age in Kano State are stunted (too short for their age) and 28.9 per cent of them severely so, which indicates long-term undernutrition. An estimated 17.1 per cent of children under five years old in Kano are two or more standard deviations below the median weight for children of that height, which points to moderate to severe wasting (National Population Commission 2009: 382). Even porridge *with* stew does not necessarily provide children with the necessary balance of essential nutrients and vitamins, and many families cannot afford to buy fruit or meat. To learn that young people in Kano experience poverty as embarrassing or even insulting disconcerted me. How

---

[1] To avoid the loaded term 'traditional', I refer to the schools I studied as either 'classical Qur'anic schools' or simply 'Qur'anic schools'. Whenever I discuss Qur'anic schools departing from the classical model (such as so-called *Tahfeez* schools, 'modernised' Qur'anic schools), I will note this specifically.

was it possible that poverty, despite being pervasive, has such a negative connotation in northern Nigeria today, even among the poor? What did this imply for the ways in which poor people relate to others who are poor and to the better-off in society? Finally, what did it mean for the young Qur'anic students with whom I was conducting my research?

Most of the students living in Qur'anic schools in northern Nigeria are – by all common definitions – poor. The *almajirai* (singular: *almajiri*), as they are called in Hausa, deriving from the Arabic term *al-muhajir* or migrant,[2] are boys and young men from primary school age to their early twenties. They leave their homes – mostly located in rural areas – to live with a religious teacher, or *malam* (plural: *malamai*), and to study the Qur'an. Qur'anic schools are common in both rural and urban areas.[3] Usually, teachers in such schools receive no salary but live off the support given by the local community, the alms received in exchange for their spiritual services, the contributions of their students, and supplementary income-generating activities. Most teachers are themselves products of the Qur'anic education system. Schools operate informally and largely outside the purview of the state. Similar schools exist across the West African Sahel.[4] Many schools follow the seasonal rhythms of the region in that individual students, and entire schools, migrate in accordance with agricultural work cycles. Many students return home during the rainy season to help their parents farm, while others visit their families for the major Muslim holidays, but some do not see their parents for years. Girls may attend Qur'anic schools as day students, but, unlike boys, they do not leave home to live with a Qur'anic teacher.

Most Qur'anic schools do not have the means to provide for their students' upkeep. Whereas in rural areas, to earn their living, the *almajirai* collect fodder and firewood or work as farmhands, including on their teachers' farms, in urban areas they must seek other sources of livelihood. Older students wash clothes, carry loads, and engage in petty trade or handicrafts.[5] Younger students are employed as domestic workers, or beg for food and money in their neighbourhoods and on the streets,

---

[2] The term echoes the Prophet's *hijrah* from Mecca to Medina, indicating its religious connotations.

[3] In Hausa, the Qur'anic schools in which the *almajirai* learn are often referred to as *tsangaya*; however, strictly speaking, this term refers only to Qur'anic schools in remote rural places. *Almajirai* can also be found in less remote areas and in urban schools, where they often study alongside day students. Such schools are commonly referred to as *makarantun allo* (literally: wooden tablet schools; singular: *makarantar allo*).

[4] Similar schools exist as far east as Darfur (Seesemann 1999).

[5] The *almajirai* in my research all positioned themselves unambiguously as either 'older' or 'younger' students, depending on whether they considered adult gender norms fully applicable to themselves (usually from about 15 years upwards). Many of them did not know their exact biological age. In Hausa, young *almajirai* (about seven to 11) are called *kolo*, adolescent *almajirai* (about 12 to 18) are called *titibiri*, and advanced students and assistant teachers are referred to as *gardi* (plural: *gardawa*).

which makes them a highly visible feature of the urban landscape. Many urbanites consider begging *almajirai* a nuisance.

Living arrangements in most Qur'anic schools are frugal to say the least, and often the teacher's (or teachers') compound constitutes a school's only premises. This means that many students spend their nights barely sheltered from the elements in canopied forecourts or in the open. Even those who can secure a place in the entrance room (*soro*) of their teacher's compound have to contend with leaking roofs, dirt, and the smell of urine. In urban areas, where water and space are scarce, Qur'anic students struggle to find places to wash and relieve themselves. Students also face difficulties as they try to earn the cash needed to buy soap and occasionally new clothes. Given the crowded conditions in many Qur'anic schools and the lack of hygiene and sanitation facilities, infections and infestations are frequent and communicable diseases spread easily.[6] Tattered clothes and skin diseases have become a trademark of the *almajirai*.

Qur'anic schools are, of course, not the only place where young northern Nigerians can learn about religion. 'Modern' Islamic schools or *Islamiyya* schools, whose teaching technologies resemble the secular education introduced under British colonial rule, became increasingly popular from the 1970s onwards, especially in urban areas. They combine Qur'anic study with instruction in other Islamic subjects. Many of them are run as private enterprises and levy set fees to cover teachers' salaries and school running costs. Qur'anic schools, on the other hand, rarely fix fees. Instead, students are expected to reciprocate the education they receive by contributing their labour and paying long-term allegiance to their teacher. This makes Qur'anic schools accessible even to the poorest.

Poverty is thus an inherent feature of the *almajiri* system. Many people find this alarming. To understand why, it is instructive to look at wider discourses about poverty, masculinity, and religion. Poverty has often been cited as a condition that predisposes boys and young men to problematic behaviours. Some authors, such as the proponents of the 'youth bulge hypothesis' (e.g. Kaplan 1994; Urdal 2004), have projected scenarios of youth exclusion fuelling frustration, which in turn translates into violence. In a global context of widespread and deep-seated fears of Islamic radicalisation and militancy, poor Muslim boys and young

---

[6] Damen et al. (2011) found that over 80 per cent of the *almajirai* participating in their study in Konduga, Borno State, had intestinal parasites. Kabir et al. (2005), conducting research with *almajirai* in Gwale, Kano State, found skin diseases to be a major problem, with 23 per cent of their respondents suffering from scabies, and 8 per cent from ringworm infections. Dr Mahmoud Nasir, whom I interviewed at the Hospital for Infectious Diseases in Kano, mentioned cholera and meningitis as major health threats for *almajirai* (21 October 2011). Eating leftover food, moreover, puts *almajirai* at risk of getting stomach illnesses (e.g. Fada 2005: 37–9).

men in particular have quickly been linked to violent outcomes (see, e.g., Beehner 2007).

Meanwhile, institutions of Islamic learning, which often cater for poor boys and young men, have become the subject of anxious attention among journalists, policymakers, and academics who examine the presumed links between Islamic education and militancy, especially in South Asia (see, e.g., International Crisis Group 2002; Fair 2007; Winthrop and Graff 2010). Influential think tanks and publishing houses such as the Brookings Institution and *Foreign Policy* have written about Islamic educational institutions as 'terrorist training schools' (Singer 2001) and 'universities of jihad' (Haqqani 2002; see also Goldberg 2000). Their teaching pedagogy has been equated to rote learning and indoctrination, which supposedly leaves boys no room for independent or critical thinking (e.g. Friedman 2001).

Not least since the rise of the Islamist terror group Boko Haram,[7] crisis discourses about boys and young men in Qur'anic schools have become widespread in Nigeria, too (including among academics; see, e.g., Onuoha 2011; Aghedo and Eke 2013). In an article in the magazine *Newsweek*, Nobel laureate Wole Soyinka (2012), for example, writes about the followers of Boko Haram that 'economic factors have facilitated the mass production of these foot soldiers' who can now be 'rendered pliant, obedient to only one line of command, ready to be unleashed at the rest of society. They were bred in madrassas and are generally known as the almajiris.'

Are we right to consider poor boys and young men – and those studying in Islamic schools in particular – tinder easily ignited by radical

---

[7] Boko Haram, which most commentators translate as 'Western education is forbidden', is an exonym coined by the people of Maiduguri and taken up widely by the media as a label for the northern Nigerian Islamist insurgency group, which gained notoriety for its repeated attacks on secular educational institutions, including the spectacular abduction of 276 schoolgirls from the Government Girls' Secondary School Chibok (in southern Borno State) in April 2014. The group itself has used the name *Ahl al-Sunna li-l-Da'wa wa-l-Jihad*, or 'People Committed to the Propagation of the Prophet's Teachings and Jihad'. Today, the insurgents are split into at least two opposing factions, one of which claims allegiance to ISIS. Violence related to the insurgency has caused bloodshed on a massive scale across the region. Borno State Governor Karim Shettima, drawing on estimates by community leaders, puts the total death toll at almost 100,000 (Tukur 2017). (Since most deaths are not reported, estimates based merely on media reporting, such as those put forward by the Nigeria Security Tracker, are likely to significantly underestimate the actual death toll.) Escalating violence since 2014 has caused massive displacement across north-eastern Nigeria and the neighbouring countries. According to the International Organization for Migration (IOM) Displacement Tracking Matrix (http://nigeria.iom.int/dtm), over two million people were displaced within Nigeria alone. According to the United Nations Office for the Coordination of Humanitarian Affairs (UNOCHA), some 200,000 people have fled across the border to neighbouring Niger, Chad, and Cameroon (www.unocha.org/nigeria). UNOCHA puts the total number of displaced persons across the region at 2.4 million. Prolonged conflict and displacement have resulted in a huge humanitarian crisis. According to UNOCHA, in 2017 over 5.2 million people needed urgent food assistance in north-eastern Nigeria alone.

religious ideas, as these discourses suggest? How do young Muslims experience poverty? What role does faith play in their lives? To my surprise, many of the older *almajirai* I met joked about their own and each other's material hardships. They boasted that not even spoiled food could upset their stomachs today after months and years of eating whatever they could get hold of. They bragged that their bodies had grown so used to the mosquitoes infesting their shabby sleeping places that they no longer felt their bites. They spoke in conspiratorial voices about the foods that only *almajirai* had managed, by the force of circumstances, to acquire a taste for, such as *kwaki*, dry cassava flakes that are soaked in water and effectively quell one's feelings of hunger, or *gajala*, which is created by mixing together various food leftovers.

I was reminded of boy scouts by these displays of toughness. Given the inevitable hardships involved in Qur'anic schooling, I was told that no *almajiri* would fail to train himself in patience. Patience (*hakuri*) is an indispensable skill and a crucial part of moral personhood in a context where individuals are expected to subordinate their wishes and desires to socially sanctioned norms and authorities, and where people's hopes and future plans are often shattered by difficult economic, social, and political circumstances. Patience and humility, moreover, are central elements of faith: God moves in mysterious ways, and the faithful are expected to accept his will unquestioningly.

Seen from such an angle, Qur'anic schools appear ideally placed to teach boys the necessary skills to become self-sufficient and socially acceptable men as well as good Muslims. The *almajirai* did not hesitate to interpret their difficulties as having an educational purpose when they were confronted with disparaging attitudes about their poverty. Inusa, for example, an *almajiri* who was roughly 15 years old, declared in one of our discussions that 'especially now that there is *boko* ['modern' school], if you come for *almajiri* education, some people think it's because you don't have food in your house, that's why you come out to beg. But it's not like that; it's because you're searching for knowledge.'

If Abdulmalik and his example of an insult offer us insights into the dominant conceptions of poverty within northern Nigerian society, Inusa's statement challenges these dominant conceptions. This suggests that the *almajirai*, and poor young people more generally, are not only recipients of the dominant norms of society. They also actively contest and reinterpret norms that disparage them. Religious discourses about the educational worth of particular experiences may thereby provide a vocabulary with which to defy stigmatising norms. Religious discourses may help to moderate feelings of inadequacy and shame triggered by experiences of exclusion, and thus help poor youths maintain a positive outlook with regard to themselves and their lives.

Yet, how sustainable are such discourses? Can they cancel out experiences of frustration entirely? And, more importantly, what do they imply for the politics of poverty and the struggle for social justice? While the *almajirai* in my research emphasised the educational value of hardship, they simultaneously sought to conceal as best they could their own financial difficulties and those aspects of their life histories that were shaped by poverty. Like Inusa cited above, many *almajirai* declared that *almajiri* enrolment had nothing to do with difficult circumstances in their rural homes. Their reluctance to link their education system to rural poverty raises questions about the chances for a politics of poverty to get off the ground.

This ties in with wider questions about the role Qur'anic schools play in the (re)production of poverty. Within policy circles, Islamic schools spark concern as presumed obstacles to universal basic education, jeopardising children's opportunities to acquire economically useful skills (e.g. Adetayo and Alechenu 2012). Most Qur'anic schools in Nigeria focus narrowly on teaching to read, write, and recite the Qur'an; specialised Islamic fields of study are the preserve of advanced learners, and in most cases 'modern' secular subjects do not form part of the curriculum. Many commentators conclude from this that the *almajirai* will lack 'the practical skills required in the real world to contribute meaningfully to modern society, or even to earn a livelihood' (Suleiman 2009).

It is true that the *almajirai*'s chances of escaping poverty as they come of age are slim. In a context of protracted economic crisis, avenues to social mobility are increasingly foreclosed to the rural poor. But can we conclude from this that the *almajirai* would be better off in 'modern' secular schools, as meritocratic discourses about such schools as 'springboards for social mobility' (Levinson and Holland 1996: 5) have it? What role do wider social relations play in the (re)production of disadvantage?

This book traces the trajectories of boys and young men through the Qur'anic education system. It makes their experiences its focal point, while embedding these experiences within the socio-economic, political, and religious/cultural context of contemporary northern Nigeria. Drawing on material from long-term ethnographic and 'participatory' fieldwork with Qur'anic students and their communities, the chapters in this book address questions that have been answered only cursorily so far. Why do boys and young men enrol in Qur'anic schools rather than in 'modern' education if this choice is likely to perpetuate their poverty? What experiences do they have in Qur'anic schools, and how do they deal with the destitution and denigration that inevitably accompany life as an *almajiri*? What role do religious discourses play for them, and to what extent do the *almajirai* seek to challenge the status quo? Finally, what consequences does the Qur'anic education system have for the future lives of the boys going through it, and what can this reveal about the wider processes underpinning protracted poverty in northern Nigeria today? While this book provides a detailed empirical account of the Qur'anic education system in northern Nigeria, it also uses the *almajirai*'s experiences as a prism through which to explore wider questions about the purposes and pitfalls of education, about the meanings of poverty and exclusion, and about the role that religion plays in the lives of poor boys and young men.

There are few ethnographies of Islamic schools that pay attention to the experiences of their students and to their wider social and economic contexts (for notable exceptions see Eickelman 1985 and Boyle 2004 on Morocco; Starrett 1998 on Egypt; Bano 2012 on Pakistan; see also the edited volume by Hefner and Zaman 2007). In-depth studies of Islamic schooling in sub-Saharan Africa are even rarer, even though questions about the role of education in social mobility and the reproduction of disadvantage are particularly pressing on the subcontinent, given both its youthful population (e.g. UNFPA 2014) and the high incidence of poverty. The works that exist tend to approach Islamic learning from either an Islamic studies perspective (e.g. Brigaglia 2009; Seesemann 2011; Tamari and Bondarev 2013) or a historical perspective (see especially Brenner 2000 on 'modern' Islamic schools in Mali; Ware 2014 on Qur'anic schools in Senegal; see also the edited volume by Launay 2016b).[8] While these works offer a range of important insights on the historical transformation of religious education systems in the region as well as on their doctrinal and epistemological underpinnings, they reveal little about Islamic students' present-day experiences.

A central argument I make in this book is that bringing insights from education studies, poverty research, and childhood and youth studies to bear on debates about young people in Islamic schools can allow us to develop a more profound understanding of the workings of religious educational systems, their students' experiences and the implications for wider society than is allowed for by the existing literature. If we want to understand the role played by institutions of religious learning in social reproduction and/or the (re)production of poverty and disadvantage, it does not suffice to look at them in isolation or at their curricula only. Rather, as anthropologists and sociologists of education suggest (e.g. Willis 1977; Bourdieu and Passeron 1990 [1977]), we have to look at the wider social and economic contexts in which educational decisions are taken, including religiously motivated ones (e.g. Bano 2012). Also, we need to consider the factors that determine who can translate particular forms of knowledge and skills into gainful opportunities in the future. In this book, I describe how Qur'anic education becomes a way forward for poor boys and young men in the context of a declining rural economy, a public education system in disarray, and frequent family break-ups. If the *almajiri* system is likely to (re)produce poverty in the long run, we

---

[8] For a detailed literature review, see Chapter 4.

cannot understand this without reference to the adverse terms on which its students participate in society, and especially in the labour market.

Another consideration highlighted by education scholars is that educational experiences are inherently gendered (e.g. Stambach 2000). To understand the appeal of the *almajiri* system to rural parents, we must study their ideas about the gender-appropriate upbringing of boys. Also, by studying the *almajirai*'s schooling experiences along the lines of gender, we can understand the boys' emerging self-conceptions and struggles to conform to normative notions of masculinity. Such an analysis can shed light on the *almajirai*'s at times problematic relationships with other members of society – notably women – while simultaneously rebutting stereotypical depictions of male Islamic students as inherently prone to violence.

Furthermore, I argue that it is not sufficient to study the curricula and doctrinal orientations of Qur'anic schools to understand what their students learn. As both education scholars and scholars of childhood and youth have argued insistently, young people are not passive recipients of experience (e.g. James and Prout 1997 [1990]), but are actively engaged in constructing the social worlds around them. This means that they do not mechanistically or linearly learn what they are being taught in school (e.g. Starrett 1998: 11ff.; Levinson and Holland 1996: 1); rather, they actively engage with their schools' wider environments and make sense of the messages they receive through school in light of these broader experiences. Schools, then, are only one among many settings within which children acquire particular dispositions. In this book, I draw on these insights to highlight both the contextual factors that shape the experiences of young Qur'anic students and their 'capacity for action' (Mahmood 2001: 210) in dealing with these experiences. Being looked down upon by others in society because they are poor and lack 'modern' knowledge is a crucial experience for the *almajirai*. In this context, they eagerly take up religious discourses about the meritoriousness of asceticism and Qur'anic erudition promoted through their schools to maintain a positive view of themselves. Religion becomes a means to cope better with challenging circumstances. Yet, in a context where inequality and consumerism are pervasive, religious justifications for living in deprived conditions cannot entirely cancel out feelings of shame about being poor, or aspirations for urban, cosmopolitan lifestyles and 'modern' forms of knowledge, which are, however, difficult to achieve for the *almajirai*.

Insights from poverty research, which draw attention to the inherently social nature of experiences of poverty, can elucidate the implications of poverty-related shame for the ways in which the *almajirai* engage with others in society as well as for the forms of politics in which they may (or may not) engage. Struggling for recognition, the Qur'anic students seek to improve their relative position within society by hiding their poverty and by distancing themselves from others who are weak. Rather than rallying for redistribution and radical change, they pursue a respectable position for themselves at the cost of nurturing solidarity with people who are also negatively affected by the current configuration of power in northern Nigeria. The scorn that poverty attracts undermines both radicalising tendencies and positive social change. While this book holds on to the idea put forward by scholars of childhood and youth that young people are competent 'social actors' (e.g. James and Prout 1997 [1990]: vii), I hold this notion in productive tension with the emphasis that both studies of chronic poverty and seminal studies of education (see, e.g., Willis 1977; Bourdieu and Passeron 1990 [1977]) place on the wider structural power relations that constrain their 'capacity for action' (Mahmood 2001: 210).

Finally, methodologically and epistemologically, this book takes up the central tenet of childhood and youth studies that it is only by listening carefully to what young people have to say that we can understand their experiences and, in turn, the wider social implications of these experiences (e.g. Boyden 1997 [1990]). Capturing young people's experiences can be taxing, especially in a context where the age difference between researcher and research participants is compounded by differences in religion, ethnicity/nationality, socio-economic status, and gender, as in my case. Scholars of childhood and youth have urged us to think creatively about what methods can allow us to adjust to young people's preferred forms of communication so as to reduce inevitable power differentials (e.g. Boyden and Ennew 1997; Morrow 2001; Barker and Weller 2003) and to let them direct the research towards their most pressing concerns (e.g. Alderson 2001). This work has sought to overcome inevitable access challenges through both long-term ethnographic fieldwork and the use of 'participatory' methods, including the production of a 'participatory' film with and about almajirai.

A later part of this introduction gives an account of how these methods produced detailed insights into the lives and concerns of the almajirai. In the following section, I explore in more depth how I bring insights from education studies, poverty research, and childhood and youth studies to bear on the study of Qur'anic education in northern Nigeria. This is followed by a discussion of what the anthropology of Islam can contribute to our understanding of the almajiri system, situating the present study within these wider bodies of literature.

The (re)production of disadvantage through education

Education studies inform this book in that they put questions about the production and reproduction of inequality and disadvantage through education at the centre of the analysis. Early Western-based studies have focused primarily on how class inequalities become entrenched through schooling, for example by legitimising a skewed appreciation of (class-based) cultural styles, or by creating '"failure" as a social label' (Jeffrey et al. 2008: 9; see also Willis 1977; Bourdieu 1984; Bourdieu and Passeron 1990 [1977]). Education, in this reading, is a means through which the powerful can bolster their dominant position, not least because dominated groups end up taking an active part in their continued subordination, for instance by developing oppositional attitudes towards schooling or by curbing their aspirations for educational success (e.g. Willis 1977: 175). Bourdieu proposes the notion of 'habitus', which he defines as 'a system of durable, transposable dispositions' (1990a: 53), to capture the ways in which subordinated groups eventually 'cut their coats according to their cloth' (ibid.: 65) and stop pursuing 'what is already denied to them' (ibid.: 54).

Whereas an emphasis on class inequalities prevailed in the early works of Bourdieu and Willis, against the backdrop of changing social realities, with Fordism and blue-collar employment on the decline in Western countries and various forms of 'identity politics' gaining prominence, later authors have broadened the focus of their enquiries. They have stressed that various axes of social division operate simultaneously. These include not only class and race/ethnicity, but also gender and religion, which are crucial markers of difference in the context of the present study (see Gewirtz and Cribb 2003; Levinson and Holland 1996 for historical overviews; Starrett 1998: 12 on religious differences).

Furthermore, calls became louder to leave behind the grand theorising and latent determinism of the early approaches, and to acknowledge instead local variation, the indeterminacy of outcomes, and people's 'agency'. Levinson and Holland (1996), for example, propose to analyse educational practices as geared towards producing a locally and historically defined 'educated person', and emphasise that educational institutions are at best 'a contradictory resource for those who would fit the young to a particular vision of society' (ibid.: 1), as within them even hegemonic definitions of the 'knowledgeable person' can be challenged. Taking these criticisms on board, I contend that some of the concepts developed to explain the tenacity of class inequalities can nonetheless productively be transposed to other contexts of inequality/disadvantage. In this work, I draw, for example, on the Bourdieusian notion of 'habitus' to understand how families come to desire forms of education that appear to reproduce their own disadvantage (see Chapter 4).

While the insights offered by the anthropology/sociology of education can help us understand the political nature of what it means to be 'educated' in particular contexts, and draw attention to unevenly distributed chances of acquiring such knowledge (Chapters 3, 4 and 8), I argue that it is not enough to look merely at the processes surrounding 'education', even if we define such processes widely, if we want to understand how disadvantage and poverty become (re)produced. This is particularly true for the example of the *almajirai*, who, as subsequent chapters will explore, are not merely 'learners' but also workers who are adversely incorporated into the spiritual services economy (see Chapter 8) and into household economies as domestics (see Chapter 5). Finally, the *almajirai* provide the backdrop for negative projections that perpetuate their low status (Chapter 2). Arguably, we need to broaden our focus to include such processes. The next section, drawing on insights from chronic poverty research, proposes ways of thinking about such wider structural processes.

'Social exclusion' and 'adverse incorporation'

In recent decades, poverty researchers have increasingly sought to challenge narrow income- and expenditure-based definitions of poverty, and to defy the widespread assumption that poor people are poor because the processes of social and economic change taking place in their societies (and globally) have failed to reach them, as modernisation theories would have it (e.g. Ruggeri Laderchi et al. 2003). The insights of this growing body of literature are useful to understand how disadvantage becomes entrenched. Researchers at the Chronic Poverty Research Centre have put forward the conceptual pair of 'social exclusion' and 'adverse incorporation' to capture the causal processes underpinning chronic poverty (see Hickey and du Toit 2007). Social exclusion has been defined as 'the process through which individuals or groups are wholly or partially excluded from full participation in the society in which they live' (Deakin et al. 1995: 129). Adverse incorporation, on the other hand, denotes 'particular forms of interaction involving the state, market, community and household' and highlights 'the terms of inclusion in these institutional forms and . . . the relations that keep people poor over time' (Hickey and du Toit 2007: 4). I argue that, in combination, these two concepts can help us capture both the experiences of young people living in poverty and the processes that produce and sustain poverty over time.

These concepts acknowledge that poverty is a multidimensional experience, and one that is not conclusively defined by a lack of material possessions (see, for example, Sen 1999; Ruggeri Laderchi et al. 2003). What is more, they emphasise the relational and dynamic nature of poverty, thus drawing attention to its political nature. Arguably, poverty is not a 'residual' and static phenomenon; rather, disadvantage is produced through the 'active dynamics of social interaction' (Kabeer 2000: 84; see also de Haan 2011), including through processes of economic exploitation and symbolic devaluation.

It has rightly been queried whether the notion of 'social exclusion', which has emerged from concerns in European countries about the predicament of particular segments of society – the unemployed, people with disabilities, or older people, for instance (for a genealogy see Silver 1994; de Haan 1998) – is applicable to 'majority world' contexts where poverty is widespread and exclusion thus the norm (e.g. Hickey and du Toit 2007: 3). The concept begs the following question: exclusion from what? Not only do different societies define exclusion differently (see Silver 1994), but, what is more, defining 'normality' (or the absence of exclusion) is arguably particularly difficult in 'multipolar societies', where a conflict may exist 'between what is normal and what is desirable' (Ruggeri Laderchi et al. 2003: 23).

Given its wide remit, fluid boundaries, and context-dependent nature, the political utility of the term 'social exclusion' is indeed limited, not least because it risks diluting 'the political will to remedy the serious inequalities suffered by those at the extremes of exclusion' (Last 2000a: 219). Yet I argue that it can nonetheless prove useful as an analytical tool that draws attention to the social dimensions of experiences of poverty, to the role of society-wide criteria of accomplishment, and to the unevenly distributed chances of living up to these. This is particularly the case in contexts, such as in Nigeria, where differences in access to income, health, or education, and to the opportunities accompanying these, are enormous.

It has been argued that feelings of inadequacy are a central feature of people's experiences of poverty. Amartya Sen (1983: 159) contends that 'shame', alongside obvious deprivations such as starvation and hunger, is at the 'irreducible absolutist core' of the idea of poverty, a proposition seconded by Walker et al. (2013). Poverty-related shame, they argue, 'occurs as a reaction to the sense of failure in living up to societal expectations which, in turn, become internalised as personal aspirations' (Walker et al. 2013: 217).[9] Various authors describe powerfully how people's experiences of deprivation are exacerbated by knowing that others in society enjoy what they do not – or what they no longer have access to (e.g. Ferguson 1999: 236ff on feelings of 'abjection' on the Zambian Copperbelt; see also Katz 2004).

---

[9] Admittedly, the circumstances and behaviours attracting shame vary over place and time, and the feelings accompanying poverty locally may be better captured by other terms. Historical notions of shame in Hausaland have little to do with one's ability to procure material goods. *Kunya*, which means modesty, self-restraint or shyness (see Gaudio 2009: 208) as well as shame, refers to behaviour considered appropriate to a person's age, gender, and social status. *Kunya* also refers to a reluctance to publicly display affection, especially affection associated with sexual relations (see Last 2000b: 378). While poverty may not evoke shame in the sense of *kunya* in northern Nigeria, it certainly attracts disdain. Arguably, shame/disdain arising from a failure to procure material goods is most strongly felt in societies 'where consumerism is increasingly seen as the mark of success' (Chase and Walker 2013: 752).

Young people in particular are vulnerable to experiencing a gap between aspirations/desires and opportunities. This is the case not least because they are frequent targets of marketing efforts, 'creating among children and youth the desire for particular goods that are beyond their economic reach' (Hart 2008a: 20; see also Everatt 2000). Young people are also 'increasingly exposed via the international media to images of successful adulthood based upon education and professional employment', which raises their own and their families' aspirations and gives rise to a sense of failure if they do not achieve them (Jeffrey 2009: 496; see also Stephens 1995; Ruddick 2003; and Chapter 3). I draw on the concept of 'social exclusion' to capture the issues of stigma and low social standing that shape the daily experiences of boys in Qur'anic schools in northern Nigeria, who are unable to live up to their society's new standards of achievement (see Chapters 3 and 8).

A further criticism levelled at the notion of 'social exclusion' is that it arguably betrays an underlying 'moral meta-narrative' of inclusion as a desirable goal. While we are justifiably concerned about processes of exclusion, we cannot jump to the conclusion 'that "integration", "incorporation" and "inclusion" are necessarily panaceas for chronic poverty' (du Toit 2005: 41). Rather, we should carefully investigate the terms on which poor people participate in mainstream society. The concept of 'adverse incorporation' can help capture the often disadvantageous terms of this participation.

Building on the earlier work of exponents of 'dependency theory' and Marxist structuralism (e.g. Gunder Frank 1966; Dos Santos 1970), who focus on the problematic consequences of larger processes of societal change and capitalist economic restructuring, the concept of 'adverse incorporation' pushes us to think about the detrimental terms on which poor people often participate in mainstream society. For example, with reference to poor young people's integration into labour markets, the concept of 'adverse incorporation' draws attention to potentially exploitative conditions. Du Toit argues in relation to the South African labour market that '[a]ccounts of social exclusion can all too easily form part of an analysis that sees exclusion as the result of "extraneous" social factors – racism, ideology, policy, or politics – excluding (or de-incentivising) particular people from beneficial participation in the workings of an economy that is seen as value-free and intrinsically neutral' (du Toit 2005: 41). But, in fact, it is the workings of this very – capitalist – economy that lead to impoverishment (e.g. Bracking 2003).

Despite the origins of the concept of 'adverse incorporation' in 'dependency theory' and economic structuralism, its proponents have convincingly argued that its use can be extended beyond the economic and political realms to include analyses of cultural and symbolic power structures. Subsequent chapters explore how the concept of 'adverse incorporation' can help us understand, for example, the *almajirai*'s position within public discourses about them and the symbolic realm (Chapter 2), within an educational landscape that fosters aspirations yet offers few opportunities to realise them (Chapter 3), within domestic work arrangements and patron–client relationships (Chapter 5), and, finally, within the spiritual economy (Chapter 8).

The politics of cultural and economic (in)justice

The concepts discussed in the previous section help us understand the weak position in which poverty traps young people. I now turn to concepts that help theorise the difficulties they are likely to face when trying to overcome this position. Nancy Fraser (1996; see also Fraser and Honneth 2003) suggests thinking of different forms of disadvantage – or, in her terms, injustice – as a spectrum, with primarily economic forms of injustice (exploitation, marginalisation, deprivation)[10] at one end and primarily cultural ones (cultural domination, non-recognition, disrespect)[11] at the other. Yet, the distinction between economic and cultural forms of injustice is heuristic rather than real, given that different forms of injustice tend to coincide. Those social groups in the middle range of this imagined spectrum, which Fraser terms 'bivalent collectivities' (1996) or 'two-dimensional categories' (Fraser and Honneth 2003), suffer from both injustices simultaneously. As noted earlier, material deprivation connotes negatively in many places, exacerbating the injury inflicted upon poor people by their lack of material means. This indicates how central the simultaneity of cultural and economic injustices is to experiences of poverty.

Fraser's distinction between economic and cultural forms of injustice can help conceptualise the logics of action that follow from different forms of injustice:

Where disadvantage is largely economic, disadvantaged groups are likely to mobilise around their *interests*, and to formulate their demands in terms of *redistribution*. Where disadvantage is largely valuational [i.e. where people are regarded, and treated, as worth less than others], mobilisation is more likely to be around the question of *identity*, and demands to be formulated in terms of *recognition*. (Kabeer 2000: 86)

---

[10] Fraser (1996: 7) defines exploitation as 'having the fruits of one's labor appropriated for the benefit of others'. Economic marginalisation means 'being confined to undesirable or poorly paid work or being denied access to income-generating labor altogether'. Deprivation refers to 'being denied an adequate material standard of living'.

[11] For Fraser (1996: 7), cultural domination means 'being subjected to patterns of interpretation and communication that are associated with another culture and are alien and/or hostile to one's own'; non-recognition refers to 'being rendered invisible via the authoritative representational, communicative, and interpretative practices of one's culture'. Disrespect is defined as 'being routinely maligned or disparaged in stereotypic public cultural representations and/or in everyday life interactions'.

But what about groups that suffer from both economic and cultural disadvantage? Arguably, they find themselves trapped in 'particularly intractable forms of poverty' (Hickey and du Toit 2007: 2–3) as they need to straddle claims for redistribution of resources on the one hand, and claims for recognition of their dignity on the other. Yet, in practice, these claims risk being in tension with each other. If redistribution policies, for example, leave the underlying causes of inequality untouched, they risk 'creating stigmatized classes of vulnerable people perceived as beneficiaries of special largesse' (Fraser 1996: 46). Whatever increase in justice or equality is achieved on the redistribution front is lost on the recognition front if certain groups are singled out as 'needy', and thus risk being reviled as scroungers. Similarly, enhancements in status do not automatically translate into improvements in one's economic position, if, for example, in the attempt to recognise a group's 'agency' and freedom, paternalistic forms of support are withdrawn alongside paternalistic domination (Fraser 1996: 49ff.).[12]

'Adverse terms of trade' and symbolic violence

Fraser's notion of 'bivalent collectivities' or 'two-dimensional categories' is helpful to understand the logics that work against the interests of poor people as they try to improve their situation. How do poor people negotiate the tricky relationship between recognition and redistribution claims? I have described earlier in this chapter how the young Qur'anic students in my research, like other poor people, perpetuate discourses that disparage poor people, and engage in behaviours that are apparently detrimental to an agenda of social justice. Struggling for recognition, they cast *almajiri* education as a positive choice made to honour cultural and religious commitments, while simultaneously disguising the poverty underpinning enrolment. Arjun Appadurai argues that one of the major factors locking poor people in poverty is their inability to develop politically enlightened visions that pursue recognition and redistribution equally rather than at the expense of each other: 'poor people have a deeply ambivalent relationship to the dominant norms of the societies in which they live,' he writes (2004: 66). While a degree of irony may permit them 'to maintain some dignity in the worst conditions of oppression and inequality', at the same time they often show 'fairly deep moral attachment to norms and beliefs that directly support their own degradation'

---

[12] Fraser (1996) illustrates this using the example of coverture: that is, the legal doctrine subsuming the legal rights and obligations of a married woman under those of her husband. While the dismantling of the protections of coverture enhanced women's status, she argues, it simultaneously 'harmed some women economically by depriving them of traditional grounds for claiming support from husbands and fathers in a context where such support was still needed by most women' (ibid.: 51).

(ibid.: 66). What does this imply? The poor, 'neither simple dupes nor secret revolutionaries', attempt 'to optimize the terms of trade between recognition and redistribution in their immediate, local lives' (ibid.: 66). However, without a long-term vision of change, or what Appadurai calls a 'capacity to aspire', they often trade recognition for redistribution on adverse terms.

Appadurai's notion of 'adverse terms of trade' between recognition and redistribution can usefully draw attention to the logics of action that may give rise to contradictory behaviours that produce negative outcomes for poor people. Yet, his approach is problematic in that it seems to suggest that chronic poverty is the fault of the poor, and that the non-poor are somehow endowed with more capacity to develop politically enlightened visions of the future than the poor (a position that seems to imply a form of 'false consciousness'). If only the poor knew how to aspire to the right things, this theory seems to suggest, they would be able to pull themselves out of poverty by their own bootstraps.

The Bourdieusian notion of 'symbolic violence', which puts wider power structures (rather than people's presumably unequal 'capacities to aspire') centre stage, can provide a more fruitful approach. Bourdieu defines symbolic violence as 'the violence which is exercised upon a social agent with his or her complicity' (Bourdieu and Wacquant 1992: 167). Accordingly, 'symbolic violence' is particularly powerful and insidious because it operates at the level of taken-for-granted assumptions about the social world, thus obliterating common oppositions 'between coercion and consent, external imposition and internal impulse' (Bourdieu and Wacquant 2004: 272–3).

What is useful about his approach is that he does not assume that poor and non-poor have different capacities for developing lucid perspectives on their condition, as Appadurai seems to do. Instead, he states that even the dominant are dominated by their own domination (e.g. Bourdieu and Wacquant 2004: 273). Yet, the strength of this approach is also its weakness. While the notion of 'symbolic violence' is useful to understand situations in which domination seems to go both unrecognised as such and unchallenged, it tells us little about the conditions in which oppressed people may be lucid about the relations of domination that affect them negatively, or about the circumstances under which change may be possible. Bourdieu's work has repeatedly been criticised for neglecting these aspects (e.g. Reay 2004; Sayer 2005). In this work, I therefore combine a focus on 'symbolic violence' with an emphasis on young people as social actors, who, though constrained by the wider power structures in which they are embedded, are capable of reflexivity, if not transformative social action. The next section explores how childhood and youth studies, and their focus on young people as 'social actors', have influenced this work.

Young people as 'social actors'

Some notable exceptions withstanding (e.g. Mead 1928), the social sciences have paid little attention to young people for most of their history. This has changed during recent decades, not least in recognition of the demographic weight that young people constitute today. According to the World Bank (2006: 33), '[t]he current cohort of young people in developing countries' (defined here as 12–24-year-olds) is, at around 1.3 billion, 'the largest the world has ever seen'.[13] Not only are young people the demographic majority in many places, youths, especially in Africa, have also been discussed as a social group that is more affected than others by political and economic crisis (e.g. Jeffrey 2009). Comaroff and Comaroff (1999: 284), for example, write that 'generation' has become 'the dominant line of cleavage' in South Africa, as 'most of those who experience postcoloniality here as privation ... are young'.

Today, a growing body of literature is exploring childhood and youth as social and historical constructions, and is examining the roles young people play as social actors within their societies. The 'discovery' of young people by social scientists has often been accompanied by an eagerness to counter the idea that young people are passive victims of the larger crises affecting their societies (see, e.g., Abbink and van Kessel 2005; Honwana and De Boeck 2005; Christiansen et al. 2006, Panelli et al. 2007) who invariably succumb to risk (e.g. Boyden 1997 [1990]; Meintjes and Giese 2006). In the African context, various authors have emphasised how young people engage creatively with their – often rather bleak – circumstances, for example by fashioning particular forms of 'popular culture' (e.g. Behrend 2000; Gondola 1999; Weiss 2002), through creative attempts to make a living, notably in the street economy (Cole 2004; Moyer 2004; Sommers 2010), and through migration (e.g. Mains 2007; Langevang and Gough 2009). Notions of young people as 'social actors' have also underpinned analyses of their unconventional interventions in the political sphere (Diouf 1996; De Boeck and Honwana 2005) and their participation in violence (Honwana 2009; Utas 2005; Vigh 2010).

---

[13] Arguably, 'children' and 'youths' are not merely biological categories, but situational concepts that vary across time and between social groups (see James and Prout 1997 [1990]). The Hausa word for 'children' (*yara*) can also mean 'dependants', highlighting that categories such as 'childhood' and 'adulthood' are closely related to social status in northern Nigeria (see Last 2004). An important transition for boys is their circumcision (at around age seven), after which they are considered old enough to be sent away from home. Towards the end of puberty, gender norms governing adult behaviour begin to apply fully, and young men – then called *samari* (singular: *saurayi*), or youths, rather than *yara*, children – stop entering the houses of other men. Adulthood begins for both women and men with their first 'dependant' – for women their first child, for men their first wife (Last 2000b: 366).

This book embraces the idea that young people are 'social actors' by highlighting instances when the *almajirai* 'refuse to be reduced to the status of obedient subject' (Gomez-Perez and LeBlanc 2012: 12). Earlier parts of this introduction have emphasised how the *almajirai* use religious discourses about the educative value of hardship to counter denigrating discourses about their poverty, thus adding to the work of others who have emphasised how young people actively construct their religious identities (e.g. Hemming and Madge 2011). Chapters 6 and 7 explore in greater depth how the *almajirai* embrace pious self-conceptions to cope with poverty-related shame and widespread stigma and rejection, and relate this to wider debates within the anthropology/sociology of religion.

While, in some instances, the *almajirai* cogently challenge the powers that be, in other instances they are complicit with structures that affect them (and others) negatively, for example when they hide their poverty to avoid shame, or when they establish their own social respectability against the backdrop of others whose social standing is low. I therefore propose that, while taking young people seriously as social actors, we have to be mindful of the larger power structures within which they are embedded, and of the ways in which 'specific relations of subordination create and enable' their 'capacity for action' (Mahmood 2001: 210). Rather than simply celebrating young people's 'agency' as an expression of 'resistance' and 'resourcefulness', I look closer at the contradictory effects of this 'agency', a topic I explore in greater depth in Chapter 7.

Finally, while it is important to highlight age hierarchies and young people's relative powerlessness vis-à-vis adults in northern Nigeria, it is also important to study how age relates to other vectors of social division, including socio-economic and educational status and gender. Several sections in this book explore how the *almajirai* are positioned relative to other young people in northern Nigeria, including girls, those who attend 'modern' schools, and their employers' children (see Chapters 5 and 7). With these considerations from education studies, poverty research, and childhood and youth studies in mind, I now turn to the insights that the anthropology of Islam can provide into Qur'anic schools and their students' experiences.

Islam, epistemology, and everyday religiosity

Recent scholarship has problematised juxtapositions of Islam in Africa as either 'traditional' and Sufi or 'reformist' and Salafi. Otayek and Soares (2007: 7), for example, argue that, despite the importance of both Sufism and reformism, 'most Muslims in Africa today are neither members of Sufi orders nor reformists or Islamists'. According to the Pew Forum (2010: 158), while 19 per cent and 9 per cent of Nigerian

Muslims identify with the Sufi orders *Tijaniyya* and *Qadiriyya* respectively, 56 per cent declare that they do not belong to any Sufi order. What is more, to assume a homogeneous 'traditional' Sufi Islam is problematic. Brigaglia (2007), for example, shows Sufis to have been major reformers of Islamic education in Nigeria, making the association of Sufism with 'traditionalism' misleading (see also Chapter 3). In a similar vein, Masquelier (2009) argues that Nigerien Muslims who identify as *'yan darika* (literally: sons (i.e. members) of a Sufi order) do not actually 'share a unified vision of Islam and, in fact, exist as a group only in the context of their opposition to Izala reformism' (ibid.: 2).[14] She urges scholars to leave behind dichotomist visions of Islam and to pay attention instead 'to the fluid, shifting, and heterogeneous nature of Muslim discourses and practices' (ibid.).

Such an approach is helpful in understanding the realities of the Qur'anic schools where I conducted my research. While the spread of Islam in the region is closely linked to Sufi figures, notably Uthman dan Fodio (1754–1817), the founder of the Sokoto Caliphate, it would be misleading to subsume classical Qur'anic schools summarily within the *turuq* (Sufi orders, singular: *tariqa*). Not all *malamai* and *almajirai* with whom I conducted research were affiliated to a *tariqa*, and many schools did not engage in any explicitly Sufi practices (such as collective *dhikr*, or the recitation of divine names). I was told that students with an interest in the *turuq* should pursue it further after finishing their Qur'anic studies. In addition, the attribute 'traditional', with which the label 'reformist' is often opposed to categorise divergent approaches to Islam, sits uneasily with the realities I observed. Some of the *malamai* portrayed themselves self-consciously as both cosmopolitan and 'modern', and their students eagerly sought to distance themselves from what they considered to be backwardness or 'village habits' (see Chapters 6 and 8; see also Thurston 2016c: 21–2).

How, then, can we characterise the Qur'anic educational practices studied in this book that have a long-standing presence in West Africa? Ware (2014) has argued emphatically that such educational practices have historical roots throughout the Muslim world, and that labelling them as 'traditional' falsely suggests a syncretic, culturally tainted '*Islam noir*' and a lack of Islamic authenticity. Seconding this, Launay (2016a: 3) highlights that categorising 'educational systems as traditional or modern is a feature of an ideology of modernity intrinsically tied to the kind of education that colonizers of whatever stripe tried to impose on their subjects'. I concur with these authors that the term 'classical' is more appropriate when speaking of the Qur'anic schools I studied.

---

[14] *Izala* is short for *Jama'at Izalat al-Bid'a wa-Iqamat al Sunna* (Arabic), which means 'Society for Removing Heretical Innovation and Establishing the Sunna'.

In recent years, a lively debate has developed among scholars about the epistemic regime underpinning classical Qur'anic education. In his pioneering study of the reform of Islamic education in Mali, Brenner argued that classical Qur'anic schools are built on an 'esoteric episteme', which distinguishes between 'public' and 'secret' knowledge. According to Brenner (2000: 7), 'all knowledge is not meant to be available to all persons'. The resulting 'hierarchy of knowledge is intimately related to the initiatic nature of its transmission. Islamic knowledge can be legitimately acquired only through personal transmission' (ibid.). Brenner contrasts this 'esoteric' episteme of classical Qur'anic schools with the presumably 'rationalistic' regime of 'modern' Islamic education.

Brenner puts his finger on some important features setting classical Qur'anic education apart from 'modern' Islamic education, notably its emphasis on personal transmission and its acceptance of the 'secret' status of certain types of knowledge, which I explore in greater depth in Chapter 8. Yet, it has rightly been argued that much of what is transmitted in classical Qur'anic schools is 'emphatically exoteric' (Launay 2016a: 10), making it problematic to subsume the entire education system under the label 'esoteric'.

In his seminal book *The Walking Qur'an*, Ware (2014: 4) proposes an alternative approach to understanding the epistemic difference between classical and 'modern' Islamic schooling. Classical Islamic knowledge, Ware argues, is 'embodied knowledge', and Qur'anic schooling is purposely 'designed to produce specific sorts of bodily sensibilities' (ibid.: 5). 'Modern' Islamic education, in his view, has become uninterested in the body and concerns itself merely with 'discursive knowledge' (ibid.: 4).

Considering what Qur'anic study usually looks like, Ware's call to pay attention to the body makes immediate sense. Young students in Qur'anic schools in Kano usually crouch in tight rows on prayer mats on the floor, clasping their wooden boards as they rock back and forth, each following their own rhythm, reciting out loud the portion of the Qur'an assigned to them. For most of the time, their bodies are kept alert by the vigilant presence of the *malam* or *gardi* (assistant teacher, plural: *gardawa*) and his whip, which swiftly comes down on any student whose attention slips. The study of older *almajirai* or *gardawa* is less tense. They tend to choose their study spots freely, and they sit in any position in which they are comfortable. No whip hovers over their heads. Yet, as soon as they crouch in front of the *malam* to have him correct what they have learned, they, too, stoop, lower their gaze, and humbly receive his verdict on their performance.

Bodily discipline is undeniably crucial to Qur'anic learning. Yet, arguably, an emphasis on the body is not unique to the classical tradition of Qur'anic learning (see, e.g., Masquelier's (2015) critique of Ware), and rather than distinguishing between 'embodied' and 'disembodied' forms of knowledge, as Ware does, we should pay attention to the ways in which different forms of schooling discipline the body in distinctive ways (see, e.g., Launay 2016a: 4; see also Mahmood 2001: 214 on the role of bodily comportment for learning pious conduct in a 'reformist' tradition). Finally, while epistemology is important in understanding how classical Qur'anic education works, to whom it appeals, and how it differs from other approaches to Islamic learning, a central argument of this book is that we must also look at people's socio-economic realities if we want to understand their educational choices (see Chapters 4 and 8). These critiques notwithstanding, the perspective advocated by Ware highlights important issues surrounding the body and its disciplining in Qur'anic schools, issues that I will explore in greater depth in Chapters 4 and 8.

Finally, while it is important to explore the disciplining projects pursued through schooling, it is also important to acknowledge their necessarily incomplete reach (see above on the politics of schooling). This ties in with wider debates within the anthropology of Islam about piety, ethical self-fashioning, and the limits of both. Recent work (e.g. Hirschkind 2001; Mahmood 2001; 2005) has drawn attention to the ways in which people seek to cultivate piety by working on themselves and their bodies. These studies have effectively challenged narratives of Islam as a monolithic regulatory system acting on individuals from the outside, and have highlighted instead how ordinary people perform and inhabit religious norms in their daily lives.

Yet, such approaches have been criticised for projecting a totalising 'image of Islam as a perfectionist project of self-discipline' (Schielke 2009: 24) that does not reflect the reality of most Muslims' everyday lives. As Schielke (ibid.) argues, most Muslims are 'sometimes but not always pious', just like the rest of humankind. Furthermore, at times people might face considerable uncertainty about what exactly moral or pious conduct would entail (e.g. Marsden 2005: 260–1). A growing number of scholars seek to acknowledge such 'issues of ambivalence and fragmentation' (Schielke 2009: 26). Soares and Osella (2009: 11), for example, urge that in addition to pious self-fashioning, '[s]truggle, ambivalence, incoherence, and failure must also receive attention in the study of everyday religiosity' (see also Janson 2014: 12; Marsden 2005; Masquelier 2007; Otayek and Soares 2007).

Such an approach is useful to understand the *almajirai*'s behaviours. They undoubtedly spend much time and energy striving to act as, and be perceived as, devout Muslims. This does not, however, prevent them from also engaging in activities less centred on piety. Many *almajirai* regularly play football and watch TV, even though their *malamai* clearly oppose such practices, considering them at best a waste of study time and at worst a morally corrupting vice (see Chapter 3). Also, portraying themselves as more-than-averagely devout Muslims does not prevent the *almajirai* from aspiring in great numbers to non-scholarly careers (see Chapter 9).

Structure of the book

The structure of this book is modelled on the *almajirai*'s trajectories through the Qur'anic educational system, exploring first the circumstances in rural northern Nigeria that underpin the enrolment of boys as *almajirai*, and then following them to their schools and shedding light on their experiences there. I end by taking stock of the *almajirai*'s skills and knowledge and tracing their trajectories after leaving school. Patently, the trajectory suggested in this book only appears to be chronological. In fact, the different 'stages' of an *almajiri*'s trajectory presented here are snapshots of different young people at different stages in their *almajiri* 'careers' taken around the same time. Rather than following *almajirai* over their life course, I collected most data during a total of 13 months of fieldwork, conducted from July to September 2009, and then again from January to November 2011. Some additional information was gathered 'remotely' in May and June 2017 with the help of Sadisu, an *almajiri* who had participated in the film project and with whom I have stayed in close touch since leaving Kano. I emailed him questions which he discussed with friends and peers, sending me detailed responses. This allowed me to learn not least about how the *almajirai* have been affected by Boko Haram and the current recession in Nigeria. However, the bulk of my data stems from my own earlier fieldwork. In Chapter 9, I reflect on the implications of ongoing social, economic, and political transformations for how we can interpret this data.

Most *almajirai* originate from rural areas. Many move to urban areas, at least during the agriculturally idle dry period, and return to the countryside for the months of the farming season. My own 'trajectory' began in urban Kano, where I had conducted most of the fieldwork in 2009, and where I spent three months learning Hausa at Bayero University Kano in early 2011. As the rains set in and many *almajirai* began returning to rural areas for the farming season, I moved to Albasu, a small rural town in Albasu Local Government Area (LGA) in the east of Kano State, where I lived for four months from May to September 2011. At the end of the rainy period, when the *almajirai* began preparing for their dry season migratory tours, I returned to Kano City, where I lived at Sabuwar Kofa within the Old City for another two months before returning to the UK.

In this chapter, I introduce the research setting and offer insights into the challenges of 'participatory' research, including video production, in a religious school setting. Chapter 2 sketches the discourses circulating about Qur'anic schools in Nigeria, and explores why the *almajirai* are such a salient theme in the popular imagination. By identifying misconceptions and tracing their origins, Chapter 2 sets the stage for an empirically informed discussion in the subsequent chapters of the actual problems and challenges of the *almajiri* system.

Chapter 3 situates the *almajiri* system within the wider historical context of northern Nigeria's changing educational landscape, arguing that an enlarged range of educational options have not necessarily translated into greater choice for the poor, even though they have increased aspirations and desires. Many people believe that Qur'anic students are hostile towards 'modern' secular education or '*boko*'. This chapter tells a different story, highlighting that 'modern' education of meaningful quality, though desired by many, is actually available to few. Chapter 4 turns to the place of the *almajiri* system within families' educational strategies, examining closely the circumstances leading poor rural households to consider *almajiri* enrolment. Using the Bourdieusian notion of 'habitus', this chapter seeks to understand how people come to conceive of an educational choice made in very constraining circumstances as a positive decision taken to honour religious and social commitments.

Chapter 5 leaves behind the rural areas where most *almajirai* originate and follows them to the urban areas where they attend Qur'anic school, some all year around, others particularly during the dry season. If we are concerned about the extent to which the *almajirai* become frustrated with and alienated from mainstream society, we need to understand the terms on which they relate to this society. By exploring the *almajirai*'s experiences working as domestic helpers in the households of the better-off, this chapter sheds light on the terms of these relationships. Chapter 6 then asks what the *almajirai* make of their close-range experiences of inequality. Ashamed of their poverty, they portray *almajiri* enrolment as a choice motivated primarily by religious commitments. This, however, belies the role of structural constraints on their lives. Arguably, the politics of poverty or redistribution and the politics of dignity or recognition follow conflicting logics for the *almajirai*. Chapter 7 looks at the social and political implications of poverty and stigma. It provides a counter-narrative to accounts of the *almajirai* as disconnected from wider society and dominant notions of morality. Yet, at the same time, it raises questions about the likelihood of solidarity and social cohesion developing among similarly powerless groups in northern Nigeria.

Whereas Chapters 5 to 7 explore the *almajirai*'s experiences and struggles for a respectable position within society, Chapters 8 and 9 ask more specifically what skills and knowledge the *almajirai* acquire, and how what they learn prepares them for their future roles in society. Chapter 8 looks in particular at the religious knowledge the *almajirai* acquire, and at the opportunities it opens up for them within northern Nigeria's 'prayer economy'.[15] Finally, Chapter 9 asks what consequences Qur'anic education has beyond the 'prayer economy' for the *almajirai*'s future lives and for society more broadly. Drawing on the *almajirai*'s experiences, I then reflect on the options for action available to poor boys and young men more generally (in northern Nigeria as well as elsewhere) at this particular historical moment, when growing consumerism and a widening gulf between the well-off and the deprived have exacerbated the negative connotations of poverty.

The research setting

Nigeria's population, estimated at more than 180 million in 2015 (National Population Commission 2016), is split relatively equally between Christians and Muslims. While Muslims live in all parts of the country, their concentration is highest in the northern states. Socio-economic inequalities map to some extent onto regional and religious divides, with the – predominantly Muslim – north lagging behind the – predominantly Christian – south (see, e.g., National Bureau of Statistics 2012; Oxford Poverty and Human Development Initiative 2013). The 2006 census found Kano State to be the most populous state in Nigeria, with over nine million inhabitants, most of whom are Hausa Muslims. The city of Kano, an important commercial hub, is Nigeria's second largest city after Lagos, with more than 2.8 million inhabitants in 2006. The majority of Kano State's population live in rural areas, most of them depending on small-holder, rain-fed subsistence agriculture for their livelihood (see Chapter 4). Rural-to-urban migration, both seasonal and permanent, is a frequent strategy to seize employment opportunities in the manufacturing and service sectors of Kano and to escape hardship in the countryside (Mustapha and Meagher 1992; Mortimore 1998). In 2001, 'full' shari'a law was reintroduced in Kano and 11 other northern states.[16]

Around 66 per cent of the population of Kano State are considered to have been living in 'absolute poverty' in 2010 (National Bureau of

---

[15] Murray Last (1988: 196; see also Soares 1996) uses the notion of 'prayer economy' to refer to the exchanges that are frequent in northern Nigeria of money (or material support) for prayers, blessings, and spiritual medicine.

[16] Islamic personal law and other Islamic civil law have been in force in northern Nigeria without interruption since precolonial times. After the return to democracy in 1999, wide parts of the population of northern Nigeria demanded the reinstatement of Islamic criminal law, which under colonial rule had been applied in name only – the British regulated the penalties – and stopped being applied entirely upon independence in 1960. The initial national and international outcry about the reinstatement of 'full shari'a' subsided as it became clear that harsh corporal punishments would not be carried out and that Islamic law would not be applied to non-Muslims (see Ostien n.d.). As shari'a has failed to bring about social justice, many northern Nigerian Muslims are disenchanted with the way in which it is implemented today.

Figure 1.1 Kano City (photograph: Susan Elden)

Statistics 2012).[17] Poverty and the deplorable state of 'modern' education (see Chapter 3) partly account for the choice of *almajiri* education. While reliable data does not exist, many believe that Kano hosts the largest number of *almajirai* of all northern Nigerian states (e.g. Abubakar 2009). This has been attributed not only to the state's size but also to the promise of a livelihood in spiritual service provision: that is, a livelihood in saying prayers, reciting the Qur'an, and producing charms and 'potions' (*rubutun sha*) (see Chapter 8).

In urban Kano, I stayed for nine months in total just inside the Old City wall (*cikin birni*) near Sabuwar Ƙofa (New Gate; see Map 2 and Figure 1.1). From there, I went on regular expeditions to a Qur'anic school near Tashar Kasuwar Rimi, a motor park inside the Old City (Malam Gali's school), and to another school near Ƙofar Famfo (Malam Maisittin's school). In both Qur'anic schools, I conducted interviews during the early days of my research, and then, upon invitation by the teachers, I returned regularly both for extended conversations and to teach English. I also regularly visited an NGO supporting *almajirai* (CAESI or Child *Almajiri* Empowerment and Support Initiative)[18] in

---

[17] 'Absolute poverty' is defined here as living on less than 54 Naira (approximately US$0.32) per day.

[18] The NGO aimed to extend support to *almajirai* in Kano, by offering 'modern' education and meals to *almajirai* from different Qur'anic schools in Sharada, Kano Metropolitan, on Thursdays, Fridays, and Saturdays, among other things. In 2010, they cooperated with NAPTIP (National Agency for the Prohibition of Trafficking in Persons), UNICEF, and Radio Nigeria Kaduna to facilitate a 13-episode radio programme broadcast nationally in which *almajirai* spoke about their education and experiences, and that included songs, drama, and street interviews. Recordings are available online at www.unicef.org/nigeria/media_5617.html.

Sharada, where I gave English lessons on several days per week. Finally, I sought out and interviewed men who had lived as *almajirai* at some stage of their life, as well as government officials, the spokespersons of NGOs and religious associations, and health and university staff to understand the wider situation.

The immediate neighbourhood (almost entirely Hausa Muslim) of the house in which I was staying constituted a major site for my research (see Map 3). The house sat at the entrance to a police housing estate (*bariki*) to one side, and bordered a middle-/upper middle-class quarter on the other. Right next to our house, which I shared first with a British VSO volunteer and a British PhD student, and later with a Ugandan VSO volunteer, lived a Qur'anic teacher with his *almajirai*. He was hosted there by a wealthy patron, and since his school did not have sufficient space to shelter all its students, the *almajirai* 'spilled over' into the neighbourhood. During the day, they could be found squatting on mats in the canopied forecourt of our house, busily bent over their boards, copying down their next lesson from little bundles of paper with the Qur'an printed on them,[19] or relaxing in the shade of a tree in front of the nearby mosque where their teaching took place. At night, they spread their sleeping mats not only in the mosque but also in the entrance halls of neighbouring houses (ours included), and finally in the open on the concrete floor in front of their teacher's compound.

The neighbourhood is characterised by a stark socio-economic divide, with the *almajirai*, who often struggle for the daily means of survival, on one side, and the families of the northern political elite (for example, relatives of the Sultan of Sokoto, and a Kano shari'a court judge) on the other. Middle-rank policemen, formal sector employees, and businessmen make up the middle ground. It is no coincidence that people at both ends of the socio-economic spectrum live together in such proximity. For the *almajirai*, living in a fairly well-to-do neighbourhood means that they have income and employment opportunities as domestic workers and street vendors. For the people in the neighbourhood, the *almajirai* present a readily available pool of cheap labour that they can draw on for all sorts of odd jobs and errands (see Chapter 5).

The house in which I lived had been rented by Europeans, several of them researchers, for over 20 years by the time I moved in, and was known locally as 'the Europeans' house' (*gidan turawa*). The children and *almajirai* in the neighbourhood were keenly aware of the fact that Europeans lived there, that they tended to have exotic habits (importantly, refusing to beat even the most mischievous children; our hammock and my guitar were further points of attraction), and that they

---

[19] As a sign of respect for the Qur'an, in their day-to-day study, students rarely handle a complete Qur'an, but use little paper bundles containing parts of it instead.

needed to learn both Hausa and cooking (i.e. Hausa dishes). Consequently, neighbourhood children and young *almajirai* looking for enter-
tainment periodically invaded our compound. On these occasions, I
could get an idea of what an urban childhood at Sabuwar Ƙofa looked
like and I could observe the relationships between *almajirai* and the children from the neighbourhood, as well as improve my Hausa and cooking
skills, which were a concern to the girls coming to visit.

As I had come to research a topic as sensitive as the *almajiri* system, the
fact that the neighbourhood had virtually been 'ploughed' by researchers
(Werthmann 2004)[20] turned out to be to my advantage. Trust was an
essential ingredient for my research. As people had been in contact not
merely with Westerners before, but also with researchers, they were fairly
relaxed about my presence and questions, and it was even possible to
experiment with a range of 'participatory' methods, including photogra-
phy and 'radio interviews'. Given the spatial constraints to which I was
subject – I could neither follow the *almajirai* to their income-generating
activities nor, as a woman and non-Muslim, participate in lessons taking place inside the mosque – I had to be inventive in order to learn
about those aspects of the *almajirai*'s lives that I could not easily observe.
The pictures the *almajirai* at Sabuwar Ƙofa and at Malam Gali's school
near Tashar Kasuwar Rimi took with disposable cameras in 2009, and
which I discussed with them, offered me valuable snapshots of these
otherwise inaccessible aspects (cf. Punch 2002; Gabhainn and Sixsmith
2006). Through 'radio interviews' that the *almajirai* at Sabuwar Ƙofa
recorded during that same period, I could gain insights into the views
of children who were otherwise shy about speaking in front of me, as an
adult and a foreigner. As I used to tape-record our conversations and
to demonstrate how the recorder worked when asking the *almajirai* for
their consent, they started taking pleasure in recording and re-playing
their own voices. Eventually, they started playing 'radio', and when I
encouraged them to 'broadcast' a radio programme about the *almajirai*'s
views on their education system, they took off with my tape recorder and
began enthusiastically interviewing each other, delivering eloquent and
passionate 'radio speeches' and even visiting other Qur'anic schools to
interview the students there (cf. Young and Barrett 2001; Frankel 2007).

My experiences in my rural field site, the LGA of Albasu, were
markedly different from those at Sabuwar Ƙofa. For fear that people
might perceive tape recordings and photographs as an attempt to illic-
itly sneak information out, the District Head discouraged me from using
them there. Our film crew was able to film in Albasu only after I had

---

[20] Researchers who temporarily stayed at Sabuwar Ƙofa include Douglas Anthony, Con-
erly Casey, Rudi Gaudio, Alaine S. Hutson, Matthias Krings, Brian Larkin, Jonathan
T. Reynolds, Constanze Schmaling, Katja Werthmann and Pete Kingsley.

Figure 1.2 Albasu (photograph: Hannah Hoechner)

produced a letter of recommendation from Kano State's Commissioner of Information, who supported the project.

Albasu, in whose administrative capital, the town of Albasu (see Maps 1 and 4 and Figure 1.2), I lived for four months, is remote, poor, and largely dependent on agriculture, and its 'modern' education is of low quality. Most of my data on the contexts and circumstances in which boys become *almajirai* stems from Albasu, where I worked with several Qur'anic schools both in Albasu town and in Daho, a village some 20 minutes by motorbike east of Albasu town. I also visited villages in Kunchi, an LGA in the north-west of Kano State (see Map 1), where I interviewed fathers whose sons live as *almajirai*. Kunchi, largely dependent on agriculture, is one of the poorest LGAs in Kano State (Ministry of Education 2008).

Albasu LGA, with a population of roughly 190,000 in the 2006 census, sits on the border with Jigawa State in the extreme east of Kano State. It is off the main road leading east from Kano through Takai and Kachako into Jigawa State (Birnin Kudu) and eventually onwards to Yobe and Borno States. Even its capital, the town of Albasu (roughly 18,000 inhabitants),[21] has no direct public transport to Kano on most

---

[21] As no up-to-date population figures are available for Albasu town, I extrapolated from 2006 census data (overall population of the LGA) and primary school enrolment figures

days. 'You don't go to Albasu unless you go to Albasu,' I was told: it is not en route to any other major destination. At the time of my research, Albasu was not connected to electricity, and, unlike other similar-sized settlements in the area, it does not have a market day, which indexes its low levels of economic activity. Only a limited range of consumer goods are available in Albasu.[22]

In Albasu, I lived in the house of the 'traditional ruler' or District Head (*Hakimi*) – as part of the family, as it were. As I enjoyed the hospitality of the '*manya*', the rich and powerful (literally: the big ones), people inevitably associated me with this elite, sometimes more than I would have wished. However, being the District Head's protégée opened important doors for me. It legitimated my presence in Albasu at a time – May to September 2011 – when political turmoil had heightened suspicions towards outsiders. Goodluck Jonathan had just won the presidential election in April 2011, whose results large parts of the population in the north contested, and the Nigerian security apparatus was patching together its response to increasing Boko Haram-related violence. In this context, people had every reason to mistrust a white woman, newly arrived in the community, who was asking questions about Qur'anic education.

Living in the District Head's house, moreover, offered many opportunities to get to know people in the community. More women made courtesy calls to the District Head's wife than to any other compound. Women also stayed around the compound as they waited for the District Head's arbitration in a marital dispute. For me, this meant opportunities to be introduced and to become familiar with otherwise difficult-to-meet women, whom I could then seek out on later occasions. More people stood in some form of employment or patronage relationship with the District Head's house than with any other household, meaning that a vast number of domestic workers (cooks, cleaners) and other service providers (drivers, gardeners, animal minders, guards, hair plaiters, NYSC members[23] who doubled as private teachers for the District Head's grandchildren in the afternoons), as well as suppliers of all kinds of products (groundnut oil, caps, sweets), dropped in at some point or

---

(2010–11). I used the percentage of all primary school students in Albasu LGA who are enrolled in Albasu town as a proxy for the percentage of the entire LGA population living in Albasu town.

[22] There is a health centre (*asibiti*) in Albasu town, staffed by two members of the National Youth Service Corps (NYSC). The closest hospital equipped to provide more than primary healthcare is 30 minutes away by *acaba* (motorbike) in Takai (costing 300 Naira or approximately US$1.80 for a return journey). That is also where anything more than basic drugs can be bought.

[23] These are recent university graduates serving for one year in the NYSC. In a bid to foster the NYSC members' commitment to the Nigerian nation, they are posted across the country, and often to regions with which they are unfamiliar.

another. Through the network surrounding the District Head's household, I was introduced to several young men who had lived as *almajirai* and to women whose sons were enrolled as *almajirai*. Owing to the District Head's intervention on my behalf, I was able to set up English and literacy/numeracy classes for *almajirai* (in Albasu and Daho; in Albasu, most students attending my classes were from Malam Nasiru's and Malam Ahmed's schools) as well as for married women.[24] Through these classes, I could both gain a foothold in the community and establish relationships with people who would later become important informants.

Growing close where inequalities loom large

During the early stages of my research, I encountered comparatively few obstacles. I managed quickly to conduct a wide range of interviews with Qur'anic teachers, their students, former *almajirai*, and *almajirai*'s parents and relatives in Kano, Kunchi, and Albasu. Leaving one's home to search for knowledge is a well-known theme among the constituencies of the *almajiri* system, and the fact that I had come all the way from the UK to Nigeria (and eventually to as remote a place as Albasu) to learn about Qur'anic education there was welcomed by many of my informants. Furthermore, aware of negative discourses circulating about the Qur'anic education system, my informants appreciated that I sought to represent their perspectives.

Despite these initial 'successes', I soon struggled to develop the contacts I had established with the *almajirai* into deeper relationships. Even though the 'participatory' methods I used allowed me to access data that would have been difficult to elicit in a 'conventional' interview setting, they did not necessarily result in sustained close relationships. Friendships do not traverse gender boundaries in northern Nigeria, or they do so very rarely.[25] As a woman, 'befriending' the *almajirai* was thus not an option readily available to me. Also, I often felt like a fifth wheel in the Qur'anic schools I visited. As mentioned before, as a woman and a non-Muslim, I could not enrol as an *almajira* myself or even observe, let alone participate in, lessons taking place in a mosque. My interest in

---

[24] Together with a woman from Albasu in her mid-twenties who had not only attended *Islamiyya* school extensively (one of very few women in Albasu to have done so) but also held a secondary school certificate, I ran evening classes in the District Head's house over the course of three months for about 50 married women on four days a week. While she taught Islamic subjects – recitation of the Qur'an, *ahadith* (the traditions of Prophet Muhammad), and the Arabic alphabet – I was responsible for teaching basic '*boko*' ('modern' secular) literacy and numeracy.

[25] In Hausa, the word used to refer to a woman's close friend is *kawa* (female); a man's friend is his *aboki* (male). Friendship bonds between the sexes are not provided for linguistically.

Qur'anic learning, moreover, inevitably raised questions about my intentions, if not among the teachers and *almajirai* themselves, then certainly among the bystanders and passers-by, whose opinion weighs heavily as gossip can make or break a Qur'anic teacher's reputation. Did I intend to convert to Islam? And if I didn't, why did I want to learn the Qur'an? Many people in this context believe Islam's holy book to be full of mystical secrets that convey power upon anyone who masters them (see Chapter 8). Why, if not for financial gain, would one give away these secrets to a non-Muslim?[26]

Although, during my English classes, I regularly got to see a considerable number of *almajirai* in a wide age range (six to 12 years in Daho; from ten years upwards in my other classes), teaching inevitably put me in a position of authority, extending still further the respectful distance that most *almajirai* kept, given my status as an adult and a 'senior' (even though, as an unmarried woman at the age of almost 30, I was a rather unconventional adult, and despite my extremely lax teaching style, which led my students on several occasions to lecture me on appropriate 'disciplining techniques').

Most Qur'anic teachers let me teach their students only on their weekend days – Thursday and Friday – which are lesson-free in most Qur'anic schools. The remaining days of the week are usually long and exhausting for the *almajirai*, leaving them little time to 'hang out' with a researcher or take English lessons.[27] The timetable of my neighbour's Qur'anic school at Sabuwar Ƙofa, which Sadisu, who studied there, described to me in detail, illustrates how densely packed the *almajirai*'s schedule usually is: classes begin after the morning prayer, with a first break around 7.30am, when students flood the neighbourhoods in search of breakfast and to perform their domestic morning duties in the households employing them. Sessions resume at around 9am and last until 11am, when

---

26 I eventually found a *malam* who agreed to teach me the religious basics, including ablutions and memorisation of short surahs. In exchange, I taught him English. Things got complicated, however, once I had mastered the essentials necessary to perform the daily prayer, as the *malam* claimed that the next necessary step for me to gain more knowledge was to start or to try praying, making me suspect that he was secretly hoping to convert me.

27 In the school in Daho, I was allowed to teach on as many days per week as I wanted (usually four to six days) as long as the lesson schedule did not clash with the *almajirai*'s Qur'anic studies and work obligations. I got to know this school through ESSPIN (the DfID-funded Education Sector Support Programme in Nigeria). Its students had attended an ESSPIN 'Tsangaya cluster school' for some months until it stopped operating. The students, most of them fairly young (17 students aged approximately six to 12 years), were keen to acquire or to continue 'modern' education, and their teachers consented willingly to me picking up from where the ESSPIN teacher had left off. In the ESSPIN pilot schools, secondary school leavers from the respective communities teach *almajirai* a condensed version of the primary school curriculum. Their timetable is agreed with the *malamai* of the participating Qur'anic schools. Classrooms are provided by the local community.

students take off again in search of food and cash. The school then runs an afternoon session between the *la'asar* (at about 4pm) and *magariba* (sunset) prayers, after which students break for dinner only to resume lessons again after the *isha'i* (night) prayer.

On Wednesdays and Sundays, the students' progress is evaluated and new lessons are assigned. In the morning, one by one the *almajirai* recite to their *malam*, or to a *gardi* acting as an assistant teacher, the verses written on their wooden board; they will have memorised these over the preceding days. If the *malam* or *gardi* is satisfied with a student's effort, he sends him to wash his board.[28] For young students, he then writes down the next lesson. More advanced students copy it themselves from sheets of paper with the Qur'an printed on them. During the Wednesday afternoon lesson, the *malam* or a *gardi* reads out to each *almajiri* the verses newly written on his board, familiarising them with the pronunciation and correcting potential spelling mistakes. Boys are then left to study their new verses, which usually means crouching behind their boards and repeatedly reading aloud what is written on them, trying to engrave the text in their memory. If a boy forgets the pronunciation of a particular passage, he may consult the *malam* or a more advanced student (*gardi*). If a boy is quick to memorise all the verses assigned to him, he may ask for additional verses.

The first – shorter – surahs of the Qur'an are memorised by all students. As they reach the Qur'an's longer surahs, memorisation becomes more difficult, and students risk getting jumbled up or forgetting previously memorised passages. Students then either switch completely to learning only to read and recite correctly rather than committing to memory, or they progress by memorising only parts, leaving out particularly difficult passages. Once they have reached the end of the Qur'an (first *sauka*; literally: alighting), some students go on to a second reading (second *sauka*) when they memorise all the surahs, without missing out any sections.

Most lessons are spent reading or memorising, the exception being Wednesdays and Sundays, when new portions of text are assigned. Night lessons (9–10pm) provide another exception to the usual rhythm, as here every student recites by heart without a board the surahs he knows already (*tilawa*) so as to preserve them in his memory. As by this time of night many boys are exhausted, the lesson is performed standing, so nobody can fall asleep.[29]

---

[28] Conversely, students who make repeated mistakes risk beatings and the imposition of extra hours.

[29] On Tuesdays, the usual night lesson is replaced with a session dedicated to supplications. First, some widely known *addu'a* (invocatory prayer) is repeated silently by all students. This is followed by a sermon by the *malam*, who makes specific intercessions and gives moral advice to his students. During the early morning session on Friday,

In addition to being kept busy in this way from Saturday to Wednesday, even on Thursday and Friday – their 'weekend' – the *almajirai* do not necessarily have much free time, as these are also the two core days when they earn their living. In urban areas on Thursdays and Fridays, *almajirai* can be seen wandering around the markets, streets, and motor parks in packs, begging for alms. In rural areas, Thursday and Friday are the days when *almajirai* pursue agricultural tasks for their own benefit rather than to benefit their teachers. Much of Friday is spent with the week's most important prayer and the preparations for it (bathing, dressing smartly, going to one of the larger mosques). How could I fit into the *almajirai*'s busy schedule?

It turned out that becoming a 'patron' or employer for the *almajirai* was the most natural way of fitting into both their schedule and the cultural frames available locally for relationships between better-off adult women and poor young *almajirai*. Two of my neighbour's *almajirai*, Sadisu and Naziru – who would later become core participants in my research – were working as domestics in the house I moved into in urban Kano. While initially I felt uncomfortable employing my (future) research participants, for the *almajirai*, being workers and 'clients' came fairly naturally: this was how they related to all the women in the middle-/upper-class neighbourhood where I was living and where their school was located. Finally, such employment arrangements were crucial to the *almajirai*'s economic survival (see Chapter 5).

Eventually, I not only 'kept' the two boys already working in our house, but also employed, on an ad hoc basis, various other *almajirai* from the neighbourhood, to fetch water for me or to run errands. Over time our relationships developed into a familiar 'protector'/patron–'protégé'/client bond. This implied not only time spent discussing neighbourhood events and gossip, but also moments to talk about the *almajirai*'s current worries and future plans.

This research situation meant that I learned about important aspects of the *almajirai*'s lives, including their Qur'anic lessons and experiences 'inside the classroom', mostly through their narrations rather than through my own first-hand observations. A further disadvantage was that the socio-economic difference between us became a central element of our relationship and a backdrop to all our exchanges. In matters concerning money, I was not always sure to what extent the *almajirai* adjusted the information they shared with me to be sure that I would not withdraw my own support or my promises of support in the future (cf. Crick 1992; see also Hoechner 2017). Clearly, the patronage element in our relationship, the expectations for material gain that came with it, and finally the *almajirai*'s fear that they might lose me as a patron if they

---

takara is done: that is, a complete reading of the Qur'an, divided into parts that are read out in low voices by different students simultaneously.

displeased me played a crucial role in how the film project we pursued together evolved, to which I now turn (for a detailed discussion of the filmmaking process and the quandaries it entailed, see Hoechner 2015a; 2016).

Filmmaking experiences

After some months of fieldwork during which I continually encountered negative stereotypes about the *almajirai*, I had the idea of producing a documentary film together with some of the Qur'anic students I had begun to know better. I thought that, through a film, they would have an opportunity to make their views known about their education, and about how society treated them. A film project, moreover, promised to provide opportunities not only to spend time with the *almajirai*, but also to learn about what they would want to document and communicate. The idea was to involve boys and young men living as *almajirai* in every step of the project, from scriptwriting to editing. Through training, they should not only be able to take control of the project as far as possible, but also learn skills that would potentially be useful to them in later life.

I secured funding and support from the Goethe Institute Kano, the patronage of Kano State's Commissioner of Information, and permission from three different Qur'anic teachers to let their students participate, provided the project occupied them only on their 'weekend days', Thursday and Friday. The project involved nine teenage *almajirai* from three different schools, among them my protégés from Sabuwar Kofa, Sadisu and Naziru, and several *almajirai* who attended my English classes in Kano and Albasu. Over the course of three months, the project unfolded as follows: first we met for various scriptwriting sessions, accompanied by long discussions about the topics the youths wanted to cover and messages they wanted to get across to the public. Then we met for practical filmmaking training with two professionals from the Kano film industry, 'Kannywood', followed by shooting sessions at the Qur'anic schools of the participating *almajirai*. Next came laborious editing sessions at the Goethe Institute, and then finally a glorious, well-attended premiere with high-ranking government officials, students and teachers from several Qur'anic schools, and a large, interested public present (Figures 1.3, 1.4 and 1.5). The *almajirai* had been involved in all stages of the film production, had performed all tasks more or less independently, and, under the guidance of two film professionals, had taken most directorial decisions themselves. It was by any account a remarkable achievement.[30]

[30] The finished film is available online with the ebook version. See www.cambridge.org/gb/academic/subjects/politics-international-relations/african-government-politics-and-policy/quranic-schools-northern-nigeria-everyday-experiences-youth-faith-and-poverty?format=HB#BfuEqQSh4ldSye3b.97 (Resources tab); and also at www.youtube.com/watch?v=A-SDeFX5rfI.

Figure 1.3 Filmmaking: studies (photograph: Hannah Hoechner)

Figure 1.4 Filmmaking: 'nasty' neighbourhood children (photograph: Hannah Hoechner)

Figure 1.5 Film screening: the Commissioner talking (photograph: Hannah Hoechner)

The docudrama we produced tells the story of Aminu, who is sent to Qur'anic school in the city because his father believes he will progress better in his studies away from home (Figure 1.6). Aminu struggles to find a place to sleep, enough food to eat every day, and money to buy soap. He is bullied by an older student in his school, abused by his employer, and denigrated by people in his neighbourhood. But against the odds, he eventually manages to secure reputable employment as a shop assistant and succeeds in his Qur'anic studies. The film's most critical message is for the communities in which the *almajirai* live, who treat them condescendingly, fail to support them, and consider them as labour power rather than as people.[31] The *almajirai* received much praise for their film, which received considerable media attention, and numerous people declared that the film had made them see the *almajirai* in a new light. It seemed that all had gone well.

The production process had been a veritable goldmine of information for me. I could learn about the *almajirai*'s experiences and perspectives not merely from the stories they contributed during the scriptwriting process, and through discussions about the way they would like to see their lives and identities represented on screen, but also from long days

[31] The youths came to defend the cause of the *almajirai* against a society failing to do them justice with a fervour that I have not encountered in any of my other interactions with *almajirai*. The personalities of the participating *almajirai* (most were fairly outspoken), the setup of the project, which created a space to verbalise and collate grievances, their roles as 'spokespersons', and the encouragement they received from the accompanying adults probably all contributed to this outcome.

Figure 1.6 '*Duniya Juyi Juyi* – How Life Goes' DVD cover

spent together and countless informal conversations, for example in the evenings after training. After long days of work, we would all sit on our veranda around our dim electric torch (the electricity supply as erratic as usual), discussing the events of the day and sharing stories from our lives as well as the feeling of being part of something important and meaningful. Incidentally, the film project also gave me an easier entry into the *almajirai*'s schools, where I visited them regularly, not least to discuss practical issues arising from the film project. Often, I ended up staying and chatting about everything and anything for long hours.

Yet, the film project was also revealing in other respects. Concretely, it exposed how weak the *almajirai*'s position is within society. More generally, it brought to light the limits and potential contradictions of 'participatory' research with a group as poor and powerless as the *almajirai*. From the beginning, it had been clear that the participating *almajirai* would act in as many capacities as possible, and that we would try to cast other children's roles with *almajirai* from their schools and with children from the neighbourhood, not least because we did not have the funds to engage many professional actors. But finding and training lay actors for adult roles was difficult, as those likely to perform best in the roles we needed (Qur'anic teachers and *almajirai*'s parents, who are often rather conservative, and nasty employers, who are by definition uncooperative) were least likely to agree to participate. The *almajirai* greeted enthusiastically the decision that we eventually took: we would engage locally famous Kannywood actors to act in the roles we were otherwise struggling to fill. They would be paid for their participation – not much by their standards, but a very significant amount by *almajirai* standards.

We decided not to pay the participating youths for fear of commercialising the project unnecessarily and detracting from the idealistic enthusiasm and curiosity about filmmaking skills that sustained it, at least in the beginning (evidenced, for example, by the way in which the *almajirai* spent their free time writing down stories they wanted to include in the script, or learning the English film vocabulary they had noted down during the day). Also, we feared that payment would exacerbate the inequality between the select few *almajiri* 'participants' and the many *almajiri* 'non-participants'. Boundaries between them were fuzzy, especially during the early stages of the project. As we met for training at the premises of an NGO (CAESI) that supported a large number of *almajirai*, non-project boys listened in at the training sessions and contributed ideas to the script. During the shooting, various students from the three participating Qur'anic schools stepped in as actors. Would it be ethical to pay for the work of some and not of others?[32]

---

[32] We sought, of course, to make sure that the *almajirai* did not suffer financially from their participation in the project by paying for food and transport costs, and I compensated

The participating youths did not come forward with their grievances, arguably to avoid displeasing me.[33] Yet, after the project ended, I discovered little by little that they had been debating among themselves for some time whether it was fair that they had contributed so much work and energy and had not been paid in the same way the professional actors were paid. Rumours and gossip in their neighbourhoods, communities, and schools further spurred the disgruntlement some youths harboured. They were accused, I learned, of being either dupes, agreeing to 'work' for free for me and/or for the Goethe Institute (which, it was presumed, would make a lot of money one day by selling the film), or liars, who had hidden the money I presumably paid them so they would not have to share it. The attendance of Kano State's Commissioner of Information at the screening ignited such rumours further: if the '*manya*' (the big and powerful) were there, surely there must have been money involved as well!

Such reasoning makes immediate sense if one takes into consideration the socio-political context. Politics in Nigeria have been characterised as 'spoils politics' (Allen 1995), suggesting that officials relate to their constituencies mainly through the redistribution of resources. The NGO sector in Nigeria is viewed by many as a vehicle for personal enrichment rather than the pursuit of the common good (see, e.g., Smith 2007). In the northern part of the country, interventions sponsored by Western donors frequently spark suspicion and trigger questions about the motivations underpinning them. For instance, the campaign launched in northern Nigeria in 2003 to eradicate polio was interpreted by some as 'part of a plot by Western governments to reduce Muslim populations worldwide' (Yahya 2006: 186). Rumours, Yahya (ibid.: 187) maintains, should be understood as 'commentary on broader political experience'. Seen in this light, the suspicions with which the film project and I were met become intelligible. However, suspicions and rumours could also – and could especially – flourish in a context where the *almajirai* have little social power to speak out against them (see Chapter 2).

I am quite convinced that the *almajirai* did not doubt that the film – which posited highly critical messages for richer members of society – was an efficacious means to communicate some of their concerns to the audience they hoped to reach: a wealthy, 'modern', urban audience that would otherwise rarely bother to listen to the *almajirai*'s views. One of the youths, for example, took a copy of the film to his employers so that they would 'learn from it' and 'correct their behaviour' towards him. Another

those *almajirai* who pointed this out as a problem to me for the income they forewent by not working during the project days.

[33] I had agreed to pay for the costs of some of the youths' secular education, which they had just started or intended to start soon. I suspect that they were afraid that I might change my mind if they upset me.

commented after the screening that people employing *almajirai* in his neighbourhood had 'understood certain things' thanks to the film. Yet, the fact that their 'voices' were being 'heard' was not the only concern that mattered to the *almajirai*. They also desired not to feel fooled, and not to be regarded as foolish or be called a liar. Finally, they hoped and expected to benefit materially, highlighting that 'recognition' is rarely the only problem poor and powerless people face.

On the subject of involving young people in research, Robson et al. (2009: 467) remark that 'in reality, ethical practice often means trying to balance different demands for which there are no easy answers'. While I acknowledge that ideally a 'participatory' project like the one described here needs to address redistributive questions in addition to questions of 'recognition', I have not yet found a satisfying answer to the question of how this could be achieved. We organisers believed that the project would provide the *almajirai* with useful and potentially marketable film-making skills, thus improving their economic position in the long term. Yet, we were gradually forced to realise that the envisaged benefits of the project may well fail to materialise. As some *almajirai* come from what is probably the most conservative segment of society, the film industry as a potential future employer is not necessarily a realistic scenario for them. For instance, one of the youths said that his parents would never allow him to get involved in the film business, which some people consider 'immoral'.[34] The question of payment also presents a lasting quandary. Had all the youths been paid 'compensation', what (if any) amount would have gratified those claiming that their labour was being exploited? Would 'payment' have led to more suspicion on the part of envious bystanders? Could those who doubt that Westerners do anything not primarily self-interested have been convinced that this was a not-for-profit project aiming to make *almajirai*'s views and experiences public?

Given the current enthusiasm for 'participatory' methods both in 'development' research and practice (e.g. Chambers 1997) and in research involving young people (e.g. Boyden and Ennew 1997; Morrow 2001; Barker and Weller 2003), it is important to point out their potential pitfalls (cf. Rahnema 1992; Cooke and Kothari 2001; Robson et al. 2009). Yet, despite all the caveats discussed here, I have little doubt that, ultimately, positive aspects prevailed in the *almajirai*'s experiences of the project. Until the end, there were moments when they stormed my house with new scenes they wanted to include, when they beamed

---

[34] Controversies surround, for example, Bollywood-style singing and dancing in films, the free mingling of the sexes, and Western-style clothing, particularly when worn by women (McCain 2013). During the Shekarau administration (2003–11), the Kano State government cracked down heavily on filmmakers and actors, especially female actors, pushing many film artists to relocate to other states.

with pride about their work and responsibilities within the project (for example, when giving press interviews), or when they reminisced about getting to know Hausa film celebrities personally. Since my departure from Kano, the film has been screened at national and international film festivals, and it won an Africast 2012 Award, which its director Abdullahi was invited to accept at the prize-giving ceremony in the capital Abuja. None of the participating youths had travelled that far before, nor had they spoken in front of a comparable audience. The prize money did its bit, I think, to propitiate whatever grudges the *almajirai* may still have held.

To sum up, this chapter has sketched the contours of the Qur'anic education system (the *almajiri* system) in northern Nigeria and has situated it within wider debates on Muslim youth and Islamic education. Such debates are often emotionally charged and built on weak empirical ground, shortcomings that the present study seeks to address. A core argument of this book is that education studies, poverty research, and childhood and youth studies provide suitable lenses through which to understand the workings of religious educational systems, their students' experiences, and their implications for wider society. Such insights can fruitfully complement the work of historians and Islamic studies scholars, and yet they have rarely been brought to bear on Islamic education systems, notably in Africa. This introductory chapter has outlined how I mobilise these respective bodies of literature to understand the situation of the *almajirai* in Kano.

The following chapters will trace the trajectories of boys and young men through the Qur'anic education system, highlighting their experiences while situating these solidly within the socio-economic, political, and religious/cultural context of contemporary northern Nigeria. The preceding paragraphs, in which I discussed the long-term ethnographic and 'participatory' fieldwork through which the data for this book was collected, have provided a foretaste of how easily the *almajirai* were scorned by their communities. Given their structurally weak position, it does not take much for the people around them to declare them dupes and liars, and to treat them accordingly. The next chapter explores this theme in greater depth by questioning contemporary discourses circulating about the *almajirai* in Nigeria.

2 Fair game for unfair accusations?
Discourses about Qur'anic students

[W]e daily witness him [the *almajiri*] in torn, dirty looking cloth, hungry stomach, and unkept (sic) body. His image is a source of concern to many modern malams [Islamic scholars] who strongly feel that he is giving Islam a bad picture; his status to others is not more than that of an eyesore or a pest. (Tilde 2009, commentator on gamji.com, a news site publishing commentary on northern Nigeria)

Are you treated well when you go out begging? I mean the people of the houses where you go to beg, do they treat you well or do they send you away when you come to the house?
Inusa (aged 15): Most of the houses do that [send us away] . . . it's just because of hatred.
Why do you think people don't like almajirai?
Dahiru (aged 20): It's because the *almajirai* are dirty. If an *almajiri* is a little boy, because there is no one to take care of him, they tend to be dirty.
But you are not dirty.
Inusa: It's because some are dirty that they think all of us are dirty.

Scruffy-looking boys with begging bowls are a visible feature of the landscape in many towns and cities across Muslim West Africa. In northern Nigeria, they have become shorthand for the Qur'anic education or *almajiri* system. Many perceive the young Qur'anic students as a hapless but harmless public nuisance. Adolescent *almajirai*, on the other hand, appear in the public imagination as ready recruits for radical groups such as Boko Haram, as potential '[b]utchers of Nigeria' (Soyinka 2012), and as 'monsters' in the 'breeding'.[1] They are also looked upon as ready recruits for politicians seeking to 'rent' a crowd or mob for a rally or riot, especially around election time and during times of heightened ethnoreligious tension (e.g. Garba 2015). The *almajirai* stir many emotions. This chapter surveys these emotions and the controversies surrounding the *almajiri* system, thus introducing the wider contexts within which the Qur'anic education system operates today.

---

[1] 'Rehabilitating our almajiris' (2011).

Discourses about the *almajirai* arguably bear important resemblances to a 'moral panic'. This concept, first developed by Stanley Cohen (2002 [1972]), refers to phenomena characterised by 'concern...about [a] potential or imagined threat', 'moral outrage' towards those considered responsible, 'widespread agreement...that the threat exists, is serious and that "something should be done"', an 'exaggeration' of the size of the phenomenon in question and of its negative consequences, and, finally, volatility: 'the panic erupts and dissipates suddenly and without warning' (Cohen 2002 [1972]: xxvi–xxvii).

As this chapter will show, the *almajirai* have been a staple in Nigerian public debates at least since independence. This sits uneasily with the notion of 'panic' as a one-off 'spasmodic' event (Cohen 2002 [1972]: xxxvii) and volatile phenomenon. Also, as far as discourses about the *almajirai* are concerned, it will become clear in this chapter that there is no 'widespread agreement' on what exactly it is that is under threat. On the contrary, that the figure of the *almajiri* can be charged with very different meanings and emotions, that it can signify very different threats, and that it can be mobilised to put blame on a range of different actors contribute to the salience of this figure. The *almajirai* appear to be simultaneously at the nexus of a range of different astonishingly long-lived 'moral panics'.

Where the notion of 'moral panic' is most productive is in pointing out the ways in which the (media) salience of certain phenomena can reveal broader issues and power struggles. As Cohen (2002 [1972]: xxxvii) puts it, '[s]uccessful moral panics owe their appeal to their ability to find points of resonance with wider anxieties'. The aim of this chapter is to identify these anxieties, while also seeking to uncover the political functions and implications of particular discourses about the *almajirai*. Hall et al. (1978) use the concept of 'moral panic' to draw attention specifically to the disciplining work accomplished by media frenzies: with respect to discourses about 'mugging' in Britain in the early 1970s, they argue that, by means of a 'moral panic', 'a "silent majority" [was] won over to the support of increasingly coercive measures on the part of the state' (ibid.: 221). This chapter explores how discourses about the *almajirai* lend legitimacy to particular forms of treatment by the state as well as by the wider public. The question that remains to be answered is this: why the *almajirai*? What makes them such a salient theme in the popular imagination?

First of all, the *almajirai* are male. Whitehead and Barrett (2001: 8) suggest that 'whenever larger social and public concerns raise their head...very quickly the issue of boys/men comes to the fore; usually how to change them, control them, provide them with purpose, or simply avoid the worst excesses of anti-social male behaviour. What emerges, in fact, is a moral panic around men and masculinity.'

Secondly, the *almajirai* are young. Arguably, discourses about young people often address and open up for debate issues at the heart of the social imaginary (Durham 2004). Comaroff and Comaroff (2006: 268) describe youth as:

> complex signifiers, the stuff of mythic extremes... simultaneously idealizations and monstrosities, pathologies and panaceas... [Y]outh stands for many things at once: for the terrors of the present, the errors of the past, the prospect of a future... In all of these tropic guises, of course, they are figures of a popular imagination far removed from more nuanced social realities.

The claim that children or youths are 'lost', or, given the circumstances under which they grow up, have 'lost out' on certain experiences deemed essential for their life stage, may reveal wider fears about the social reproduction of society (see Durham 2004: 591).

Finally, discourses about the *almajirai* touch on wider debates about schooling, which, given its importance for the socialisation of children, easily stirs up emotions. As Stambach (2000: 3) writes, 'schools are often pivotal social institutions around which the configuration of society as a whole is imagined, contested, and transformed' (cf. Starrett 2006). In brief, ideas about boys and young men, childhood, youth, and education are closely tied to social, economic, and political conditions, while inferences about wider societal concerns can be drawn from prevailing ideals and notions of deviance.

Debates about West African Qur'anic education systems have been analysed in some depth only for Senegal, where international children's rights organisations have a strong presence (Perry 2004; Ware 2014). Building on local critiques of the system, a coalition of Western aid workers, missionaries, Senegalese activists, and concerned individuals has been campaigning against the system in Senegal since the 1990s (see, e.g., Human Rights Watch 2010). Donna Perry (2004) analyses the 'global civil society' actors involved in this campaign and their discursive strategies.[2] By contrast, she spends little time scrutinising local actors and their reasons for positioning themselves in particular ways in debates about the *talibés*, as male Qur'anic students are called in Senegal.

Rudolph Ware points out the historical precedents of current negative discourses about Qur'anic schooling in Senegal. 'This kind of caricature of the *daara* [Qur'anic school] did not originate with human rights groups,' he claims. 'Attacks on Qur'an schools were a major component

---

[2] Perry (2004) argues that the 'global civil society' actors involved, afraid of being accused of cultural imperialism, strategically frame the plight of the *talibés* in structuralist terms. As they invoke poverty, structural adjustment, and population growth as the reasons why a once well-functioning practice has presumably been derailed, they avoid criticising more cultural aspects of the practice.

of French assimilation policy and the colonial *mission civilisatrice* (civilizing mission) in Africa' (Ware 2014: 40). Importantly, he attributes current misunderstandings about Qur'anic education to the epistemological shifts associated with Islamic reformism and pro-Salafi movements in West Africa. Salafi-oriented intellectuals 'shared in the colonial discourse of modernity', Ware argues (ibid.: 69), and sought to replace the 'embodied' practices surrounding Qur'anic learning with 'abstract' knowledge, 'divorce[d] from its particular embodied bearers' (ibid.: 205).

It is important to recognise the influence of colonial legacies and global actors on discourses about the *almajirai*, even though international children's rights advocates are far less vocal in northern Nigeria than they are in Senegal, and even though British colonial administrators there arguably held ambiguous attitudes towards Qur'anic schools (see Chapter 3). Epistemological shifts and the rise of 'reformist' Islam play an important role in discourses about Islamic learning in Nigeria as in Senegal. However, the majority of authors contributing to current discourses about the *almajirai* in Nigeria are contemporary Nigerians steeped in present-day concerns, who do not limit themselves to questions of epistemology. By analysing the ways in which contemporary Nigerians debate the *almajiri* system, we can learn about some of their concerns and fears.[3]

The *almajirai* figure in debates about such vexing questions as poverty and the distribution of power and resources, anxieties about raising children as 'modern' citizens of a united Nigeria, and claims to religious legitimacy and cultural superiority. The Qur'anic students are frequently 'othered' in such debates, a process I conceive of as 'adverse symbolic incorporation'. They serve as a projection screen onto which competing images of what is 'appropriate' and 'normal' are thrown. Yet, as the *almajirai* serve in most situations as a counter-image of what is desirable, being incorporated in this way works to their disadvantage. Negative projections compound their low social status and make the *almajirai* vulnerable to scapegoating.

The data for this chapter stems from a range of sources. I surveyed media records (national and international English-language news, and internet sources including blogs and online forums), official narratives, and institutional publications (from local and international organisations working with children), as well as local academic texts.[4] There are

---

[3] For an earlier version of the argument made in this chapter, see Hoechner (2014b).

[4] I collected the newspaper material through keyword searches (*'almajiri'*) on individual newspapers' homepages, including both Abuja- and Lagos-based newspapers, and via the online newspaper database allAfrica.com. Most articles were published between 2009 and 2012. I collected blog and online forum entries via the Google search engine using *'almajiri'* as a search term. Most articles I analysed were either editorials/letters

obvious limits to the use of newspapers and blogs as a proxy for public opinion or discourse, especially in a context where large segments of the population cannot read English[5] and lack the resources to buy newspapers or access media online.[6] Also, the nature and quality of the 'knowledge' produced through newspapers, blogs, and online commentaries can be problematic. As newspaper sales in Nigeria are low, so are journalists' salaries. It is common practice for politicians to sponsor journalists to cover or omit certain stories (see Walker 2016: 201ff.). The anonymity and cost-free nature of online commentaries and entries in online forums make them widely accessible to both readers and writers. Yet, for these very reasons, it is difficult to know who uses them and whose opinion they represent.

To counterbalance these uncertainties, where possible I combine reflections based on written material with observations made during fieldwork. Furthermore, I concentrate in my analysis of written sources on major newspapers, and on statements by authors who are well-established public figures or can at least be clearly identified by their full name. However, I also quote some online commentaries and material from online forums whose authors are unidentifiable. I do so when I find views to be both recurrent and particularly problematic. I argue that spontaneous, impulsive, un-self-censored thought – as opposed to thought-out opinions, which their propagators are prepared to defend – are worth analysing in their own right: they can reveal people's underlying stereotypes and fears.

The next section starts with some general reflections on perceptions and generalisations that can help us understand why people notice the *almajirai* only in particular ways and moments, pointing to the mechanisms turning probabilities into 'truths'.

'Whoever best fits the stereotypes wins'

The *almajirai* have attracted many labels. Policymakers and development workers concerned with universalising basic education categorise them with reference to their absence from formal schools as 'out-of-school'

to the editor, featuring personal opinions and anecdotes, or reports on the occasion of political events, such as former President Goodluck Jonathan's launch of the so-called 'Almajiri Model Schools' (see Chapter 3 and below).

[5] Only about 74 per cent of 15–49-year-old men and 54 per cent of 15–49-year-old women are literate in Roman script (National Population Commission 2009: 35–6).

[6] Print newspaper sales are low, but freely accessible online news sites are frequently consulted by the internet-using public, which has grown substantially since smartphones have entered the market. The number of internet users in Nigeria has grown from less than 1 per cent of the population in 2000 to over 47 per cent in 2015. This is well above the African average for 2015 of 22.5 per cent internet users (International Telecommunication Union n.d.).

children and uneducated (e.g. Aderinoye 2007; UBEC 2010: 8). Children's rights' advocates talk about them as 'child beggars'[7] and 'street children'[8] who are 'neglected', 'exploited', or 'abandoned' (e.g. Okoye and Yau 1999; NCWD 2001). In the context of Boko Haram-related violence, many look at the *almajirai* through a security lens as a 'time bomb'[9] and 'menace' (Olagunju 2012; see also West Africa Insight 2010; Onuoha 2011). Labels reveal people's ideas about 'how [other] people fit into different spaces in the social order' and about 'the terms on which society should engage with them' (Moncrieffe and Eyben 2007: 2; see also Goffman 1975). But labels also develop a logic of their own as they influence how we perceive our environment.

Scholars of humanitarianism have argued that humanitarian logics of action require target groups to be construed as 'needy' and 'pure' victims, as this makes it possible to sustain narratives of humanitarian action as disinterested, uncontroversial, and universally salutary (Redfield and Bornstein 2011: 13; Malkki 1996: 378). Labels such as 'neglected', 'exploited', and 'abandoned' cast the *almajirai* in the role of passive victims who need to be 'saved' from the abusive treatment of their parents and teachers. Not only do these labels distort the *almajirai*'s lived realities; they also obscure the fact that some boys enrol as *almajirai* of their own accord.

What is more, many of the labels used for the *almajirai*– 'street children', 'child beggars', 'out-of-school children' – de-gender the *almajirai* ('children' rather than 'boys'), thus obscuring the fact that the *almajiri* system is reserved for boys, and that ideas about gender-appropriate upbringing are an important part of parents' motivations for enrolling sons in the system. To mature into men, boys are expected to learn how to cope with hardship and to stand on their own feet.

Labels, moreover, filter our observations. Perception 'is more complicated than simply seeing, hearing, and sensing' (Mills 1997: 141). As more information exists in our environment than we can possibly assimilate, we focus on those pieces of information that chime with our preconceptions. We not only perceive 'evidence' selectively, as psychologists have shown; we also tend to seek and interpret 'evidence' in ways that bolster our pre-existing beliefs, expectations, or hypotheses (Nickerson 1998: 175). These features of human cognition beg the following questions: which *almajirai* are registered as *almajirai*? In which situations and places do *almajirai* appear on people's radar? Which *almajirai* vanish from notice, and when? Which boys are 'wrongly' classified as *almajirai*?

---

[7] 'Child beggars of Nigeria's Koranic schools' (2008).
[8] Almajiri Education Foundation (n.d.).
[9] 'Almajiris: Nigeria's ticking time bomb' (n.d.).

People easily generalise from individual observations, as hinted at by Inusa when he notes that, because some *almajirai* are dirty, people assume that all *almajirai* are dirty. 'Whoever best fits the stereotypes wins', Fonseca (1995: 238) writes about Roma in Europe who are considered 'genuine' only when they resemble exoticising images. Mismatching information is easily discarded. Many people considered unkempt looks to be a precondition for being a 'real' *almajiri*. For example, in the course of scriptwriting for the 'participatory' film project I organised with nine *almajirai*, we discussed what a 'typical' *almajiri* would look like: Auwal, one of the participating youths, stated that often people would not believe that he was an *almajiri* given the (smart) way in which he dressed.

Pragmatic factors contribute to selective perception. People are more likely to register *almajirai* carrying begging bowls as *almajirai* than those without, and they are more likely to recognise *almajirai* wearing scruffy clothes as *almajirai* than those dressed well. Sigona (2005: 752) writes about Roma in Italy that 'Roma beggars... are much more visible than statistically representative'. Similar points can be made about the *almajirai*: they go unnoticed when they look and behave like any other boy. The *almajirai* whom people see are those who fit the stereotype and thereby confirm it: those who belie it are invisible. Labels such as 'street child' or 'child beggar' obscure the fact that many *almajirai* neither live on the streets nor engage in begging, or, if they do, they often combine it with other livelihood activities.

Many of the *almajirai* I was close to expressed distress about the difficulties they face in dressing well and being clean, and access to food was a recurrent concern. Students not yet old and strong enough to do paid physical work and who therefore have no resources to buy food are particularly vulnerable. Thus, there is certainly truth in the associations described in the paragraphs above. Yet, reducing the *almajirai* to scruffy food scroungers is just as problematic as ignoring the problems they face in terms of accessing food and adequate clothing. It overlooks that their struggle is as much for dignity as it is for material improvements to their situation. Also, the difficulties of the *almajirai* that are less visible to the outside observer are easily dismissed.

As a consequence of equating *almajirai* with 'street children,' most people's concern is with urban *almajirai* (cf. Perry 2004: 63, 66, who comes to a similar conclusion for Senegal). For example, one member of a committee set up by former Kano State Governor Rabi'u Kwankwaso to advise his government on *almajirai*, and to which I presented my research, asked me why I went to a rural area for my research given that the problem of the *almajirai* was an urban and peri-urban one. Such thinking ignores the *almajirai*'s frequent seasonal movements between rural and urban areas. It also pays no heed to the difficulties the *almajirai* face during their sojourns in rural areas. Widespread poverty in rural areas makes it difficult for the *almajirai* to earn the necessary cash to buy soap and clothing. Despite villagers' roles as food producers and their greater acceptance of the *almajirai*, accessing food is also a challenge in rural areas, especially during seasonal times of scarcity.

Chambers (1983) has prominently argued that little is done to alleviate rural poverty because the rural poor are peripheral to urban centres of power, resources, and 'knowledge' production. A similar argument can be made about the *almajirai*. It is when they are in urban areas that they come within the ambit of journalists, academics, policymakers, and Nigerians belonging to different socio-economic strata or to a different religion. Whereas they 'blend in' in rural areas (and are difficult to tell apart from other poor rural boys), when they come to the cities they are noticed as misfits. The young *almajirai* to whom I was teaching English and literacy in the rural community of Daho said that they were insulted much more frequently in urban than in rural areas. This indicates their greater acceptance in rural locales.

In a similar vein, I would argue that the *almajirai* attract much more attention when moving about in public spaces (on streets or at traffic junctions, for instance) than when they work or spend time in private spaces (for example, within households). This might help explain the relatively strong focus on begging in criticisms of the system. However, if we want to protect the *almajirai* from humiliating experiences, we also need to pay attention to the abuse they suffer in their roles as domestic workers (see Chapter 5).

While many *almajirai* are thus not immediately noticed as such, many young beggars and poorly dressed boys are taken to be *almajirai* regardless of whether or not they live in a Qur'anic school. The *almajirai* in my research complained about boys pretending to be *almajirai* who 'collect money from people that want to buy something and just run away with the money' (Tanimu, aged ten). Conversely, people identifying with the *almajiri* system emphasised that equating *almajirai* with hapless, squalid young children did the 'true' system injustice. For example, the *malam* at Sabuwar Kofa, whom I asked for his opinion on young boys enrolled as *almajirai*, suggested that they were orphans and exceptions. Commonly, boys are not enrolled as *almajirai* before they are circumcised, which is done at around age seven. The *malam* himself did not accept enrolments from boys below the age of ten.

In summary, stereotypical representations of the *almajiri* system should be taken with a pinch of salt: what is noticed depends on the lens of the viewer. How people think or write about the *almajiri* system reflects their position within society and the wider societal concerns that disquiet them. By analysing discourses about the *almajirai*, we may learn about such concerns. This is what the next sections explore.

Almajirai as antithesis of development and modernity

Concerned discourses about the *almajirai* can be traced back to the 1960s and the early years of Nigeria as a newly independent state, when modernist nation-builders called into question the ability of the Qur'anic education system to forge a 'modern' citizenry for a united Nigeria (Abdurrahman and Canham 1978: 63; Csapo 1983). These nation-builders were confronted with a challenging colonial heritage. During the colonial period, the historically Muslim Northern Region and the predominantly non-Muslim Eastern and Western Regions had been administered separately, and were characterised by markedly different approaches to education. Whereas missionaries set up 'modern' schools in the southern parts of the country, during almost 60 years of indirect colonial rule in the Northern Region, the British neither reformed the existing precolonial Islamic education sector nor introduced 'modern' education on any noteworthy scale. The needs of the colonial administration were met by employing secular-educated southerners and by offering 'modern' education to only a small section of society. Regional differences in 'modern' education at the time of independence had a 'knock-on effect' on subsequent development. According to Mustapha (2006: 8), 'a destabilizing inequality in educational attainment was built into the fabric of the Nigerian state'.

While educational disadvantage affects the vast majority of young people in northern Nigeria, this issue is often discussed with narrow reference to the *almajirai*. Former President Goodluck Jonathan (2010–15), for example, called the *almajirai* 'dangerous to national development' and declared that 'the time has come for the nation to build on the moral foundations of the traditional school system by providing the Almajiri with conventional knowledge and skills' (Adetayo and Alechenu 2012). Newspaper headlines such as 'Almajirai: A National Emergency' (Ayuba 2012) and 'Almajirai, Street Kids and a Nation's Future' (Olagunju 2012) imply an immediate connection between the *almajirai* and the fate of Nigeria.

The *almajirai* are considered a stumbling block on the way to a 'modern' Nigeria. 'We are modern now; we don't send our children on *almajiranci* [to live as *almajirai*],' I was told by an official of the LGEA (Local Government Education Area) in Kunchi, a rural community where I conducted interviews in 2009, when I asked whether any boys in his family were *almajirai*. The *almajirai* are imagined as relics from the past, 'stuck in a time warp' (Fabiyi 2008), and their schools are likened to typewriters in an era of computers (Tilde n.d.). The *almajiri* system, it is claimed, needs 'to be overhauled in order to conform with the new economy and modern realities',[10] and its students are considered to lack

---

[10] 'Almajiris: towards creating brighter future for the street kids' (2012).

'the practical skills required in the real world to contribute meaningfully to modern society, or even to earn a livelihood' (Suleiman 2009). In fact, educational disadvantage in northern Nigeria extends far beyond the *almajirai*, as is attested by the low secular school enrolment rates for girls, or the poor achievement of even those children who do attend secular school (see Chapter 3). In terms of skills and future prospects, not much sets the *almajirai* apart from other poor undereducated youths from rural households. The fact that the *almajirai* defy the increasingly globalised norms of 'modern' childhood arguably contributes to the persistence of the idea that they are in fundamental opposition to 'modern' Nigeria and that they in particular constitute a problem for 'development'.

'Modern' children for a 'modern' nation

According to Boyden (1997 [1990]: 190), 'modern' Western ideals of childhood as a protected phase of economic dependence, embedded within the nuclear family and the formal education system, have become a 'good' for 'global export'. These ideals have become enshrined in international children's rights legislation[11] and have influenced social policy doctrines. Also, I would argue that they have been embraced, in theory if not in practice, by many 'modern', urbanised, better-off Nigerians. The *almajirai*'s apparent defiance of 'modern' norms of childhood reinforces their association with 'backwardness'.

While there are certainly problems with the way in which many *almajirai* grow up, a one-size-fits-all approach to childhood ignores the fact that the blueprints of 'modern' childhood are not accessible or affordable to all, and they may contradict culturally valued ideas about child-rearing. Often a failure to fit into what is considered a universally valid model is construed as problematic, leading invariably to pathological results. This ignores the fact that young people may prove astonishingly resourceful and resilient when confronted by risk. It also leaves little room for *almajirai*'s own perceptions of what constitutes a risk in their lives (cf. Boyden and Cooper 2007).

As the *almajirai* do not live within nuclear families, they are often thought to grow up outside appropriate adult care and control and without sufficient support (cf. Perry 2004: 68, who finds that similar

---

[11] Nigeria has been a signatory to the United Nations Convention on the Rights of the Child since 1991, but due to resistance by different segments of society, the Convention was not domesticated until 2003. To date, not all states of Nigeria have passed the so-called Child's Rights Act into law (e.g. UNICEF 2017). Several commentators consider that its norms prohibiting child trafficking are applicable to *almajirai* (Department of State 2009; Olujuwon 2008). In a similar vein, the committee tasked with monitoring the implementation of the 'African Charter on the Rights and Welfare of the Child' found in 2015 that the practices of classical Qur'anic schools in Senegal, especially their students' 'forced begging', violated the charter (Right to Education 2015).

tendencies prevail in discourses on *talibés* in Senegal). Many Nigerians unfamiliar with the system believe the *almajirai* to be 'quasi-orphans' (COCFOCAN n.d.) and 'forsaken by their parents' (Shehu n.d.). For most *almajirai*, life in school is considerably harsher than at home. Yet, we cannot conclude from this that they do not know or experience parental care. Across West Africa, fostering is a common and valued child-rearing strategy. While the *almajirai*'s hardships are to some extent deliberate, most parents seek to ensure a minimum of care by placing sons with teachers who are either relatives or close family acquaintances. Blanket assumptions about a lack of parental care make it more difficult to identify those boys who indeed cannot count on their family's support, such as orphans or boys from disbanded families, who may be particularly vulnerable.

The fact that students often farm with their teacher and, if they earn an income through other means, contribute financially to his livelihood has been equated with abuse and exploitation (e.g. Abubakar 2009; Saidu 2010). We have to take *almajirai*'s complaints about their workloads seriously. The young *almajirai* I taught and befriended in the rural community of Daho – aged between six and 12 years – concurred that at school they have significantly more work to do than at home. However, classifying all work done by children as harmful ignores the fact that many poor families have no choice but to demand work contributions from all their members, including the youngest, and that work can also teach children important livelihood skills (see Boyden et al. 1998).

The street as a corrupting space is a recurrent theme, albeit not a new one; this is shown by Fourchard (2006), who traces concerns about the corrupting influences of the street on children back to the colonial period.[12] Begging has been criticised for being 'harmful to both [the *almajirai*'s] physical and mental health with attendant physical and psychological consequences' (Okoye and Yau 1999: 45). According to Aluaigba, an academic at Bayero University Kano, street begging exposes *almajirai* 'to all sorts of vile and deviant behaviors and immoral acts because they interact freely with people of low virtue like prostitutes, drug addicts and gamblers' (Aluaigba 2009: 22; cf. Rosemberg and Andrade 1999: 114).

The *almajirai* themselves are highly critical of begging, which they say exposes children to verbal and physical abuse by the people they beg from and increases their risk of being injured in traffic. The *almajirai* also acknowledge that *'yan daba*, members of urban gangs, may lure *almajirai* into their orbit (see Chapter 7), which corroborates Salaam's (2011)

---

[12] Fourchard (2006) shows how, in the late colonial period, children's activities on the street – such as working, hawking, and trading – became increasingly seen as dangerous and were made the object of government interventions. Incidentally, it was mainly poor children who performed such activities.

finding that many *'yan daba* have at some stage lived as *almajirai*. Yet, a focus on the street as a corrupting space and locale where so-called 'people of low virtue' gather should not detract our attention from the role ordinary people and their insults play in making begging a problematic experience for the *almajirai*.

Many outside observers wonder about the incidence of sexual abuse by Qur'anic teachers and among students in *almajiri* schools.[13] Given the sensitive nature of the issue and the silence surrounding it, it is difficult to come to definitive conclusions. When I asked one of my closest informants whether he or any of his friends knew of any case of sexual abuse in a Qur'anic school, he denied this emphatically. On the other hand, he knew of a young *almajiri* who had been sexually assaulted by a man in the neighbourhood, and pointed out that young boys may be vulnerable to being seduced with gifts and money.

It is thus undeniable that there are problems and dangers relating to the circumstances under which many *almajirai* grow up. However, it is important to note that risks are often located in the *almajirai*'s wider social environments rather than in their schools, and that frequently ordinary people are the sources of abuse. What is more, many narratives construe negative outcomes as an automatic and inevitable result of *almajiri* enrolment and so lose the power to explain these outcomes. Not every child living away from his parents is 'abandoned'; not every form of work carried out by children amounts to 'exploitation'; not every begging child falls prey to corrupting influences. To assume that the *almajirai* inevitably succumb to adversity ignores their resourcefulness in navigating the risks they encounter. It is important to investigate the factors moderating and mediating their experiences. Recourse to religious discourses, for example, can attenuate humiliating experiences, such as the frequent abuse the *almajirai* are exposed to when begging. Finally, we have to keep in mind the fact that the *almajirai* know their ordeal to be temporary: eventually, they will graduate from the *almajiri* system and its concomitant hardships.

Backward parents, brutish children, and Boko Haram

Cohen (2002 [1972]: xii) writes that an important element of a 'successful moral panic' is 'a suitable enemy: a soft target, easily denounced, with little power and preferably without even access to the battlefields of cultural politics'. In the case of the *almajirai*, a 'suitable enemy' is swiftly found: their poor rural parents. Many people describe the *almajiri* system as a case of 'culture gone awry'. The notion that the parents of *almajirai* are backward and negligent and 'defy every effort aimed at

---

[13] See, for example, 'Mixing the modern and the traditional' (2014).

addressing' the system (Kumolu 2012) is a recurrent theme in discourses about the *almajirai*. For example, Bala Muhammad, former head of *A Daidaita Sahu*, a Kano State directorate created to promote morals and good behaviour, chides 'parents who have more children than they can afford and see Koranic schools as a means to rid themselves of the extra burden' (Abubakar 2009). Aishatu Jibrin Dukku, Nigeria's Minister of State for Education at the time, claimed that the *almajirai*'s parents are 'so insensitive to the welfare of their children that they dispatch them to unknown places to take care of themselves'.[14] The *almajiri* system has been ranked on the same level of child abuse as female circumcision and the killing of twins and child witches (Owuamanam et al. 2012). While poverty, combined with one of the highest fertility rates in the world,[15] effectively limits the resources with which families can support their children, we cannot deduce from this that parents are careless or callous towards their offspring. Many parents sincerely believe *almajiri* enrolment to be the best option for their children, given the available alternatives (see Chapter 4).

Discourses about cold-hearted parents declare rural families responsible for whatever the *almajirai* go through. If they suffer, this is because their parents made 'poor' choices for them. By conceiving of the *almajiri* system as a cultural 'evil' and the product of a presumed 'culture of poverty' (cf. Lewis 1959), both the ways in which other members of society contribute to abuse and the basis of the *almajiri* system in material circumstances can be ignored. Similarly, many people describe begging as a cultural problem, arguing that the *almajirai* loiter on the streets because they prefer begging to 'work'. Hajiya Fatima Bello Aliyu, Kano State's Special Advisor to the Governor on Child Welfare until 2011, whom I interviewed, argued vehemently that people should not give to begging *almajirai* as 'giving would perpetuate the system'. It would 'reinforce the begging habit in them', they would 'grow up thinking there's nothing wrong with begging', and they would become 'drains on society'. She proposed that, instead, *almajirai* need to be 'cut off from the source'. As she framed the issue, it was inconceivable that some *almajirai* beg out of necessity rather than choice.[16]

Yet, many people are not merely afraid that the *almajirai* may become 'drains on society' one day. The circumstances of their upbringing, and

[14] 'Nigeria's 10mn child beggars' (2009).
[15] According to the National Bureau of Statistics (2016: 3), the total fertility rate in Kano State was 7.5 children per woman in 2015. This is just below the fertility rate of Niger Republic (7.6 children per woman), which in 2015 was the highest in the world (World Bank n.d.).
[16] Interview with Hajiya Fatima Bello Aliyu, Special Advisor to the Kano State Governor on Child Welfare under the Shekarau administration, 2 February 2011. The exact wording might have been slightly different, as I am reconstructing our conversation from my notes.

their presumed failure to acquire economically useful skills, are often presented as sufficient conditions to make them inherently dangerous. Saudatu Sani, a federal legislator from Kano State, for example, claims that '[t]he pathetic life' the *almajirai* live 'breeds heartless criminals' (Abubakar 2009). The current spate of Boko Haram violence in northern Nigeria has carried such modes of thinking to their extremes. Given the group's declared hostility towards and repeated attacks on 'modern' educational institutions, many in and outside Nigeria have considered Qur'anic schools their natural allies, and have jumped to the conclusion that the Islamist group finds easy recruits in such schools (e.g. Comolli 2013; Griswold 2014).

How well founded are assertions that the *almajiri* system and Qur'anic schools are aligned with Boko Haram? The existing evidence suggests that the reality is more complex than many commentators on Boko Haram would have it. Firstly, the constituencies of the *almajiri* system are not univocally antagonistic to 'modern' education. On the contrary, most of the *almajirai* aspire to 'modern' knowledge and most of their parents do not oppose it. Secondly, few young people are 'pure' *almajirai*: it is common for children to combine different educational options or to switch between them. As I have already pointed out, many poor young people from rural households struggle to acquire economically useful skills, whether or not they are *almajirai*.

I did not encounter Boko Haram sympathisers in the Qur'anic schools where I conducted my research, nor did I hear about any cases of *almajirai* leaving Kano to join Boko Haram. Of course, this may be linked to timing and geography: at the time of my research (2009–11), the Boko Haram insurgency still sounded like a remote phenomenon to most people in Kano, and as first and foremost a Borno-related affair.[17] In any case, this was how my *almajiri* informants perceived the situation as the 2011 Durbar or *Hawan Sallah* approached, the annual end-of-Ramadan celebration that usually features beautiful horse parades and large crowds of onlookers in Kano.[18] When I confided to the *almajirai* I knew best that I worried about the risk of a Boko Haram attack on Kano during this event, they were surprised: 'Boko Haram is in Kano?!' In their minds, Boko Haram concerned north-eastern Nigeria and maybe Nigeria's Middle Belt (a region often riddled with ethno-religious tensions), but certainly not Kano. Their genuine surprise about my warning highlights how little presence Boko Haram had in their everyday lives, at least at that time, and how far off their horizon was recruitment into Boko Haram.

[17] This quickly changed, however, and on 20 January 2012, Kano was the target of a large-scale attack claiming over 250 lives.

[18] Eventually, the Kano State government cancelled the 2011 Durbar festivities, citing the 'ill health of the Emir of Kano Alhaji Ado Bayero' (Aliyu 2011).

Of course, this does not mean that the *almajirai* and *malamai* in Kano may not share some of the grievances motivating their counterparts in north-eastern Nigeria to join Boko Haram. Indeed, one of the *malamai* I was close to declared that he could sympathise with the Boko Haram insurgents' cause. In his view, Nigeria lacked both justice/righteousness (*adilci*) and manners (*da'a*). Even with a secondary school certificate, ordinary people in Nigeria would not be given a job – not even a job sweeping up rubbish. Another *malam* asked me upon my return visit in August 2012 whether I was spreading the message that there is 'no righteousness [*adilci*] in Nigeria', and that God would curse the perpetrators.

Whereas some of my interlocutors could identify with the grievances fuelling the Boko Haram insurgency, hardly anyone condoned their methods. The *malam* mentioned in the previous paragraph judged Boko Haram to be erring for taking justice into their own hands rather than trusting in God to bring about change. That Boko Haram indiscriminately kills fellow Muslims particularly alienated my informants: anyone killing fellow Muslims could not claim to be acting in the name of God. The *almajirai* have been just as vulnerable to Boko Haram's indiscriminate violence as everyone else. Many of the *almajirai* who go to school at Sabuwar Ƙofa regularly attend Kano's central mosque, which was attacked by Boko Haram on 28 April 2014, killing over a hundred people (e.g. Ross 2014). I was told that, at the height of the Boko Haram crisis, parents were reluctant to enrol sons as *almajirai* in Kano, because schooling in the city (as opposed to rural localities) increased their risk of being harmed in a Boko Haram attack.[19]

Authors describing the *almajirai* as somehow more prone to indoctrination than other members of society in a similar structural position forget that most *almajirai* are not insulated from wider society and the opinions that reign within it. It certainly matters to them what their *malam* thinks, but they also listen to the radio and to podcasts circulating via mobile phones (which several of the older *almajirai* own); they care about their employers' and friends' opinions and they listen carefully to what is said in the Friday mosque. After the 26 August 2011 bomb blast at the UN headquarters in Abuja, which killed 25 people and injured over a hundred, the *almajirai* participating in the film project reported that in the Friday mosque they attended the attack had been condemned, and Islamic sources had been cited to back up this condemnation. If their social environment does not espouse Boko Haram's messages and violent means, it seems odd that the *almajirai* should start doing so by themselves.

Nothing in my data suggests that, at the time of my research, the *almajirai* were any more likely to join Boko Haram than other young

---

[19] Unlike in north-eastern Nigeria, where villages were frequently attacked by Boko Haram, in Kano State most attacks targeted Kano City itself.

men in Kano. What does the data collected on Boko Haram itself suggest? Arguably, we have reason to believe that Boko Haram recruits its members from diverse educational backgrounds (see, e.g., Mercy Corps 2016). At the beginning of the insurgency, young university graduates attracted attention as they demonstratively tore up their graduation certificates when joining the group. A report by the International Crisis Group (2014) documents that the educational trajectories of known Boko Haram members are diverse and it is not uncommon for them to include time in 'modern' educational institutions.

Finally, Boko Haram developed as an offshoot of the Salafi movement in Nigeria (Anonymous 2012). Salafis, however, are 'reformist' and have long been critical of classical Qur'anic schools (this is discussed in more detail later in this chapter and in Chapter 8). Such subtleties disappear in accounts declaring that classical Qur'anic schools are the principal 'breeding grounds' for Boko Haram.

How about *almajiri* views of wider international Islamist and jihadist movements? The *almajirai* I was close to surprised me several times with their interpretations of, and reactions to, current events. One day, for example, I was walking back to Albasu with a group of adolescent *almajirai* who had taken me to their *malam*'s field to teach me how to plant beans. Among them was Usman, a cheerful and open-hearted youth I knew fairly well, and who eagerly followed my English classes (he had pursued secular education up to junior secondary school (JSS) level before enrolling as an *almajiri*). I was telling the youths the news of the day: Osama bin Laden had been killed. A series of questions followed: was he Muslim? Who killed him? The Americans? Why did they just kill him? As I tried to explain the event, Usman chipped in, declaring off-handedly that he too would 'go to America on jihad one day. To contribute to the greatness of Islam.'

How can we understand Usman's comment? Should we worry that he is a 'radical' and potential jihadist? I argue that reading 'radicalism' or a 'propensity for jihad' from this thoughtlessly made comment would be pointless. Usman did not entertain any particular interest in international jihadism, and, before our conversation, he was aware neither of bin Laden's death nor of its political significance. Rather, statements such as Usman's reveal how different the frame of reference is through which many northern Nigerians interpret current events. Many perceive American foreign policy – and the American 'War on Terror' in particular – as an aggression and a hate campaign against Islam more than anything else. In this context, figureheads such as Osama bin Laden can easily be promoted to the status of freedom fighters who are to be emulated, even though, ultimately, few know what precisely they stand for. This is true not only for the *almajirai*, as the allegedly 'massive increase in the number of baby boys called Osama' in northern Nigeria after the September 11 attacks suggests (cf. Masquelier 2007 on similar trends in

Niger; Seesemann 2007 on Kenya).[20] The cult surrounding Che Guevara would probably be an appropriate Western analogy for northern Nigeria's 'Osama craze'. Few people would find it reasonable to believe that Western youngsters who admire Che Guevara would actually join a guerrilla movement.

To date, the claim that the *almajirai* participate in violence, whether interreligious or sectarian, has been investigated systematically on only one occasion: namely, in the aftermath of the Maitatsine crisis of the 1980s. Members of an Islamic sect, condemning elite corruption and the enjoyment of Western consumer goods, had risen up against the police, resulting in hundreds of deaths. The insurgents were believed to be mainly boys and young men enrolled in Qur'anic schools (Lubeck 1985; Hiskett 1987; Winters 1987). A federal government-constituted Tribunal of Inquiry established that children aged ten to 14 years, unaccompanied by their parents, were among the followers of Mohammed Marwa (nicknamed Maitatsine, or 'the one who curses').[21]

Detailed empirical knowledge about the actual membership of Boko Haram is yet to emerge, and while the conflict is still ongoing, its changing dynamics will continue to influence the recruitment processes, making it difficult to come to definite conclusions (see, e.g., Higazi 2015, who details how people in areas under Boko Haram control were forcibly recruited; see also International Crisis Group 2014; Amnesty International 2015b). Meanwhile, existing scholarship on Boko Haram has urged us to acknowledge the complex genealogy of the group, and to resist the temptation of offering single-factor explanations (e.g. Thurston 2016b; Walker 2016; Mustapha 2014). Poverty, inequality, intra-Muslim and intra-Salafi power struggles, and alienation from a political elite that is widely considered to be corrupt and insufficiently Islamic have all been discussed as factors contributing to the insurgency. Even though some authors suggest otherwise, the shortcomings of the *almajiri* system are clearly an unsatisfying explanation for a phenomenon as complicated as Boko Haram.

The politics of numbers: inflated figures and fears of domination

In 1975, Kirk-Greene wrote that 'the psychological fear of discrimination, of domination... the fear of not getting one's fair share, one's desserts... has been constant in every tension and confrontation in political Nigeria' (1975: 19–20). Fears of 'not getting one's fair share' were

---

[20] 'Osama baby craze hits Nigeria' (2002).
[21] See the *Report of Tribunal of Inquiry on Kano Disturbances (Maitatsine)*, published by the Federal Republic of Nigeria in 1981 (cited in Awofeso et al. 2003). In addition, the police are on record as having lined up and shot at least a hundred *almajirai* in Kano (personal conversation with Murray Last, 23 January 2014).

nourished further by the tremendous oil wealth that surged into the coffers of the federal government from the 1970s, and that now, with the oil price at a historical low, is at risk of drying up. Numbers in this context are highly political: the relative sizes of different population groups matter as they determine the allocation of resources to both states and local governments. In a context where 'resources are scarce (and getting scarcer) – resources such as jobs, land or access to the political posts that offer huge rewards – the competition between groups is fierce simply because these resources are usually allocated on the basis of which community the applicant belongs to' (Last 2007: 608).

Religion, which is highly politicised in Nigeria, has become a crucial dividing line in such conflicts over resources and political power. While precise figures do not exist – the last census enquiring about religious affiliation took place in 1963 (see Ostien 2012) – Muslim and Christian populations in Nigeria are estimated to be roughly equal in size (United Nations 2009; Pew Forum 2010). This stokes fears of domination within each group. While large religious minorities can be found in both parts of the country, overall Muslims prevail in the north whereas Christians prevail in the south. Ethnic divides map to some extent onto religious and regional divides, with most northern Nigerian Muslims being Hausa or Fulani (Hausa and Fulani make up 29 per cent of the total population of Nigeria according to World Factbook n.d.). Whereas *almajirai* can be found across the northern states (including in non-Hausa areas), they are hardly present in the southern part of the country.

Guesses about the size of the *almajiri* phenomenon echo more deep-seated concerns in this environment. Most guesses grossly overestimate the actual number of *almajirai* in Nigeria. The only official statistics that exist, compiled by the Ministerial Committee on Madrasah Education, estimate enrolment in Qur'anic schools throughout Nigeria to exceed 9.5 million, with more than 8.5 million in the northern part of the country (UBEC 2010). How many of these students are *almajirai*, however, is subject to speculation, as the existing statistics do not differentiate between day students (who stay with their parents, potentially attend 'modern' school in addition to Qur'anic school, and include female students) and 'boarding' students.

Despite the ambiguity, many journalists, bloggers, and government officials take '9.5 million *almajirai*' as a given, and some estimate even higher numbers. Often, authors do not specify to whom exactly they refer with their numbers, and it seems that many do not reflect on what their writings imply. Many use the terms '*almajirai*' and 'child beggars' synonymously, which means that older youths and *almajirai* who do not beg should not be included in their estimates, making the high figures even more unlikely (see Table 2.1).

Migration, especially during the agriculturally unproductive dry season, is a common strategy of Sahelian peasant households to reduce

Table 2.1 *Estimates of* almajiri *numbers*

Source	Estimated number of *almajirai* in 2011–12
Leadership[22] (newspaper)	'up to **20 million child beggars**, popularly called Almajirai . . . in northern Nigeria alone' (This would imply that all boys/male youths aged six to 17 years are *almajirai*, plus over eight million others.)
Vanguard[23] (newspaper)	'**30 per cent** of Northern youths are almajiris'
Business News[24] (news site)	'Kano has about **1.6 million** destitute Almajiris' (Given a total state population of just below 9.4 million according to the 2006 census, roughly 17 per cent of whom are males between the ages of six and 17 (approximately 1.6 million), this would equate to the entire population of boys/male youths within this age bracket in Kano State.)
The Punch[25] (newspaper)	'Borno has overtaken Kano as the state with the highest number of almajiris with **1.9 million child beggars**' (According to the 2006 census, the total population of Borno State is just below 4.2 million. Even if we assume that all *almajirai* in Borno are recent immigrants and have not been captured by the census, this estimate would imply that about one in three people in Borno State is an *almajiri*.)
Weekly Trust[26] (newspaper)	'Government statistics of 10 million almajirai in the North sounds speculative. Official statistics published by the Kano State government in 2006, for instance, revealed that there were **over three million almajirai in the state alone**' (The author probably refers to the ITQE census carried out in Kano in 2003 (see, e.g., Ministry of Education 2008). The census enumerated all students of Islamic education institutions, including girls, *Islamiyya* and *Ilimi* school students,[27] and non-boarding Qur'anic students. It put the total number of children and youths participating in the Islamic education sector in Kano at 3,004,981.)

their subsistence burden (Mustapha and Meagher 1992; Mortimore 1998). Where cultural and ethnic groups are spread across several states, national borders do not limit migration. An estimate of the total population potentially sending boys as *almajirai* to Nigeria therefore has to look beyond the country's border at related groups in neighbouring states. However, even a generous estimate of the total population potentially enrolling boys as *almajirai* does not support the high figures circulating in the Nigerian popular media discourse (see Table 2.2).

[22] 'A nation of 167m in a world of 7bn' (2011).   [23] See Kumolu (2012).
[24] See Alabo-George (2012).   [25] 'FG missteps on almajiri school scheme' (2012).
[26] See Ndagi (2012).
[27] *Ilimi* schools are schools for adult learners teaching a range of Islamic subjects.

Table 2.2 *Maximum number of 'possible'* almajirai *in northern Nigeria*

Maximum number of 'possible' *almajirai* in northern Nigeria in 2011–12 (approximate figures)[28]	
Hausa, Fulani, and Kanuri population of Nigeria	56.1 million
Hausa, Fulani, and Kanuri population of Niger Republic	11.2 million
Fulani population of Cameroon	2 million
Kanuri population of Chad	1 million
Fulani population of Benin	0.7 million
Total population potentially enrolling boys as *almajirai*	71 million
Percentage of male population between six and 17 years old[29]	17 per cent
Boys and young men theoretically eligible to become *almajirai* (17 per cent of 71 million)	**12 million**

The IQTE (*Islamiyya*, Qur'anic, and *Tsangaya* Education) census carried out in Kano State by the Office of the Special Advisor on Education and Information Technology in 2003 found 1,272,844 students enrolled in '*Tsangaya*/Qur'anic schools' across the state, with 537,562 of them attending school in urban areas and 735,282 in rural areas (Office of the Special Advisor 2005). The census captured neither students' gender nor their residence, and it did not ask about attendance at other educational institutions. The total figure thus includes girls as well as boys living with their parents and potentially attending *Islamiyya* or secular (*boko*) schools in addition to Qur'anic schools, which suggests that the actual number of *almajirai* in Kano is significantly lower than 1,272,844.

The fact that the publicised numbers are rarely based on reality (nor even on people's reasoned reflections on reality) should be clear by now. It seems that many authors simply do not do any maths when putting forward large numbers. Alonso and Starr (1987: 3) say of statistics in the United States that '[e]ven when the numbers misrepresent reality, they coordinate our misperceptions of it. The process is thus recursive.' This holds equally for the *almajiri* system. Inflated numbers both reflect the sense of crisis surrounding the system and further inflame anxieties.[30]

---

[28] All estimates for the size of the ethnic groups in question are gleaned from World Factbook (n.d.). Last (2009: 6) adds for consideration that 'Hausa' is a social rather than a genealogical label: 'the numbers calling themselves Hausawa rises and falls for politico-economic reasons, and has no reference to, say, the birth-rate'.

[29] Based on the proportion of male children/youths aged six to 17 years in Kano State in 2011 as a proportion of the projected total state population in 2011. Projections were obtained from the Ministry of Education of Kano State (Ministry of Education 2011). For want of age-specific population statistics for the entire population in question, I use the Kano estimate as a proxy. All numbers are rounded up.

[30] Cf. Bray (2003) and Meintjes and Giese (2006), who make similar arguments about inflated numbers of orphans and vulnerable children in South Africa.

Exaggerated numbers resurface when people discuss the state's response to the *almajiri* phenomenon. Some authors are concerned that state action is insufficient in the face of the huge mass of *almajirai* they imagine to exist. For example, in an opinion piece in the *Weekly Trust*, Ndagi, who believes that the 10 million guess underestimates the real number of *almajirai* in northern Nigeria, considers the recent attempt by the federal government to include *almajirai* in Universal Basic Education (UBE) initiatives by building so-called '*Almajiri* Model Schools'[31] insufficient:

> Even when we take the official figure of 10 million almajirai for granted, it is obvious that the new initiative can only cater for just a handful of this figure. If government builds 100 Model Almajiri schools as planned for 10 million pupils, my poor knowledge of arithmetic tells me there would be one hundred thousand almajirai in each of the schools. (Ndagi 2012)

Some online commentaries and comments in online forums – where people write more impulsively, and under the cover of anonymity – also have a more resentful edge. Many raise alarm about population growth and voice fears of 'losing' federal resources to 'undeserving' northerners. As people imagine uncontrollably large numbers of unkempt 'child beggars', they envisage solutions in the form of family planning and birth control, often pointing out the costs the state would otherwise have to incur. With reference to the '*Almajiri* Model School' initiative, for example, one commentator on the homepage of the Lagos-based newspaper *The Punch* argues that: 'Providing schools for the almajiri kids without abolishing the culture that ensures their "mass production" is crazy & amounts to an endorsement of the parents' reckless planlessness & irresponsibility' (Owuamanam et al. 2012). Several commentators claim that it would be 'unfair' to devote federal or national resources to supporting the *almajirai* since they are a 'northern problem'. Another commentator on *The Punch* website 'hope[s] the President realises that the "Almajiris" that are supposed to be in the streets of nonnorthern [sic] states are being curtailed by their individual families. He should

---

[31] These are over a hundred boys-only formal boarding schools built by the federal government across Nigeria. While laying emphasis on Qur'anic memorisation, they integrate religious and secular curricula and offer vocational training. Using Hausa as the language of instruction and communication (arguably to discourage the local elites from enrolling their children), and following the Islamic calendar (with Thursday and Friday as weekend days), they seek to reach out to boys who would otherwise live as *almajirai* ('Almajiri integrated model school' 2013). While the schools are a step in the right direction, they alone cannot address northern Nigeria's massive educational challenges, and questions remain, for example over the ways in which pupils for these schools are selected and whether similar provisions will be made for 'out-of-school' girls. Also, misappropriations have been reported since these school structures have been taken over by the respective state governments (UBEC 2015).

therefore provide the same amount of money being provided for the north to the governments in the south' (Adetayo and Alechenu 2012).

The discourses about the *almajirai* described here reflect wider political anxieties about the distribution of power and resources within Nigeria, and mirror a sense of competition between regional, ethnic, and religious groups over such assets. Moreover, in statements such as those above, moral and financial responsibility for poorer segments of society is disclaimed by referring to them as 'irresponsible' and therefore undeserving, unduly siphoning off national resources. The next sections explore how, in a context of increasing competition over religious legitimacy, the *almajiri* question serves to negotiate claims to religious and cultural superiority.

Contests over religious legitimacy

Like other parts of the Muslim world, postcolonial Nigeria has seen the fragmentation of religious authority (see, e.g., Thurston 2015). New fault lines have superseded the inter-Sufi tensions of earlier decades (see, e.g., Paden 1973). Since the late 1970s, Nigeria has witnessed the emergence – and subsequent fragmentation – of mass anti-Sufi and pro-Salafi 'reformist' movements (e.g. Loimeier 1997; Kane 2003; Brigaglia 2015) and the rise of a substantial Shi'ite faction, as well as the emergence of a series of more marginal sects, some millenarian in orientation, with Boko Haram as the latest addition to the list (see Mustapha and Bunza 2014).[32]

Initially, religious revival was limited to particular elite social groups (educated people, intellectuals, and students). However, since the 1980s, it has swept across wide sectors of the population (Fourchard 2005: 343–4). Societal transformations leading to growing socio-economic stratification provided the backdrop to this religious change. The oil boom of the 1970s and the subsequent economic slump pushed large segments of the population into poverty, especially in the northern part of the country and in rural areas (see Mustapha 2014: 169ff.). Meanwhile, structural adjustment hollowed out the health and education sectors and nurtured corruption. These processes were accompanied by the growing individualisation of society. Islamic ideologies of reform – most prominently formulated by the *Izala* (see Loimeier 1997; Kane 2003) – offered a powerful vocabulary to people frustrated with the established social, economic, and moral order to call for change. They have been said to challenge 'traditional' redistributive practices and to provide ethics that match

---

[32] While these developments have polarised the religious arena in important ways, there is also 'a large body of "neutral" Muslims today who, wary of the turmoil unleashed by sectarianism, shun any sectarian affiliation' (Mustapha 2014: 4; see also Chapter 1).

the new individualistic and acquisitive economic spirit (e.g. Kane 2003: 237).

A context of protracted political and economic crisis has arguably heightened the stakes involved in the search for religious righteousness. According to Last, the coming of the apocalypse 'is not an extraordinary idea' among Muslims today (2008b: 42). For Muslims, the religious integrity of the Muslim community (*jama'a*) is an issue of real concern, and attempts to ensure its piety, and to 'purify' Islam by removing unlawful innovation (*bid'a*) (a major endeavour of the 'reformist' movements) or by fighting Western-style 'immorality', are beset by a sense of urgency (Casey 2008; Last 2008b). This is evidenced, for example, by the keen implementation of shari'a law in Nigeria's northern states since 2000 (see O'Brien 2007; Thurston 2015).

Differences in religious views often manifest themselves, and are argued about, with respect to pressing social questions, such as the 'proper' upbringing of girls, or the 'right' educational system. The *almajiri* system provides one such area for debate in which competing claims to religious legitimacy can be negotiated. A person's position vis-à-vis the *almajiri* system has become a touchstone of her or his religious disposition among northern Nigerian Muslims. Supporters sometimes treat it as an indicator of a Muslim's religious 'authenticity' and accuse critics of having succumbed to 'Westernisation'. In a commentary on gamji.com, a news site with a focus on northern Nigeria, for example, A. M. Gusau accuses Senator U. A. Tafidan Argungu, an advocate of the Child Destitution Bill, which would ban children from begging, of revealing 'a deep seated disgust for a surviving indigenous institution that has not fallen under the sway of colonial and neo colonial estates' (Gusau n.d.).[33] Former Kano State Governor Ibrahim Shekarau was careful to adopt a conciliatory tone towards the *almajiri* system (see Iguda n.d.) so as not to alienate the tradition-oriented *'ulama*, which is still an influential electoral constituency in Kano. One of my neighbours at Sabuwar Ƙofa, a middle-aged policeman whom I approached for help when arranging for a sick *almajiri* to be taken to hospital, lamented to me that 'nobody takes care of them. Their parents just send them. But if I say I am against the system, they will say I'm not a good Muslim.' Critics of the *almajiri* system risk being accused of being anti-Islam, which may explain why so few local NGOs and even fewer international NGOs have launched campaigns to change the system.

On the other hand, many reform-minded Muslims in Nigeria criticise the *almajiri* system as a cultural accretion to Islam. Islam permits begging only in acute emergencies, they claim. Bambale (2007: 7), a

---

[33] The bill aimed to establish a national commission with which *almajiri* schools would have to register. *Malamai* who failed to do so or who allowed their students to beg would have been punished with two years in prison. Several new versions of the bill have since been tabled by different senators, but none has been passed into law yet.

lecturer at Bayero University Kano, for example, accuses the *malamai* of the *almajiri* system of having 'misunderstood or manipulated' Islamic injunctions 'to suit their personal needs'. This has resulted in 'an atmosphere of unnecessary begging among a vast number of people including those that are not even almagirai [sic] or needy' (ibid.: 8). The *almajirai*, like other powerless groups, are at the receiving end of arguments about religious differences. The youths involved in the film project, for example, told me about the *'yan Izala*– a term often used broadly to refer to Salafi-oriented Muslims, whether or not they are formal members of the Islamic reform movement *Izala* – that 'if an *almajiri* begs at their house, they don't give to him, they might even beat him'.[34]

Criticisms of the *almajiri* system are also framed in ethnic terms. By criticising the *almajiri* practice as a 'Hausa' cultural aberration, Muslims from other ethnic groups in Nigeria lay claim to the 'right' way of being Muslim. '[T]hat begging is an accepted occupation among the Hausas and that very large number [sic] of Hausa "beg" should not necessarily be misconstrued as an indication that Islam supports begging,' argues Ogunkan (2011: 127), an academic at Ladoke Akintola University of Technology, Oyo State. According to him, 'begging is not in any way embedded in Islamic injunctions' (ibid.; see also Fawole et al. 2011).

Hashim and Walker (2012: 2) write about Kano that 'the poor acceptance of diversity among Muslims...has created two classes of Muslims...with one considered indigenous and "authentic" and the other consisting of Muslims of minority ethnicities who are rendered "second class" Muslims'. By querying whether begging is permissible within Islam, non-Hausa Muslims may challenge the self-perception and self-presentation of some Hausa Muslims as Nigeria's 'better' Muslims. Interestingly, participants in such debates do not seem to be aware that begging forms part of Qur'anic education systems across the Sahel and well beyond Hausaland.

Conclusion: easy scapegoats and adverse symbolic incorporation

Most *almajirai* do not know what the national and international media write about them, or how the wider Nigerian public discusses their education system. But they are acutely aware of the discourses circulating locally about *almajirai*. They know very well that the people in the urban neighbourhoods to which they come to study talk about them as urchins and hoodlums, and, since the rise of Boko Haram, also as potential recruits for the Islamist insurgency. While they feel fairly well accepted within their rural communities, most *almajirai* I worked with – from very

---

[34] Not all Salafi-oriented Muslims identify with the *Izala*, and, in fact, the pro-Salafi community is itself highly fragmented (Thurston 2015: 39).

young ones to those who were almost adults – had experienced rejection and contempt in urban areas, ranging from insults and 'donations' of spoilt food to physical assaults. They were painfully aware of negative opinions about them and frequently voiced their distress about being denied even a minimum amount of respect as human beings. Bashir, an *almajiri* at Sabuwar Kofa in urban Kano (aged 12), felt that they were treated as even less than animals, for no reason other than being *almajirai*:

> Some of them don't think *almajirai* are human. To some, a dog is better than an *almajiri*[35] . . . To some, an *almajiri*, as long as he is an *almajiri*, they just take him to be a bad person. They think he is an animal, that a donkey is even better than an *almajiri*.

What is worse, as the *almajirai*'s reputation is predominantly bad, it is easy to claim that they are responsible for negative incidents – quarrels, thefts, and so on – in their neighbourhoods. Accusations chime with people's preformed opinions and therefore seem plausible. In addition, as newcomers and strangers at their places of study, the *almajirai* lack strong spokespersons (*gata*) to stand up for them and to defend their interests. Accusing them carries little risk of stepping on the toes of powerful protectors.[36] This is something that the *almajirai* involved in the film project were upset about. Without someone answering for them nearby, they felt that they had become fair game for unfair accusations. Auwalu, for example, stated during the scriptwriting stage of the film:

> Some offences, it's not an *almajiri* who committed them; it's the people/kids from town ['*yan gari*]. But they'll just say an *almajiri* committed it, if there's a school close by, they'll just go and tell the *malam*: look what your *almajirai* did, whereas it wasn't them who did it. The people from the neighbourhood don't see their own children's faults.

The boys and young men involved in my research understood very well the logics that turned the *almajirai* into an easy target for people looking for a scapegoat, and were keenly aware of what was at stake in creating particular representations of their education system. This became apparent especially during the production process of our film. For example, Kabiru, one of the participating youths, decided that his message to the public included in the end credits of the film should be 'either speak good about us or keep quiet!'

How can we conceptualise the social logics underpinning negative representations of the *almajiri* system? Researchers at the Chronic Poverty

---

[35] Unlike cats, which might be kept as pets, there is little sympathy for dogs in Hausa society. They are considered polluting, and Prophet Mohammed also disliked them (personal communication with Murray Last, 7 December 2010).

[36] The children in my neighbourhood at Sabuwar Kofa had understood this very well: on two occasions, I witnessed how young thieves in my house attempted to put the blame on my neighbours' *almajirai* after they had been discovered.

Research Centre propose the conceptual pair of 'social exclusion' and 'adverse incorporation' to capture the often detrimental terms on which poor people participate in mainstream society (Hickey and du Toit 2007). Rather than regarding poor people as 'left behind', such an approach pays attention 'to the ways in which particular groups or individuals are linked to larger social totalities . . . that shape their economic and social lives' (ibid.: 4). Poverty, according to this reading, is the result of particularly harmful social relations. I argue that the notion of 'adverse incorporation' can productively be extended to the symbolic realm (cf. Fraser 1996). For example, people routinely project onto powerless groups those characteristics from which they would like to distance themselves (Bauman 1990: 143). Low-status groups may play an important role in the construction and consolidation of 'mainstream identity' by serving as a backdrop for negative projections that devalue and subordinate them. Finally, low-status groups may serve the more powerful in society as scapegoats.

As I have demonstrated in this chapter, the *almajiri* system continues to be contentious in Nigeria. Controversies flare up, especially in relation to the allocation of resources to 'solve the problem' (for example through the '*Almajiri* Model Schools' proposed by former President Goodluck Jonathan), reflecting a sense of competition between different (ethnic, regional, or religious) groups over such assets. Through statements about the *almajirai*, people may position themselves within larger debates, which makes the young Qur'anic students a salient theme. The *almajirai* figure in debates about religious righteousness, where people discuss what is religiously ordained and acceptable behaviour with reference to the practice of begging. They are also invoked in discussions about the causes of the current political and economic crisis in Nigeria, and about societal responsibility for the poor.

The *almajirai* are frequently 'othered' in such debates, as I have argued. By construing the *almajirai* as being in breach of the rules of 'appropriate' behaviour, different segments of society may validate their own attitudes and actions. People imagining the *almajirai* as 'undeserving' may reject responsibility for the poor more widely, and people can affirm their own 'modernity' by viewing the *almajirai* and their parents as 'backward'. People branding the constituencies of the *almajiri* system as religiously misguided may confirm their own religious virtue by distancing themselves from the 'errant'. Finally, if the *almajiri* system can be declared responsible for problematic outcomes such as the current Boko Haram crisis, there is no need to seek more complicated, potentially uncomfortable, explanations. The *almajirai* are versatile figures in all these debates, which explains their salience. Yet, their symbolic incorporation into public discourse is mainly adverse, as the *almajirai* serve, first and foremost, as a counter-image to what is considered 'normal', desirable, and religiously ordained.

While I agree with Ferguson (1999: 85) that myths are worth analysing in and of themselves, they also need to be contrasted with empirical realities. Why do families opt for the *almajiri* system? What do the *almajirai* learn over the course of their enrolment? What are they likely to do after leaving the *almajiri* system? These questions must be answered on empirical grounds, since some of the popular answers provided so far craft their own realities, corroborating Hall et al.'s (1978) claim that 'moral panics' are politically productive. For the boys and young men living as *almajirai*, being the backdrop for people's imaginations can have negative consequences: people act in accordance with their assumptions and prejudices. Accusations levelled at the *almajirai*, even if they are unfounded, make immediate sense to people considering them hoodlums and miscreants. Furthermore, low status can engender even lower status. As *almajirai* often lack the power to refute unjustified accusations, these feed negative stereotypes, which may give rise to fresh accusations. Stereotypes about the *almajirai* as backward, gullible, and dirty can further facilitate their 'adverse incorporation' into the economy. As I explore in Chapter 5, the people employing the *almajirai* for domestic work can justify poor pay with the 'civilising mission' they are presumably pursuing by employing them.

Finally, framing the *almajiri* system as a problem of backward or neglectful attitudes is dangerous as it gives rise – and legitimacy – to government policies that penalise the poor rather than address their grievances (cf. Wacquant 2003). Since the escalation of violence associated with Boko Haram, there have been increasingly frequent calls for restrictions on the *almajirai*'s mobility, and bans on begging have been enacted in several states.[37] Seeking to deconstruct empirically unsound but socially productive stereotypes, the following chapters contrast the discourses about the *almajiri* system discussed here with ethnographic evidence.

[37] Attempts to control Qur'anic schools through punitive legislation date back to the colonial period, starting with efforts by the Kano Native Authority to regulate their movement as early as 1959, and attempts by the Kano State government to make registering with the state compulsory after the Maitatsine crisis in 1980 (Yusha'u et al. 2013: 130). Kano State Governor Rabi'u Kwankwaso (2011–15) set in motion a legislative process to 'ban all street begging and enable the state government to evacuate Almajirai from the streets' (NSRP n.d.). In February 2016, the state government made headlines when it proclaimed that it had deported 'no fewer than 60,000 almajirai' found begging in Kano to their states of origin (Elazeh 2016). Plateau State outlawed street begging by school-aged children in 2009 (e.g. 'Plateau govt bans street begging' 2009).

3 'Secular schooling is schooling for the rich!'
Inequality and educational change in northern Nigeria

Nowadays, if you have only the Qur'anic studies, there are places that when you go there, people will think you are nobody. (Ibrahim, *almajiri* in Kano, aged about 24)

Secular schooling is schooling for the rich! The poor won't succeed with it since the rich buy the exam results. (Isa, *almajiri* in Albasu, aged about 18)

Thursday afternoon in Albasu, a small rural town in eastern Kano State, northern Nigeria: the official part of our English class is over. This is when the *almajirai*, the young Qur'anic students I am teaching on their 'weekend' days – Thursday and Friday – present me with their vocabulary lists. They assemble an eclectic mix of English expressions, such as 'far stronger' or 'making the world better'. The *almajirai* do not learn English in their schools. Few people in their close social environment speak it competently, and those who do seem to have no time to spare for translations. My students ask me for the meaning of words they pick up from various places: from the scribbled notebooks of friends attending 'modern' secular school, from the imprint on the back of a Western-style second-hand T-shirt, from bits of discarded newspaper, from scraps of conversation they overhear on the streets or on the radio, and from sentences thrown at them by secular-educated youngsters in the neighbourhoods of their schools. Through my English classes I learned about the *almajirai*'s feeling of being excluded – excluded from knowledge that has an ineluctable presence today in northern Nigeria, but also from the social status that comes with such knowledge.

Another day, another setting. I am invited to the house of Kano State's Special Advisor to the Government on Child Welfare, who welcomes me to an imposing compound near the Race Course, in one of Kano's wealthiest neighbourhoods. We discuss the *almajirai*'s plight, and she presents what she considers the appropriate government response: *almajirai* should be obliged to attend 'modern' secular school. 'Sometimes you have to be a bit dictatorial about things,' she explains, given that 'no child wants to go to school. They wouldn't go by themselves.'[1] As she puts it, the *almajirai* fail to learn English because they refuse to attend 'modern' school. In a similar vein, many in Nigeria today explain the *almajiri* system in terms of 'backward' attitudes and a stubborn rejection of 'modern' knowledge. The challenges poor people face when trying to access 'modern' education of meaningful quality,[2] and their sense of exclusion when they fail to overcome these challenges, are mentioned less often.

After I note down the Special Advisor's policy ideas, our conversation drifts off into calmer waters. We talk about her children. She tells me proudly that her son at the age of four already schools in French, speaks English with his mother, converses in Arabic with his father, and learns Hausa from his nanny. This is necessary, she laments, to prepare the boy adequately for today's 'competitive world'.

Education scholars have long emphasised the inherently political nature of education. Definitions of what it means to be 'educated' in a particular context, and the distribution of opportunities to acquire the requisite knowledge and skills to count as 'educated', reveal wider societal power relations (e.g. Willis 1977; Bourdieu 1984; Bourdieu and Passeron 1990 [1977]; Levinson and Holland 1996). 'Modern' education, characterised by classroom-based instruction, age grading, certification, and the teaching of secular subjects, came to dominate such definitions of the 'educated person' (Levinson and Holland 1996) in many places around the world over the second half of the twentieth century. Arguably, 'modern' education has become 'one of the defining features of modern childhood' (Crivello 2009: 1). National schemes such as the Nigerian Universal Primary Education (UPE) and Universal Basic Education (UBE) campaigns launched in 1976 and 1999 respectively, and global initiatives including the 'Education for All' (EFA) movement started in 1990 or the Millennium Development Goals adopted in 2000, which seek to universalise basic education, attest to the central place that 'modern' schooling has come to occupy today within both government and development discourses (cf. Froerer and Portisch 2011: 335).

Liberal assumptions about the role of 'modern' schools as 'meritocratic springboards for social mobility' (Levinson and Holland 1996: 5) underpin this hegemony. Upward mobility, in this logic, is considered

---

[1] Interview with Hajiya Fatima Bello Aliyu, Special Advisor to the Governor on Child Welfare under the Shekarau administration, 2 February 2011. The exact wording might have been slightly different, as I am reconstructing our conversation from my notes.

[2] Of course, what exactly 'quality' means lies in the eye of the beholder. Dominant definitions of 'quality' have been criticised for their materialist and secularist biases, evaluating schools merely with regard to their ability to impart economically useful skills (see Newman 2016: 21ff., 245ff.). I use the term 'quality' here in a limited sense to refer to the ability of 'modern' schools to deliver what they propose to deliver: knowledge of secular subjects. Chapter 4 explores the meanings of education in a more fundamental way.

'an outcome of talent and effort' (ibid.: 4). Statements such as that of the Commissioner cited at the beginning of this chapter attest to the belief that is widespread in policy circles that if poor children only attended 'modern' schools, their future would look brighter. This chapter sheds critical light on such meritocratic discourses about 'modern' education. Many people in northern Nigeria have a more critical perspective on it, and even though they may aspire to 'modern' knowledge, in a context where chances to learn are unevenly distributed, to many people meritocratic discourses ring hollow.

What does the reality of 'modern' education look like for young people in disadvantaged contexts? Ruddick (2003: 335) remarks that, ironically, Western models of childhood and youth, such as 'modern' schooling, 'are being exported to non-Western contexts in which resources to adequately reproduce these forms are sadly lacking'. 'Modern' schooling, which is sufficiently adapted to local priorities, affordable, and of acceptable quality, is unattainable for many. Porter (2009: 1–2) observes that, by prioritising quantity over quality, in many countries the push to expand primary school enrolment has resulted for the children of the poor in 'swollen classes, lacking even the most basic educational resources, supervised – sometimes – by underpaid, barely trained teachers'. A focus on 'bums on seats' (ibid.: 1–2) rather than learning relevant to children's current lives and likely futures carries the risk that children fail to learn even the basic skills necessary to participate in a 'modern' economy.

In addition, rising participation in 'modern' education has, ironically, been accompanied by declining opportunities for formal sector employment in many areas (e.g. Demerath 1999; Jeffrey et al. 2004; for an early observer, see Dore 1976). While the jobs for which 'modern' education presumably prepares children become more and more scarce, 'modern' schooling also puts at stake children's participation in 'traditional' productive activities (e.g. Rival 1996). As the ideologies underpinning such schooling typically devalue and dismiss manual work (e.g. Rao and Hossain 2012; for a Western context, see Willis 1977), 'modern' schooling arguably 'deskills' young people for agricultural livelihoods already rendered difficult by economic restructuring (e.g. Katz 2004; see also Froerer 2011). This leaves poor young people and their families struggling more and more to prepare for an uncertain future.

A range of authors explore how young people unable to realise the presumed benefits of 'modern' education make sense of their experiences. Jeffrey et al. (2004), for example, illustrate how educated unemployed youths in North India embrace an 'educated habitus' to distinguish themselves from others and to make a point about the worth of their education, even though it does not help them access desired white-collar employment. Conversely, other authors show how disenchantment with the formal schooling available locally leads young people to distance themselves from ideals of the 'educated person' that emphasise 'modern' education, and to turn to 'traditional' or religious ideals instead (e.g. Demerath 1999; 2000; Rao and Hossain 2011; on oppositional youth identities in Western contexts, see Willis 1977; Bourgois 1995).

This chapter adds to the debates outlined here by tracing educational changes in northern Nigeria over the last century, and by exploring how people at the receiving end of these changes deal with, and make sense of, their situation.[3] Under colonial rule, only a small segment of society was given access to 'modern' secular education. During a brief period in the late 1970s and early 1980s, secular education became fairly accessible to poor people, and reservations about what was considered a colonial import constituted a major factor hindering enrolment. Today, increasing acceptance on principle has been counteracted by the state's withdrawal from public service provision after structural adjustment. Money plays an increasingly important role in accessing 'modern' education of worthwhile quality. Meanwhile, even though the 'hegemony' of 'modern' education is incomplete in northern Nigeria today, the prestige of once highly valued forms of knowledge, such as the 'habitus' inculcated in the schools of the *almajiri* system, has considerably decreased. Religious knowledge as it is taught in classical Qur'anic schools is juxtaposed today with both religious and secular forms of 'modern' knowledge taught in 'modern' secular (*boko*) and 'modern' Islamic (*Islamiyya*) schools respectively. However, the multiplication of forms of knowledge, while enlarging the range of educational options available, has not necessarily translated into greater choice for the poor, even though it has increased aspirations and desires.

After tracing educational changes in northern Nigeria over the past century and sketching out the diverse educational landscape resulting from it, this chapter investigates the *almajirai*'s positioning vis-à-vis 'modern' secular knowledge. It is a commonplace that people frequenting Qur'anic schools in northern Nigeria do not appreciate secular knowledge – a commonplace that nurtures, for example, suspicions about the presumed participation of the *almajirai* in the Islamist insurgency led by the group Boko Haram, which has gained notoriety for its condemnation of and attacks on 'modern' secular schools. My research provides a counter-narrative to such discourses.

While the parents I interviewed in my research had genuine regard for religious knowledge and made sure that their children acquired it, most were not opposed to 'modern' secular knowledge. Also, most young

---

[3] For an earlier version of the argument made in this chapter, see Hoechner (2011).

people were keen to achieve secular knowledge. However, in a context where access to prestigious knowledge is stratified, they struggled to access 'modern' education that is affordable and of acceptable quality.

In this context, like youths in other parts of the world who are unable to realise the presumed benefits of 'modern' education, the *almajirai* sought to maintain a positive outlook on themselves and their future. Far from rejecting 'modern' education, they emphasised its desirability. At the same time, however, they found ways of making their lack of access to it more bearable for themselves, for example by emphasising their own religious or moral credentials (see Chapter 7), by pointing out the presumed moral shortcomings of secular-educated youngsters, and by pinning their hopes on future opportunities to acquire the desired knowledge.

Education in precolonial and colonial Nigeria

'Islam . . . arrived in West Africa on the back of a camel,' write Abdur-rahman and Canham (1978: 44), pointing to the importance played by the Muslim faith both in the economic life of the region and in the vivid intellectual and social exchanges it facilitated across the Sahara. Adopting Islam allowed traders to 'identify with the larger world of Islam' while simultaneously facilitating 'credit and finance' (Paden 1973: 47). Kanem–Bornu, covering part of present-day north-eastern Nigeria, became Islamic in the eleventh century via trans-Saharan trade routes connecting it to North Africa, Egypt, and Sudan. In the Hausa city states further west, Islam was slower to become dominant. Beginning in the fifteenth century, it was the religion of the ruling elites. Yet, until the nineteenth century, its influence outside the capital cities and the ruling families was limited. The Fulani-led jihad of Uthman dan Fodio in 1804–8, launched against what were perceived as un-Islamic, syncretistic practices, and the ensuing establishment of the Sokoto Caliphate (Last 1967), strengthened the hold of Islam among the wider population.

While basic Qur'anic education may have been available locally, given the scarcity of scholars in the early days of Islam in the region, advanced Islamic knowledge was acquired by moving away from home to live with a renowned scholar in one of the emerging centres of learning (Kane 2016: 13). This meant that students often travelled great distances – 'tens if not hundreds or thousands of miles' across the Sahel to study with a shaykh with expertise on a particular book or subject (ibid.: 23). As elsewhere in West Africa, craft occupations were largely hereditary in Hausaland, which meant that boys and young men from scholarly households prevailed among Islamic students. Also, the time and mobility required by Islamic scholarship effectively limited extensive study to youths from privileged households that could afford to forego a student's labour power for extended periods of time (Last 1993: 120).

Scholars could pursue a career in teaching, or, if they failed to attract students, they could live by trading in spiritual services (Last 1993: 125). A further option was politics. Religious knowledge has been a political asset since the early days of Islam in the region. Muslim rulers, by submitting to the restraints of a written code, exposed themselves to the judgements of intellectuals educated in that code (ibid.: 124–5). Religious scholars became particularly influential in the Sokoto Caliphate. As the main literate class prior to colonialism, they were the only ones eligible for government positions such as secretary, judge or imam within the Islamic state (Last 1993: 124; Umar 2001). At the same time, the high mobility of religious scholars was essential for creating ideological and political coherence across the vast territories belonging to the Caliphate. As Lubeck (1985: 372) argues, 'Islamic networks and Qur'anic schools', spanning the entire Caliphate with their migration routes and networks, 'were integral to the expansion, reproduction and ideological integration' of the Islamic state.

British conquest and 'indirect rule' in Northern Nigeria from 1903 set in motion social and political changes that altered the configuration of the Islamic education system in important ways. Several developments transformed its position within society substantially during this period and, incidentally, boosted enrolment. Colonialism instigated the gradual ending of slavery, which had been a central pillar of economic life in Hausaland until then (see Lovejoy and Hogendorn 1993). As slave raiding subsided, travel became less dangerous, and new transportation networks further eased travel (e.g. Lubeck 1981: 71). Through the increased movement of Muslim traders and workers, Islam grew, and so did demand for Islamic education (cf. Reichmuth 1989: 41–2 on the expansion of Islam in western and central Nigeria during this period). The ending of slavery also created novel opportunities for social mobility for freed slaves, many of whom turned to religious education as an avenue to high status. While status distinctions did not vanish completely, the prestige accruing to the religiously learned, as well as the geographical mobility that characterised religious scholarship, helped obliterate memories of servile origins (Last 1993: 120; cf. Ware 2014: 163–4 on Senegal).

The gradual ending of slavery finally unleashed new economic pressures. Former slaves often found it difficult to secure a living, which added to the attractiveness of Islamic teaching as a livelihood (Last 2000b). In addition, with slave labour becoming unavailable, households struggled to produce enough grain to feed all their members during the agriculturally idle dry season. Under these circumstances, more teachers and students left their homes during the dry season to move to urban areas (see, e.g., M. F. Smith 1954: 132), thereby easing the subsistence burden of their rural households during times of scarcity. Migrant Qur'anic students have long been a readily available labour pool for the urban handicraft industry during the dry season (Lubeck 1981; 1985), while they could be put to work on their teachers' fields during the farming season, arguably providing a substitute for slave labour in large parts of West Africa (Bledsoe and Robey 1986: 215–6). Finally, British conquest boosted Qur'anic school enrolment by spurring beliefs in the coming of the apocalypse, which heightened parents' concerns that their wards should acquire religious knowledge in a timely manner (Last 1970; 2000b). Meanwhile, for a range of reasons, colonial policies largely left the Islamic education system to itself.

Colonial officials held ambiguous attitudes towards Islam and institutions of Islamic learning. The Mahdist uprising in Sudan (which also attracted followers in northern Nigeria; see Mustapha and Bunza 2014: 78; Paden 1973: 68) was still fresh in people's memories and served as a warning (Hubbard 1975: 154; Thurston 2016a). Frederick Lugard, High Commissioner of the Northern Nigeria Protectorate and later Governor General of the Colony of Nigeria, wrote about Islam: 'It is a religion which renders Africans liable to wild bursts of religious frenzy' (cited in Philips 2004: 58). Meanwhile, others in the colonial administration, including Richmond Palmer, who strongly influenced British policy in Northern Nigeria in the 1910s and 1920s, deemed Islam to be both a conservative and a 'civilising' force, which, if handled and transmitted well, would ensure political stability (Hubbard 1975: 155).[4]

Such divergences notwithstanding, colonial officials agreed that policies towards Islamic schools were part of wider struggles to stabilise and prolong indirect rule, and that educational policy had to be designed in a way that would preserve to the greatest extent possible the legitimacy of indirect rule and of its local partners, while simultaneously training enough African staff to man the Native Administration (e.g. Thurston 2016a: 120). This, moreover, had to be accomplished at minimal cost, as the British sought to keep financial liability for their colonies to a minimum (e.g. Tukur 2016: 332ff.). For fear of antagonising Muslim constituencies, missionaries, who provided 'modern' education in many other parts of the colonised world, were discouraged from opening schools in Muslim parts of Northern Nigeria.

---

[4] This echoes ideas about '*Islam noir*' prevalent among French colonialists. Ware (2014: 37), for example, argues that French colonial policy in Senegal, which limited interference in Qur'anic schools there, resulted from racist ideas about 'African Islam' as 'docile', 'quietist', and therefore unthreatening to the colonial endeavour. In line with such thinking, colonial rulers sought to insulate presumably 'peaceful' Muslims south of the Sahara from the 'unruly' Arab Muslims in the north (see also Kane 2016: 140; Seesemann 2011: 11).

For financial reasons – but also for political ones – the British never provided 'modern' secular education on any noteworthy scale in Northern Nigeria. Colonial officials, notably Hanns Vischer, a former missionary who chaired the Northern Provinces' Education Department for several years, worried that Western educational institutions would 'denationalise' African subjects, and eventually turn them against the colonial regime. In southern Nigeria, self-assertive opponents to colonial rule had emerged from mission schools, making colonial rulers wary of repeating the experience (Hubbard 1975: 155; see also Fafunwa 1974; Umar 2001). In addition, because of its association with both colonialism and Christianity, secular education was arguably unpopular among large parts of the Muslim population (e.g. Umar 2006: 58–9).[5] Meanwhile, a number of government schools were established from 1910 to train the sons of the local elite for positions in the Native Administration in a context where the British presence on the ground was very thinly spread (see, e.g., Mamdani 1996: 73).

Until the 1930s, British colonial officials, desirous both of co-opting and controlling Islamic schools and of increasing the appeal of the newly opened government schools for the local elite, made several attempts to integrate Islamic and secular education, drawing on experiences from elsewhere in the British Empire (notably in Sudan; see Thurston 2016a: 121). These attempts included efforts to integrate Arabic and Qur'anic teaching into government schools, the opening of a school mainly for Islamic studies (the Kano Law School, opened in 1934 and renamed the Kano School for Arabic Studies in 1947), and training courses for *malamai* to include secular subjects in their schools. Yet, according to Hubbard (1975: 158), despite the innovative character of some of these interventions, 'ultimately they amounted to very little'. The political rationales of the time favoured other outcomes. Educational institutions closely resembling British models were deemed most effective for training a local elite that could staff the Native Administration, and Islamic elements were considered useful merely to attract students (ibid.: 159). As far as the wider population was concerned, preserving the status quo was deemed politically most expedient. By 1940, 'the government and Islamic schools were nearly as separate . . . as at the beginning of the century' (ibid.: 158).

Despite its narrow base, the introduction of 'modern' education had a substantial impact on the *'ulama* (religious scholars), as it gradually undermined their 'monopoly over literacy' and thus their access to

---

[5] Tukur (2016: 347), however, cautions against coming to too definite conclusions in this respect: as the British kept secular education out of the reach of the wider populace, its actual (un)popularity was never put to the test.

prestige, positions, and resources (Umar 2001: 129). Before the arrival of the British, most written communication in the region had been in Arabic, using Arabic script. Yet, after conquest, Frederick Lugard, then High Commissioner of the Northern Nigeria Protectorate, decreed that Hausa should be the administrative language. Furthermore, Roman was to replace Arabic script. The use of *ajami* (Hausa written in Arabic script) was discouraged, arguably to spare colonial officials the effort of learning yet another 'language' (Dobronravine and Philips 2004: 107ff.). Colonial rulers were ambivalent about introducing English into government schools, fearing that it would 'denationalise' Africans, and, like Arabic, give them access to anti-colonial propaganda published elsewhere (Philips 2004: 76). Yet, the numbers of southerners in the administration – who risked importing nationalist ideas to the north – were also to be kept low (ibid.). Eventually, English instruction was introduced region-wide in government schools from the late 1940s (Hubbard 2000: 129; Tibenderana 1983: 532).

Many of the *'ulama* were arguably reluctant to accept, and acquire, these new forms of knowledge encouraged by colonialism. Government institutions that were purposefully created to train *'ulama* – such as the Kano Law School/School for Arabic Studies – smacked of increased government control over religious actors. Also, given how unpopular government schools were in Northern Nigeria, *'ulama* who became involved risked alienating their clientele (Hubbard 1975: 164). Arguably, by the time they enrolled their children in government schools, few people could foresee the precise course that political developments would eventually take, and the tremendous importance 'modern' education would assume within a united, independent Nigeria (Hubbard 2000: 231). Yet, if only to hedge their political position and privileged relationship with the colonial power, many Native Administration officials made sure that their wards acquired 'modern' education, as such an education could secure them administrative posts (see, e.g., Tibenderana 1983). Nearly all the students at Katsina College, which was set up as a teacher training college but eventually became one of the best 'modern' educational institutions in Northern Nigeria, had ties to the Native Administrations (Hubbard 2000: 239). Many of the graduates of Katsina College found themselves inheriting power from the British as they envisaged political independence for Nigeria. Suddenly, educated northerners were urgently needed 'to represent the North at the Federal level and ... to fill political and government posts in the North' (ibid.: 232).[6]

---

[6] Arguably, literacy in Arabic retained political significance within the shari'a courts (Philips 2004: 80), even though criminal matters were withdrawn from their jurisdiction at independence.

Education in independent Nigeria

At the time of independence in 1960, 'modern' secular education had thus gained only a tenuous foothold in Northern Nigeria, while the classical system of Islamic education operated relatively unabated. Yet, in the post-war period, providing suitable education for Muslim constituencies had already become an important part of the political agenda of northern teacher-politicians. Nationalist northerners under the leadership of Aminu Kano – a graduate of Katsina College – launched initiatives to modernise the Islamic education system by including secular subjects and 'modern' teaching methods in religious schools. The political overtones of their projects and their close association with the opposition party NEPU (Northern Elements' Progressive Union) provoked resistance on the part of the authorities, however, and their efforts were blocked (Bray 1981: 59).

After independence, Ahmadu Bello, another Katsina College graduate and the premier of the Northern Region, took up the cause of improving educational provision in the north and rekindled efforts to modernise Islamic schooling. During the 1959 elections, he campaigned for an increase in assistance to Qur'anic schools, among other things (Thurston 2016a: 127). One of the first steps of his government was to set up a committee to assist the Islamic education system. It has been argued that Bello's religious as well as 'modern' credentials as both a descendant of the founders of the Sokoto Caliphate and a 'modern' school graduate permitted him to rally support from a wide range of constituencies for his project of religious educational reform (see Thurston 2016a: 125–6). Connections with leaders in the Arab world further boosted his popularity (ibid.). After his assassination in 1966, however, the developments he had set in motion ground to a halt (Reichmuth 1989: 42). When the Civil War (1967–70) ended, Nigeria was transformed into a federation of smaller states. Responsibility for education was devolved to state governments, and thereby fragmented.

The developments in the Islamic education sector since the 1970s mirror larger societal transformations, which have led to increasing socio-economic and religious stratification. The oil boom of the 1970s and the ensuing economic downturn, accentuated by structural adjustment and rapid population growth, impoverished large parts of the population, notably in the rural areas, and increased income inequality. Many authors find that these structural changes transformed the Qur'anic schooling system fundamentally, pushing formerly predominantly rural-based schools (*tsangaya*; plural: *tsangayu*) into the urban centres of the region, while simultaneously eroding their previous support structures.

Religious reform and fragmentation from the late 1970s, stoked by conditions of societal crisis, transformed religious schooling practices further. Education was at the heart of the reform agenda – of the Sufi religious/intellectual elite seeking to keep in step with changing social realities by opening and promoting 'modernised' Islamic schools (Brigaglia 2007: 180–1), but also of newly emerging religious movements such as the Salafi-oriented *Izala* (see Umar 1993; Loimeier 1997; Kane 2003). Chapter 8 discusses the religious underpinnings of these developments in more detail. Suffice to say here that such reform efforts have resulted in a much enlarged range of religious educational institutions.

In Kano, a number of *Tahfeez* schools have opened; these are 'modernised' Qur'anic day schools. More important, though, are *Islamiyya* schools, which have made a major appearance on the educational scene, notably in urban areas. These are privately run community schools using 'modern' teaching methods. Desks, chairs, books, and pens, as well as age grading and formal certification, replace the wooden boards, prayer mats, and flexible learning groups of the classical Qur'anic schools. *Islamiyya* schools offer lessons in a broad range of Islamic subjects, and emphasise the practical knowledge required for 'correct' religious practice. For example, they familiarise students with the intricacies of performing ablutions and prayers, and teach them the appropriate supplications (*addu'a*) for specific situations. Beyond these shared general characteristics, though, *Islamiyya* schools are very diverse in terms of their curricula, degree of formalisation, quality,[7] and timetables. In Albasu, some of the *Islamiyya* schools have registered with the government, operate mostly in the mornings, teach the government-sanctioned curriculum, and receive – albeit limited – state support in exchange. Others operate without any state supervision and mostly in the afternoons, including secular subjects in their syllabuses if and as they see fit.

Most *Islamiyya* schools, despite being supported to some extent by community spirit, are also economic enterprises whose teachers rely for their livelihood on the money they receive from parents and students in the form of school fees (cf. Brenner 2007 on madrasas in Mali). This makes them somewhat less accessible than the Qur'anic schools. In theory, *Islamiyya* schools require students to buy uniforms, but not all enforce this rule if students cannot afford them. In my rural field site of Albasu, many students attended school without uniforms. In theory, *Islamiyya* schools also expect students to purchase books and writing materials, but again, most teachers are lenient if students cannot afford all the required items.

Islamiyya schools have become both popular and widespread in northern Nigeria, especially in urban areas (Bano et al. 2011: 7). According to

---

[7] Arguably, the quality of teaching in many *Islamiyya* schools today is poor (see, e.g., Boyle 2004: 119ff.).

estimates, among all religious educational institutions, *Islamiyya* schools account for the largest student body in Kano today, with over 60 per cent of students at primary and secondary levels in the three LGAs surveyed by Bano et al. (2011: 19).[8] *Islamiyya* schools are popular particularly for the education of girls. Most girls and women in northern Nigeria – some notable exceptions notwithstanding[9] – acquire significantly less education (both religious and secular) than their male counterparts. Girls do not normally board with a *malam*, as boys do, and they are generally kept closer to home and under greater control, to protect their sexuality. In line with parents' concerns about their daughters' sexuality, girls are often married off young to ensure that they 'do not get spoilt' (*'kar ta lalace'*) before marriage (cf. Masquelier 2009: 181 on similar concerns in southern Niger). Before marriage, for many girls, school attendance must compete with work obligations. Married women in *purdah* (female seclusion) rarely attend school, though husbands may engage a private teacher or teach their wives themselves – provided they have enough money or knowledge and time (Hutson 1999: 48). In this context, the imperative is for girls to learn the basics of Islamic practice before marriage, and *Islamiyya* schools are deemed best placed to deliver this knowledge. There are clear gender differences in enrolment, which become more pronounced as children grow older. Slightly more than half the students in *Islamiyya* schools in Kano State are girls, whereas in both Qur'anic and secular schools they are clearly outnumbered by boys (Bano et al. 2011), who are expected to delve deeper in their studies, whether religious or secular. Once they marry, men will be held responsible for the education of their wives and children.[10]

Efforts to universalise basic education, and Islamic schooling

As the petroleum boom flushed state coffers with cash (Lubeck 1981: 76), Nigeria launched its first Universal Primary Education (UPE) campaign in 1976, aiming particularly to reduce regional and gender imbalances in formal education. But the boom was short-lived, and from 1981 oil revenues decreased, limiting the resources available to fund UPE

[8] In terms of absolute numbers of schools, however, Qur'anic schools rank first. This is because *Islamiyya* schools cater on average to almost five times as many students as Qur'anic schools (Bano et al. 2011: 19).

[9] Hutson (1999), for example, documents the roles of notable female Sufi scholars in twentieth-century Kano, whose success has been facilitated by their elite family background. Many women's halls of residence in schools and universities are named after Nana Asma'u, Uthman dan Fodio's daughter, who is an icon of female scholarship in northern Nigeria (Boyd and Last 1985).

[10] The Boko Haram crisis may have given enrolment in *Islamiyya* schools yet another boost. A close informant, with whom I discussed the issue, argued that parents consider it particularly urgent today that their children receive solid religious knowledge (see also Chapter 8), to 'immunise' them against religious aberrations such as Boko Haram.

(Csapo 1983: 95–6). In 1986, structural adjustment was initiated, which slashed education funding (Baba 2011). Moreover, the success of the UPE campaign was constrained by chaotic implementation and waning political will under subsequent military regimes (e.g. Bray 1981; Tahir 2001).

In 1999, another campaign was therefore launched to achieve universal basic education (UBE). Aiming to provide 'free, universal basic education for every Nigerian child of school-going age' (UBE 2003: 5–6), the UBE programme set out to address the persisting inequalities. To reach all children, including nomadic children, children with disabilities, and *almajirai*, this second campaign included an emphasis on non-formal forms of education (e.g. Ojuah and Arikpo 2011).

Although overall enrolment rates have risen,[11] inequalities are still severe, with girls and children growing up in the northern part of the country, in rural areas, and in poor households being far less likely to attend primary school than their male, southern, urban, or better-off counterparts. According to the 2013 Demographic and Health Survey, the primary net attendance rate in the south-eastern zone of the country was 81.4 per cent in 2013, whereas in the North West (which is where Kano is situated) it was as low as 47.2 per cent. Some 71.2 per cent of all 6–12-year-olds were enrolled in primary school in urban Nigeria in that year, compared with a mere 51.8 per cent in rural areas. While 50.7 per cent of all 6–12-year-old boys in the North West attended primary school, only 43.8 per cent of girls did (National Population Commission 2014: 26–7). In 2013, the net primary school enrolment rate of children from households within the lowest wealth quintile was 27.1 per cent, whereas that of children from the highest quintile was 70.4 per cent (ibid.: 27).

According to the 2013 Demographic and Health Survey, Kano State is mid-table in terms of school enrolment, with 59.5 per cent of primary school-aged children attending primary school in the state compared with 59.1 per cent nationwide. Net attendance in secondary schools is 43.3 per cent. Attendance ratios are higher for boys than for girls, with 60.5 per cent of 6–12-year-old boys attending primary school, compared with 58.6 per cent of girls. Some 50.8 per cent of 13–18-year-old boys attend secondary school, but only 35.6 per cent of girls do (National Population Commission 2014: 26–7). Enrolment is significantly lower in rural than in urban LGAs (Ministry of Education 2008).

In a context where participation in secular education is low, state and private actors have sought to take advantage of the ubiquity and great popularity of religious educational institutions to achieve UBE goals. It

---

[11] Net primary school enrolment increased from about 51 per cent in 1990 to 61 per cent in 2008 (National Population Commission 2011a). By 2013, it had fallen back to 59 per cent (National Population Commission 2014).

is estimated that over 80 per cent of all children and youths aged six to 21 years in Kano State attend some form of Islamic education either in addition to attendance in a secular school or as their only educational experience (Ministry of Education 2008). The UPE initiative of the 1970s hardly aimed for synergy with the Islamic education system, but, in the past decades, policymakers have attempted to harness the potential of institutions of Islamic learning to achieve UBE goals (e.g. Arewa House 2000; Usman 2008; UBEC 2010; Yusha'u et al. 2013). This included encouraging Islamic educational institutions to register and accept the state-sanctioned curriculum in exchange for assistance with teachers' salaries and learning materials. In Kano, while most Qur'anic schools still operate informally and pursue an exclusively Qur'anic curriculum, some of the day schools have registered with the government, teach the state curriculum, and receive support from the state and/or international donors in exchange. *Islamiyya* schools, which increasingly include secular subjects in their syllabuses, are a major pillar of UBE efforts in Kano State today, even though there remains a great number of purely religious *Islamiyya* schools.

In addition, several initiatives have been taken that explicitly target the *almajirai*. At the federal level, a committee was set up in 2010 to push for further integration of 'modern' subjects in religious schools, better integration of Islamic subjects in secular schools in Muslim areas, and the establishment of integrated '*Almajiri* Model Schools' (UBEC 2010; 2015; Olatunji 2010; Bilkisu 2011). At the state level, under Governor Ibrahim Shekarau (2003–11), older *almajirai* in Kano were offered vocational training to provide them with viable livelihoods. Under Governor Rabi'u Kwankwaso (2011–15), a research and consultation process was initiated to develop a coherent strategy on the *almajirai* (Kano State Government 2012). However, this appears to have given way to a more punitive approach, including a ban on street begging and efforts to deport *almajirai* found begging to their states of origin (see Kano State Government n.d.; Elazeh 2016). Several international donors have established and/or supported pilot schools where students from Qur'anic schools learn modern subjects (UNICEF and DfID, for instance; see Antonisis 2012; ESSPIN n.d.). Yet, as these efforts have been limited in both scope and scale, the everyday reality for the vast majority of *almajirai* has, so far, remained unchanged.

On balance, the state has remained a minor actor on the Islamic education scene. Private actors, sometimes supported by the state, but mostly relying on their own and community resources, have borne the brunt of educational reform and renewal. Yet, privatisation has meant that poverty has increasingly come to determine children's educational trajectories. The remainder of this chapter sheds light on 'modern' secular education and the relationship the *almajirai* and their parents and teachers have with it. As suggested in the introduction, it is a commonplace discourse that those associated with classical Qur'anic schools do not appreciate secular education. In the following, I propose an alternative narrative that emphasises both the diversity of educational trajectories and the exclusionary nature of the secular education on offer today.

Educational trajectories and fuzzy categories

For the sake of simplicity, in this book so far, I have used the term *almajiri* to refer to a boy acquiring Qur'anic knowledge first and foremost. Yet, a closer look at actual educational trajectories reveals that this category is anything but clear and unequivocal. Many people in northern Nigeria appreciate various strands of knowledge, including secular education, and, if their means permit it, they try to expose their children to a range of different educational experiences. Some families 'distribute' their children over the different educational institutions available to them. Also, children – especially boys, whose educational trajectories are usually longer than those of girls – frequently combine and/or switch between different educational options. This means that '*almajirai*', male '*Islamiyya* school students', and male 'secular school students' are not neatly separable demographics, even though many boys who become *almajirai* grow up in particularly vulnerable circumstances (see Chapter 4).

As school timetables vary, it is possible for children to combine attendance at different educational institutions throughout the day. Qur'anic schools operate various shifts, the first early in the morning after the *asuba* prayer (approximately 5.30–7.30am), and the last in the evening after the *isha'i* prayer (about 8–10pm). Qur'anic school attendance can therefore easily be combined with attendance at other educational institutions. Qur'anic schools often have sessions in the late morning (9–11am) and/or late afternoon as well (between *la'asar* and *magariba* prayers, from about 4pm to 6pm), where *almajirai* constitute the majority of students. But the afternoon slot is also popular with children attending secular school in the morning. Similarly, secular school students may attend *Islamiyya* schools operating afternoon shifts. Some children attend all three educational institutions every day: Qur'anic school at daybreak, secular school during the morning, and *Islamiyya* school in the afternoon. Saturdays and Sundays, and secular school holidays, also offer opportunities for secular school students to go to Qur'anic and *Islamiyya* schools.

For *almajirai* who have to work or beg to provide for their subsistence and who are usually expected to attend all their school's 'shifts', combining different educational options is rather challenging. I have, however, met *almajirai* (in Albasu, Daho, and Kano) who attended *Islamiyya* and/or secular schools while living as 'full-time' Qur'anic students. What is more, many boys do not live as *almajirai* all through their childhood and youth; instead, either voluntarily or forced by circumstances, they switch between different educational options – for example, they might attend primary school for some years before enrolling as an *almajiri*, or interrupt secular education for some time to acquire Qur'anic knowledge as an *almajiri*.

I do not have systematic quantitative data to assess how many *almajirai* of particular age groups have attended secular school and up to what level. But from the life stories I collected, it emerges that among young *almajirai* there are hardly any children with secular school experience, while among older students there are many who attended secular school for some time, but then dropped out to join the ranks of the *almajirai*. To give an example, none of the 17 young *almajirai* I was teaching in Daho, who were of primary school age, had yet attended secular school; however, seven of the nine youths participating in the 'participatory' film project I organised during my research had attended secular primary school. Two of them had even started junior secondary school (JSS) and one had finished senior secondary school (SSS). In short, switching between different educational institutions is routine today in northern Nigeria.

Secular education: worth the investment?

As hinted at in the previous sections, poverty is a major factor determining educational participation. While basic education is officially free, in reality it implies not only direct costs (e.g. contributions to the parent–teacher association, collected at the beginning of each school year) but also considerable indirect expenses, as well as opportunity costs. Indirect costs arise, for example, as students need to purchase textbooks, writing materials, and uniforms.[12] Some must pay for transportation to and from school. Schools also levy (semi-official) fees for the maintenance of school facilities, which are often in a deplorable state, to buy furniture, medicine for sick students, fuel for the grinding machine (to prepare food for boarding students), or prizes for the end of year ceremony.[13] Teachers also ask for small sums from students to cover the expenses of chalk, brooms, report cards, and other sundry running costs. Teachers may also extort money as a form of punishment, and, for example, charge students who arrive late for class.

[12] School uniforms cost around 500 Naira (approximately US$3). The cost of books and writing materials depends on the level of schooling. Private secondary schools in Kano levy around 10,000 Naira per year (approximately US$60) for a complete set of books and notebooks. In Albasu, students were recycling the books of older siblings or friends, and hardly any student owned all the books she or he was supposed to have.

[13] Interview with the head teacher of Girls Arabic Secondary School Albasu, 27 September 2011.

Expenses thus add up, and leave families wondering whether the secular education on offer is worth incurring the constant drain of money. Several *almajirai* confided to me that they dropped out of secular education because of a lack of money. Furthermore, secular education is at best a risky investment in children's economic futures, for its promised pay-off in terms of salaried employment is unlikely to occur. Parents are aware of this: one father in Kunchi, a rural community in northern Kano State where I conducted a range of interviews in 2009, declared to me that even 'modern' education would not enable his son to escape his economic conditions.

Post-primary education often requires students to travel long distances daily or to board, and children from families lacking both financial means and the right connections cannot easily transition from one level of schooling to the next. I was told on several occasions that children did not proceed to secondary school even though they would have liked to and even though they performed well in primary school because they could not secure admission. Admission letters are a scarce good as the number of secondary school places is limited. According to Musa Salihu, Education Commissioner in 2008, due to a shortage of classrooms and qualified teachers, Kano State could accommodate a mere 60 per cent of secondary school aspirants in that year.[14]

Scarce secondary school places are often distributed based not on merit, but on 'purchasing power', as the quote at the beginning of this chapter suggests. Exam results are a matter of luck, purchasing power, and connections, which causes frustration among those who do not have them and diminishes respect for the state school system.[15] Fatima, a woman I befriended in Daho, for example, said to me that her son's *boko* school teachers were hypocrites (*munafukai*): they would drop a boy's name from the list of students who have passed an exam successfully and put someone else's name instead if that person paid them. I heard similar complaints from many others in both Kano and Albasu. Many ordinary Nigerians perceive the state-run education system to be little more than yet another enrichment scheme for a corrupt government elite.

---

[14] 'Classroom shortages threaten primary education targets' (2008). The 'survival rate' of children through primary school – that is, the percentage of students that will likely persist to the end of primary school – was 82 per cent in Kano State in 2010. Yet, only 39 per cent of children enrolling in primary school were likely to 'survive' until the first year of junior secondary school, suggesting that drop-outs are particularly likely to happen at the end of primary school (Ministry of Education 2010: 28).

[15] Secondary school entry exams are multiple choice tests, and the ones I saw were entirely unrelated to students' (and even teachers') standard of knowledge: how were children supposed to tell the difference between 'rugged', 'slopey', 'smooth', and 'bumpy' if they hardly mastered simple greetings in English? Some schools write the exam answers, which they receive in advance, on the board, and pay the invigilators off. The *almajirai* schooling with the CAESI miraculously all 'passed' their JSS entry exam: they had been shown the exam answers in advance.

In addition to direct and indirect costs, formal education also implies opportunity costs, for example in the form of foregone income from children's labour (cf. Tomasevski 2005). Secular schools, operating mainly morning shifts, clash with rural children's agricultural work obligations (and not only in northern Nigeria; cf. Admassie 2003). The timing of their school holidays does not reflect the peak times of the farming season either (field preparation and sowing before and after the first rains around April/May, and harvest when the rains stop around September). The poor fit between the agricultural and the school year may force rural children to be absent from 'modern' secular school for long stretches of time and eventually to drop out. This is what happened in the case of Nura and Danjuma, two boys, about 11 and 13 years old, whose mother Fatima I befriended in Daho, a rural community close to Albasu. The boys had attended secular school for about three years, but work obligations – collecting fodder for the family's two cows, and helping their older brothers with the farm work – had kept them busy during the rainy season. After an extended period of absence, their teacher had dropped their names from the register. At the end of the farming season, their parents intended to have them join their neighbours' *almajirai* for their migratory tour during the dry season.

Children's high levels of mobility also make it difficult for them to continue in secular education. It is not only *almajirai* who migrate seasonally: boys from rural areas, for example, may accompany their fathers as errand boys and apprentices when they migrate to the urban centres of the region during the dry season. Fostering is common, including of girls, especially as children are essential to the ability of women in *purdah* to trade. All these circumstances necessitate school changes, and if these are difficult to accomplish, children are likely to drop out. The *almajiri* system, on the other hand, in which every student progresses at his own pace, is well adapted to both school changes and students' extended periods of absence.

Universal basic education: a mixed blessing

Even for those young people who are presumably benefiting from the expansion of enrolment, the UBE agenda appears to be a mixed blessing. Corroborating the argument made in Chapter 2, in terms of skills and future prospects, little differentiates the *almajirai* from other poor undereducated youths from rural households. In Nigeria, even children who attend secular school hardly learn to read and write in Roman script or to calculate on paper, despite these being declared goals of secular education. For example, according to a national survey from 2010 testing functional literacy and numeracy among children who had attended primary school in Nigeria, 46.3 per cent could not read a simple sentence in their preferred language at all. If children not enrolled in formal education are included, the share is even higher, especially in the north: 71.7 per cent of all children aged five to 16 years in the North West and 83.1 per cent of children in the North East could not read a simple sentence. In the South West, in comparison, 62.7 per cent of children could read an entire sentence, and a further 16.1 per cent could read at least parts of it. Some 28.9 per cent of children with primary education in Nigeria could not add two single-digit numbers on paper correctly. Only 39.4 per cent of all 5–16-year-old children in the North West and only 27 per cent of children in the North East managed to do so, while 88.7 per cent of children in the South West could (National Population Commission 2011b: 47, 51).[16]

A look at the capabilities of their teachers explains why many Nigerian pupils perform so poorly. Johnson (2008), reporting on a capabilities assessment carried out in 2008 among the entire population of primary and junior secondary teachers in Kwara State, Nigeria,[17] found that the overwhelming majority lacked even basic literacy and numeracy skills. Low levels of education spending and high pupil per classroom ratios also contribute to poor learning outcomes (e.g. Ministry of Education 2008). In Albasu, teachers frequently go on strike, for instance because their salaries are not paid on time. This means that lessons are cancelled. According to one secondary school student in Kano, if teachers do show up, some go straight to the staff room to sleep. Secular school students often spend their time playing *langa*, a jumping and wrestling game popular with children, or collecting fodder on the school grounds.

Qur'anic schools have the reputation of not sparing the rod on their students (see Last 2000b). Yet, curiously, I heard far more complaints about the violence dealt out in secular schools. I met several mothers and other relatives who considered enrolling their sons or boys they cared for as *almajirai* because they were discontented with the beatings they received from their secular school teachers. Boys had been beaten so severely – for 'transgressions' such as getting the answers wrong in an exam or not having a school uniform – that they refused to attend.

Last (2000b: 362) writes that physical punishment in both Muslim and Christian (state-run or mission) schools across Africa has long been tolerated because schooling was closely linked to the promise of social advancement, which gave beating a certain moral legitimacy. Yet, the

---

[16] As the statistics are based on written tests in Roman script, they test a particular set of skills: the ability to read and write in Roman script and to do paper-based calculations using Roman numbers. We cannot conclude from them that children lack literacy and numeracy altogether, as results may well have been different if tests had been administered in *ajami* (Hausa written in Arabic script), or if children had been asked to add numbers in their heads.

[17] Kwara is considered to be one of the better-performing Nigerian states in terms of education, and certainly as a state that performs better than Kano.

fact that parents disapprove so strongly of the physical punishments generously meted out in state-run secular schools, while simultaneously tolerating the hardships and violence involved in *almajiri* education, points to widespread disenchantment with the former: they largely fail to fulfil their promise of social advancement in exchange for the hardships they inflict on students. Private schools have become the norm today in northern Nigeria for those who can afford them. At Sabuwar Kofa, for example, most neighbourhood children attended expensive private secular schools, as well as *Islamiyya* schools.

Views on 'modern' secular education

Contrary to received ideas about the presumed extreme 'conservatism' of northern Nigerians, throughout my research I did not meet anyone who considered secular education as *haram* (forbidden), and I met few who thought it was not worthwhile (cf. Brigaglia 2008, who comes to a similar conclusion). Several youths commented, however, that their own or their schoolmates' parents did not understand the use (*amfani*) and importance (*muhimmanci*) of secular education since they had not attended it themselves, and consequently they had no interest in enrolling their children in it. Most teachers let me teach their students 'modern' or secular subjects exclusively on the days of their weekend (Thursday and Friday), in order to preserve the remaining days for the Qur'anic studies that the students had been sent to attend by their parents. At the same time, several of the Qur'anic teachers I got to know well sent their own children to secular schools.

Most of the *almajirai* themselves saw 'modern' education in a very positive light, and were convinced of its importance for an economically successful life – a life to which they aspired. They deemed 'modern' education important in order 'to progress', because it would 'help them on earth', and, as Ibrahim put it, whom I cited at the beginning of this chapter, because 'if you have only the Qur'anic studies, there are places that when you go there, people will think you are nobody'. Sadisu, who was from a poor Kano neighbourhood and without rural links, declared that for someone like him, who did not have a village future ahead, and who might find himself in Abuja or even Lagos one day, 'It's indispensable that you get secular education.' Kabiru explained that secular knowledge could not be considered Western (*ilimin turawa*) any longer as it was spread all around the globe: if one had a chance to acquire it, one should do so.

The *almajirai*'s enthusiasm about 'modern' secular education, however, could not eclipse their judgement when it came to the quality of the secular education poor youths like them were likely to acquire, and they were realistic about how much of a change such an education would be likely to make to their future prospects. Isa, whom I quoted at the beginning of this chapter, told me that secular schooling was 'schooling for the rich': poor people could not succeed with it, since the rich bought the exam results. Also, in his view the teachers in government schools were often ignorant of the subjects they were teaching and had secured their position through connections rather than qualifications.

It was also pointed out to me that the teachers and students at secular schools did not match up to the moral standards of their counterparts in Qur'anic schools. But this was stated as a point of honour (and self-legitimisation) rather than to challenge their legitimacy altogether. One *malam*, for instance, commented disapprovingly about secular school students that they were playing football in the afternoons. Many *malamai* disapprove of football because they find it irreverent towards the Prophet's grandson Hussain b. 'Ali b. Abi Talib, who was beheaded at the Battle of Karbala, and whose rolling head a football apparently evokes (e.g. Haruna and Abdullahi 1991: 114).[18] One of the *almajirai* participating in the film project complained that secular school students did not learn religious knowledge properly, which predisposed them to behaving 'immorally' (for example, having sex outside wedlock). But such criticisms never amounted to an outright rejection, did not call into question the legitimacy of secular knowledge per se, and were made alongside comments on the desirability of such knowledge. I argue that they have to be understood in light of the *almajirai*'s struggles to construct a positive self-image, emphasising their own moral worth and religious credentials.

Admittedly, my research might underestimate remaining resentments against secular education on ideological grounds, as people opposed to anything 'Western' might have avoided meeting me or talking to me, and as interviewees may have concealed critical views, thinking that they would make me uncomfortable. Several people I spoke to felt that secular knowledge comes second in importance to religious knowledge. Whereas parents may find it excusable to let their children's secular education slide, most felt strongly about ensuring that their wards acquire some Qur'anic knowledge.

Various people in Albasu stated to me that, in the past, people did not value secular education, but that now most had come to understand its benefits. Yet, increasing acceptance in principle has been thwarted by state withdrawal from the education sector since structural adjustment. Whatever the role of remaining resentments against secular education, given the financial difficulties poor parents face in trying to enrol and sustain their children within it, we cannot jump to the conclusion that it

[18] His *almajirai* confided to me that they seized the opportunities of their visits home to play football, and went to watch football matches at the public TV parlour in Albasu on their days off – without their teacher's knowledge or consent (cf. Schielke 2009 on the context-dependent and fragmented nature of pious conduct).

is necessarily a dislike for such education that makes children drop out or enrol as *almajirai*.

Finally, we have to be careful not to reduce critical views on secular education to a sign of 'backwardness' or 'blockheadedness'. Demerath (2000), writing about 'modern' education in Papua New Guinea, for example, encourages us to understand the oppositional attitudes to school he observes among students as a wider social critique of the individualistic and competitive behaviours that 'modern' schools encourage and reward (ibid.: 226–7). In a similar vein, negative attitudes towards secular education in northern Nigeria originate – in part at least – in contemporary social and political conditions. Boko Haram, for example, links its rejection of '*boko*' (secular education) to the corruption and depravity of today's elites, most of whom are secular school products (see Last 2008a).

Conclusion: new aspirations, few occasions

I started this chapter with a description of how *almajirai* seek to learn English so that they, too, can participate in what other members of society take part in. English is necessary for such mundane things as reading a newspaper or understanding the menu of one's mobile phone. English is also necessary to make status claims. Many of the people I interacted with in Kano used language, consciously or unconsciously, as a means of exclusion and differentiation. Although I answered in Hausa, some would insist on speaking English to me despite the presence of others, often *almajirai*, who clearly did not speak enough English to follow the conversation. Situations such as these leave their mark.

Several of the *almajirai* participating in the film project approached me for support in their aspiration to acquire, or further, a secular education. They also daydreamed about university admission (in case I became a university lecturer in Nigeria and could help them secure admission, and even a doctoral degree). Several of those who had attended primary school for a number of years expressed regret about their parents' decision to interrupt this education to enrol them as *almajirai*. Former *almajirai* are likely to make up a large part of the clientele of adult evening schools.[19]

Many of the students, aware that they were missing out on something they deemed important, consoled themselves with the thought that they would be able to pursue 'modern' education sometime in the future. One *almajiri* at Sabuwar Kofa (whose parents were adamant about Qur'anic schooling being more important than secular education) resolved the

---

[19] This impression is based on visits to two different adult evening education centres in Kano City and on information from older and former *almajirai*.

tension between his need (and wish) to obey his parents and his sense of frustration about being denied a valued opportunity to learn by reinterpreting his obedience towards his parents as a service to God:

If your parents took you to Qur'anic school, and you refuse to study and say you only prefer *boko* [modern studies], what will you tell Allah in heaven?...After I complete my school, I can go to *boko*, because my parents will not give their consent for me to go to *boko* now. I have to obey them, because it is said that 'whoever obeys his parents, obeys Allah'...we still have hope that we will go to *boko*. We will not lose hope. ('Radio interview')

Despite his 'resolution' to obey his parents, the boy eagerly took up my offer to teach him English on his lesson-free days. Two of the youths participating in the filmmaking project showed a similar spirit of 'defiance' when discussing what to do if their *malam* did not allow them to attend secondary school at the time they hoped to enrol. They would move on to a Qur'anic teacher who gave permission, they proclaimed.

Economic, political, and social changes over the last century have accentuated the importance of 'modern' forms of knowledge in order to acquire status in northern Nigeria. The educational landscape has become increasingly diverse with the introduction of secular education by the British and its expansion through two UPE/UBE campaigns in 1976 and 1999. 'Modernised' Islamic schools have gained much ground since the 1970s, and today constitute a central feature of the educational landscape in northern Nigeria. Classical Qur'anic learning, on the other hand, has been pushed to the margins. In this context, children's educational trajectories are highly diverse, as young people try to straddle different forms of schooling. An enlarged range of options, however, has not translated into greater choice for everyone. Money plays an increasingly important role in accessing education in a context where private actors have assumed a central role for educational provision, and where state support has been on the wane.

As enrolment in 'modern' education is spread unevenly, it is important to ask how young people experience their inability to comply with the putative standards of 'modern childhood'. In Chapter 1, I proposed to analyse experiences of poverty through the notions of 'social exclusion' and 'adverse incorporation', which emphasise how poverty is produced 'through the active dynamics of social interaction' (Kabeer 2000: 84). Arguably, the rise of 'modern' education, which has nurtured new aspirations and altered society-wide standards of achievement, has exacerbated the relative position within society of those who do not have access to it. Inequitable educational change has brought about new experiences of exclusion for poor boys such as the *almajirai*. Poverty, as the *almajirai* – and other children unable to access 'modern' forms of knowledge – experience it, has little to do with not having been 'reached' by 'modern' developments. Rather, poverty means being perpetually reminded of one's failure to live up to society's new standards of achievement. Arguably, the *almajirai* are 'adversely incorporated' into an educational landscape that fosters aspirations yet offers few opportunities to realise them.

How do young people deal with such experiences of exclusion? I have described in this chapter how the *almajirai* seek to uphold a positive outlook on themselves and their future by pinning their hopes on future opportunities to acquire prestigious knowledge. Subsequent chapters will pursue this question further and explore how the *almajirai* counter difficult experiences by emphasising their own moral and religious credentials (see Chapters 6 and 7). These observations tie in with the overarching argument of this book that Muslim boys and young men do not inevitably react to experiences of exclusion by turning to radicalism and violence, even though this is what many people assume.

To deconstruct simplistic narratives about exclusion turning into violence, it is important to ask about the experiences of poor boys and young men. However, this enquiry should also engage with the factors that give rise to such experiences. Tales about the presumed 'backwardness' of rural parents, their alleged inability to appreciate the benefits of 'modern' education, or their putative disregard for their sons' wellbeing, though widespread, are unsatisfying, as this chapter has sought to show. Meritocratic discourses about 'modern' education that reduce educational success to a question of 'talent' and 'effort' detach this education from the social context in which it is acquired. They thereby risk obscuring the structural inequalities governing access to meaningful and relevant 'modern' education, as well as the large disparities in the opportunities young people are likely to encounter in their future lives. The next chapter, which explores how boys become *almajirai*, puts the structural conditions constraining the room for manoeuvre of poor peasant households centre stage.

4 Peasants, privations, and piousness
How boys become Qur'anic students

'I am not hungry [*na koshi*].' Samaila's words, with which he declined to eat from the plate pushed in his direction, were barely audible. Not hungry? But *almajirai* are *always* hungry, except maybe after they have just licked their fingers clean after a big bowl of sticky millet porridge (*tuwo*). The Qur'anic schools where they study don't usually provide food for them, and, living away from their parents, many *almajirai* therefore rely on begging to feed themselves.

It was the middle of the afternoon and I knew for a fact that Samaila had not had lunch before accompanying me to his father's compound. Could he, a slight 11-year-old, seriously be too full to eat the *taliya* his stepmothers offered him? By common consent, the *almajirai* consider this dish of shredded spaghetti flowing in an oily tomato and meat sauce a treat. Not that the *almajirai* were picky eaters. The young *almajirai* (6–12 years old) to whom I taught English and literacy/numeracy skills in the village of Daho, for example, declared that they liked every single Hausa dish I could name – much to my bafflement as their English teacher. I had wanted to practise food names and the English phrases 'I like . . .' and 'I don't like . . .' with them. We didn't really get around to practising 'I don't like'. The only food the *almajirai* in Daho said that they didn't like was food that had gone off. Sometimes, however, when they were very hungry, they would even eat food that had been kept overnight and had started to smell sour.[1] So why did Samaila refuse his stepmothers' *taliya*?

I got to know Samaila through his grandmother Nafisa, a middle-aged widow who worked in the household of the District Head of Albasu, with whom I lodged during the four months I spent in this rural town. Employed to cook, Nafisa spent over 12 hours in the house of the

---

[1] The *almajirai* believed that people gave them spoiled food as an act of contempt. Arguably, young children are often sent to gather food remnants to give to *almajirai*, and they might be unaware that what they give away is inedible. The young boys I was teaching in Daho told me that they go to sleep hungry about twice a week. It was only the very young ones among them who were given food from the *malam*'s house in case their begging was unsuccessful. The *almajirai* I befriended in urban Kano knew of fellow students so hungry that they would dry and re-boil food that had gone off.

District Head every day: ample time for us to become close and for me to find out about her life and that of the grandchildren in her care. Nafisa, a proud woman with a strong sense of right and wrong, did not usually mince her words. In a context where many people measure very carefully what they say aloud – not only to honour norms of self-restraint and modesty, but also to stay out of trouble – I found Nafisa's company extremely refreshing, and often sought her out to talk. On her few days off, I accompanied her to her farm,[2] and on some evenings I visited her at home.

Nafisa's life had not been easy. Many of her children – over ten of them – had died in infancy, leaving her with three adult daughters but no male descendants. After the death of her husband, Nafisa had continued to live in the latter's family compound. Yet, without the support of a husband, the responsibility for supporting her daughters and grandchildren in times of need fell on her. Her daughters' marriages had been anything but stable, and during the times they found themselves without husbands, they moved back in with Nafisa, who provided for them with the little that she earned in the District Head's household and with the yield from her small farm. Nafisa also cared for Yunusa, another of her grandsons: he was a jolly little fellow of about three years old who followed Nafisa at every turn. His mother had left him with Nafisa when she remarried, to a man who preferred not to have the little boy move in along with his new wife.

When I told Nafisa that Samaila had turned down his father's new wives' invitation to eat, she was not surprised. In any case, she said, they had offered him food only because I was present. In the past, she told me with indignation, Samaila's stepmothers had eaten in front of the boy without offering him anything. Food is usually eaten communally in Hausaland. In a context where open confrontation is shunned, not inviting somebody to join in while eating is tantamount to telling him that he is not welcome. Samaila's refusal to eat the *taliya* he was offered was, in turn, a refusal to forget the poor treatment he had received previously from his father and his new wives.

Since divorcing his mother, Samaila's father had assumed very little responsibility for the boy. As Samaila's mother remarried in another

---

[2] Most married women live in seclusion and therefore do not usually farm, although they may own farmland. As a widow, Nafisa was comparatively less constrained by restrictions on female mobility, and partly cultivated her land herself. Even though men are formally considered the household provider, in practice, women actively contribute to the household budget. Almost all women in Albasu (whether married or not) had some kind of trade (*sana'a*), ranging from the production of groundnut oil and livestock rearing to the preparation of foods for sale (to be hawked by children) and cap-making. The fact that married women spend most of their time inside their husband's compound therefore should not be taken to mean that they are economically inactive (see Callaway 1987; Hill 1969; Schildkrout 1982; Pittin 1991; Werthmann 1997).

village, this responsibility fell largely onto Nafisa, with whom Samaila lodged whenever he came back to Albasu – including the time when I got to know him. For the farming season, he returned to his home town, and, in the absence of any other close male relatives of the appropriate age, he helped his grandmother Nafisa with the farm work. For the rest of the year, he lived as an *almajiri* in Takai, a nearby town, where Nafisa had enrolled him. Nafisa, despite her very limited budget, had been the one to buy whatever supplies Samaila needed for his *almajiri* education. When I asked her about secular education, she merely reminded me that there was nobody to pay for it.

If I discuss Samaila's (and Yunusa's) situation here in some detail, this is because his is not an isolated case. Like him, many boys who enrol as *almajirai* have no place that they can consider as 'home' any longer, for example because their parents have divorced or passed away, or because their new stepmothers or stepfathers do not welcome them. Like Samaila, many *almajirai* have nobody to provide the necessary resources for them to pursue a 'modern' education. Like him, many *almajirai* return home during the rainy season when their parents need their help with the farm work. *Almajiri* schools leave it up to their students whether they stay at school or return home during this period – unlike most 'modern' schools, which are poorly adapted to their students' seasonal absences.

Yet, when speaking to people who rely on the *almajiri* system about their reasons for opting for this form of education, few foreground the constraints they face. Instead, most emphasise the moral, social, and religious dispositions and skills that *almajiri* enrolment is expected to instil. Among the rural populations enrolling boys in the *almajiri* system, Qur'anic scholarship is highly regarded, and hardship is considered to be of educational value for their social and moral training. Nafisa did not tire of praising Samaila's progress in his Qur'anic studies. When I asked her why she had taken him to Takai, she did not refer to his parents' divorce or her strained financial situation, but explained to me that if one lets boys stay at home, they do not take their studies seriously. Without hesitation, Nafisa declared that, unless his father came to claim him, she would also enrol Yunusa as an *almajiri* once he had grown a little older. In this way, she would make sure he would grow up to become a 'good person'.

In a context in which many people have come to look at educational choices through the lens of 'human capital theory' (developed by, *inter alia*, Becker (1993 [1964]), and popular today in development as well as in education studies), the decision to educate children in purely religious institutions has often been met with bewilderment. In the eyes of people trained to think about education as a process whereby knowledge is stored in children for future use and benefit – mostly defined in narrow economic terms – such decisions make little sense. As a consequence, religious school enrolment has often been explained as a consequence of either 'irrational' preferences – that is, religious fundamentalism and blockheadedness – or deprivation, assuming that people turn to religious options only when they are barred from accessing secular alternatives, which are believed to be more lucrative and thus preferable (see Newman 2016: 13–4 on such assumptions in the literature on Senegal; Bano 2012: 101–2 on Pakistan). While we must take seriously the very real inequalities governing access to different educational options in northern Nigeria, explanations such as those invoked here are unsatisfactory as they fail to do justice to the complexities of educational decision-making, or to the genuine appeal that religious education – and the pedagogical practices that go with it – may hold (cf. Gérard 1999; Brenner 2000: 236–7; Ware 2014; Bell 2015). The previous chapter showed that people value different forms of knowledge simultaneously, and that they seek – their circumstances permitting – to expose their children to several educational experiences. Various researchers have shown that the purposes pursued through education extend well beyond narrowly defined economic goals (see, e.g., Levinson et al. 1996; Brenner 2000; Bell 2015). Then how can we understand educational choices such as Nafisa's?

The anthropological/sociological and historical literature on Qur'anic education in Muslim West Africa offers some important clues. Several authors emphasise the cultural and religious underpinnings of Qur'anic schools, claiming that particular ideas about the proper upbringing of Muslim children – and notably of boys – motivate the system (Sanneh 1975; Last 2000b; van Santen 2001; Perry 2004; Ware 2014: 42ff.; Newman 2016: 119ff.). Others place more emphasis on its economic and social utility, arguing that in rural areas the students of Qur'anic schools provide hard-to-find farm labour for their teachers in exchange for what we may call cultural/religious and social capital (Cruise O'Brien 1971; Saul 1984; Bledsoe and Robey 1986; see also Wilks 1968). Historians have noted that, after the gradual ending of slavery under colonial rule, Qur'anic students replaced the agricultural labour of freed slaves (Bledsoe and Robey 1986: 215–6; Last 2000b). As travel became less dangerous, Qur'anic schools moved to urban areas during the months of the dry season, when agricultural activity is slow, allowing peasant households to reduce their subsistence burden during times of scarcity (Lubeck 1985; Last 1993).

While seasonal rural-to-urban migration has a long history in the West African Sahel, many authors find that structural changes since the 1970s have increasingly pushed Qur'anic scholars and their students into the urban centres of the region. Food shortages during the dry season, and deteriorating economic conditions more generally, especially in rural areas, have been declared responsible for these changes. Structural adjustment, recurrent droughts, and rapid population growth have exacerbated economic pressures on scarce resources (see, e.g., Lubeck 1985; Winters 1987; Reichmuth 1989; Last 1993; Khalid 1997; Umar 2001). Worsening structural conditions have undermined both the ability of Sahelian peasant households to provide adequately for the young and the capacity of the community to offer support (see, e.g., Mohammed 2001; Sule-Kano 2008). Increased individualism, growing mistrust, and strong criticism from reform-oriented Muslims have also been among the reasons put forward to explain dwindling support structures and declining prestige as well as diminishing returns of *almajiri* education in terms of employment within the spiritual economy (see Lubeck 1985; Sanankoua 1985; Winters 1987). Finally, difficult economic conditions and the spread of secular education have made it increasingly difficult for *gardawa* (advanced or adult Qur'anic students) and former *almajirai* to find jobs within the non-religious sectors of the economy.

As I argue throughout this book, the *almajiri* system today promises neither access to political power nor high social status; its former economic viability has largely been undermined and its religious merit has come under attack. Nonetheless, demand for the system persists. Why do people value an educational system that appears to contribute to their own marginalisation? While the existing literature captures well the structural forces weighing down on rural peasant households, it tells us little about people's attempts to make sense of these constraints. Some authors emphasise the cultural and religious ideas underpinning Qur'anic education (e.g. Ware 2014); however, this is often at the expense of the social and economic contexts within which such ideas emerge. How can we conceptualise educational choices such as *almajiri* enrolment in a way that takes seriously people's reasoning about the value of the education they choose, but that simultaneously acknowledges the social and economic contexts in which such reasoning takes place?

Making a virtue of necessity?

Pierre Bourdieu's work (e.g. Bourdieu 1984; Bourdieu and Passeron 1990 [1977]) has been very influential within anthropological and sociological thinking on the question of how education perpetuates inequality and disadvantage (e.g. Willis 1981; Levinson et al. 1996; Jeffrey et al. 2004). His notion of 'habitus' in particular has been popular for capturing situations like that of Nafisa and her grandsons, who appear 'to make a virtue of necessity' (Bourdieu 1990a: 54) and view an educational choice made in very constrained circumstances as a positive decision taken to honour religious and social commitments.

Bourdieu proposes the notion of 'habitus', defined as 'a system of durable, transposable dispositions' (1990a: 53), as a tool to analyse how people internalise and embody their social positions, including the low status and limited opportunities that potentially accompany them. According to him, the dominated develop dispositions that prevent them from attempting to achieve 'what is already denied' to them; instead, they 'will the inevitable' (Bourdieu 1990a: 54). The notion of 'habitus' seeks to capture both 'the experience of social agents and . . . the objective structures which make this experience possible' (Bourdieu 1988: 782, as cited in Reay 2004: 439). Arguably, 'habitus' thus offers 'a means of viewing structure as occurring within small-scale interactions and activity within large-scale settings' (Reay 2004: 439).

Bourdieu himself uses the concept of 'habitus' largely to understand class inequalities and their reproduction (e.g. Bourdieu 1984; Bourdieu and Passeron 1990 [1977]). Yet, a range of authors within the anthropology and sociology of education have also applied it to other forms of inequality, including gender inequalities (e.g. Connolly 1998; McNay 1999) and ethnic or racial disadvantage (e.g. Archer and Francis 2006). The malleability of the notion of 'habitus' makes it potentially applicable in situations like that of Nafisa, Samaila, and Yunusa, where different forms of disadvantage coincide. For Nafisa and her grandsons, the negative consequences of socio-economic deprivation, rural location, and social vulnerability compound each other.

While the notion of 'habitus' as the repository of wider societal power relations can shed light on important aspects of the decision-making processes underpinning *almajiri* education, several caveats have to be kept in mind. The first relates to the close relationship that Bourdieu establishes between 'habitus' and social reproduction; in this regard, his work has been critiqued for its latent determinism (see, e.g., Willis 1977; 1981). While Bourdieu argues that 'habitus' 'goes hand in hand with vagueness and indeterminacy' (Bourdieu 1990b: 77, as cited in Reay 2004: 433), he nonetheless expects structures of domination to be largely reproduced.

His work acknowledges a limited number of openings in which change becomes possible. These include, for example, when 'habitus' is taken out of the 'social world of which it is the product' and thus stops being 'like "a fish in water"' (Bourdieu and Wacquant 1992: 127; see McNay 1999: 106). This arguably creates disjunctures that make change possible.

However, some critics have gone even further, and have argued that situations of mismatch between the 'social world' and 'habitus' are not the only moments in which people at the receiving end of societal power relations may reflect critically on their condition. As Sayer (2005: 29) argues, 'reflexivity is certainly not the preserve of academics but is common to people regardless of their social position'. If parents or care-givers and *almajirai* themselves may be seen to make a virtue of necessity, for instance when they declare hardship to be a valuable form of char-acter training, this does not mean that they are oblivious to the social and economic conditions in which particular educational decisions are taken, or that they are incapable of aspiring to anything other than what the 'objective conditions' make inevitable (e.g. Bourdieu 1990a: 64–5). Nafisa, for example, unhesitatingly acknowledged the role that finan-cial constraints played in her educational decisions when I enquired why she did not enrol her grandsons in one of the secular schools in Albasu.[3]

If many of my research participants discussed *almajiri* enrolment pri-marily as a deliberate child-raising strategy motivated by religious and moral considerations, leaving aside structural factors, we cannot con-clude from this that they do not reflect on these factors, or that these factors do not play a part. Rather, we have to consider carefully the rea-sons for these silences. People are likely to switch, depending on the situ-ation, between acknowledging the material pressures limiting their room for manoeuvre, and portraying their situation as the result of deliberate action motivated, for instance, by moral or religious considerations. In a context where poverty carries negative connotations, keeping up appear-ances is a way of eschewing poverty-related shame.

A final caveat we have to bear in mind when using Bourdieu's work is that it risks downplaying the intrinsic values of religion, which he portrays extensively as an instrument of power (e.g. Bourdieu 1971).[4] As will become clear throughout this chapter, we cannot use people's 'objective conditions' alone (read as material and social circumstances) to determine who enrols boys as *almajirai*, although these conditions play an important role. *Almajiri* education is not merely 'virtue made of necessity', but also a positive choice of its own. If we want to account for this, we have to take people's religious commitments seriously in their own right. Having said this, a sensibility to 'habitus' can help us exam-ine how particular religious ideas and aspirations have emerged histor-ically, and in which social worlds (or 'fields') they have currency – and where they seem out of place. People in urban areas, for example, are more likely to honour their religious commitments by enrolling their sons in *Islamiyya* or local Qur'anic schools than by sending them away

---

[3] Despite his tender age – around three years at the time I met him – Nafisa repeatedly sent Yunusa to the informal English classes I offered (free of charge) in Albasu, which reflected her concern for his education and appreciation of 'modern' knowledge.

[4] Newman (2016: 28) rightly points out that 'the conceptualisation of religion as capi-tal... tends to reduce its pursuit to instrumentalist ends'. This ties in with wider cri-tiques of Bourdieu's work for his heavy reliance on market analogies (see Sayer 2005: 16), which are little suited to capture the non-instrumental logics motivating people's actions.

as *almajirai*. Taking these theoretical considerations as a starting point, this chapter analyses the processes underpinning *almajiri* enrolment, by drawing on ethnographic observation in a 'sending area' (the rural town of Albasu), personal life histories of current and former *almajirai*, and in-depth interviews and casual conversations with their parents and caregivers.

While in other aspects of my research being female obliged me to be inventive in order to establish a rapport with my research participants, in my research on the reasons underpinning *almajiri* enrolment being a woman was an asset, echoing the experiences of earlier female researchers studying northern Nigeria since the 1940s.[5] It may seem counterintuitive to acclaim female mobility in a context with one of the strictest regimes of female seclusion or *purdah* (Hausa: *kulle*) within the Islamic world (see Callaway 1987; Robson 2000), yet, on balance, many more people and spaces are considered off-limits for a man than for a woman. A man would probably be denied access to the wives and compounds of men to whom he is not related. The 'only' restrictions on female mobility are those ordained by 'shame' (*kunya*) and those imposed by male 'guardians': husbands in the case of married women, and male relatives in the case of unmarried women. Several authors have demonstrated the negotiated nature of such controls on female mobility, with women exercising much more agency than conventionally assumed (see Werthmann 1997).

As a single Western woman, I ended up with the 'best' of both worlds: endowed with an imaginary carte blanche from my 'guardians' back home (who apparently had allowed me to come to Nigeria on my own), unmarried (and thus not bringing shame to a potential husband visibly not in control of my movements), and non-Muslim (and thus less bound by what people considered Islamically ordained), I could be close to a wide range of people. By virtue of being a woman, I could enter people's houses freely and befriend the women inside. I made ample use of this opportunity, and willingly accepted the numerous invitations of the women attending the evening classes I gave in Albasu to visit them during the day when married women are conventionally expected to remain inside their compounds. The *malamai* whose schools I visited frequently, moreover, suggested I befriend their wives, which I did with pleasure. While I spoke to a large number of both men and women in my research, much of the data I draw on in this chapter comes from conversations with women such as Nafisa: mothers, grandmothers, aunts, and sisters of *almajirai*.

[5] For example, Mary Smith, Polly Hill, Enid Schildkrout, Barbara Callaway, Elsbeth Robson, Heidi Nast, and Katja Wertmann.

Interestingly, my conversations with women brought to the fore more easily the structural factors underpinning *almajiri* enrolment, factors that received little or no mention in my interviews with men. This may be because I interviewed them earlier on in my research, when I was less familiar with the context and thus less able to ask specific questions. It may also be because as a woman myself, I built up trusting relationships more easily with other women, with whom I could interact frequently, casually, and unconstrained by northern Nigeria's strict regime of gender segregation. Women and mothers may also be generally more sceptical about *almajiri* enrolment, and therefore less inclined to foreground legitimising discourses. The youths participating in the film project, for example, agreed that most mothers were not happy to see their sons leave as *almajirai*. But if men were reluctant to discuss constraining circumstances with me, this may also be because as heads of households they were – at least theoretically – responsible for the well-being of the children under their authority, and therefore more concerned with upholding a discourse that would legitimise their enrolment decisions. Women, on the other hand, did not hesitate to reveal instances when care arrangements had broken down, pointing out larger questions around poverty-related shame and concealment strategies.

Disbanded families, unstable marriages, and 'evil stepmothers'

Maraya – sai karatu! An orphan's only option is to study!

Nafisa, who made the statement above, was referring to the sons of her daughter's new husband when she stated that 'an orphan's only option is to study!' The man's previous wife had passed away, leaving him with several now motherless children.[6] That their father was alive and well did not prevent Nafisa from declaring these children 'orphans' (*maraya*).[7] Tellingly, after their mother's death, all three sons of the man in question had been enrolled as *almajirai*. This section explores the particular vulnerability of children who grow up without a mother nearby, and how this relates to *almajiri* enrolment.

---

[6] Unlike in other parts of sub-Saharan Africa, HIV/AIDS is not a major cause of parental death in West Africa and Nigeria, and HIV/AIDS infection rates are comparatively low – 3.1 per cent of the Nigerian population in 2015 (UNAIDS 2015).

[7] Whereas the term *maraya* is rarely used for adults who are 'merely' single orphans, it is commonly used for children in such situations. Children without a complete set of parents are considered particularly vulnerable as the roles of mothers and fathers are complementary. As one of my informants put it: 'The one who lost his father lost his [economic] support and the one who lost his mother lost [social/emotional] protection.'

Divorce is frequent and easy to achieve in Hausaland. Unlike Christianity, Islam does not regard marriage as a lifelong and, in principle, unbreakable bond. Consequently, less stigma is attached to divorce (Werthmann 1997: 151, 166). For a divorce to be effective, a husband merely pronounces the formula of repudiation (*na sake ki* – I have divorced you). However, unless he has already divorced his wife in this way two previous times, she may return within a period of three months. Women can – and do – also prompt their husbands to divorce them, for example by 'fleeing' to their parents' house and refusing to return, an act called *yaji*, which is a term also used for hot spices (see Callaway 1987; Werthmann 1997). Leaving a husband in a 'hot' temper, however, mostly means that women must leave their children behind.

The people in my field sites considered poverty, men's sexual 'greediness', and women's presumed 'materialism' and lack of serenity the main reasons for high divorce rates. The youths participating in the film project, for example, declared that some rich men easily lose patience with their wives' misdemeanours. But the youths also accused girls from poor families of caring only about money when choosing their husbands, and of lacking moderation when making material demands on them. They also acknowledged that poor parents may decide to marry their daughters off into problematic arrangements for financial reasons, and that men sought marriage even when they did not have the means to sustain a family. Women in Albasu stated that some men lost interest in their wives once their bodies began to wear the marks of several pregnancies. They also discussed fights with or because of co-wives (the Hausa word for co-wife is *kishiya*, from *kishi*, or jealousy) and the husband's inability to take care of the basic needs of his family (food, soap, clothes) as important reasons for divorce.

Smith found that, in the 1950s, Hausa women married about three to four times on average before menopause (1959: 244). Comprehensive data on current divorce rates does not exist as most marriages are divorced outside a court, making data collection difficult. Uwais et al. (2009: 20), drawing on interviews with bus drivers and *amalanke* pushers (cart-pushers), who traditionally carry a bride's possessions upon both marriage and divorce, estimate that over 75 per cent of marriages in Kano City end in divorce. The repeated efforts by the Kwankwaso administration of Kano State to marry off widows and divorcees at state expense illustrate the sense of crisis enveloping divorce in Kano.[8]

High divorce rates beg the question of what becomes of the children from dissolved marriages. According to orthodox Maliki law, which most

---

[8] 'Another 1,000 divorcees, widows up for wedding in Kano' (2013); see also Solivetti (1994). See Thurston (2015: 49) for a discussion of the political character of such mass weddings.

northern Nigerian Muslims follow at least nominally, a divorced mother is entitled to custody of her sons until they reach the age of seven, and of her daughters until they reach the age of puberty. If she remarries, custody is given to the children's maternal grandmother. The children's father is obliged to provide financially for the children's upkeep (Owasanoye 2005: 422–3). However, these rules are rarely followed to the letter.[9]

In practice, divorced mothers have very little control over their children. Fathers may either decide to keep them all, even small children (once they have been weaned), or demand some or all of the children from their mother at any point in time. While fathers are theoretically obliged to provide financially for children living with a divorced mother or with maternal relatives, they often fail to do so, and women may be reluctant to lodge their claims for fear of having their children taken away from them. From the perspective of mothers, it is often they who must shoulder the financial burden of raising children, at least while they are small, whereas fathers lay claim to them, particularly the boys, once they are old and strong enough to add to the household's labour pool.

The example of Azumi, a boy of around 14 years whom I befriended in the household of the District Head of Albasu, illustrates this logic well. Azumi had been under the care of his mother after his parents divorced, and she had enrolled him as an *almajiri* in Albasu. Azumi seemed to enjoy his stay in Albasu, which was considerably larger than his home village and where his daily needs were taken care of by the household of the District Head, for whom he worked as a domestic. The District Head's wife and I were making plans for him to enrol in *boko* school in addition to *Islamiyya* and Qur'anic school when, at the beginning of the rainy season, his father requested his return to help him with the farm work. Although he was unhappy about leaving, Azumi dared not refuse his father's request.

It was not only requests from children's biological fathers that put divorced mothers at risk of having their children taken away. In addition, divorced women of child-bearing age are under substantial pressure to remarry quickly so as not to risk their moral reputation, and not to be a burden on their parents or relatives whom they move back in with (see Werthmann 1997; cf. Mahmood 2005: 179ff. on divorcees in Egypt). Few men are willing to shoulder the additional burden of providing for the children a woman brings with her from a previous marriage. Consequently, children not claimed by fathers are often redistributed to relatives in a context where fostering is common practice (see, e.g.,

---

[9] I met girls living with their mother in the household of their stepfather, girls staying behind with their father after their mother had left the household, boys living with their divorced mothers, and boys staying in their father's compound without their mother.

Werthmann 2002: 116). An additional option for boys is to be enrolled as *almajirai*.

My informants considered children staying with their father after their mother had left the household to be vulnerable to neglect and abuse by their father's new wives and co-wives (cf. Pittin 1986: 50). The same holds true for maternal orphans – and maternal mortality rates are high. In 2008, the Kano State Health Service Management Board estimated that the maternal mortality ratio in the state was 1,600 deaths per 100,000 live births; this is more than twice the national average (Federal Ministry of Health 2011; Galadanci et al. 2010).[10] If a boy has no mother, his father's other wives accuse him of being responsible for the mischief of their own children; as a group of women from my class in Albasu explained, such children have no one to defend them.

Often, other women in the household notice if a child suffers at the hands of a stepmother. In Daho, a village near Albasu that I visited frequently, I witnessed a dispute between Hauwa and her daughter-in-law, whom Hauwa reproached for beating four-year-old Ali too much (Ali was her stepson and Hauwa's grandson who had stayed behind after his mother had left the household). Recounting the incident, Hauwa grumbled that nobody had any plans to take Ali anywhere, so his stepmother should better come to terms with his presence. But sympathetic relatives, or fathers, intervening on behalf of 'motherless' children may also consider enrolment as an *almajiri* to be a preferable alternative to abusive conditions at home, and they may advocate or decide that a boy be taken to Qur'anic school. For example, Tabawa, a woman attending our evening classes, made sure that her younger brother was enrolled as an *almajiri* after their mother died as she felt that their father was beating the boy too much. While Qur'anic schools are known for not sparing the rod on their students either, the beatings meted out in such schools are commonly considered benign – presumably they ultimately make a child a better Muslim. Beatings from spiteful relations – like beatings from secular school teachers – on the other hand, are looked upon critically.

It is difficult to know how large a share of overall *almajiri* enrolments is made up of boys from disbanded families, not least since this is not

---

[10] According to the National Demographic and Health Survey, the maternal mortality rate for Nigeria as a whole was 545 per 100,000 live births in 2008 (National Population Commission 2009). World Health Organization estimates are considerably higher at 867 in 2010 and 814 in 2015 (World Health Organization 2015: 74). With 1,600 deaths per 100,000 live births, Kano State tops even Sierra Leone, the country with the highest maternal mortality rate worldwide in 2015 (1,360 deaths per 100,000 live births). The average maternal mortality rate in the 'developing regions' of the world was 239 and that in 'developed regions' 12 per 100,000 live births in 2015 (World Health Organization 2015).

an aspect of their life history *almajirai* willingly reveal (see Chapter 6). But given that boys from such families are more likely to be moved back and forth between relatives and more likely to lack somebody to assume financial responsibility for their education, they are certainly more likely candidates for *almajiri* enrolment than boys from stable households.

Subsistence agriculture and food scarcity

The current pattern of smallholding agriculture in Kano developed largely at the beginning of the twentieth century as aristocratic estates based on slave labour were gradually dissolved, with former slaves setting themselves up as independent farmers (Mustapha and Meagher 2000: 4; see also M. F. Smith 1954). Land previously too unsafe to settle became available as slave raids on farmers subsided (Tiffen 2001: 14). At the same time, the colonial regime began taxing the peasantry on an unprecedented scale, steadily siphoning off resources; this situation would come to an end only in the late 1970s (Mustapha and Meagher 2000: 35). This 'haemorrhage' through taxes was supplemented in the late colonial and early independence period by the work of marketing boards, which extracted surpluses from the production of cash crops, especially groundnuts (ibid.: 31), leading Mustapha and Meagher to wonder whether the fate of the rural population would have been less bleak if its resources had not been appropriated on such a massive scale.

During a brief period during the 1970s and early 1980s, rural populations experienced real improvements in their living conditions as oil wealth was used to finance infrastructure projects including rural electrification and water supply schemes. Such expenditures, however, were slashed when the oil boom economy ran aground and when, in 1986, structural adjustment was initiated (Mustapha and Meagher 2000: 48). Many infrastructure projects have since fallen into disrepair. Structural adjustment squeezed livelihoods in rural Kano as input and consumption prices rose even faster than crop prices. Farmers who produced less grain than they consumed, and were thus obliged to buy additional grain, were harmed by high prices. While wealthy peasant households could take advantage of new market opportunities, many poor households could not, which increased differentiation and inequality (ibid.: 50; Meagher 2001).

Today, in contrast to most of the last century, smallholding farmers in northern Nigeria are largely free from government exactions. Yet, as Abba noted as early as 1983, comparatively speaking 'the farmer in his mud house is relatively worse off than before' because 'now *some* live in large cement houses with asbestos roofs and electricity and plumbing and have cars' (Abba 1983: 203). Growing inequality and stratification among the rural population, as well as between cities and countryside, is likely to affect subjective experiences of poverty. Moreover, a number of structural changes have likely exacerbated the difficulties faced by the poor rural majority.

Massive demographic growth, with the Nigerian population more than quadrupling since 1950 (United Nations 2009), has increased competition, especially for fertile and conveniently located farmland (a trend already noted by Polly Hill in the 1970s; Hill 1977; see also Mustapha and Meagher 1992). Kano State has one of the highest population growth rates (3.5 per cent per year) among the Nigerian states. The population of Albasu grew at 3.4 per cent per annum between 1991 and 2006, the years in which censuses were conducted. Rainfall has become less reliable (Sawa and Adebayo 2011) and soil quality has deteriorated in places, also because resources to buy fertiliser are lacking (Mustapha and Meagher 1992; Mortimore 1998).

Often, several men from the same lineage, especially fathers and sons, form a farming unit (*gandu*) to pool resources and relieve individual insecurity (see Hill 1972). Most rural households engage in a range of different economic activities to spread risk and diversify income. Livestock is raised (chicken, guinea fowl, goats), but mostly for sale rather than for consumption as meat is a luxury not many can afford. Wild foods are collected, mostly for consumption, but they are also sometimes marketed (for example, moringa tree leaves (*zogale*) and mangoes (*mangwaro*), and the fruits of locust bean trees (*dorawa*), shea trees (*kadanya*), or tamarind trees (*tsamiya*)).

Most households farm for subsistence as well as for sale. The main crops grown in Albasu are early and late millet, guinea corn, maize, beans, and groundnuts. People may also plant watermelons, capsicum, sesame, cassava, and henna in smaller quantities. While millet and guinea corn are the staple food crops, none of the planted varieties are purely a cash crop. All are part of the local diet and can be marketed if the need for cash arises (see, e.g., Hill 1972: 26–31). Special crops (such as onions, tomatoes, rice, and sugar cane) are cultivated on irrigable farmland (*fadama*), which is, however, scarce around Albasu.

Non-farm activities have long been central to the livelihood strategies of rural households in a climatic zone where rainfall is unreliable and droughts intermittent (Meagher 2001: 43). Cash can be raised for emergencies through trade and craftwork, to purchase foodstuffs or to buy farming inputs (Hill 1972: 30). While traditional crafts such as weaving and pottery have declined in the face of competition from imported industrial goods, Meagher finds that 'economic restructuring since the mid-1980s has tended to reinforce the importance of non-farm incomes'

(2001: 43). For example, men engage in the retail selling of agricultural products or industrial goods not available locally, such as toiletries, household goods, school supplies, or processed foodstuffs.[11]

While many households struggle for their existence year-round, hunger is most acute during the months of the rainy season. This is when stocks run low because seeds are needed for planting,[12] household members return home for farm work, and the new harvest is not yet in. Malnutrition rates are high. Food-insecure households may therefore enrol boys as *almajirai* to reduce their subsistence burden. This is often interpreted as a sign of parents' callousness towards their sons, but I also met parents who decided to enrol boys as *almajirai* because they could not bear to see them suffering. Jamila, for example, a poor peasant's wife, told me that her sons had been sent to Qur'anic school because there was not enough food in the house:

We left them in God's hand. If they get something from begging, they eat. If they don't get anything from begging, [at least] we won't see it. Only once they come home, if they put on weight, we'll see it, if they come emaciated [*awaje*] we'll also see it.

It would be misleading, however, to assume that all *almajirai* come from food-insecure households. Indeed, it is not necessarily the poorest households in a community that enrol their boys as *almajirai*. For the 'ultra-poor' (Last 2000a), even the limited expenditures required to enrol a boy as an *almajiri* may be burdensome. A wooden board on which to write the Qur'an, a bowl for begging, a sleeping mat, and a gift for the *malam* (mostly in the form of grain) need to be provided, and transport costs must be covered. Sympathetic relatives may pay these if parents cannot afford them. Nafisa, for example, paid for her grandson Samaila's expenses. A family not only 'financially poor' but also 'poor in people' may struggle, and I met youths in Albasu who did not have the funds to return to their Qur'anic school after the farming season.[13]

Several of the Qur'anic teachers I met (one of them was among the wealthiest people of his village, owning several horses and other animals) sent their own sons to schools where they either begged or farmed for their livelihood. The son of one of the Qur'anic teachers I was close to in Albasu begged for his food – despite living at home where there was food

---

[11] Meagher (2001: 49) attributes the economic viability of such retail trade not to increased purchasing power but to the increasing inability of rural dwellers to pay high transport costs and to purchase such items themselves in one of the urban centres.

[12] Often the previous year's harvest is used, reducing yields and increasing the risk of disease (see Ajeigbe et al. 2010).

[13] Cf. Bano (2012: 102) on the material and social resources (transport money, acquaintances in town) required to enrol a child in a madrasa in Pakistan.

available.[14] The perception even of fathers who did not enrol their own sons as *almajirai* was that a particularly strong commitment to religious knowledge rather than poverty – combined with the belief that this could best be acquired away from home – determined who opted for *almajiri* enrolment. This confirms the argument that we have to take seriously in their own right the religious and moral/social commitments leading to *almajiri* enrolment, and cannot reduce them to a mere reflection of material circumstances. At the same time, we should remain conscious of the wider contexts – beyond food scarcity – in which such choices are made.

The rhythms and requirements of peasant households

Most children in rural northern Nigeria work, often for several hours a day and in addition to schooling (see, e.g., Robson 2004, writing about Zarewa village, southern Kano State).[15] It is mostly boys who till their families' fields, but girls also help with labour-intensive tasks such as planting. Both boys and girls care for livestock, gather firewood, wild foods, and fodder, process agricultural food crops, and help with house construction and repair works. Children also complete daily household tasks such as fetching water and running errands. Girls also look after younger siblings. In addition, children, especially girls, hawk (*talla*) produce or wares, either to contribute to their family's subsistence on behalf of their – mostly secluded – mothers, or to earn cash for their own marriage expenses (Robson 2004: 201–6).

The availability of children – especially sons – of a suitable age to engage in work influences household decisions about children's educational trajectories. I met fathers who enrolled all their sons as *almajirai*, but my sense was that some children – either girls or boys too young to be enrolled as *almajirai* – will usually be kept at home to perform daily chores beyond the 'reach' of women in *purdah*, such as fetching water or running errands. Boys whose help is required in agriculture or trade to ensure their household's survival have few opportunities to attend 'modern' school. However, *almajiri* enrolment may be tailored around such work demands. Sons can be – and are – summoned back during the farming season when labour demands peak.

On the limited *fadama* (irrigable lowland areas), farming is possible year-round. Work in rain-fed agriculture, however, is more seasonal.

---

[14] His mother had left the household, though – I am not sure she would have agreed to this arrangement!

[15] Poor urban children do not work in agriculture, but they, too, help with household chores, run errands, mind younger siblings, and trade for themselves, their mothers, or their households. Boys may work alongside their fathers or other men, and, in an ideal scenario, learn their trade at the same time.

There are tasks specific to the dry season, such as house and roof repairs and the maintenance of fences, and livestock droppings have to be swept up and carried to the fields as manure (from March). But the 'peak season' begins with the first rains (around April or May) and ends about two months after the rains have stopped (around November). Labour demand is greatest for ridging, sowing, repeated weeding, and harvesting – tasks that have to be performed within a certain time frame to be effective. Other jobs (such as building and repair works) are less time-bound and can be done gradually. The *almajirai* insisted that there was little demand for hired labour (*kwadago*) outside the peak season and that there were very few opportunities to earn an income apart from gathering firewood (*itace*) and corn or guinea corn stalks (*kara*).

Once the harvest is in and stored and labour demands subside, many young men leave the rural areas and head for the cities for *ci rani*, to 'eat away the dry season' (see Mustapha and Meagher 1992; 2000; Mortimore 1998; 2003). Many Qur'anic schools also follow the rhythm of the agricultural seasons, with intense study, including nightly study sessions, during the agriculturally less busy dry season, and a more lax lesson schedule or holidays during the farming season. Urban Qur'anic schools release their students to return to rural areas during this period to help their parents or teachers farm.

While most senior *malamai* are settled – i.e. they have a family, a compound, and a stable livelihood – junior teachers and students are often highly mobile. During the dry season, young aspiring teachers (from about 18 years upwards) with several *almajirai* under their care may leave their wet-season abode where they were attached to a stationary senior *malam*. They either move to a fixed dry-season residence (changing from year to year, but often located in an urban area), or start a migratory tour that will only end with the return of the rains. During their travels, they lodge with stationary *malamai* in the villages they visit. At the end of the dry season, they mostly return to the 'home base' school from where they departed.[16]

Young men from rural areas may migrate to the urban centres during the dry season in order to earn some cash, either to start a family or to support an already existing one,[17] and they attach themselves to a Qur'anic teacher to set themselves up (see Lubeck 1985; Khalid 1997). Gathering the resources to launch an adult career – that is, to build a room for prospective bride(s) and children, and to marry – presents a real challenge to adolescent boys and young men in a largely eroding rural economy where opportunities to earn cash income are scarce.

---

[16] Transport fares are usually covered using saved-up revenues from selling crop surpluses. Villagers may also subsidise the travel of *almajirai* they have grown close to.

[17] In the latter case, his wife and children stay behind in the husband's parental household.

The cities offer petty income opportunities as street vendors and odd-job men. Moreover, for older youths with sufficient means and determination, moving to an urban area as an *almajiri* may be a strategy to acquire (belatedly) some 'modern' secular knowledge. I met several Qur'anic students in their late teens and early twenties who attended adult literacy evening classes in Kano – a rare opportunity in rural areas.

The Qur'anic schooling system thus synchronises well with the work rhythms of peasant households. This is true not only over the seasons, but also during the day. Qur'anic schools hold their first lesson in the early morning hours and break to free their students for agricultural tasks before the midday heat sets in. Mid-mornings and afternoons are mostly lesson-free, at least in rural schools during the farming season, and many schools hold sessions after dusk, when they do not compete with their students' other work obligations.

Given how well integrated the *almajiri* system is with peasant households' work rhythms, its students acquire agricultural knowledge as a matter of course. The *almajirai* in Albasu could satisfy my curiosity about Hausa plant names and their uses without hesitation. On the occasions when the *almajirai* I befriended in Albasu took me to their fields, I was impressed by the ease with which they performed their tasks. When I commented on his speed of planting, Buhari declared with some pride '*aikina ne*': his skilfulness should not surprise me given that 'this was his work'. The *almajirai* monitored and corrected each other's work. Abbas, for example, rebuked his younger brother Mustapha for planting seed beans too close to each other: 'These are beans!' Both Malam Nasiru and Malam Ahmed, the two *malamai* I visited most frequently in Albasu, had allocated their students small plots of land where they grew their own crops for sale. The returns allowed them to buy soap, clothes, or shoes. Kabiru, one of the older *almajirai*, raised his own goat.

Almajirai staying in urban areas permanently do not achieve a mastery of agricultural tasks to quite the same extent. Sadisu (whose parents live in Kwanar Huɗu, a slum area within urban Kano, and who stayed at Sabuwar Ƙofa all year) stated plainly that he did not know how to farm. Some people considered that staying in urban areas all year round would deskill students, and not only in terms of practical agricultural knowledge. One father, for example, confided to me that he wanted his sons to study in rural areas – even though he believed that they would have more time to study in an urban area where no agricultural tasks could distract them. He feared that once his sons had acquired a liking for the bright lights of the city, they would not be able to endure village life and its hardships. To use the language of Bourdieu, he considered that if boys were to handle village life like 'a fish in water' (Bourdieu and Wacquant 1992: 127), it was necessary to cultivate the appropriate 'habitus' carefully, and not to put it at risk by exposing them to city life.

'Seek knowledge, even as far as China!'

So far in this chapter, I have focused largely on the circumstances of rural peasant households. Yet, *almajiri* enrolment is not limited to peasant households, which once again underlines the fact that we cannot neglect the significance that religious, moral, and social considerations hold in their own right and independent of underlying material circumstances. The first round of fieldwork, which I conducted from July to September 2009 almost exclusively in urban Kano, coincided with the rainy season. This meant that many students from peasant households had returned to rural areas to help their parents or teachers farm. Yet, I still encountered *almajirai* in Kano. Rather than being farmers, most of their fathers were engaged in business (as traders in clothes, phones, or goats, owners of provision stores, or bus drivers, for example). Some worked as Qur'anic teachers, and some for the local government. Moreover, not all of those *almajirai* who leave during the rainy season leave to work in agriculture. Malam Ahmadu, for example, the Qur'anic teacher I lived next door to at Sabuwar Kofa, sent some of his students home and did not accept new enrolments until the rains had stopped because he didn't have enough space to shelter them all during the rainy season.

The remainder of this chapter explores the social, moral, and religious aspirations underpinning *almajiri* enrolment. The first question we must answer is what drives parents to send their sons away rather than enrol them in a local Qur'anic school (of which there are plenty in northern Nigeria). Several practical considerations play a role. Fathers would not necessarily have time to support their sons in their studies, I was told. Having too many friends would distract a boy. Being exposed to different teachers with different strengths, and to new circumstances and new people in general, is believed to broaden a student's knowledge. A well-known *hadith* (a saying of the Prophet Mohammed) invites believers to search for knowledge even as far as China (see Fortier 1998: 218).

Finally, parents told me that boys at home would be distracted from their studies by their participation in the daily reproductive activities of the household (cf. Fortier 1998: 218 on Mauritania). While this did not match the experience of younger boys – for example, the *almajirai* I taught in Daho (six to 12 years old) lamented that their workload at Qur'anic school was higher than at home – older youths agreed that as *almajirai* in the city they had more time for their studies than at home, where family obligations tied up their time. The main explanation for sending boys away, however, can be found in the pedagogical expectations underpinning the system.

Self-reliance and provider roles

Boyden et al. (1998) indicate that the path to adulthood in many societies is secured by making contributions to the good of the family or household rather than through children's evolving autonomy, as Western thinking has it (see also Durham 2008). Children are expected to increasingly take over responsibilities for others as they grow up, rather than being gradually 'released' into an independent adult life. In socioeconomic contexts where families often depend on the economic and/or labour contributions of all their members, including the youngest, it is essential to socialise children into contributor roles.

While both girls and boys are socialised into such roles in northern Nigeria, expectations vary with gender. Whereas girls are trained to become homemakers and mothers, boys are expected to become self-reliant and responsible breadwinners. Accordingly, the *almajiri* system encourages boys to learn early on to take care of themselves and of others materially and financially. Rather than being provided for by their teachers and parents, the students contribute towards their teacher's livelihood and bring presents when they visit home. Being left without means of sustenance is intended not only to 'steel' the character, but also to teach a boy how to stand on his own feet.

I gained the impression that for young *almajirai* – on whom not too many expectations rest – helping others was first and foremost an opportunity to receive credit and praise. I hardly ever got the chance to carry my bag myself from the *malam*'s house in Daho to the *Islamiyya* school building where I gave literacy and numeracy classes to his *almajirai*, as one of the boys would always insist that he be allowed to carry it for me. When I asked what the boys would do if they had a lot of money, Nazifi, aged about nine, blurted out that he would buy new *Sallah* (Eid) clothes for his father! Sadisu (aged 14 in 2009), who studied at the Qur'anic school next door to where I was living during my stays in urban Kano, clearly took pride in being able to shoulder the burden of providing for himself:

My parents bring clothes for me, I have enough now. So even if they want to bring something for me, I tell them not to. They also bring food for me . . . Now, I don't want them to bring food for me again, because I want to fend for myself. ('Radio interview')

For older *almajirai*, the expectation from families that they would contribute to the household was somewhat more burdensome. They were torn between their own wish to live up to these expectations and a genuine enjoyment of the provider role on the one hand, and the implications such demands had on their resources and room for manoeuvre on the other. When I enquired whether anyone in his family would be able to support Naziru (aged 17) financially in his plans to enrol in *boko* school, Sadisu (aged 16), who was also present, explained that 'it was now time for them to bring rather than take from their parents'. Pressure to support families back home is particularly intense for boys without older male siblings. After his father's death, it fell on Auwal (aged about 18) as the eldest son to till his family's fields, and he returned home even though he had just gained a hard-won place in secondary school.

'Proper' personhood

At the time when I was taken to school, me, I didn't know how to say my prayers, where east is, what ablutions are, how to fast, how to live among people. (Abdullahi, early twenties)

Abdullahi, a participant in our film project, implies in this playful narration of his life course that Qur'anic school played a vital role in socialising him in his religious duties, as well as in teaching him how to become a suitable social being. The two are largely inseparable. In Islam, the *umma* is considered collectively responsible for the conduct of all its members. The religious transgressions of an individual thus constitute a social problem to some extent. While the training of both boys and girls aims at forming disciplined Muslims, the religious education of boys is considered more consequential and therefore given greater weight. Upon marriage, it is the men who will be held responsible for the conduct of their wives and children.

Many Muslims in northern Nigeria consider that Islam requires complete and unquestioning submission to God's laws. Many 'traditional' Muslims also view respectful behaviour and obedience towards one's social superiors (*manya*) as an extension of such religious compliance, and a necessary ingredient to ensure social order (see, e.g., Last 2000b; Ware 2014).[18] Several fathers commented to me that boys were sent out to study the Qur'an so that they would learn 'respect' for their parents, as experiencing the hardship and strict discipline of the Qur'anic school makes them appreciate what they have at home. The perceived ability of a teacher to ensure 'character training' or a 'moral upbringing' (*tarbiyya*)[19] and to teach religion (*addini* – in an applied sense,

---

[18] 'Reformist' Muslims arguably have a somewhat different approach to authority (see, e.g., Janson 2014; Masquelier 2009; Chapter 8).
[19] Whereas my informants used the Hausa-nised term *tarbiyya* broadly to refer to moral and social 'character training', it can also refer more specifically to the 'spiritual training'

going beyond mere Qur'anic recitation)[20] was central to my respondents' accounts of what they considered to be good schools.

In the northern Nigerian context, children are seen as 'beings who require disciplining in order to become human' (Last 2000b: 374). Undisciplined children are perceived as animal-like, as 'they simply sleep, eat and drink' (ibid.: 374). Without 'external shaping' in the form of discipline and physical hardship, including physical punishment, 'a child is scarcely human, and certainly not a proper Muslim' (ibid.: 376; see also Fortier 1998; Schildkrout 2002 [1978]; for comparable notions of childhood in Western history, see Jenks 1996: 70ff.; Valentine 1996).

Language reflects this concept of personhood. Nafisa, for example, said of her grandson Yunusa that she was planning to take him to Qur'anic school as an *almajiri* so that he would 'become a person' (*ya zama mutum*). One qualifies as a 'proper' human being only once one is capable of (and responsible for) following God's laws. Young children (below the age of about seven), on the other hand, are incapable of committing either faults or sins (cf. Starrett 1998: 103).[21] When I asked a group of young people in Albasu to enlighten me about Hausa swear words, the older youths present told me that they could not pronounce any for me without putting at stake whatever rewards they had previously earned in the sight of God. The little boys present, however, could say swear words with impunity, I learned, and eventually I got the examples I was asking for.

Many 'tradition'-oriented adults in northern Nigeria are concerned that demonstrations of love may 'damage' a child's character. Parents are particularly afraid that their deep affection may lead to the child being spoilt, a sentiment that gives rise to a 'strong tradition of public restraint or emotional reserve' between parents and children (Last 2000b: 378). While parents are concerned about avoiding 'spoiling' – and ensuring the disciplining – of both boys and girls, the practices through which they seek to ensure good outcomes vary. Girls are usually kept closer to home, although both boys and girls may be fostered with relatives (see, e.g., Goody 1982; Bledsoe 1990). Additionally, boys may be sent to Qur'anic school to ensure that they are exposed to the necessary hardship. The

---

tariqa (Sufi order) initiates undergo 'with the aim of purifying one's self and achieving mystical union with and experiential knowledge of God' (Seesemann 2011: 72).

[20] The term *addini* is also often used to refer to the practical details of 'correct' religious practice, as contained, for example, in the *ahadith*. Classical Qur'anic schools do not, however, teach these at elementary level (see Chapter 8), and the *addini* referred to here has a broader meaning.

[21] From the age of about seven, children are encouraged to participate in prayer. See also the *hadith* cited by Starrett (1998: 103): 'Play with your son [for] seven [years], then discipline him [for] seven [years], then be his friend [for] seven [years], then give free rein to him.'

distance ensures that parents do not interfere, and makes it difficult for boys to escape from school and run back home. While it is recognised that parents are reluctant to be too harsh, this is perceived as a weakness. One of the *malamai* I was close to explained his decision to teach *almajirai* rather than students from the neighbourhood: in his experience, nearby parents could not help but interfere in his teaching. Rather than blaming them, he took this to be a structural problem that could be solved by sending boys away. One student claimed that one studies better away from home because, at home, enjoying one's parents' support, one may simply decide to drop out of school if one feels treated badly by the teacher.

Not only most fathers but also several of the mothers I interviewed stressed discipline and hardship as their motives for advocating that a boy be enrolled as an *almajiri*. Mairo, one of three wives of a poor farmer in Albasu, for example, hoped to secure her husband's permission to enrol her seven-year-old son Muhammad as an *almajiri*. Of the five children she had given birth to, three had died early. When I got to know her, she had a little daughter, still a toddler, and Muhammad. To make sure that he would acquire good manners (*tarbiyya*) and religious knowledge, she wanted to put aside her own strongly felt desire to be close to him.

The fact that many of the fathers enrolling their sons as *almajirai* have gone through the system themselves – and have come out on the other side 'unscathed' – lends it a certain legitimacy (Last 2000b: 375; see also Ware 2014: 43). Several fathers told me how much they themselves had suffered as students; however, they argued that the conditions nowadays are slightly less tough – people are richer and give more, more profitable activities are available to the *almajirai* to earn a living, particularly in the cities, and the physical infrastructure of the schools has improved. While being relieved that the deprivation nowadays is not quite as harsh as when they were students, fathers made a conscious choice to expose their sons to hardship.

It is interesting to note that the *almajirai* only partly bought into discourses describing children as inherently feral and in need of disciplining. The young *almajirai* at Sabuwar Ƙofa with whom I conducted research in 2009 portrayed *almajiri* enrolment as a strategy designed to remove boys from problematic influences. While they also brought up the danger of becoming spoilt as a reason for enrolment, they linked this danger mainly to specific external corrupting influences rather than to some intrinsic characteristics of children, thus shifting the blame away from themselves, and providing a reason why not every child has to become an *almajiri* if he wants to escape 'spoiling'. Naziru, for instance, suggests that parents enrol small boys as *almajirai* because leaving the child at home is risky. If you leave a child, he is going around with spoilt children... if the child is following the spoilt children, going to watch football, and going to roam about, and going to play rough play – instead of allowing your child to do all this, it's better to bring your child to Qur'anic school. ('Radio interview')

When conducting group interviews with younger *almajirai*, I sometimes encouraged them to enact particular situations to make it easier for them to convey their experiences. In a small role play about *almajiri* enrolment, the boys invented a drunkard, a gambler, and a criminal as corrupting influences justifying a father's decision to send his son away.

While hardship is considered desirable to some extent, parents nonetheless try to ensure appropriate care arrangements on a practical level, for instance by placing boys with relatives: I met *almajirai* who were related to their *malam*, or to one of his wives. I also met boys who were sent with siblings (or to a school where an elder sibling studied already), or at least with boys from the same village. In all the schools where I conducted research, there were 'clusters' of students who came from the same area or village. Yet, while the senior stationary *malamai* with whom *almajirai* stay during the rainy season are likely to be known to parents, in many cases the young *malamai* or *gardawa* who take them on migratory tours during the dry season are not.

Finally, parents tend to take into account their sons' temperament and ability to withstand hardship when making enrolment decisions (see Last 2000b: 382). I befriended a family in Albasu, for example, whose oldest son had been enrolled as an *almajiri* for some 13 years before returning emaciated and without having acquired much Qur'anic knowledge. The second eldest son was subsequently enrolled in *boko* school, and *almajiri* education became a consideration only when he could not secure secondary school admission. The family's third son, on the other hand, a charming but mischievous boy, was to be sent to *almajiri* school for some time so that he would take his secular school studies seriously afterwards. For similar reasons, Larabiyu enrolled her son (from whose father she was divorced) as an *almajiri* after he returned from his father's place, where he had lived for some time. Nobody had taken care of his education there, and therefore he had got into the habit of secular school vagrancy, she told me. She hoped an episode of *almajiri* enrolment would get him back on the straight and narrow. Moreover, she did not have the money to enrol him in a secular school at the time.

In brief, *almajiri* education is often chosen as a means to inculcate a particular 'habitus' in boys. It is not an inevitable stage of boyhood let alone of childhood – indeed, it is deemed inappropriate for girls – although it certainly draws on narratives about the educational nature of hardship and pain that are widespread and well-known in Hausaland.

Privation, pain, and punishment

Physical exertion and even pain do not necessarily carry negative connotations in Hausaland. Pain is considered a necessary and inevitable part of daily life: people may not even make an effort to avoid it,[22] and some forms of pain are considered educational. With the exception of very young children, children crying from physical or emotional pain are usually quickly hushed. For example, when Khalidu (aged about eight), who had just learned that his sister had died in childbirth, started crying, his teacher told him to be quiet, and to pray for her. When I tried to console a young *almajiri* who had injured himself, putting my arm around him and asking about the pain, the boys standing nearby, somewhat bewildered, laughed at the situation. When I talked about circumcision with some of the youths involved in the film project, I wondered what they considered preferable: to circumcise when a boy was still an infant, or when he had grown up a little. They agreed that an infant would suffer less, but that remembering the pain involved was important for a boy to learn to empathise with others.

The *almajirai*'s deprived living conditions, and especially the fact that many young students beg daily for food, have often been decried as problematic and detrimental to their studies. Yet, among supporters of the system and segments of the rural population more widely, a certain degree of physical discomfort, including hunger, is considered necessary for one's mind to stay alert and focused (cf. Ware 2014: 8). Eating to full satisfaction every day is considered to numb the mind, and eating for pleasure is also a privilege reserved for the powerful. 'Eating' (*ci*) plays a central role in metaphors of power, the word 'eating' being used to describe situations such as winning a victory, conquering a place, or having sexual intercourse with a woman (see Last 2000b: 374; see also Robson 2006). An important implication of marriage, which marks the beginning of respectable adulthood for men, is that one has secure access to the food prepared by one's wife. Young *almajirai*, conversely, are expected to learn humility and endurance, and therefore they must toil to fill their stomachs with the leftover food they receive when begging.

I saw teachers sharing food with very young *almajirai* (six- to seven-year-old boys in Daho) in cases when they did not receive anything from begging, and with older students or *gardawa* who helped them with their teaching load. The large majority of students, however, received

---

[22] For example, one day I set out to loosen the braids of a woman who had come on a visit to the house of the District Head and who was about to have her hair braided anew. As I had no experience of this task, I asked her to let me know if I caused her pain. She laughed at me, saying, 'You [Westerners] don't like pain!' and queried whether I would be able to stand having my own hair braided.

food from their *malam*'s house only if they were sick. For the rest of the time, they relied largely on what they (or their fellow students) got from begging.[23] Giving and receiving food leftovers is a routine practice in Hausaland. Leftovers cannot be kept: refrigerators are scarce and the electricity supply erratic. When I discussed with the *almajirai* participating in the film project their opinions on a ban on begging, they raised the question of what would happen to food leftovers if no one came to collect them. That would be '*almubazzaranci*', they explained: letting food go to waste unnecessarily. Eating leftovers is not generally considered demeaning. The *malam*'s wives and I were regularly offered a taste of the food the young *almajirai* in Daho had brought back from their begging rounds, and occasionally we accepted a handful. Giving and receiving leftovers that have gone off is, of course, a different matter altogether, but according to the *almajirai*, this is a problem mostly in the urban areas, where some donors have little regard for the *almajirai*. Suffice to say that for many poor rural parents, accepting that their sons beg for food has very different connotations than it has for Western, urban, or southern Nigerian observers who condemn it as 'child neglect' and 'abuse'.

In addition, while we should not disregard poverty when considering the scruffy appearance of some *almajirai*, their tattered clothes and bare feet are also to some extent external markers of the humility and asceticism they are supposed to learn and embrace. As Mahmood (2005) has argued about veiled women in Egypt, clothing practices are thought to help produce particular desirable subjectivities.

The *almajirai*'s schedule is deliberately designed to be tough. Usually, they start their first lesson after the first morning prayer at dawn and are kept busy until after the evening prayer. Time spent sleeping is time lost to one's studies: this is how Malam Nasiru, whose school in Albasu I visited regularly, justified why he made his students study deep into the night during the dry season, and why he woke them up again after midnight for another study session.[24] During lessons, students crouch on the floor behind their wooden board, always within reach of the vigilant whip of an older student or assistant teacher (*gardi*). When a student's concentration slips, a lash will remind him to focus. Pain in this context is used as a 'technique of memory' (Last 2000b: 383), through which 'truths are seared into the long-term memories of the young' (ibid.: 384;

---

[23] Even when food was scarce, *almajirai* expected other *almajirai* to share it out. The youths participating in the film project described vividly how young *almajirai* would cover their begging bowl with one hand when dishing out small amounts to their peers with the other (*dille*) if good luck had dealt them a filled bowl. Some *gardawa* would share out rice in portions of 'five rice grains', I was told. Handing out rice by the grain was considered more acceptable than not sharing it at all.

[24] Angels are believed to wander the earth at night, which makes the middle of the night the best time to find a sympathetic ear for one's prayers.

see also Fortier 1997; Ware 2014: 42ff.). But it is not only attention that is policed through physical pain. So are mistakes and misdemeanours. This ties in with wider ideas about punishment and the maintenance of social order in Hausaland.

Last (2000c: 328) writes that 'there is general agreement that severe punishment is just, and that justice is the key characteristic of good government. Preachers and poets alike stress hell and the severity of Allah's judgement... Teachers and adults generally are not expected to spare the rod (or the leg-irons) on the young.' Furthermore, in times when 'the world's end [may be] imminent', the religious *umma* should police moral trespasses all the more and 'live extra-righteously now' (Last 2009: 1). One *almajiri* with whom I discussed questions of social and moral order justified the severe corporal punishment included in shari'a law with reference to the even severer punishment offenders had to expect from God: after all, they would be better off in the afterlife if they paid as much of their debts as possible in this world.

As studying is perceived as a religious service and duty, for *almajirai* it is almost impossible to justify a refusal to learn and study hard if not with reference to a student's laziness and stubbornness. Naziru, for instance, argues that a good student

knows that whatever he does, he is doing it for himself. He knows that if he is not serious with his studies, he is cheating himself and he is also cheating his parents, and he is also cheating his teacher, because they will say he is not teaching him well. ('Radio interview')

An interpretation of studying as a personal responsibility towards God also lends even greater legitimacy to students' relative powerlessness vis-à-vis their teacher. Habibu (aged 11), for instance, in a 'radio speech' justifies the physical punishment of students as it is they who will reap the benefits of a successful education:

An *almajiri* is not supposed to be taken from one school to another just because his father sees that he is being beaten... because the studies are going to be useful to him, not to his father. ('Radio interview')

Nonetheless, none of this prevents the *almajirai* from passing judgement on what they consider unacceptable punishment, especially with regard to the practices of other *almajirai*. For example, two of Malam Ahmadu's students (both in their late teens) sneered at Mukhtar, one of their fellow students who was aged about 18 and aspired to become a *malam*. They argued that if he did not reduce the number of beatings he dealt the three young students under his supervision, he would not be able to make *almajirai* stay with him (*riƙe*). They reasoned that one should teach through advice, not through beatings.

Conclusion: like fish in water?

This chapter has sought to understand why boys become *almajirai*. Using Bourdieu's notion of 'habitus', it has explored both the social and economic circumstances in which *almajiri* education becomes a desirable option for parents, and the cultural and religious discourses through which people justify the enrolment of boys in this education system. I have argued that *almajiri* education corresponds well to the economic requirements of Sahelian peasant households. The rhythm of Qur'anic schooling synchronises with agricultural work cycles, which means that households can call on the labour of boys and youths enrolled as *almajirai* during peak work times, and reduce their subsistence burden during times of scarcity. Given how well integrated the *almajiri* system is with peasant households' work rhythms, many *almajirai* acquire agricultural knowledge as a matter of course. However, their acquisition of skills for a rural livelihood has to be assessed against the backdrop of a largely declining rural economy (see Chapter 9).

The *almajiri* system also offers redress for a number of difficult situations. Many poor households struggle to gain access for their children to 'modern' education that is affordable and of acceptable quality. High divorce and maternal mortality rates, as well as rural poverty, make it difficult for some children to stay at home. For adolescent boys and young men struggling to gather the necessary resources to transition into adult life, the *almajiri* system offers an opportunity to migrate seasonally or permanently to the cities, where petty income opportunities are easier to come by than in rural areas.

While the vagaries of subsistence agriculture, as well as difficult social and economic circumstances, in many instances provide the backdrop against which *almajiri* education becomes an option, most people explain their decision to enrol boys in the Qur'anic schooling system with reference to the social, moral, and religious dispositions and skills they expect their sons to learn as *almajirai*. Arguably, the harsh discipline of the Qur'anic school moulds boys into good Muslims, as they learn what it means to show respect and be humble. Incidentally, in an environment where people are expected to subordinate their personal aspirations to socially sanctioned norms and authorities, and where people's plans are frequently thwarted by adverse external circumstances, being able to endure and to accept one's fate are indispensable skills. What is more, hardship is said to train boys in endurance and to teach them to take care of their own needs, and eventually of those of their family, which is a crucial skill for their future roles as breadwinners and heads of families.

Bourdieu's notion of 'habitus' captures well the ways in which people seem to make 'a virtue of necessity' when foregrounding religious and cultural arguments for *almajiri* enrolment, while relegating to the background the structural constraints to which they are subjected. Rather than reducing *almajiri* enrolment to the result of either 'deprivation' or 'fundamentalism/backwardness', approaching *almajiri* enrolment through the lens of 'habitus' allows us to take seriously people's reasoning about the value of the education they choose, and to simultaneously acknowledge the structural contexts in which such reasoning takes place.

Yet, when thinking about *almajiri* education through the lens of 'habitus', we must be careful not to forget that 'making a virtue of necessity' does not prevent people from reflecting critically on the conditions that create this necessity in the first place, or from aspiring to change. If people leave out certain elements in their accounts of *almajiri* education, we cannot conclude from this that they are not aware of them. The following chapters pay close attention to the role played by negative connotations of poverty, and poor people's struggles to keep up appearances in this context, for the way in which people speak (publicly) about *almajiri* education.

Second, while material and social circumstances, or what Bourdieu calls the 'objective conditions', certainly matter for understanding *almajiri* enrolment, we have to refrain from assuming a linear or mechanistic relationship between the two. Many people value the moral/social and religious training associated with *almajiri* education for its own sake. Chapter 8 explores in more detail the religious narratives underpinning *almajiri* education, and contrasts these with alternative religious narratives, drawing attention to the social worlds or 'fields' within which they have currency.

Finally, in the introduction to this chapter, I queried what happens to the 'habitus' supporting *almajiri* education when it is taken out of the – mostly rural – contexts in which it appears 'like a fish in water'. What happens when the *almajirai* come into contact with 'social worlds' that are at odds with those of which they are the 'product'? And what are the implications of such disjunctures for social reproduction and the perpetuation of this 'habitus'? The next chapters pursue this theme further. Following the *almajirai* into town, I explore their encounters with people from very different social backgrounds, and trace how such encounters affect the *almajirai*'s perspectives of themselves and their education system, as well as their future aspirations. The next chapter starts off this enquiry by looking at the *almajirai*'s experiences in urban middle- and upper-class households, where they often work as domestic helpers.

5   Inequality at close range
Domestic service for the better-off

Aminu is sweeping. Bent forward, his eyes fixed on the floor, he takes great care to let no dry leaf or fallen twig escape the rough brush of his tattered broom. The boy, in his mid-teens and visibly experienced in his task, is focused. He barely notices the two younger children approaching. Dressed up in starchy school uniforms, their satchels strapped tightly to their backs, they make their way across the courtyard to the compound gate, ready for school. As they reach Aminu they pause for a moment, puff themselves up. Several insults then rain down from them onto Aminu, who is still bent over his broom. Wearily he looks up at the two children, determined not to rise to the provocation. He continues sweeping. Then a woman enters the scene, her attention having been drawn by the commotion. She barely waits for the two young children to finish their complaints about Aminu, who, they claim, obstructed their way to school by sweeping where they needed to pass. She proceeds straight to the attack: if he does not treat her children with due respect, he can immediately pack his bags and leave; she has no use for ill-mannered employees. Aminu, not daring to straighten up now, his posture all submissiveness, his broom frozen in mid-air, quickly abandons his attempt to defend himself. Instead he begins pleading with the woman to forgive him, to let him keep his post. As the employer shepherds her own children to the gate, she tells Aminu sneeringly that proper parents take care of their children (like she does) and do not dump them elsewhere as *almajirai* (like Aminu's parents did). She then turns her back on Aminu, who, resigned, resumes sweeping.

Aminu's real name is Iƙiramatu, and together with eight other Qur'anic students or *almajirai*, he wrote the script for the film scene described here. The woman is a professional actress whom we engaged (with funds from the Goethe Institute Kano, which supported our 'participatory' film project) to play a spiteful employer of *almajirai*. The children aren't hers but belong to households in the neighbourhood of Sabuwar Ƙofa, where I lived during my time in Kano City and where we filmed the scene. The storyline is fictional; the characters are acted. Yet, both storyline and characters are also to some extent real. The two neighbourhood children playing in the scene came to the set in their own uniforms, with their own satchels. Both go to school while their mothers employ

Figure 5.1 Filmmaking: domestic work (photograph: Hannah Hoechner)

other children, including *almajirai*, to clean, fetch water, and run errands for them. Iƙiramatu, the protagonist, is an expert domestic worker, who has been employed in various households in the neighbourhood since his arrival at the Qur'anic school there. He has even worked in the home of one of the youngsters who act as the children of Aminu's employer in the film.

Also real are the *almajirai*'s grievances about their relationships with the better-off people in the urban neighbourhoods of their schools that they sought to communicate through the film, and that are revealed – albeit in a somewhat overstated, 'movie-like' fashion – by the scene at the start of this chapter. The *almajirai* with whom I conducted my research agreed: bad treatment originates first and foremost with 'the rich' and those holding high status in society (Hausa: *masu kuɗi, masu girma*). Most *almajirai* are from poor rural families and have low status in the urban areas where they come to study. Even though many urban schools of *almajirai* are not located in 'rich' neighbourhoods, most students will come into contact with people from more privileged segments of society during their sojourns in urban areas, not least because such households are more likely to be able to afford domestic helpers. Despite the risk of poor treatment, many young *almajirai* seek domestic employment, the alternative – to live off what they get from begging – being even less appealing.

Domestic work arrangements bring people at opposite ends of the socio-economic spectrum intimately close together, and thus reverse trends towards the increasing spatial segregation of different socio-economic strata that is spurred, for instance, by processes of gentrification and ghettoisation. Dickey (2000: 466) argues that domestic service in South Asia 'provides one of the clearest markers of class distinctions. The ability to hire servants is a sign of having achieved middle- or upper-class status.' According to her, 'domestic service interactions constitute the most intense, sustained contact with members of other classes that most of their participants encounter' (ibid.: 463). Through such interactions, members of different strata negotiate, enact, and potentially contest their relative positions within society. By looking at domestic work arrangements, we can trace how reduced physical distance affects the social, emotional, and economic distance between members of different segments of society.

Often, children are employed as domestic helpers. Mostly they possess the requisite skills because they carry out similar tasks in their own homes (e.g. Bourdillon 2009). They are likely to work for lower pay and be more malleable than adult employees (e.g. Klocker 2011). UNICEF (1999: 2) estimated that, at the turn of the century, child domestic workers constituted 'the largest group of child workers in the world'. West Africa has a long history of children working in households other than their own. In fosterage arrangements, children are placed with members of the extended family or other acquainted adults. Children are 'circulated' for several reasons: to provide childless households with children, to reinforce bonds between different households, so that they can attend school or pursue apprenticeships, to facilitate their acquisition of housekeeping skills (girls), or for 'character training' (e.g. Goody 1982; Bledsoe 1990; Jonckers 1997; Hashim 2005; Notermans 2008; Hampshire et al. 2015). Fosterage serves 'to distribute the economic costs and benefits of children' (Bledsoe 1990: 74). Most fostered children are expected to perform certain domestic and other tasks for their guardians, for which they or their parents receive material and symbolic support from the foster household.

The historical practice of fosterage to procure domestic helpers has undergone considerable transformation over recent decades, and has given way to increasingly commodified and market-based arrangements. Arguably, many households in West Africa today eschew the reciprocal relationships underpinning fosterage arrangements. The labour of fostered children is not free, as Jacquemin (2009: 13) notes for Côte d'Ivoire: 'the reciprocity expected has a considerable financial cost in a period of recession and also has a high symbolic cost'. According to her, many urban households now 'prefer to employ an unrelated girl that they pay a salary as this is much cheaper . . . than using the services of a "little niece"' (ibid.). In many cases, the distinction between familial and employment relationships is kept deliberately blurred (Jacquemin 2004; Klocker 2011; Thorsen 2012). For many young domestic workers, the changes described here have resulted in poor and precarious working conditions, which human rights organisations denounce in strong terms as 'child trafficking' and 'child slavery' (e.g. Anti-Slavery International 2003; Human Rights Watch 2003; Terre des Hommes 2003; ILO-IPEC 2004).

Blanket condemnations obscure the great diversity of child domestics' work realities and the potential access to economic, social, or cultural capital that domestic service relations may open up for them. For instance, employers may pay school fees, provide support during difficult circumstances, or help employees find better-paying jobs as they grow older (Wasiuzzaman and Wells 2010; Thorsen 2012). Yet, many young domestic workers grow up to see their hopes frustrated. They feel let down by their employers and relegated to a place at the bottom of the social hierarchy. The juxtaposition of a spatial and emotional intimacy resulting from a worker's integration into his employers' private space with a distance resulting from class and other hierarchies adds another layer of complexity to domestic work arrangements. Unlike in most other work settings, workers and employers relate to each other at close range. Adams and Dickey (2000: 2–3, 17) suggest that this triggers a 'dynamic of self–other contrast', as ways must be found to justify workplace hierarchies. Ideas about what it means to be civilised, moral, and pious play an important role in contestations over the relative status of both sides and the tangible terms of the employment relationship.

The material presented in this chapter corroborates the arguments made in Chapter 1 about poverty as produced through the 'active dynamics of social interaction' (Kabeer 2000: 84). I have proposed to analyse the processes that support protracted poverty through the conceptual lenses of 'social exclusion' and 'adverse incorporation'. The latter in particular can usefully draw attention to the ways in which not only exclusion from, but also participation in, the institutions of mainstream society can produce problematic results for poor people. Hickey and du Toit (2007: 12), for instance, caution that even though clientelistic systems may 'integrate all the participants in the network of exchange relations', lower-status groups are usually included on disadvantageous terms (see also Morgan et al. 2010).

This chapter asks about the terms on which the *almajirai* relate to the people in the urban neighbourhoods of their schools. As Qur'anic students who come to town primarily to pursue their religious education, they used to be the habitual recipients of alms, and townspeople could gain religious standing by supporting *almajirai*. Yet, as the religious merit of the classical Qur'anic education system has increasingly come under attack from those calling for Islamic reform and the modernisation of Islamic education, the *almajirai*'s role as legitimate recipients, and even claimants, of charity is being redefined. It has become largely impossible today for *almajirai* to survive on charity alone. Begging, moreover, exposes *almajirai* to verbal abuse and even physical assaults. Many *almajirai* complain of being chased away, or given food leftovers on the brink of going off. Domestic work for neighbouring households can constitute a comparatively easy way of earning money.

The large majority of young domestic workers in West Africa – an estimated 80 per cent – are girls (Thorsen 2012: 4). In northern Nigeria, on the other hand, it is mostly young male Qur'anic students who are employed as domestic workers. While girls may be fostered to members of the extended family, female live-in domestic servants without family connections, as can be found in the households of the better-off in other parts of West Africa, are rare in northern Nigeria. Concerns about protecting female sexuality play a role in this. Also, given the ubiquity of Qur'anic schools, *almajirai* constitute an alternative and readily available pool of cheap labour for domestic tasks.

Socio-economic inequalities and strict seclusion of married women across the social spectrum in Kano foster demand for children's labour (see Schildkrout 2002 [1978]; Robson 2004).[1] As many women are largely confined to their compounds, children make the daily reproduction of the household possible. Unencumbered by the gender norms restricting the movements of adults, children can be called upon to clean, shop, or run errands. As most of the urban households that can afford to do so educate their own children in 'modern' secular (*boko*) and 'modern' Islamic (*Islamiyya*) schools today, demand for the labour of the *almajirai* is reinforced. During schooldays, children of school age are away for most of the morning and afternoon. 'We, that's the time we are free,' says Ibrahim, Iƙiramatu's schoolmate at Sabuwar Ƙofa, explaining the timetable of their Qur'anic school.

Some households establish durable relationships with individual *almajirai*, who may be in charge of washing and ironing clothes, cleaning the house and compound, fetching water each day, or doing the daily shopping. Others employ *almajirai* on an ad hoc basis for all sorts of odd jobs and errands: for example, to catch runaway chickens, to repair a mud wall that has crumbled under the rain, or to clear out a blocked sewer. *Almajirai* are also engaged to provide basic spiritual services. They

---

[1] The practice of purdah or female seclusion reaches beyond geographical and socio-economic divides, and the wives of rural peasants are just as likely to be secluded as the wives of the urban upper classes (see Callaway 1987). The practice of *purdah*, however, is stratified to some extent. The wives of Qur'anic teachers (*malamai*) and traditional rulers are almost completely secluded (*kullen dinga*), while most other women go out occasionally, though mostly accompanied and only with their husbands' permission (*kullen tsari*) (Callaway 1987: 57; see also Robson 2000).

say prayers, recite Qur'anic verses, or fabricate 'potions' (*rubutun sha*) that aim to improve the fortunes of a particular employer or household. Almost all *almajirai* I met had some experience working as domestics. Towards the end of puberty, however, gender norms governing adult behaviour begin to apply fully. Young men then stop entering the houses of other men and seek other forms of employment. But until that age, domestic employment is one of the most accessible ways of earning a living for boys, or of earning at least an occasional meal or a place to sleep in a neighbour's entrance room (*soro*). As many Qur'anic schools lack facilities to shelter all their students, young *almajirai* may have little choice but to seize such opportunities.

That domestic work arrangements nevertheless cause discontent will become apparent over the following pages as I describe the ambiguity inherent in them. This ambiguity makes it possible for employers to limit their obligations towards employees. The contest over relative status and material entitlements is fought in a wide range of arenas, and it is a contest that the *almajirai* tend to lose. Why is there so little advantage for them in their employment terms? I propose an answer based on the relative distribution of power between the *almajirai* and their employer-patrons. Yet, arrangements in which tangible benefits are distributed unevenly are in need of justification. While employers seek to defend and legitimise the status quo, the *almajirai* attempt to challenge it, and to win at least a moral victory. Many consider their wealthy employers to be inconsiderate and ungenerous. Does this mean, though, that their experiences radicalise the *almajirai*, as many in Nigeria and beyond assert? The conclusion to this chapter offers some reflections on this question. It also connects the *almajirai*'s experiences to larger societal changes affecting the relationships between richer and poorer segments of northern Nigerian society today.

If the *almajirai* get more of a hearing in the pages that follow than their employers, this is firstly an outcome of my data. I collected data on employers' views and behaviours during over a year of ethnographic fieldwork largely 'along the way'. Data with *almajirai*, on the other hand, was collected through a wide range of methods (see Chapter 1), which generated powerful and nuanced insights into their concerns. Secondly, perspectives on domestic work arrangements are necessarily subjective. This chapter is interested in showing the *almajirai*'s perspectives.

Ambiguous relationships: between market transaction and intimate personal ties

Domestic work often occupies the grey area between personal relationships based on mutual commitment and market transactions based on the exchange of services for compensation. Within the former, working conditions are flexible, remuneration takes the form of gifts and favours, and employees have reason to hope for support in the longer term. The latter are mostly short-term, impersonal contracts with set conditions and payments, which can be terminated at any time. The *almajirai* unanimously preferred personal relationships with employers to monetised one-off transactions.

One-off market transactions do not hold the promise of longer-term livelihood support. On the other hand, informal arrangements can – with luck – be developed into more durable support structures. In an ideal case, the *almajirai* argued, households would take an *almajiri* in as a 'son of the house' (*dan gida*). They would offer him a space to socialise and relax during the day and a place to sleep at night, provide a reliable food supply, and listen to his worries and difficulties. They would sponsor him through secular education, provide new clothes for him at *Sallah* (Hausa for *Eid al-Fitr* and *Eid al-Kabir*, the two major Muslim holidays), and help him find better-paying income opportunities once he grew older. In brief, ideally an *almajiri* would find himself if not substitute parents then at least committed patrons in town (cf. Jacquemin 2009, whose young interviewees in Abidjan unanimously stated their desire 'to feel like a member of the family' in which they were working).

What the *almajirai* envisage resembles classic patron–client relationships in Hausa society, which '[consist] in ties of mutual loyalty, interest and assistance. The inferior or client frequently performs political or domestic services for his superior or patron, while the latter takes care of him politically . . . and also assists him economically' (Smith 1957: 13). Patron–client relationships can provide a substitute for kinship networks for those, including immigrants, who lack 'effective support from kinsfolk in the community' (M. G. Smith 1954: 32). Kinship terms are often used to express such relationships. Patrons, for example, are frequently referred to as 'fathers' or 'mothers of the house' (*uban daki* or *uban gida* for male patrons; *uwar daki* or *uwar rana* for female patrons), and their respective clients figure as 'sons' or 'daughters' (*dan arziki, 'yar arziki, dan gida*). That patrons/parents and clients/children are so closely related within the Hausa cultural idiom provides a clue to why the *almajirai* project parent-like roles onto their employers.

Indeed, some *almajirai* develop close personal bonds with households in the neighbourhoods of their school. Salisu (aged about ten), a bright young *almajiri* at Malam Nasiru's school in the rural town of Albasu, could mostly be found at Hauwa's house during his free time. Hauwa was newly married to a man who spent most of his week in Kano City to pursue a master's degree. As the only wife and without children, Hauwa was fairly lonely in her compound, and visibly rejoiced in Salisu's company and in the information he delivered to her about the outside world. For example, he would immediately report to her when I had arrived back in town from one of my trips to Kano. Her compound was not far from Salisu's school, which I visited frequently. Through Salisu, Hauwa could almost instantaneously track my movements, and she sent the boy after me with an invitation to visit her compound as soon as I took my leave from his school.

Auwal's (aged about 17) relationship to Fatima, a vigorous and cheerful woman in her forties, provides another illustration of how close a bond some *almajirai* develop with their employers. When I came for the first time to the school of Auwal and the other boys who had been following my English classes at the CAESI, the first stop was the obligatory visit to their *malam*'s (Qur'anic teacher's) house. However, the second visit on our tour of the neighbourhood was the house of Auwal's *uwar daki*, his long-term employer. I was surprised to find out that it was her telephone number he had put on the attendance sheet which the Goethe Institute (which sponsored our film project) had asked me to pass around during our training sessions to register attendance. Auwal did not own a phone himself at that time. Ignorant of this, I had called the number he had written down on several occasions when trying to get hold of him. Fatima now told me laughingly that she had been the person answering all these rather futile phone calls. Even though Auwal had stopped working for Fatima as he grew older, he still visited her regularly, and considered her a source of support that he could rely on if needed.

If these two examples constitute a 'gold standard' of sorts for *almajirai*'s relationships with employers, most *almajirai* found themselves in less positive arrangements. Scholars of domestic work have argued that employers often deliberately leave the nature of their relationships with servants undefined, drifting in the grey space between personal relationships and market transactions, which may serve to mystify relations of domination (e.g. Shah 2000). Domestic workers occupy a liminal zone that makes it possible to appropriate them 'in labor as well as in person' (ibid.: 89). Klocker (2011: 214) describes similar conditions for young domestic servants in Tanzania, who 'attained neither the benefits of familial membership (protection, security, love, nurturance, and access to education) nor the advantages of being an employee (set working conditions and wages)'. Many *almajirai* find themselves in arrangements of an undefined nature. Work schedules and pay are the foremost arenas within which ambiguity makes itself felt. Arrangements about working hours are rarely made explicit and the *almajirai* complain that often employers do not respect the timetable of the Qur'anic school, demanding that a boy works for them during school hours. The youths participating in the film project lamented that:

Some of our employers...mistreat you. Some send their own children to [secular] school. But you, you're expected to stay and work for them. If you say it's time for your own studies, they'll complain: 'We're helping you, you good-for-nothings, first you go to the market, then you can go to your school.' If you tell them, you'll be late, they don't care. (Scriptwriting)

Remuneration is another source of recurrent discontent. Shah (2000: 101) writes that being remunerated through gifts and tips rather than a contractual wage 'necessarily relegate[s child domestics] to a subordinate position where they have to be obliging and servile to their masters beyond what is required in contractual wage relations'. This was the case for the *almajirai*, as the payment they received was often minimal and seldom fixed. One *almajiri* I was close to at Sabuwar Kofa received no formal payment from the household in whose *soro* (entrance hall) he slept and for whom he fetched water every day. Instead, they stepped in on several occasions to cover his expenses, such as the transport costs to visit home, or the money needed to sew new clothes at *Sallah*. Meals were the most common form of remuneration. But even the food given was sometimes perceived as second-class. One boy, for instance, commented about the people for whom he worked and who paid him with food that he was rarely given meat, although he was the one being sent to buy it, so he knew exactly what the rest of the household was eating.

If vague and flexible arrangements concerning working hours and pay fed the illusion of a personal relationship based on mutual care and affection (within which tight agreements would seem inappropriate or unnecessary), most employers made sure that boundaries and differences between household members and employees were nevertheless maintained. Due to their own strained resources, or because they considered the *almajirai* beyond the scope of their responsibility, employers also sought to keep their material obligations towards them in check.

A true 'son of the house'?

While the *almajirai* aspired to relationships with their employers that resembled those of a son to his parents, their employers were hardly ready to grant them son-like status. This becomes most apparent when we compare the *almajirai* with their employers' children. In a society where status comes with age, children are used to being treated as having low status compared with adults, but being treated as having low status in comparison to other children has a different quality to it. Jacquemin (2004: 393) queries how young maids in Côte d'Ivoire can ever feel 'like a daughter' to their employers when every day they see their 'boss's children well dressed, going to school, playing, studying, watching television and handing out orders'. Given that the *almajirai* face very similar conditions, it is doubtful whether they can feel like true 'sons of the house'.

Both *almajirai* and their employers' children were very familiar with their respective roles and enacted status differences with ease. I witnessed this on various occasions in the household of a local elite family in Kano that I visited frequently. While domestic workers and employ-ers' children were playmates on an equal footing in certain situations (for example, making a bow and arrow together or playing football in the yard), in others they performed the roles pertinent to their respec-tive status position without hesitation. They could smoothly slip back and forth from an egalitarian to a hierarchical relationship. It came very naturally to the household's children to issue instructions to the child domestics – their peers with respect to age – and the latter accepted them as a matter of routine. Talatu, for example, who was much younger than both Sulaiman and Lawan, the two *almajirai* employed in the house-hold, sometimes requested that they should greet her as social inferiors are supposed to offer greetings to their superiors.[2] On another occa-sion, Talatu's older brother Abubakar, about to pass his leftover food to Sulaiman, changed his mind at the last moment. Rather than giving Sulaiman his plate so that he could take it to his usual eating spot where he would share it with the other child domestics, he ordered him to sit down and eat while he watched. (Sulaiman obeyed until little enough was left to be scooped into his hand and quickly carried away to his peers.)

Bourdillon (2009: 4) writes that: 'In many cases, other children in the household look down on child employees and contribute to the abuse.' Abuse and derision from their employers' children and other children in the neighbourhood was a pressing concern for the *almajirai*. The follow-ing draft scenes for the film, where the protagonist they invented suffers various forms of abuse, exemplify this:

[An *almajiri*] begs from a house, and some boy [from the neighbourhood] ridicules him, and hits him. Then [the neighbourhood boy's] older brother comes out. He doesn't enquire what is happening, he just starts beating [the *almajiri*]. The *almajiri* starts crying; he is exhausted and walks off.
The children of the neighbourhood often call an *almajiri* to come running but then you'll see there's nothing to be given to him, it's just abuse. (Scriptwriting)

Almajirai are likely to be asked to perform tasks that the children of their employers do not do. Khalid (cited in Amzat 2008: 61–2), writing about urban Sokoto in north-western Nigeria, states that almost every-one, including those opposed to their presence, 'rely on the labour of the almajirai, especially for chores they would not saddle their own off-spring's [sic] with'. The *almajirai* were keenly aware of the fact that their employers' children did not sully their hands with the work the *almajirai* were asked to do.

---

[2] 'Proper' greetings usually imply genuflecting and bowing towards the person being greeted (cf. Nast 1998 on the importance of body postures for enacting hierarchies in the Emir's palace in Kano).

Another domain within which inequalities between the *almajirai* and a household's own children become apparent is education. As previously discussed, the assumption that *almajirai* are opposed to 'modern' education is widespread but incorrect. Often economic reasons prevent them from attending. A vehement opponent of the *almajiri* system once told me that in his view the most promising strategy to end it was to encourage households to take in an *almajiri* as an employee and protégé, as, over time, a relationship would develop, and the employers would eventually see to it that 'their' *almajirai* received a 'modern' education. The *almajirai* mentioned some of the people in the neighbourhood for whom they worked or had worked who wanted them to achieve 'modern' secular education. This did not mean, however, that their employers were ready (or able) to commit significant resources to 'their' *almajirai*'s education. Sani's case exemplifies this. In 2009, he told me that:

In the house where I work, and other people that are nice to me, they asked me to ask my teacher and my brother if they would allow me to go to *boko* school, but my brother said no and my teacher also said no.

In 2011, the situation had changed somewhat. As Sani had done his first *sauka* (the graduation after completing a first 'reading' of the Qur'an, which includes learning to write and recite it) and had progressed well in his Qur'anic studies, his father agreed to 'modern' education. As he was concretising his enrolment plans, the youth voiced concerns about the actual commitment of his employers – a family with whom he had been 'staying' for some six years. 'Some people don't stick to their promises,' he declared. He was also concerned that the family may soon move to another ward within the city, leaving him and his secular studies in limbo.

Sani might also have been strategic in his comments to make sure I would pay for his schooling as I had once proposed. If this was his strategy, it reflects his lack of trust that the arrangement with his employers would work out according to his interests. Looking for a school (other than Sabuwar Ƙofa's poor-quality government school) in which he could enrol, Sani took me to several fancy private schools around the neighbourhood, which he knew because some of the residents' children attended them. Most of these schools charged fees well beyond my means (over US$375 per term), and their secretaries gave me bewildered looks when I confirmed that it was indeed Sani, aged 17 at that time, whom I wanted to enrol in their primary school. Sani's employers considered putting him in the government school in the neighbourhood, while their own children attended private school. This confirms Bourdillon's (2009: 4) finding that when child domestic workers do receive some education, it is usually inferior to that of their employers' children.

That their employers' commitment is limited becomes most apparent if an *almajiri* falls ill and his labour thus becomes temporarily unavailable. Then his employers quickly lose interest in him, as the youths participating in the film project complained. Abdullahi, in his early twenties at the time, lamented that once an *almajiri* falls ill, many employers 'dump' (*ajiye*) him at his *malam*'s place, and are not heard from again: 'Often people care about your *healthy* self only, and not about you *yourself*'. An interview with the Head of the Paediatrics Section at Murtala Muhammad Hospital, Kano's largest public hospital, confirmed this: it was not their employers but fellow students or their *malam*'s wives who would accompany *almajirai* to hospital in the rare cases that they came at all. In most cases, they would first seek the (cheaper) services of traditional healers, or self-medicate with drugs bought over the counter from a pharmacist, and go to hospital only when already very ill.[3]

In brief, discontent was widespread – so widespread that one of the urban *malamai* I got to know well told his *almajirai* that they should look for other forms of livelihood (*sana'a*), and not for employment in the houses of the rich. One youth explained that he decided to sell soft drinks rather than continue working as a domestic because employers would make the *almajirai* do things at their convenience, even if they had class or other obligations.

Why do the *almajirai*'s domestic work arrangements cause so much frustration? Why do the *almajirai* rarely manage to secure employment on more favourable terms? Different expectations of the young employees and their employers partly explain the discontent, I think. The former seek to establish long-term intimate personal relationships and even family-like bonds, and they feel let down and betrayed when their patrons 'default' on their presumed obligations. The latter, by contrast, appear to assume more ambiguous positions. As I have argued throughout this chapter, employers benefit from vague arrangements, for example regarding working hours and pay, which are possible within more personalised arrangements. At the same time, limiting their commitment to cash-for-service exchanges allows them to eschew longer-term obligations. For some households, this may be a necessity given their own constrained resources; others may conceive of the *almajirai* simply as beyond the scope of their responsibilities. Also, with changing definitions of what it means to be educated, fewer people think it worthwhile to support and sustain the *almajiri* system on religious grounds. Another reason lies in the *almajirai*'s weak bargaining position.

[3] Interview with Dr Binta Jibr Wudil, Head of the Paediatrics Section at Murtala Muhammad Hospital, 5 April 2011. To mobilise the support of faraway parents takes time. Some parents, moreover, lack funds to pay for drugs and treatment. If an *almajiri* suffers an injury or falls ill, he thus tends to depend on the goodwill of friends and teachers to help him out with expenses for drugs and treatment.

A weak bargaining position

Going on 'holiday' is risky for *almajirai*. A boy who spends the rainy season at home to help his parents farm, for example, may come back to find his job has been taken by someone else during his absence. This reveals how weak the *almajirai*'s position within their employment relationships is. Earlier in this chapter I pointed to the similarities between the relationships the *almajirai* seek to establish with their employers and 'traditional' Hausa patron–client relationships. Patronage and clientelism have long been discussed as the bane of African politics and social relations, stalling social mobility and trapping poor clients in relationships of dependence and servitude.[4] Such a blanket condemnation is unhelpful as it obscures that clients – like the *almajirai* – may have good reasons for seeking patronage relationships, for example to avoid more detrimental commodified forms of interaction and exchange (cf. Mustapha and Whitfield 2009). To understand why their position within such relationships is nevertheless weak, it is helpful to ask about the specific conditions determining how power is distributed between patrons and clients. Cheeseman (2006) provides a useful framework for doing so. He proposes to analyse patron–client relationships in two dimensions. The first dimension concerns the degree to which they are personalised: that is, what proportion of patronage is channelled through individuals. If patronage is diffused or bargained for collectively, it does not necessarily create personalised ties of submission and dependence (Whitfield and Mustapha 2009: 220). The second dimension concerns how competitive patron–client relationships are: that is, the extent to which the recipients of patronage 'are able to choose between, or periodically change, the source of patronage. This is of great importance because it determines how responsive patrons are likely to be to local needs and demands' (Cheeseman 2006: 33).

How do the *almajirai* fit into Cheeseman's matrix? Their relationships to their patrons are highly personalised and in many cases involve only one *almajiri* per household, ruling out collective forms of bargaining. Also, the *almajirai* are competing for employer-patrons rather than the other way around, which means the latter are under little 'competitive pressure'. Given the oversupply of potential clients ready to fill their posts, the *almajirai* are in a weak bargaining position. Their age may set them apart from potential competitors as domestic service is foreclosed to those to whom adult gender norms apply fully. Also, their identity as religious scholars may distinguish them from other potential young clients as people can gain religious standing by supporting *almajirai*. Yet, this identity has come under attack, and in a society where over

---

[4] For an influential contribution to this debate, see Chabal and Daloz (1999).

40 per cent of the population are under the age of 15 years (British Council and Harvard School of Public Health 2010: 13), youth alone hardly works as a 'unique selling point'. Moreover, we should not forget that in a society where seniority commands respect, being young compounds the effect of other axes of inequality, with the effect that young *almajirai* enjoy very little social status. In sum, the terms of the *almajirai*'s incorporation into clientelistic systems are mostly adverse.

Strategies of distinction

In a context where religious norms emphasise generosity and the equality of Muslims before God, it takes some effort to rationalise and defend highly unequal relationships. What idioms do employers use to justify employment terms that favour them rather than their employees? And how do the *almajirai* seek to challenge these terms?

Hansen (2000: 53–4) describes the strategies that upper-class employers of domestic servants in Tamil Nadu, India, use to justify difference as morally acceptable. Since arguing that 'money makes poor people the way they are . . . would weaken the "rightness" of the moral differences that keep the relatively privileged on their side of the class divide', the better-off collapse character and socio-economic status into one concept, she writes (ibid.: 55–6). Shah echoes this, arguing that urban employers in Nepal want domestics from rural areas as these are considered honest, loyal, meek, and obedient. (Incidentally, such qualities make it easy to appropriate their labour.) As a flipside of their association with meekness and loyalty, rural children are stereotyped as 'ignorant, dirty, and . . . uncivilised', which 'provides urbanity with a civilizing role and further adds a cultural dimension and rationale for the servant's subordination' (Shah 2000: 95).

Similar dynamics are at work in northern Nigeria. Rurality connotes negatively for most urban dwellers, including the *almajirai* themselves. The youths with whom I produced the film, for example, talked with some condescension about people who lacked exposure to urban life, including parents who failed to understand the purpose of the film project. 'Villager' (*ɗan kauye*) serves as an insult among *almajirai*. Yet, their efforts to distance themselves from their (mostly) rural origins are not necessarily successful, and negative connotations remain. Frequently, the *almajirai* are labelled backward, gullible, and dirty, including by the people in the households where they work. The teenage son of an upper-class family I visited frequently in Kano, for example, repeatedly insulted his little brother, using comparisons with the *almajirai* working for the household: 'Are you an *almajiri* or what, to put on such a dirty kaftan?' 'You smell like an *almajiri*! You stink just like Dauda and his like!' In our film, Aminu's employer offers the boy employment when he first comes to her house on the condition that 'from now on, you'll bathe, and wash your clothes, so you too look like other people'.

Anthropological scholarship has forcefully argued that discourses about 'dirt' expose wider conceptions of the social order and attempts to enforce it (see, e.g., the seminal work of Mary Douglas 2001 [1966]). Arguably, 'dirt is not inherently "dirty"' (Masquelier 2005a: 10). At times, it points to 'metaphorical' and not to 'literal pollution', which makes it 'a situational, rather than substantive, category' (ibid.). In the examples in the previous paragraph, invoking inappropriate looks and smells serves first and foremost to belittle and subordinate, rather than to objectively evaluate hygiene standards. This buttresses Masquelier's finding that '[b]ecause dirt often stands for deviance, anyone that cannot, will not, or should not fit into a particular social system or pattern can be defined as "dirty"' (Masquelier 2005a: 10).[5] Conceiving of the *almajirai* as 'dirty' thus justifies difference, and garnishes employment relationships with 'civilising' overtones.

People housing or employing *almajirai* regularly interpret their actions as a way of taking responsibility for the needy, or as a means of honouring their religious commitments through 'facilitating' the *almajirai*'s religious studies, rather than as a labour contract. Some people support *almajirai* unconditionally. Yet, most *almajirai* are expected to reciprocate the 'charity' they receive in some way or another, be it through prayers for a 'benefactor's' advantage or the provision of other spiritual services, or by carrying out domestic work. In one scene in our film, two upper-class women discuss their opinions of *almajirai*. One of them states:

Their parents grew tired of them, they farm, grow food, sell it to us, then they send their children and want us to feed them?

While the protagonist of the film, Aminu, is providing crucial services in the woman's household, his employer dismisses this, and casts their relationship as one in which she is expected to feed him magnanimously. While this scene caricatures upper-class behaviour, it originates from a shared understanding between the *almajirai* and the professional actresses involved of how some people define themselves vis-à-vis the *almajirai* working for them. The better-off employers of *almajirai* with whom I interacted frequently described themselves as granting rather than seizing opportunities when I asked them about the *almajirai* in their households.

---

[5] As a matter of fact, Dauda, to whom the teenager cited here referred, was not an *almajiri* but lived with his parents, attended secular school, and was usually fairly well-groomed. He came from a poor rural household and frequently ran errands for the household in exchange for food. Apparently, this was enough for the youth to categorise him as both an *almajiri* and 'dirty'.

While employers may portray themselves as magnanimous benefactors, the *almajirai* emphasised the value and importance of their own work for the wider public good. The youths involved in the film project, for instance, expressed frustration that their contributions to the smooth functioning of society often went unrecognised and undervalued. What would happen if there were no *almajirai* to do all the work they are currently shouldering, they asked? They demanded that:

> people should know that, truly, if all *almajirai* were gathered up and returned home, it's their own children who will have to do all the hard work that the *almajirai* are doing now, like laundry and ironing and emptying the dustbin and so on. (Scriptwriting)

One boy said that he wanted to take a long holiday at home after *Eid al-Kabir* and so the family he was working for would have to fetch their water themselves for a while. He was hoping that they would realise how demanding his work was and provide more adequate compensation.

Conclusion: good, bad, and elusive patrons

In the context of the Boko Haram crisis, Nigerian Nobel laureate Wole Soyinka (2012) wrote that Qur'anic schools are places where terrorists are 'deliberately bred, nurtured, sheltered, rendered pliant, obedient to only one line of command, ready to be unleashed at the rest of society'. Many believe that the *almajirai*'s narrow curriculum, 'traditional' teaching style, and deprived living conditions make them susceptible to radical doctrines. In narratives such as Soyinka's, Qur'anic schools are treated as if they existed in a social vacuum. They are portrayed as discrete, self-contained units that – if left to themselves – produce angry youths ready to commit acts of violence (see Starrett 2006, who detects similar logics in American discourses about Islamic schools in South Asia). Absent in Soyinka's narrative are all the other members of society and the terms on which they relate to the *almajirai*. Yet, arguably, if we are worried about the extent to which the *almajirai* become frustrated with or alienated from other members of society, we need to understand the very terms on which they relate to them. In this chapter, I have discussed these terms of engagement in detail. What emerges is a rather gloomy picture of the *almajirai*'s struggles for recognition and decent employment conditions. Given the indifference and condescension with which they are frequently met, the *almajirai* would have every reason to resent the better-off in society. They did not refrain from voicing criticism of particular employers and of the rich more generally. Yet, does this mean that they are susceptible to doctrines that challenge the status quo?

Scheper-Hughes (1992) writes that 'bad patrons' in north-eastern Brazil serve as scapegoats for an unfair and exploitative system. 'Bad patrons' take the blame for the abysmal treatment of the poor, and thus a more thoroughgoing critique of the social relations underpinning poverty and hunger is stalled. As she puts it, '[t]he bad boss can be treated as an aberration rather than as a manifestation, the true flowering of the logic and violence of *paternalismo*. The good boss, for her part, helps smooth over, conceal, and sometimes resolve the contradictions inherent in the perverse relations of power and dominance' (Scheper-Hughes 1992: 126). Scheper-Hughes's description may be overly Manichean. Nonetheless, it offers some helpful clues to decipher the dynamics at work in northern Nigeria today. Far from challenging the fundamental status inequality that is at the basis of their relationships with their employer-patrons, the *almajirai* instead seek to ameliorate the terms of these relationships. Like Scheper-Hughes' shantytown dwellers, the *almajirai* believe in 'good patrons'. They pin their hopes for future advancement on them, and occasionally they are proven right. In a context where alternative avenues for social mobility are rare, seeking a 'good patron' appears to be the *almajirai*'s best bet. But it is nonetheless a poor bet.

In the past, patron–client relationships helped prevent dire poverty in all but exceptional circumstances. Today, patrons, whether good or bad, have become elusive. Given the number of poor young migrants to urban areas, it is difficult to gauge who falls within whose remit, and it is easy not to feel responsible. In the context of economic restructuring, poverty has also been recast to some extent as an individual rather than a collective responsibility (see Chapters 2 and 6). Despite their proximity to urban middle-class households, the *almajirai*'s expectations for support therefore often remain unmet. This is indicative of the larger crisis that has befallen societal relations in northern Nigeria. Wealthier segments of society refuse, it seems, to assume the full responsibilities inherent in 'traditional' patronage arrangements.[6] This is possible as poor young migrants are in a weak bargaining position vis-à-vis potential patrons. Also, as social relations become more commodified, it is easier to frame interactions as market transactions, and therefore detached from the wider responsibilities inherent in patron–client relationships. Finally, we should not forget that in a context of widespread poverty (see National Bureau of Statistics 2012), potential patrons may themselves

---

[6] Several civil society organisations in Kano seek to salvage such patronage arrangements to support the *almajirai*. The Kano-based Almajiri Foundation, established by Malam Kiyawa, for instance, suggests that each household should adopt one *almajiri* and take care of his personal, financial, and educational needs. I have argued elsewhere (see Hoechner 2014a) that a public code of conduct, developed with both *almajirai* and their employers, and publicised through the media, establishing good practice in terms of care for and payment of household helps, could help sensitise the population to the *almajirai*'s concerns. To date, this does not appear in any of the NGOs' action plans.

lack the means to support clients. The fact that respect for their education system is declining also reduces people's willingness to support the *almajirai*, compounding the negative effects of other processes of societal change. Chapter 8 returns to the developments outlined here and discusses how they make themselves felt within the spiritual economy. The next chapter explores how the *almajirai* engage and cope with the adverse terms of their incorporation into society.

6 Concealment, asceticism, and cunning Americans

How to deal with being poor

With the *almajirai* participating in the film project, I often sat on our veranda after the day's work was done. We discussed the progress of the project, which sought to equip the nine participating Qur'anic students with the requisite cinematographic skills to make a movie about their lives. While we were filming in public places, knots of curious passers-by and neighbourhood children instantly formed around us, with people leaning on and pushing each other, impatient to catch a glimpse of the unusual goings-on. It was impossible to exchange more than a few hurried comments and instructions. The midday heat did its bit to tire us out. When we retired into my compound, for once locking the door to be safe from the indefatigable onslaught of the neighbourhood children, everyone rejoiced in the calm and coolness of the yard, and the opportunity to chat peacefully. We made a habit out of these reunions, and even after we had concluded our film, the boys frequently called in, assembling their peers from the neighbourhood, and together we reminisced about the project. Often our conversations drifted off into various directions, and the youths seized the opportunity to find out from me what other places were like, places they had not had a chance to learn much about. We often talked about poverty in Nigeria, but on one occasion I explained that poverty also existed in the West. I described that some Western countries have elaborate social security systems, which can buffer people's personal calamities. The absence of a decent social security system in the US accounts for the many poor people in the States, I argued – despite the country's overall wealth. '*Zab*! Really?' Abdullahi exclaimed, surprised to learn that there was poverty in the US. The Americans were 'cunning' (*suna da wayo*), he concluded: in the American films he had seen, everything looked neat and wealthy. They knew how 'not to show their poor'.

Abdullahi's declaration that the Americans were 'cunning' to edit poverty out of their globally broadcast image reflects the negative connotations that poverty has today in northern Nigeria – even among poor people. I have proposed to use the Bourdieusian notion of 'symbolic violence' to capture a situation in which the poor perpetuate discourses that serve their own subordination. Like the example of an insult given by Abdulmalik at the very beginning of this book ('Your family eats their porridge without stew!'), Abdullahi's statement suggests that poverty is embarrassing and best concealed. This chapter asks how boys and youths deal with being poor in this context, and what role religion plays in their lives.

Often, religion has been portrayed as a radicalising force in the lives of the poor, particularly so where poor people are also young, male, and Muslim (for a critique of such discourses, see Bayat and Herrera 2010: 4; Esposito and Mogahed 2007: 65ff.). In the context of violent conflict related to the Boko Haram insurgency, poor Muslims in northern Nigeria have frequently been cast as prone to violence to claim their share of highly unequally distributed resources. Many authors quote statistics on the high incidence of poverty in northern Nigeria as if in themselves they could 'explain' the current crisis (e.g. Awofeso et al. 2003; Robertson 2012; Comolli 2013; Griswold 2014). Yet, what empirical evidence exists about Boko Haram refutes the 'simplistic application of economic deprivation theory' (Anonymous 2012: 118). The vast majority of poor northern Nigerians have not joined and do not support Boko Haram.

In contrast to discourses casting religion as a radicalising force, prominent thinkers within the sociology of religion have described how religion can serve to legitimise existing economic and political power relations, for example by levelling poor people's aspirations or by justifying their destitution as divinely ordained (e.g. Bourdieu 1971; Berger 1967). 'Religious capital' and the power to 'produce' particular religious discourses are indeed unlikely to be distributed evenly (Bourdieu 1971). Poor people may have little leverage over religious norms that disparage them: for example, they may view wealth as a sign of God's favour and conversely its absence as proof of his wrath or indifference. Yet, this should not detract attention away from poor people's ability to turn religious discourses to their own ends.

In the African context, the role of specific or novel religious movements and ideologies in the economic lives and opportunities of their adherents has been relatively well documented (on 'reformist' Islam and the justifications it provided for rejecting costly 'traditional' social practices such as sumptuous wedding celebrations, see Kane 2003; Loimeier 2003; Masquelier 2009; on Pentecostalism, see, e.g., Marshall 1991; Meyer 1999; Gifford 2004). In contrast, few authors take the experience of poverty, and people's attempts to come to terms with it, as the starting point of their analysis (for a notable exception, see Last 2000a; see also Hoechner 2015b). This means that little is known about the ways in which poor Muslims make use of religious discourses to reclaim dignity and resources in the face of poverty.

Drawing on the *almajirai*'s experiences in Kano, this chapter offers an empirical enquiry into how boys and young men at the lower end of society mobilise religious discourses to moderate the feelings of inadequacy and shame triggered by experiences of exclusion. It challenges the truism that Islam is ultimately a radicalising force in the lives of poor Muslim boys and young men, and nuances assumptions about its role in legitimising existing power structures. To escape the negative connotations of poverty and to cope with denigrating experiences, the *almajirai* reinterpret their deprivation as a voluntary exercise in asceticism and a necessary part of their education. However, their room for manoeuvre is constrained in a context in which conspicuous consumption is increasingly considered a marker of success and status. Discourses about asceticism notwithstanding, the *almajirai* foster hopes for urban 'cosmopolitan' lifestyles and an escape from poverty. In this context, self-assertive behaviours go hand in hand with behaviours that do not seek to challenge dominant discourses or socio-economic power structures, but instead reinforce them. The next section delineates the historical changes that have exacerbated the negative connotations of poverty in northern Nigeria, providing the context within which the *almajirai*'s experiences are embedded.

Historical meanings of poverty in northern Nigeria

It is useful to distinguish between structural and conjunctural poverty, as Iliffe (1987) suggests. The former refers to destitution caused by systemic factors, such as lack of land or labour, and the latter to the momentary deprivation caused by ill fortune or personal failure. We may juxtapose these involuntary forms of poverty with the voluntaristic poverty of the ascetic, who renounces worldly luxuries of his own free will.

Deep structural poverty in Hausaland is largely a product of the changes brought about by colonialism, which gave rise to the massive taxation of rural production, and industrialisation, which undermined traditional crafts (see, e.g., Lubeck 1981). Yet, even in precolonial times, 'a grain-based agriculture dependent upon a short and unreliable wet season bred numbers of very poor cultivators whose condition resulted less from shortage of land or accident of birth than from ill fortune, personal inadequacy, or...incapacitation' (Iliffe 1987: 34). Moreover, the situation of slaves has long been precarious (see, e.g., M. G. Smith 1954). However, in the absence of a modern transport system, which would later concentrate trade and industry in the towns, as a whole the countryside was comparatively prosperous. Poor Hausa could survive on crafts or by establishing 'a client relationship with a wealthier patron, working on his farm and performing menial tasks in return for subsistence and help in establishing an independent household' (Iliffe 1987:

34). Dire poverty or destitution, when it occurred, implied a 'lack of normal social relations, and hence lack of support (other than charity) when incapacitated' (ibid.: 42). Precolonial Hausaland also knew the voluntary poor: ascetic *malamai* who, following long-standing traditions of Sufi scholarship (see, e.g., Reid 2013), renounced the pleasures of this world to devote their lives to religion. However, historically, access to a career in Islamic learning was restricted to scholarly families.

Historically, Hausa society juxtaposed *talakawa* (poor commoners) and *masu sarauta* (wealthy office-holders), while slaves constituted the bottom stratum of society. According to Smith (1959: 241), political 'office has always been the principal road to wealth among the Hausa'. Not only slaves but also *talakawa* stood limited chances of accessing wealth and status, as occupational status, which mapped relatively neatly onto wealth categories, was almost entirely ascriptive (ibid.: 251). Particular professions were reserved to 'closed descent groups between which all movement [was] disapproved' (ibid.: 251).

While, historically, access to riches was thus unevenly distributed in Hausaland, wealth was – and still is – considered a blessing that ought to be shared to some extent. 'It is the hoarding of wealth for oneself that is questioned: miserliness suggests the wealth came not from Allah but through some evil pact or witchcraft,' writes Last (2000a: 222–3). Conversely, poverty 'implies either failure in attracting Allah's blessing or a pact that went wrong; the poor are not specially beloved of Allah' (ibid.: 223). Alms-giving in this context was (and is) not a 'charitable' act;[1] rather, one was meant to 'sacrifice' a part of one's wealth in order to earn protection from the powers causing misfortune. This was a real concern to the powerful, whose 'right to power' depended on their ability to ensure the well-being of their households or communities (ibid.: 223).

In brief, with the exception of ascetic scholarship, being poor has long been a sign of low status in Hausaland. At the same time, it was considered divinely ordained rather than self-inflicted and entailed certain expectations towards wealthier patrons, with the effect that dire destitution was limited to exceptional circumstances. To what extent have 'modern' developments altered the meanings of poverty?

People not belonging to 'ruling' families still frequently refer to themselves as commoners (*talakawa*) and attribute a range of conditions and behaviours to this status, which usually implies a lack of resources.[2] For example, a poor mother in my rural field site explained to me that she let her daughter marry a well-off doctor who treated her badly because 'he has money, and we are *talakawa*. Amina really wanted to marry him, and he brought us so much money.' People also justified their

---

[1] Incidentally, large endowments to support the poor (*waqf*) were rare (Iliffe 1987: 47).
[2] The abstract noun corresponding to *talaka*/*talakawa* is *talauci*, which means poverty.

preference for a particular politician (usually General Muhammadu Buhari) with reference to his support for 'us commoners' (*mu talakawa*), and explained their difficulties in terms of accessing and succeeding in the secular schooling system as a consequence of being a *talaka*.

Being a *talaka* is thus not a cause of shame. Also, I have never heard anyone mentioning their own or someone else's former slave status, buttressing Last's (2000a) observation that slave origin carries little stigma today.[3] Yet, as suggested by the conversations described at the beginning of this chapter, people who are destitute (*matsiyaci*; plural: *matsiyata*) are looked down upon. I have not come across anyone identifying himself or herself as being destitute, for destitution is treated as something to be concealed. Economic and societal changes and growing socio-economic inequality have exacerbated the negative connotations of poverty. With consumerism gaining momentum (see, e.g., Usman 2011), poverty attracts disdain, especially among those who are not poor.

However, certain cultural and religious discourses impose a limit on consumerist ideologies, or at least furnish those unable to engage in conspicuous consumption with the necessary vocabulary to reclaim some legitimacy and dignity. Long-standing Sufi traditions of ascetic scholarship are a case in point. Also, Islam encourages 'generosity as reciprocation for God's bounty' and enjoins the Muslim *umma* to 'purif[y] and [maintain] its wealth by giving up a portion of it in alms, and [to take] ample account of the kinsman as well as the disturbing, unknown, poor stranger' (Bonner 2005: 404; see also Salih 1999). Poverty is seen not only as putting individuals and their faith at risk as it may push them 'to cross the limits of religion and morality', but as endangering 'the security and stability of the society as a whole' (Al-Qaradawi 1994 cited in Salih 1999: 69).

Religious injunctions enjoining the rich to support the poor generously allow poor people to assess – and judge – the behaviour of the wealthy. For example, the fact that giving in secret does not seem to come easy to the rich in Hausaland gave rise to a mixture of cynicism and amusement among my respondents. The youths participating in the film project considered those donating food during Ramadan to be calculating rather than acting selflessly. They would give generously during Ramadan (when God rewards good deeds at a tenfold rate) but would stop giving once Ramadan was over, the *almajirai* scoffed. My host in Albasu explained to me jokingly when I asked her about *zakat* (required alms-giving) and *sadaka* (charity, or a freely made offering) that, despite the religious injunction to give the latter in secret, 'Nigerians want people to know, so people say, this one *yana da kirki* [he is kind]; that's why

---

[3] One of my informants suggested that remembering slave status was an upper-class practice and discouraged by Islam.

they make people line up in front of their houses when they give out *sadaka*'.

Several factors work against the interests of the poor, however. The dictates of shame (*kunya*) usually require people to exert self-constraint and modesty, meaning that the poor stand few chances of making effective claims on the resources of the rich. My neighbours' small children, who often came to visit me, for instance, would usually refuse the sweets or fruit I offered them. I learned that their father, who was an imam at the nearby mosque, had impressed upon them not to accept food from people in the neighbourhood so as not to appear greedy or gluttonous.[4]

The growing gulf between rich and poor also reinforces spatial segregation, as the better-off move to gated communities or shield their compounds with barbed wire and armed guards. This makes it more difficult for poor people to lodge claims and to get a hearing from the rich in society. Furthermore, religious reform movements have challenged 'traditional' redistributive practices in northern Nigeria. Kane (2003), for example, describes how the 'reformist' *Izala*, founded in 1978 in opposition to the Sufi orders, appealed to the *nouveaux riches* brought forth by the oil boom, who sensed that 'some traditional values and institutions hampered their economic goals and curtailed their autonomy'. Religious reformism allowed them to eschew 'costly traditional practices of wealth redistribution' (ibid.: 237).

Meanwhile, the increased movement and mixing of people in the context of urbanisation and demographic growth has contributed to the emergence of strategies to signal status that put wealth or conspicuous consumption centre stage. In a very status-conscious environment such as Hausa society, migrating means removing oneself, at least to some extent and for some time, from one's assigned position within the status hierarchy. Coming to a noisy, crowded, and heavily populated city such as Kano means encountering instances of anonymity (e.g. Last 2008: 43) and unstable hierarchies made in the present moment. In this context, demonstrations of wealth – expensive cars, flashy mobile phones, glamorous clothes – are a popular default option for those wishing to make claims to high rank. The display of one's mastery of prestigious and hard-to-attain forms of knowledge also creates instantaneous hierarchies. People may speak in English or in Arabic with a 'Saudi' accent to distinguish themselves. Most poor people, however, do not have access

---

[4] As I discussed in Chapter 1, perhaps for similar reasons the boys involved in the film project did not voice easily their financial grievances. However, certain explicitly interdependent relationships (that of a *mai gida/uwar gida* towards a *dan gida*, for example) may legitimise demands for support. After initial hesitation, the boy who was working in our house, for example, asked quite frankly for help with his educational and business projects, several of which I agreed to support. However, I gained the impression that unless there was a social relationship legitimating such claims, gifts as well as alms ought to be given freely and could not, or should not, be precipitated.

to such strategies: prestigious forms of education are mostly expensive to acquire.

How do the *almajirai* position themselves within this context and how do they manage to maintain a positive sense of self? The next sections describe their attempts to come to terms with experiences of exclusion and denigration. I also highlight the contradictory, and potentially self-defeating, effects of some of their behaviours.

Asceticism: endurance as show of faith and character?

Most of the *almajirai* I got to know well were from poor families, and most of the families enrolling boys as *almajirai* that I knew were poor. Given current political and economic conditions in northern Nigeria, the *almajirai*'s prospects of escaping poverty as they come of age are slim (see Chapter 9). Nonetheless, the young people with whom I conducted my research portrayed their deprivation as finite – a temporary sacrifice for knowledge's sake. This not only allowed them to maintain hope for a better future, but also to position themselves within the category of the voluntaristic poor.

I gained the impression that the burden of poverty was easier to carry for the *almajirai* when they could reinterpret it as a deliberate choice. Their teachers did so routinely. The *malamai* I was close to in my rural field site of Albasu considered modesty and frugality outstanding virtues. They were, for instance, reluctant at first to allow their students to participate in our film project as they objected to the presumably corrupting nature of the film industry. They argued that once the youths had acquired a taste for money, they would not study diligently any more. They themselves would not do anything for the sake of money, they claimed, but for the sake of God alone. What God provided them with in their fields was all they needed and desired. This, of course, simplified their lived realities, as cash had also penetrated their daily lives as subsistence farmers. Yet, from their declaration transpires the ideal of living uncorrupted by the temptations of money. One teacher in Albasu explained corruption among the Nigerian elites in similar terms: as their children grew up close to money, they would get used to it, and once they were old, they would put the money they received into their bank accounts rather than using it to help the poor.

The *almajirai* could also embrace frugality or asceticism as a desirable, if also necessary, virtue. Cultural norms that ascribe educative value to hardship provide a vocabulary with which *almajirai* can justify their deprived conditions, eschewing the familiar narratives of poverty and parental neglect with which the *almajiri* system is often associated. In this way, being an *almajiri* can attenuate the negative connotations of poverty. After all, have not the *almajirai* proved their outstanding religious dedication by foregoing the (presumed) comforts of home for the sake of knowledge? The *almajirai* worked towards this narrative. During the scriptwriting for our film, the boys involved in the project invoked any number of social, cultural, and religious arguments to justify enrolment as an *almajiri*. For example:

At home, he [a child] becomes stubborn, quarrelsome with other children and disrespectful towards elders. If he's told to go to school, he doesn't go. He just goes for a stroll, annoying the people in the neighbourhood.
Parents want their children to get to know their religion, and know people, and know how to live together with people.

The youths I got to know well over the course of my research joked about their own and each other's material hardships in a way that made me think of boy scout-style displays of toughness (cf. Ware 2014: 45, who describes similar behaviours among former Qur'anic students in Senegal). Ibrahim, for example, a young teacher in Daho, a village close to Albasu, who enjoyed introducing me to curious Hausa concepts, once teasingly asked me whether I knew *gajala*. That was the *almajirai*'s food, he declared, and described the 'recipe': one had to combine stews of various kinds (*miyan kala-kala*), leave the potpourri to stand overnight, and heat it up in the morning. His description of this presumed 'Hausa dish' caused amusement among the bystanders (including other *almajirai*), who were aware that *almajirai* often have to scramble together various different leftovers to fill their stomachs. Ibrahim's description took the edge off the *almajirai*'s food deprivation.

Being poor and being used to exercising 'patience' when it came to monetary expenses (or even the necessities of life) were considered some kind of '*almajiri* trademark'. For example, one evening Abubakar, an *almajiri* from Albasu, phoned me in Kano while his schoolmates were with me for the film project. He passed his mobile phone to an acquaintance who also wanted to greet me, but quickly took it back and hung up abruptly, although we were only halfway through the standard greetings. The fact that Abubakar did not want to spend his hard-earned phone credit on other people's extensive greetings caused amusement among the other *almajirai*. '*Almajiri – sai a yi hakuri!*' they explained, laughing. (An *almajiri* has only one option: have patience!) Being able to share one's phone credit generously was not a freedom the *almajirai* could currently enjoy.

Material want caused neither grief nor shame if it could be reinterpreted as a more or less self-inflicted temporary condition one had entered for the sake of knowledge. To exercise patience (*yi hakuri*) is a valued cultural skill in Hausa society. It means 'to endure pain, to refrain from letting your passions get the better of you, and to put your trust in God' (Gaudio 2009: 198). In a context where difficult economic and political conditions frequently thwart people's future plans, *hakuri* is a vital skill.

The *almajirai* invoked their own 'proven' ability to withstand hardship to set themselves apart from other young people. In one instance, for example, some *almajirai* who came to visit my house at Sabuwar Kofa were talking about their *malam*'s son, Ali; he was slightly younger than them and until now had lived with his parents and had attended a 'modern' secular school. To get him to follow in his footsteps as a Qur'anic teacher, his father now wondered about sending him away as an *almajiri*. The *almajirai* questioned whether this could prepare Ali for the task of teaching *almajirai*. As *dan birni*, a 'city boy' (as opposed to a 'villager' or *dan kauye*), he had not experienced hardship and would therefore fail to comprehend the *almajirai*'s circumstances. He would be unable to exercise enough strictness to ensure that his students studied well.

Being able to withstand hardship was also a quality invoked to redeem village *almajirai* vis-à-vis urban *almajirai*, potentially to counter the widespread association of village life with a lack of sophistication and exposure to the world more widely. Buhari, who was studying in Albasu when I met him, told me that *almajirai* staying in Kano City all year round lacked the ability to cope with village life, whereas he and other *almajirai* who migrated seasonally could deal with the challenges of both environments.

Finally, the longest-serving *almajirai* referred to their 'toughness' to distinguish themselves from *almajirai* who had joined the *almajiri* system only as teenagers (for example because they had previously attended secular school). In one instance, I talked with two of the youths involved in the film project about how the film should show people what life as an *almajiri* was like. Khalifa, an *almajiri* about their age who had recently enrolled at their school, chipped into the discussion '*lafiya kalau kawai*' ('fine anyways'), suggesting that the boys should not make such a fuss about their difficulties. One of the film youths retorted with a slight air of condescension that Khalifa had not done *kolo*: he had not experienced life as a young *almajiri*, and he therefore did not know what hunger was.

Almajirai may also take refuge in self-conceptions that place their compliance with (presumed) Islamic norms in the foreground, relegating lack of economic success to the background. When I asked Ali and Abubakar, two young men and former *almajirai* in Albasu, one of whom was a barber, how their *almajiri* education had helped them in terms of their income-generating activities, they explained it thus:

If, for example, you're a barber and charge so and so much, and then someone comes and says, how much is the barbering, and you say 40 Naira [approx. US$0.25], and you know actually it's done for 30 Naira, you see, deception has come in. Therefore, even if you assemble one million, these ten Naira that you added will spoil all this money [before God]. But if you have Qur'anic knowledge, you wouldn't do this . . . you wouldn't cheat.

The *almajirai* are certainly not alone in northern Nigeria in using Islam as their primary frame of reference. Together with other economically disenfranchised segments of society, however, they may resort to religious modes of thinking and arguing more frequently so as to maintain viable self-definitions. From the point of view of classical economics, the behaviour condemned in the quote above looks like a fairly conventional procedure to tap customers' willingness to pay. It is reinterpreted in a way that prioritises moderation in the pursuit of profit and 'honesty' over individual economic advancement. Being able to recast a lack of economic success in positively connoted religious terms may be an important resource to buffer frustration.

I gained the impression that some of the *malamai* I befriended (and the former *almajirai* cited above) had declared frugality the principle by which to live their lives. The *almajirai*, on the other hand, treated it more as a temporary necessity and corollary of *almajiri* life, which they hoped to overcome at some stage. That the *malamai* could embrace frugality so wholeheartedly might also be connected to the fact that they had achieved some degree of economic stability in their lives, if at a fairly low level. Their livelihoods as Qur'anic teachers were well established; their status as respectable adult men, with wives and children for whom they could provide the necessities of life, was secured. The *almajirai*, on the other hand, were yet to achieve all of this in a worsening economic environment. From the youths I got to know well during my research, I gained the impression that they hoped to eventually overcome the austereness of their current condition and to enjoy the trappings of 'modern' city life, aspirations to which I turn now.

The trappings of cosmopolitanism

A range of authors have explored how young Africans creatively engage with expressions of 'modernity' that offer them little or no place. It has been argued that through their imaginative practices and cultural productions, young people fashion 'imaginative links' to more desirable 'elsewheres' to which they have no access, thus simultaneously challenging and highlighting their own exclusion (Weiss 2002: 101, 104–5; see also Gondola 1999; Mains 2007; Janson 2014: 120–1). Behrend (2000: 73), for example, describes photographic studios in Mombasa, Kenya, as 'wish-fulfilling machines, offering visions of an instant utopia' that stand in marked contrast to the drudgeries of everyday life. In their photographs, urban migrants can realise the reveries of social success that they otherwise fail to achieve.

Figure 6.1 Snappy postures (photograph: Hannah Hoechner)

In a similar way, the *almajirai* in my research backed away from the frugal and ascetic 'habitus' encouraged by the *almajiri* system on a range of occasions, and instead sought to create images of themselves as worldly wise and conversant with Western-style modernity. This transpired, for instance, from the snappy postures they assumed when taking photographs (see Figure 6.1), from fashion accessories they flaunted (such as sunglasses, wrist watches, and finger rings), and from making proud and public use of (borrowed or owned) electronic appliances such as MP3 players and mobile phones. During the film production process, the participating *almajirai* seized the opportunity to snap each other behind the computer we used for editing, pretending to be busy working, even though at the time most of them hardly knew how to type (see Figure 6.2).[5] (Sadisu, the boy in Figure 6.2, has eagerly pursued

[5] Like several of the youths in Figures 6.1 and 6.2, many *almajirai* wear Western (second-hand) clothes on a day-to-day basis. Yet, as such clothes are the cheapest option available today, it would be overhasty to read a particular mindset into this. As many *almajirai* cannot afford new Hausa clothes regularly, they seek to preserve one set of such clothes (usually the kaftan and trousers that were sewn for them on the most recent *Sallah* celebration, if enough money was available then) for Friday prayers and other special occasions. The picture in Figure 6.1 was taken on a Friday, which explains why several of the youths wear their 'good' Hausa clothes. The only time I saw the young *almajirai* I was teaching in Daho dressed up in neat Hausa clothes was when I took their photograph.

Figure 6.2 'Busy' behind the computer (photograph: Hannah
Hoechner)

computer classes – made possible by different sponsors – since taking
this picture and has become so computer-savvy that he offers classes to
other youths today.)

The *almajirai* are also eager consumers of 'popular culture'. Those
who own mobile phones use them to listen to the (love) songs of Hausa
celebrities and various radio stations. Even though their *malamai* unanimously disapprove of this, most *almajirai* regularly sneak into one of
Kano's public 'TV parlours', sacrificing a couple of hard-earned Naira
for the entrance fee, to watch the Hausa and Bollywood films and football matches displayed there. According to the *almajirai*, watching TV
allows them to get 'exposure' (*waye*) or, as Sadisu put it, be 'updated
about the world'.

Ferguson (1999: 207ff.) describes how rural migrants on the Copperbelt try to distance themselves from their rural origins by adopting particular 'cosmopolitan' styles. Similarly, the ways in which the *almajirai*
fashion themselves in the situations described here reveal reveries that
sit uneasily with the rural realities in which most of their families live
and where many of them originate. And, indeed, the *almajirai* considered rural people without any experience of urban life to be 'backward'.
Some used the term 'villager' (*ɗan ƙauye*) as an insult. On one occasion,

an *almajiri* I was close to grumbled that the behaviour of a crowd of children who, attracted by the sight of a white person, came running after us in his home neighbourhood was *kauyanci*, or village behaviour.

In Chapter 4, I proposed that we should think about *almajiri* education as geared towards the inculcation of a particular rural ascetic 'habitus'. Yet, what happens to this 'habitus' once it is taken out of the contexts where it is like 'a fish in water'? The urban environments of their schools trigger new aspirations among the *almajirai* that have very little to do with the ideals of asceticism and frugality discussed earlier. In the houses where they work and on the streets where they meet other youngsters from the neighbourhood, they encounter urban and consumerist lifestyles. These leave their traces on their dreams and future aspirations (cf. Lubeck 1981: 74 for an early observer of such trends). To complicate things further, in a religious 'market' where competition for followers is growing, and where pressure is mounting to distinguish oneself from others who offer spiritual and education services, some urban *malamai* have largely relinquished ideals of asceticism and frugality. Malam Gali, a good-humoured and well-heeled Islamic scholar in the centre of Kano's Old City, whose school caters not only to *almajirai* but also to *Islamiyya* students, and whom I visited frequently, provides a good example of this. He had several cars, farms, and wives, and travelled to Saudi Arabia frequently on *hajj* and on business. He portrayed himself as a cosmopolitan and took pleasure in introducing me to acquaintances of his in London.

The *almajirai*'s narratives about enrolment as an *almajiri* as a choice, taken to honour one's religious commitments, become somewhat unstable in a context where religious role models and authority figures, such as their *malamai*, abandon asceticism, or embrace 'modern' forms of knowledge for their own offspring, or exempt their own children from some of the hardships declared 'educational' for *almajirai*. Several *almajirai* complained to me about their *malam*'s reluctance to let them attend secular school, while simultaneously he enrolled his own children.[6] *Malamai* may act in this way out of a sense of obligation towards their students' parents, who entrusted their sons to them for the sake of their Qur'anic studies. Nevertheless, seeing that their religious authority figures do not fear for their own children's spiritual and moral maturation when educating them at home and in secular schools threatens to undermine the *almajirai*'s self-narrative.

Keeping up appearances

Walker et al. (2013: 227), when asking how poor people handle poverty-related shame, found that they struggle to keep up appearances, to

---

[6] See Gérard (1999) on similar dynamics in Burkina Faso. Two of the *malamai* I was close to approached me to ask whether I could teach their children secular subjects.

conceal their poverty, and to avoid 'situations likely to publicly expose their circumstances'. This has also been argued for young people (e.g. Sutton 2009). The *almajirai* acted in similar ways. As migrants – newcomers in their places of study and far enough from home to have some control over the information 'trickling through' from their communities – they could keep to themselves the circumstances that had led to their enrolment as *almajirai*. These circumstances are sometimes experienced as embarrassing, as they are shaped by a lack of support from (supposedly responsible) social elders as a consequence of poverty, divorce, or death. At the same time, the *almajirai* could conceal to some extent the ordeals of life as an *almajiri* from the people back home.

While young *almajirai* are purposefully exposed to hardship so that their character matures, older youths are expected to have developed the requisite 'life skills' and wit (*wayo*) to do relatively well for themselves. For older *almajirai*, economic and religious reasons often combine to motivate their migration to urban areas, as cities offer not only opportunities to study, but also to earn cash. The *almajirai* try to avoid situations that make their failure to live up to the (perceived or actual) expectations of parents and other relatives apparent. Several of the older *almajirai* confided to me that they avoided going home too often because of the associated expenses. For example, when his mother remarried, Balado did not attend the wedding celebrations because he was very short of cash at the time. Guests would want to give a present to the newlywed couple – and would be expected to do so. Gifts are required not only on special occasions but more generally when an *almajiri* visits his home, as Balado explained to me when I discussed with him whether he could go to pick up his birth certificate from his mother (in order to apply for a national ID card). He would rather not arrive home empty-handed so as not to disappoint the hopes of younger siblings (cf. Thorsen 2006: 104; Langevang and Gough 2009: 751).

Younger *almajirai* are often discouraged – and even sometimes prevented – from visiting home too frequently as this is considered counterproductive for their studies and emotional well-being. Newcomers should not visit home, I was told, as this would likely make them homesick. While students who have been enrolled for longer are rarely denied permission to visit home, they, too, may refrain from doing so – for instance to avoid the financial obligations attached to home visits – and legitimately justify this decision by arguing that this is better for their studies.

Living usually quite a distance from their places of origin also allows the *almajirai* to partially conceal individual life histories and the circumstances under which they left home. Leaving home does not mean though that migrants turn into 'loose molecules' (Kaplan 1994: 46), as many migrate within networks that connect them to their home localities and through which social control is maintained, to some degree.[7] However, coming to a noisy, crowded, and heavily populated city such as Kano also means that the *almajirai* have opportunities for anonymity, and they know how to take advantage of these.

For example, on one occasion, Balado was at my house when two girls from a northern elite family living in the neighbourhood came to visit with a female relative aged about 20 who did not know Balado. While she tried to ascertain his social position, he cunningly avoided answering her questions. Rather than 'giving away' the fact that he was an *almajiri* at my neighbour's school, he declared himself to be 'the one selling petrol along the road'. When we talked about our planned trip to his father's house during *Sallah*, he said he lived 'far... you get there only by car' (suggesting overland travel) – a fairly deceptive description of the slum neighbourhood within Kano City where his father actually resides (some 30 minutes from Sabuwar Kofa on public transport).

Even schoolmates who had been enrolled in the same Qur'anic school for years and shared their daily routines with each other as friends knew very little about each other's family backgrounds. Bashir, for instance, did not know that Khalidu was orphaned and had become an *almajiri* as a consequence of parental death. They had been schoolmates for over two years and appeared to be quite close friends.

It is understandable that the *almajirai* seek to keep their life histories private in a context where giving away personal information means making oneself vulnerable.[8] As a researcher, I regularly contravened rules of respect for people's privacy by enquiring into personal circumstances and life trajectories. As expected, my informants were reluctant to give away compromising information. Often it was only after probing, or engaging other family members in the conversation, that I found out about the underlying material circumstances of a boy's first enrolment as an *almajiri*. The young people themselves often prioritised religious and cultural values over material constraints when explaining their careers as *almajirai*.

---

[7] A UNICEF researcher who has been widely quoted in Nigerian newspapers estimates that 60 per cent of the *almajirai* never return home (e.g. Purefoy 2010; Jumare 2012). Such scaremongering about the breakdown of social relations has little empirical support. Only one of the numerous *almajirai* I spoke to over the course of my fieldwork said that he had not seen his parents at all during the six years he had been enrolled as an *almajiri*. Several of the fathers I spoke to reported long intervals between their sons' visits (up to two or three years). Intermediaries commuting between home villages and the places where boys are attending school also exchange information and sometimes goods. Nowadays, many *almajirai* have mobile phones, which makes it easier for them to reach out to – and be reached by – their parents.

[8] Some *almajirai* told me that they do not usually share their father's name with their peers (despite patronyms being widely used as a means of identification). This is to make sure that no one can use it to insult or curse them.

Idris, for example, in his early twenties, had enrolled as an *almajiri* after only one month of secondary school. When I asked about the school change, he explained it in terms of the importance of religious knowledge in this world and the hereafter. Only when I probed whether any key event triggered his drop-out, he revealed that his father had died at the time. Isiyaku, in his early twenties, who had returned from *almajiri* enrolment at that time, and whom I interviewed in the presence of his mother, explained to me that he dropped out of 'modern' education to become an *almajiri* while his younger brother persisted because the latter had more of the kind of intelligence required for this type of schooling. His mother then chipped in to explain that Isiyaku had to drop out because his father was very ill at the time and the household in financially straitened circumstances.

When the script advisor, a professional from the Kano film industry, suggested that destitution was indeed a factor underpinning the enrolment of boys as *almajirai*, the boys nodded approval. Yet they also agreed to his suggestion to disregard this aspect of the system in their script. On other occasions, the *almajirai* rejected explanations invoking poverty or difficult conditions at home (such as parental divorce or death) as reasons for *almajiri* enrolment outright. Inusa (aged 15), for instance, contended that:

Especially now that there is *boko* ['modern' school], if you come for *almajirci*, some people think it's because you don't have food in your house, that's why you come out to beg. But it's not like that; it's because you're searching for knowledge.

Anas (aged 15) denied parental neglect, suggesting that:

People bring their children to Qur'anic school not because they hate them, but because they want them to have the knowledge [*ilimi*].

I am not implying that people do not mean what they say when they stress the importance of religious knowledge, or that *almajiri* enrolments are necessarily caused by acute household emergencies. Rather, my point here is that people are likely to seize the opportunity to conceal personally compromising circumstances if such an opportunity presents itself. The *almajiri* system and its ideology provide a versatile tool for such concealment tactics. Enrolment as an *almajiri* does not require an explanation in terms of personal circumstances: after all, searching for religiously enjoined knowledge is not an endeavour in need of justification.

Conclusion: redistribution or recognition?

How are we to make sense of the *almajirai*'s complex manoeuvrings vis-à-vis poverty, and what are their likely effects? In Chapter 1, I proposed to approach this question using Nancy Fraser's (1996; Fraser and Honneth 2003) reflections on different forms of injustice, and their associated logics of action. Fraser emphasises that groups suffering from cultural and economic injustices simultaneously – so-called 'bivalent collectivities' or 'two-dimensional categories' – are in a particularly weak position. They need to straddle claims for the redistribution of resources on the one hand, and claims for the recognition of their dignity on the other. Yet, such claims are likely to be in conflict with each other, and for those suffering from the double injury of material and valuational disadvantage it may be particularly difficult to formulate positions that resolve the tensions between these conflicting claims. The *almajirai* epitomise the challenges that 'bivalent collectivities' or 'two-dimensional categories' face, and illustrate how the coincidence of cultural and economic disadvantages can result in 'particularly intractable forms of poverty' (Hickey and du Toit 2007: 2–3). Using the words of Appadurai (2004), they 'trade' recognition for redistribution on 'adverse terms'.

In the context of growing socio-economic inequality and consumerism, poverty has acquired very negative connotations in northern Nigeria, even among the poor. Urbanisation and demographic growth have intensified the movement and mixing of people. Material wealth is important in this context as a sign of status as it can be displayed instantaneously. Lacking material means is experienced as embarrassing. The poor are not only economically disadvantaged but also culturally devalued. In this environment, the *almajirai*'s concerns with recognition mute demands for redistribution to some extent.

Given the negative connotations of poverty, the *almajirai* embrace discourses about themselves and the reasons for their enrolment that belie the role of structural constraints. They portray themselves as devoted searchers for sacred knowledge and cast deprivation as a voluntary exercise in asceticism and a valuable form of character-building. By making creative use of religious and cultural arguments, they manage to retain viable self-definitions. All too frequently it is assumed that poverty and religion, if combined, lead to problematic outcomes. Yet, rather than radicalising the *almajirai*, religion helps them endure difficulties and denigration. This is an important insight in a global context where Muslims, especially those who are poor, young, and male, are frequently vilified as 'foot soldiers' and 'cannon fodder' for violence.

Yet, paradoxically, in their attempts to defend their sense of self and self-worth, and to achieve recognition, the *almajirai* add fuel to the fire. By embracing self-conceptions as devout seekers of sacred knowledge, ironically they play into the hands of 'othering' logics. They adopt a narrative that prioritises the cultural and religious aspects of the *almajiri* system over its material bases. As a result, they may unwittingly buttress culturalist explanations, which, changed into the negative, evoke 'backward' educational aspirations and neglectful and ignorant parents, as well as fears of religious fundamentalism. Often, the *almajirai* are portrayed as prone to becoming nuisances, troublemakers, and – against the backdrop of Boko Haram-related violence – 'terrorist' cannon fodder.

In addition, as the *almajirai* depict themselves as devout migratory scholars who have chosen to live in deprived conditions of their own free will, a debate about the structural causes of the poverty that afflicts the constituencies that opt for the *almajiri* system is kept off the table. Such a debate, however, would be important to achieve a change for the better for the *almajirai* and their families. As long as consumerism and wealth dominate definitions of status within society, it is likely to be difficult for people suffering from the negative connotations of poverty to speak up for themselves and demand social justice. The next chapter, by situating the *almajirai* within the wider social landscape, and by sketching their relationships to other social groups, explores the chances of solidarity and social cohesion developing among people in structurally weak positions in society.

7   Mango medicine and morality
Pursuing a respectable position within society

In the backyard of the house in which I was living in Kano, just inside its old city walls, stood a mango tree. Towering over our compound walls, its imposing canopy was visible from afar, and the children in the neighbourhood of Sabuwar Ƙofa were well aware of its existence. The juicy fruits were the object of vivid desires and crafty schemes: how to ensure one's share of the fruits before we or the other kids tucked in. The mangoes were also on the minds of the young Qur'anic students schooling with my neighbour, who was the imam at the nearby mosque. Would I give them mangoes? I promised to share the fruits once they were ripe. Would I still be in Kano, though, when they had ripened? Aware that my departure from Kano was approaching, and worried that my housemates (then a British VSO volunteer and a British PhD student) were less sympathetic to their cause, the *almajirai* saw the promise of mangoes going up in smoke. They began asking for unripe fruits. I refused to hand them out, as I did not think they were very healthy. Then one day two of the *almajirai* wandered into our compound and declared that they needed unripe mangoes to treat the rashes on their heads. Skin infections are common among the *almajirai,* and crowded study and sleeping spaces in their schools offer perfect conditions for communicable diseases to spread.

Later, I would learn about their salubrious qualities, but at the time I had never heard of the medicinal uses of mangoes, and my first reaction was therefore amusement at what I thought was a particularly original attempt to get hold of the fruits. I told the boys I did not believe that unripe mangoes were medicine, but nevertheless gave them the fruits and they left. Some minutes later, they knocked on our compound door, with serious looks on their faces, and pieces of unripe mangoes distributed on their heads for me to acknowledge. Reassured that I no longer believed that they had wanted to trick me into giving them mangoes, they took off.

Just as it was important for the two boys with their mango medicine to make sure that I did not consider them liars, it was a major concern for the *almajirai* I met during my research to protect their reputation. In a context where they are frequently denigrated as thieves and troublemakers, they sought to project an image of themselves as particularly moral and pious people, which arguably helped them cope with rejection.

While most anthropological and sociological research on the ways in which people react to stigma and prejudice against them looks at adults – such as Goffman's (1963) classic work and Lamont and Mizrachi's (2013) edited volume on stigmatised minority groups – several scholars of childhood show forcefully that we have no reason to assume that young people are any less worried about the image others have of them (e.g. Jeffrey et al. 2004: 970; Hart 2008b; Mann 2012; Walker et al. 2013). The way in which young people deal with stigmatisation and prejudice has been explored, for example, with respect to young people living in poverty (e.g. Ridge 2002; Sutton 2009; Walker et al. 2013), young people affected by the AIDS epidemic and 'orphanhood' (e.g. Bray 2003; Freidus 2010), young people affected by their own or their parents' disease or disability (e.g. Haug Fjone and Ytterhus 2009; Jahoda et al. 2010), and children who are displaced or migrants (e.g. Mann 2012). Authors have emphasised how young people engage creatively with difficult circumstances, and struggle to keep up appearances (e.g. Haug Fjone and Ytterhus 2009; Walker et al. 2013) and a positive self-image (e.g. Mann 2012), despite widespread disdain. It is to this emerging body of literature that I seek to add by exploring how the *almajirai* pursue a respectable position within society in a context where they are frequently looked down upon and denigrated.

Morality and religion are two crucial domains through which the *almajirai* seek to enhance their self-image. A range of authors discuss how poor and powerless people draw on moral discourses to criticise the rich and powerful who denigrate them (e.g. Scott 1985: 22ff.; Sayer 2005: 182ff.; Hansen 2000). Children's recourse to morality to gain respect has received less attention, but has been documented, for example, with respect to refugee children (Mann 2012). As regards religion, fairly little is known about its role in the lives of young people struggling with prejudice, although some authors explore how it can help youths at the lower end of social and economic hierarchies to maintain a positive outlook on themselves (for the West African context, see Masquelier 2009: 17; Janson 2014: 89ff.). This chapter adds to these works by describing how the *almajirai* seek to portray themselves as particularly moral and pious in a context where many people look down on them. The *almajirai*'s desire to be considered respectable, moreover, provides a counter-narrative to simplistic accounts of the Qur'anic education system in Nigeria in which the *almajirai* appear as gullible and rogue and disconnected from the dominant morality of the society in which they live.

The *almajirai* emphasised their moral and religious credentials to position themselves favourably vis-à-vis the better-off in society. What did their desire for respectability imply for their relationships with others in socially weak positions? Sayer (2005: 177) points out that often the quest for respectability neither challenges existing power structures nor promotes the cause of others who lack social power. He compares the 'desire for respectability' with the 'demand for respect'. Whereas the latter is potentially liberatory, the former 'defers to hierarchy and dominant values', uses others who are weak as a backdrop against which 'respectability' is established, and thus leaves potentially problematic logics intact. Sayer's observations are useful for understanding the position of the *almajirai*. Vying for respect and material support, they were eager to furnish proof of their own status and to make clear that they were not 'at the bottom of the social pile' (Walker et al. 2013: 229). Some youths stressed their links to people higher up in the social hierarchy (*gata*) on whose support they could presumably count. Others emphasised their masculinity and moral superiority as males over females. Others again declared other poor boys and youths responsible for behaviours widely disapproved of by society, thus freeing the *almajirai* of such charges.

Conceptualisations of young people's agency as 'resistance' and 'resourcefulness' have been at the centre of much writing in childhood and youth studies in an attempt to counter the idea that young people are passive victims of the larger crises affecting their societies (e.g. Honwana and De Boeck 2005; Christiansen et al. 2006, Panelli et al. 2007; for a critique, see Lancy 2012; Gomez-Perez and LeBlanc 2012: 12). Reinforcing what was said in the previous chapter about the *almajirai*'s contradictory attempts to hide their poverty, the material presented in this chapter, which highlights instances when the *almajirai* are complicit with structures that affect them – and others – negatively, suggests that we reconsider such conceptualisations. The idea that 'agency' is akin to 'resistance' and 'resourcefulness', and thus desirable, is obvious in the way in which many authors approach the presumably constrained nature of young people's agency. Such approaches present agency quantitatively (Durham 2008: 152). As Bordonaro (2012: 422) points out, concepts such as 'thin' – as opposed to 'thick' – agency (Klocker 2007) and 'tactical' – as opposed to 'strategic' – agency (Honwana 2005), or the idea of a continuum in 'agency' ranging from 'no agency' to 'public agency' (Robson et al. 2007), presuppose that 'agency' is a desirable quantity, and thus the more children have of it the better. Whenever young people engage in activities at odds with 'iconic notions of childhood innocence, then their agency is assessed as constrained' (Bordonaro 2012: 422).

Of course, the popularity of the concept of 'agency' inscribes itself within a wider historical context. Asad (2000: 30) attributes its rise to the decline of Marxism and associated beliefs in 'historical collectivities and destinies': 'What classical Marxism conceived of as the action of a class-subject impelled by historical laws has... tended to become individualised and autonomised... All individuals, we are given to understand, have the moral capacity and responsibility to act for themselves' (ibid.: 30). Critical commentators on the enthusiastic use of the notion of 'agency' speak of 'an epic effort by social scientists to grant a certain amount of power, resistance and political influence to those who are commonly considered to be devoid of any' (Bordonaro and Payne 2012: 367).

In its common use, 'agency' thus focuses narrowly on behaviour that is considered emancipatory and progressive. To liberate the concept from its Western-centric baggage, Mahmood (2001: 210) proposes that we should understand agency 'not simply as a synonym for resistance to relations of domination, but as a capacity for action that specific relations of subordination create and enable'. This is an interesting approach as it permits us also to acknowledge as 'agency' actions that may displease liberal social scientists. We may think of what Jeffrey (2011: 249–50) calls forms of 'negative agency' – 'reactionary strategies that sustain and replenish established power structures' – or what in Bordonaro and Payne's (2012: 366) view are instances of 'ambiguous agency': young people's behaviour at variance with moral and social ideals. Finally, Mahmood (2001: 210) draws attention to the ways in which particular relations of subordination 'create and enable' specific forms of agency, thus opening up for enquiry the wider social contexts and power structures in which social agents are embedded.

This is the line of enquiry I pursue in this chapter. The next two sections explore the *almajirai*'s recourse to morality and religion to claim a respectable position within society. After this, I turn to the *almajirai*'s relationships with other socially weak groups, notably women and younger and more deprived *almajirai*, highlighting how fragile solidarity is in an environment where both respect and the material means of sustenance are scarce.

Playing moral trumps

Morality does not necessarily presuppose resources. According to Hansen (2000: 55–6), domestic workers in India often embrace morality as a domain within which they, rather than their wealthy employers, can lay claim to superiority. Money, these workers argue, can be acquired independently of character. Similarly, the *almajirai* put enormous emphasis on their moral credentials, which allow them to maintain a positive outlook about themselves despite the scorn they often experience from better-off members of society. 'Moral lessons' are part of the implicit teaching curriculum of the *almajirai*, and teachers impart moral ideas to their students by sharing their everyday lives with them. The *almajirai* in my research knew very well what their teachers' attitudes were towards certain behaviours (see below). *Malamai* also summon their students to instruct them in 'correct' behaviour or to reprimand them for transgressions. The moral training associated with Qur'anic schools figures large in parents' accounts of why they enrol their sons as *almajirai*. I gained the impression that an environment of societal disapproval encouraged the *almajirai*'s compliance with some of these 'lessons' offered through school.

The *almajirai* in my research had very clear ideas about what it meant to be an *almajiri*, and what sort of conduct one could legitimately expect from those living as *almajirai*. The youths participating in the 'participatory' film project I organised during my research engaged in extensive debates on the moral upbringing (*tarbiyya*) of *almajirai*. They felt that the accusations put forward against *almajirai* were unwarranted and that one of the core messages of the film should be that people are wrong to assume that *almajirai* are hoodlums. In their view, obedience and self-discipline were two of the *almajirai*'s core virtues, as the following passage, drafted during the scriptwriting process, illustrates:

An *almajiri* with *tarbiyya*, you will see he is diligent with his studies, and he follows the instructions of his teacher, and he doesn't fool around rudely. He goes begging well composed, and if some woman employs him, he is there on time. Whenever the *almajirai* finish their lessons, he goes straight to work, and he is very conscientious with his studies. Whenever someone tries to interfere with what his parents sent him for, he won't consent . . . whenever he sees a fellow *almajiri* misbehave, he will attempt to stop him.

Older *almajirai* would often reprimand younger ones for not behaving as an *almajiri* should. When Abubakar (aged ten), for instance, began singing into my tape recorder and fooling around, his older brother Bashir (aged 12) told him that he, as an *almajiri*, should not be singing like that. From the boys' behaviour, I gained the impression that the prestige and self-esteem deriving from the moral code of conduct pertaining to every *almajiri* was a resource they could access whenever they needed to. While they did 'take time off' from following the principles they had embraced and adopted for themselves (for example, to play football on a lesson-free Thursday outside the purview of the teacher who disapproved of their play, or to visit the public 'TV parlour', attendance at which their teacher frowned upon), the *almajirai* put an enormous emphasis on 'behaving well'. They pointed out that rough play and football were inappropriate, particularly for *almajirai*, and that boys should rather focus on their studies. Even though they were aware of their own 'trespasses', knowing that they knew how to behave well and possessed the 'moral knowledge' society often claimed they lacked helped them maintain dignity in the face of negative attitudes.

In my group interviews with younger *almajirai*, I sometimes asked them to enact particular situations. The following 'instruction' Naziru (aged 15) gives as a teacher in a role play to 'his' students reveals the link between behaving well and coping with societal rejection:

Please, if you go out to beg, I want you to always pull yourself together, because some people are used to saying, *almajirai* are not well-behaved, that they like playing rough play.

Chapter 5 argued that *almajirai* strive to establish durable relationships with urban households, for whom they provide domestic services. Employment as a domestic worker entails entering employers' houses freely and thus presupposes trust. People may also send *almajirai* whom they do not know on errands, making a leap of faith as they entrust money upfront, hoping that the chosen messenger will come back with the requested item. If a boy proves trustworthy, they may consider a more durable employment arrangement. In this context, presenting themselves as worthy of people's trust is a particular concern to the *almajirai*. The example of the two boys looking for mango medicine cited at the beginning of this chapter is a case in point. The *almajirai* also resented other children's behaviour that might undermine the *almajirai*'s reputation of honesty. Tanimu, a ten-year-old *almajiri* at my neighbour's school at Sabuwar Ƙofa, for example, complained in a 'radio interview' he recorded:

I don't like the children in town that [pretend to be] *almajirai* and collect money from people that want to buy something and just run away with the money.

Apart from projecting themselves as well-behaved and trustworthy to win people's esteem, focusing on their own 'moral credentials' also helped the *almajirai* to stay strong when treated badly. The *almajirai*'s reasoning about how to react appropriately when people gave them food that was clearly inedible when they begged – food, for example, that had been tampered with by small children, or that had been kept for too long and had turned sour – offers a striking example of this. The boys discussed how one should react when given food that was so obviously spoilt that there was no way for the 'donor' not to be aware of it, and which put the person eating it at risk of diarrhoea. They had observed *almajirai* plastering the food on the door of the people who had given it, or dropping it in front of the house. Such behaviour, Naziru asserted, would make those giving bad food realise their fault:

If you come out [of your house and see the food] and you are reasonable, you know that what you did was wrong.

While the boys were concerned that this might be interpreted as their fault, they were well aware of the public message of such an act, and its potential to embarrass the 'perpetrators' in front of neighbours and passers-by. Despite having such a potentially subversive means of retribution at their disposal, the *almajirai* reasoned that such behaviour was in fact wrong:

[The *almajirai*] misbehave. It's better for them not to collect the food if they don't want to eat it... Some of the *almajirai* move away from the house before pouring the food away. Some will go and give it to goats. (Naziru)

In the context of widespread negative attitudes towards them, to occupy the moral high ground was more valuable to the *almajirai* than to publicly retaliate against bad treatment.

Despite their determination to portray the *almajirai* in what they considered a positive light, the youths participating in the film project nevertheless acknowledged that not all *almajirai* behave in morally flawless ways. Sadisu, for instance, acknowledged that 'if we say none of us is like that [with a bad character], that would not be the truth. One would necessarily find some with a bad character.'

The *almajirai* then discussed what may put *almajirai* at risk of 'going astray'. Their explanations mostly invoked 'corrupting' factors located in their urban neighbourhoods and beyond the purview of their schools. One factor they discussed were the *'yan daba*. These are unemployed or underemployed young men from poor urban families who have dropped out of school and spend their days 'hanging out' on the street (Dan-Asabe 1991; see also Casey 2007; 2008; Ya'u 2000). According to Dan-Asabe (1991), *'yan daba* emerged from traditional hunter groups who organised to chase wild animals. As hunters they bore arms, and thus were frequently used as political thugs. '[W]ith no visible means of livelihood', they are said to engage in a range of illicit activities, including drug abuse, loitering, theft, rape, and armed robbery (ibid.: 91). Today, people use the term *'yan daba* broadly to refer to the demographic described here,[1] and liberally accuse the *'yan daba* of various vices. The *almajirai* joined the chorus of those claiming that the *'yan daba* are inherently violent, even though they found such accusations unfair in their own case. The *'yan daba* were liable to 'profligacy' (*iskanci*) and acts of violence, the *almajirai* proclaimed. One youth said that *'yan daba* would lure *almajirai* to join them by giving small gifts in exchange for errands. Once used to the *'yan daba*, the *almajirai* might consent to join in their delinquent activities.

---

[1] According to the *almajirai*, *'yan daba* usually dress in *kananan kaya* (Western-style T-shirts and jeans), combined with a *hula*, a traditional cap.

The same youth also assigned blame to the *almajirai*'s employers, stating that 'if an *almajiri* works in his employer's house, if he isn't shown any sympathy by the people for whom he works, then he can develop such a bad character'. In a mock interview with an imaginary Qur'anic teacher that the *almajirai* participating in the film project drafted, they suggested several ways in which an *almajiri* could go astray, and explained whose responsibility it was in their view to ensure that this does not happen:

Their employers send them on errands when it's time for school, but they won't tell them to go to school . . . Some [*almajirai*] become spoilt through the children of the neighbourhood . . . [They] join the children of the neighbourhood playing football in the street, even if it's time for prayer . . . Their employers should always remind them to be clean, if their clothes are dirty, they should give them soap, or money to buy soap, and if it's time for school, they should send them to school.

The *almajirai* also recognised that the setup of the *almajiri* system puts limitations on the extent to which teachers can retain control over their students. Abdullahi explained, for example, that between their study sessions the *almajirai* disappear from their *malam*'s sight. The *malam* has no way of knowing what they get up to and which student's character he has reason to be concerned about, especially when student numbers are large. A lack of parental concern could also constitute a source of risk, the youth concluded:

Some people bring their children to school, and won't monitor their behaviour any further. If [a father] comes once or twice per year, he will be made aware of what his son gets up to. But if he doesn't come at all, his son may start roving about, he may end up smoking marihuana and drinking alcohol [*shaye shaye*].

It is interesting to contrast these statements, which acknowledge risks and deviations from 'ideal' *almajiri* behaviour and were made in the sheltered atmosphere of our training for the filmmaking, with the statements the *almajirai* decided to include in the end credits of the film. There, the *almajirai* proclaimed, for example:

Through this film, I want to show people who think *almajirai* are hoodlums, that this is not true.
I want those who think *almajirai* are bad people, to know that they aren't.

These statements, which mask the more complicated positions the *almajirai* voiced off the official record, signal, I think, how closely the *almajirai*'s concerns with morality are related to their relations with other segments of society. By portraying themselves as particularly moral people, the *almajirai* aim to reposition themselves vis-à-vis those segments of society that tend to look down upon them.

Pleading religious righteousness

In a context where for many people the term '*almajiri*' has negative connotations, the *almajirai* endeavoured to emphasise their religious credentials. Some *almajirai* told me that the syllable 'Al' in *almajiri* stood for Allah, whereas 'Ma' was short for the Prophet Muhammad, and 'Jiri' for the angel Jibril. This interpretation does not reflect the word's actual etymology – the word *almajiri* derives from the Arabic term *al-muhajir* (migrant), a term echoing the Prophet's *hijrah* from Mecca to Medina. Yet, this interpretation shows how eagerly the *almajirai* sought to embrace pious self-conceptions.

To some extent, the *almajirai* perceived themselves to be trained to be more strictly practising Muslims than other people, as evidenced, for example, by Buhari's (early twenties) comments on the role of Qur'anic schools in ensuring that students pray regularly. If boys stay with their parents, Buhari argued, prayer time comes and goes, and they keep roaming about. No one makes them say their prayers. *Almajirai*, on the other hand, would be beaten if they were late for prayer. And, indeed, prayer times were strictly enforced: Buhari's Qur'anic teacher in Albasu monitored whether his students had said their prayers, and refused to accept excuses such as not finding water for ablutions in time. When visiting our house at Sabuwar Kofa, Naziru and Sadisu, two *almajirai* in the nearby mosque whom I became close to, would drop everything when they heard the call for prayer and rush off to the mosque – unlike other neighbourhood boys and even the *malam*'s sons. The boys and young men involved in the filmmaking, with whom I spent long stretches of time, also persisted with their fast during Ramadan even when feeling ill, added voluntary fasting days outside Ramadan, and were unlikely to be late for any of their daily prayers. Finally, they reviewed each other's behaviour critically, and did not hesitate to pass judgement. One of the youths participating in the film project, who had coloured his hair, was told off by his peers who lectured him about a *hadith* in which the Prophet discouraged such hairstyling. Another youth had to endure critical commentary after having gone to sleep shortly before the evening prayer on a day during Ramadan and had not woken up in time to say his prayer.

Many of the *almajirai* I got to know well tended to interpret events and evaluate behaviour with reference to Islam. When we discussed any topical or personal issue, their primary frame of reference was what they thought Islam demanded. In one instance, for example, I told Rabi'u and Muhammadu about the earthquake devastating Japan in April 2011. Muhammadu, without the slightest hesitation, replied that this was because they did not fear God. When I answered that there are not many Muslims in Japan, Muhammadu was surprised. Rabi'u eventually concluded that this must have been the reason for the earth-quake. On another occasion, Muhammadu told me that the new shoes he had just bought for the *Sallah* celebration had been stolen from the mosque while he was praying. Without further anger or frustration about the loss, he commented laconically that God would punish the thief accordingly (*'Allah zai biya masa'*).

Furthermore, in an environment of widespread disdain, religion offered a frame of reference for the *almajirai* to preserve their dignity in highly unequal relationships with other members of society. As religious students, the *almajirai* can conceive of themselves as legitimate recip-ients and even claimants of charity, meaning that they can assess the treatment they receive in religious terms. The *almajirai*'s interpretation of their begging helped them to maintain some self-respect in the face of denigrating treatment. Abdurrahman and Canham (1978: 70), who write about child-rearing in northern Nigeria, ask whether there could be any 'better way to [practise humility] than to make oneself dependent on the charity of others for food and other necessities?' Such an inter-pretation of begging as an educative practice reverberates, for example, in the statement by Inusa (aged 15) that:

some people think... you come out to beg [because you don't have food in your house]. But it's not like that; it's because you're searching for knowledge.

Before very long, most *almajirai* experience being insulted and chased away when begging. Begging by *almajirai* has been attacked as un-Islamic by Islamic reformers. In this context, it is important to the *almajirai* that an interpretation of their begging as a legitimate activity is available. Peo-ple in support of the *almajiri* system widely believe that giving alms to *almajirai* is a form of worship. One father, for instance, explained to me that *almajirai* would receive more support nowadays as everyone was searching for a way to earn rewards in heaven.

Even though they could interpret begging as religiously ordained, the *almajirai* I befriended during my research unanimously preferred work to begging. Begging makes the beggar vulnerable to the caprices of poten-tial donors, as well as to abuse. The weather is a further source of anx-iety. During the wet season, when people shut their doors against the rain, finding food is very laborious. This is also the time when food is most expensive, as stocks run low and the new harvest is not yet in. Many households prepare food only in the evening and not dur-ing the day during this 'hunger season', the *almajirai* told me. Despite the struggles involved, as the *almajirai* deemed begging morally accept-able, they preferred it to forms of money-making they considered more compromising.

In a photo exercise, for example, where the *almajirai* took pictures of what they thought was good and bad children's behaviour, Anas and

Ibrahim snapped a boy picking empty toiletry containers from a rubbish dump to be refilled and resold under false labels. In their view, this was tantamount to cheating the customers, and they claimed that he should engage in more respectable activities: 'If he's an *almajiri* he can still go and beg or get a house to work in.'

Recourse to religion thus helped the *almajirai* justify their begging, which is often disparaged in northern Nigeria. Religion also offered them a vocabulary with which to pass judgement on better-off Muslims, who are often critical of the *almajiri* system. The *almajirai* I got to know during my research criticised those who denied them support and respect for being malign and lacking faith and knowledge. One *almajiri* at Sabuwar Ƙofa (aged 15) argued in a 'radio interview' that *almajirai* in urban areas are treated worse than in rural areas because:

most of the village people are [Qur'anic] teachers, they know the Qur'an and its importance very well. In Kano, some of them are illiterate. They only have the *boko* ['modern' secular] studies.

The *almajirai* I spent time with during the film project were frustrated with the rich and ruling classes, who in their view did not live up to their obligation to provide as much for the *almajirai* as they provide for the students of 'modern' secular schools (*'yan boko*).[2] As citizens (*'yan ƙasa*), they felt they deserved to be accorded the same rights (*'yanci*). Writing about the Senegambia, Ware (2014: 47) argues that historically '[g]iving students food and charity was understood as a community responsibility, and attention to it indexed the spiritual health of the Muslims'. Referencing a similar community responsibility, Bashir (aged 18) and Nura (about 19) equated supporting *almajirai* with having strong faith – and a failure to do so with a lack thereof:

Bashir: In Nigeria, how many *almajirai* do the rich take responsibility for?
Nura: Actually, the rich in Nigeria, not all of them have faith [*imani*]. Out of a hundred, you can only get 1 per cent that have faith.

Both the *almajirai* and their teachers thought that the rich in Nigeria did not fear God enough. With Ismaila (aged about 18), I talked about the differences between the children of the poor and the children of the elites. The latter would smoke marijuana and drink alcohol, some would not pray on time and others not at all, and they would not fast during Ramadan, he told me.

Do such attitudes imply that the schools of the *almajiri* system produce easily ignitable recruits for extremist ideas, which is how the *almajirai* are frequently described? Rather than calling for any form of radical

---

[2] Given the low standards and limited resources of most government *boko* schools in northern Nigeria, it is somewhat alarming that someone would envy them for the support they receive.

change, the *malamai* I befriended in my rural field site of Albasu largely commended *hakuri*, patience, as the appropriate response for the poor (*talakawa*) vis-à-vis elite corruption, and they trusted that God would restore justice once the Day of Judgement had come. I was surprised by the serenity and equanimity that Ibrahim, a young teacher, and his senior *malam* showed when we discovered that the Kano State official whom I had asked to convey *Sallah* presents for me to their school had stolen half of them. While I was appalled, the *malam* and Ibrahim shrugged the incident off as unsurprising.

Scott (1985: 324) reminds us that, even though 'it may serve just as efficiently to produce daily compliance', 'resignation to what seems inevitable is not the same as according it legitimacy'. The *almajirai* and their teachers understood that their penury was to some degree the product of other people's actions, and they did not suspend their judgement of people higher up in the hierarchy. Often, they invoked God, whom they thought was 'on their side', to substantiate their criticisms. One boy, for instance, argued about people giving bad food to *almajirai*:

Allah said what you cannot eat, don't give it to someone to eat, even if he's a mad man. The people who are doing this do not know. May Allah show them the way. May Allah give them understanding. ('Radio interview')

He also invoked the principle of equality of all Muslims in the eyes of God to criticise those denying the *almajirai* respect by giving them bad food.

I want people to remember that the way Allah creates you is the same way Allah creates an *almajiri*, the way Allah loves you, that is the way he loves an *almajiri*, and also remember it's Allah who gave you the money for the food. But you keep the food and allow it to spoil first before you give it to an *almajiri*. ('Radio interview')

The *almajirai* were confident that God would eventually ensure justice and punish the miserliness of the rich. During the scriptwriting for our film, one of the boys drafted a frank appeal to the political leaders and wealthy members of Nigerian society:

We *almajirai* call upon you, why don't you help the *almajirai*? You should know they are also citizens of this country. Therefore, for God's sake, keep looking after them. Everything you give is your share (*rabo*) in the afterlife. But you don't care, you don't think of the afterlife... ALLAH [capitals used in the original] doesn't care a fig about your money or rule (*mulki*), you will only reap what you have sown. Therefore, better prepare before your death.

In brief, the *almajirai* found strong words to criticise the rich in society, and to demand that resources be distributed more equitably. Yet, at the same time, they pinned their hopes for justice to be restored on God rather than any worldly action, which once again confutes depictions of them as prone to violence to claim their share of resources.

Almajirai and other structurally weak groups

In many ways, the *almajirai* epitomise the challenges poor young people in northern Nigeria face more widely. Poverty is widespread, and its negative connotations affect all poor alike. Many young people who are not *almajirai* share the latter's experience of exclusion from 'modern' forms of religious and secular education, and from the status and future prospects attached to these. Yet, in some respect the *almajirai* are better off than others. Boys from 'ultra-poor' (Last 2000a) families struggle to achieve the Qur'anic knowledge that gives the *almajirai* access to self-definitions as seekers of religious knowledge (see Chapter 4).

Girls tend to receive significantly less education than boys, and are generally considered of lesser worth than boys. For example, when discussing shari'a law, the *almajirai* participating in the film project told me that if a woman killed a man, two women would need to be killed in retribution, to compensate for the man's greater 'value'. Even though other intersecting axes of hierarchy, such as class, age, and noble origin, mediate this relationship, as males, the *almajirai* have a systematic status advantage over females in northern Nigeria.

Furthermore, there is a time limit to the *almajirai*'s exclusion: they will eventually graduate first out of *kolo*, or young *almajiri*-ship (which is arguably the toughest phase), and later out of the *almajiri* system altogether. Their experiences differ, of course, to some extent from those of boys who have not been *almajirai*. Yet, once they return home, there is no stigma attached to them (see Chapter 9), but there are also categories of marginalised or maligned people whose exclusion has no 'end date' and is thus potentially interminable.

Historically, slaves and members of certain professions, especially butchers, were such groups (see Smith 1959). Today, we may count *'yan daudu*, or men who act 'like women' (see Gaudio 2009), among the 'ultra-excluded'. In a context where people are vying to be (regarded as) religiously righteous, and to fight presumed 'social evils', the policing of sexuality has moved centre stage. Sexual minorities, such as the *'yan daudu*, are not only stigmatised but physically in danger following the criminalisation of all sexual relations between people of the same gender, as well as of support, or even tolerance, for such relations (e.g. Mösch 2014).[3]

---

[3] An *almajiri* I was close to in Albasu informed me that some *malamai* tell their *almajirai* not to accept food from *'yan daudu*, because 'Islam condemns *'yan daudu*'.

Besides the *almajirai*, there are also scores of more 'conventional' beggars (*mabarata*; singular: *mabaraci*) in northern Nigeria, who must endure the denigration of begging while knowing that it is not necessarily a passing phase, as it is for the *almajirai*. After a student in my English class in Albasu proposed that '*almajiri*' should be translated as 'beggar' and I pointed out that *almajirai* are not the only people who beg, my students rattled off a whole list of words for which they wanted the English translation from me: *makaho* (a blind person), *gurgu* (a crippled person), *kuturu* (a leper), *bebe* (a deaf person).[4] As the political and commercial centre of the region, 'Kano has long attracted ... the disabled and impaired', Last (2000a: 227) argues, attributing this not least to the 'recyclable waste' the city produces, for instance in the form of food leftovers or discarded clothes. Begging is such a well-established profession in Kano that people with different disabilities (such as blindness) have developed their own organisations, with recognised heads to represent their interests (ibid.).

It is not only people with disabilities who beg in Kano, though. Adedibu and Jelili (2011: 153), who randomly sampled beggars in Kano, found that less than half of them (48.5 per cent) were physically challenged. Widows and divorcees without family support also beg, for example by the Race Course in the Government Reserved Area (GRA) (e.g. Abdu et al. 2013). *Almajirai*, moreover, are not the only young people on the streets seeking alms. Some children hire themselves out as guides for the blind (Last 2000a). Reportedly, there are also 'street boys' in Kano who are not, or are no longer, associated to any Qur'anic school. However, they are difficult to tell apart from 'real' *almajirai*, and may indeed find it convenient to be mistaken for them in order to access alms. The *malam* at Sabuwar Ƙofa told me that 'some children would simply come from their village with a bowl and beg'. Such 'fake' *almajirai* can be identified by their presence on the street during the hours *almajirai* normally spend at school. Finally, so-called *'yan daba*, who are members of urban gangs, also attract much scorn in Kano. In their vulnerability to all sorts of accusations, they resemble the *almajirai* (see my discussion of how some *almajirai* declared the *'yan daba* responsible for the vices frequently attributed to the *almajirai*). There are thus categories of people whose social status is equally low or considerably lower than that of the *almajirai*.

---

[4] Impairment does not necessarily entail exclusion from the institutions of 'mainstream' society and many of the impaired do not beg. Qur'anic schools accommodate students with impairments. Abdulgafaru, a young *almajiri* in Albasu, disabled, I suspect, by polio, not only studied alongside his able-bodied peers but also had his teachers' permission to write the Qur'an with his stronger left hand, despite the general prohibition against approaching the Holy Book with one's 'impure' left hand.

'We also have *gata*!' Claiming social belonging

I have cited statements above in which the *almajirai* claimed fair treatment as fellow Muslims and fellow citizens (*'yan kasa*). In other instances, however, they established their own respectability on the basis of narrower, more exclusive criteria. In a society in which individuals derive their social standing from the people they 'belong' to (be it family members or patrons), being unable to display such belonging means being vulnerable and defenceless. The term *gata* connotes a person or persons whom you can legitimately expect to stand up for you as well as provide materially for you. The *almajirai* with whom I conducted my research often explained the abuses they suffered with reference to the apparent absence of such guardians or protectors. During the scriptwriting process for the film, the participating boys noted that *almajirai* are often mistreated because:

> people see he [the *almajiri*] doesn't have any guardians/protectors (*gata*), and if they mistreat him, nothing will happen to them. And the *almajirai*'s teachers want to live in peace with the people from town. That's why even if *almajirai* have been mistreated, they'll tell them to have patience.

I would not go so far as to suggest that it is considered legitimate to treat someone badly for lack of *gata*. But as an explanation for bad and heedless treatment it makes immediate sense to people. Command over, and claims to, other people's respect inhere not in the individual, but in the social hierarchy to which she or he belongs. To fend off assaults on their dignity, the *almajirai* participating in the film project asserted that they too had their supporters and protectors rather than demanding that everyone should be treated with respect and dignity irrespective of whether or not he has *gata*. Buhari (aged about 20) for instance, part of the film production crew, proclaims in the end credits, where the *almajirai* spell out their messages to the public:

> I want those people who abuse *almajirai* to understand that they also have people who care about them (*gata*).

To use Sayer's (2005) terms, rather than demanding 'respect' by virtue of being human, the *almajirai* sought to establish their own 'respectability' by invoking their *gata*, thus leaving dominant social logics intact according to which respect is owed first and foremost to those who can produce evidence of belonging and support. The following sections explore the *almajirai*'s relationships with women and with other *almajirai*, underlining how the stresses of poverty put a strain on relationships among people whose social and economic status is low.

Domestic work, gender relations, and masculinity

Studies of masculinities (e.g. Cornwall and Lindisfarne 1994; Connell and Messerschmidt 2005; on 'Islamic masculinities', see Kandiyoti 1994; Ouzgane 2006) have put great emphasis on their dynamic and socially constructed nature, and on the contextual factors giving rise to particular gender performances. Rejecting essentialist and 'Orientalist' renderings of Islamic masculinity, Ouzgane (2006: 2), for example, argues that 'masculinities in Islamic contexts emerge as a set of distinctive practices defined by men's positionings within a variety of religious and social structures'. With these insights in mind, how can we understand the *almajirai*'s performances of masculine identity? I argue that in order to grasp them, it is important to examine domestic work arrangements and the *almajirai*'s position within them.

As in most parts of the world, domestic work in northern Nigeria is a predominantly female affair, but young boys and girls in Hausa society perform fairly similar tasks. Both boys and girls are sent to shop, take food to the grinding machine, fetch water, run errands, and sell their mother's wares. As they grow older, boys carry out progressively fewer domestic tasks, and adult men perform hardly any. Relinquishing the domestic 'female' sphere is considered an important step for boys to mature into men (Robson 2004: 204; Schildkrout 2002 [1978]: 359ff.; see also Masquelier 2005b).

Adulthood for males is also marked by their independence. Schildkrout (2002 [1978]: 363) writes that 'men in Hausa society, although they may in some respects remain under the authority of men of higher status than themselves, they cannot remain under the authority of women. Inevitably, then, the transition to manhood means moving out of the domain of female authority.' However, for many men it is impossible to conform to dominant norms of masculinity. In a very hierarchical and stratified society, in practice men frequently work under the authority of women who are of higher status or belong to a higher socio-economic class than themselves. Those men employed in the household of the District Head of Albasu, for instance, received orders from women – the District Head's wife and daughter – without this affecting their status as men and adults. Domestic work arrangements thus bring intersecting hierarchies of class, status, age, and gender to the fore. Domestic work is of low status, 'not least because much of it is alongside or associated with women's work in the private sphere' (Robson 2004: 208).

As discussed in Chapter 5, *almajirai* frequently work as domestics while they are young and entering another man's compound is still acceptable. In some cases, their female employers are only a few years older than they are, as women marry considerably younger than men.

In a context that sanctions male authority over women, being subordinated to female employers is delicate. Domestic employment relationships are also a source of frustration for many *almajirai*, as they entail endless struggles over employment conditions and the reach of employers' responsibilities. It would be rash to assume a straightforward causality between the *almajirai's* domestic employment situation and their behaviours and attitudes towards women, as multiple factors give rise to particular performances of gender identity (e.g. Connell and Messerschmidt 2005). What is more, in the absence of comparative research (for example with students from *Islamiyya* and secular schools), it is difficult to ascertain to what extent the *almajiri* system is responsible for producing particular attitudes towards women or whether other young men share these views. However, it would be equally rash to ignore the problematic experiences of *almajirai* while working as domestics under the authority of women.

In a context where domestic work is of low status and gendered female, I gained the impression that the *almajirai* were eager for opportunities to eschew it, and to behave as 'proper men'. During the days they spent at my house at Sabuwar Ƙofa during the filmmaking, for instance, they would not offer to help with chores such as cooking, sweeping, or fetching water, but would sit on the veranda waiting to be served. This confused me, as at least some of them had worked in our house before as paid domestic helpers and were familiar with the routines, and they had behaved considerately and helpfully on previous occasions. While the youths took care not to interfere with any 'female' tasks, they would quickly and almost aggressively step in on the occasions when I set out to undertake work considered inappropriate for women, such as carrying a heavy water bucket or generator. Once, one of the boys who worked in our compound made a point of telling me in English 'it's not correct' when he discovered me carrying a heavy bucket from the well to our house with my (male) housemate, and he quickly took over from me.

In addition, several of the adolescent *almajirai* I got to know well eagerly embraced and defended normative positions on the question of male control over female behaviour, and on various occasions commented disapprovingly on the behaviour of the women in their environment. For example, they criticised the women in their neighbourhood for being overly nosy, and snubbed them for breaking the norms of *purdah* merely to satisfy their curiosity. They also claimed that the neighbourhood women were too chatty, and would not even be quiet when told to. This was a concern for some of the youths participating in the film project, who for this reason thought it unwise to encourage the attendance of these women at the film premiere.

Remarkably, virtually all the female characters in the 'participatory' docudrama we produced together are either weak or malicious. The female employer of the film's protagonist, an *almajiri* called Aminu, is a spiteful woman who loses no opportunity to humiliate him. (The male shopkeeper, who eventually gives him work, on the other hand, is portrayed as fair and sympathetic.) The other women appearing in the film are an older neighbourhood girl who sneers at Aminu for being upset about the insults her little brother throws at him, his mother, who holds no edifying advice for him but weeps helplessly at his departure, and a sister of his employer, who treats *almajirai* with snobbish contempt. To some extent, women came off worse in the film than the *almajirai* had intended, I think. For example, during the scriptwriting, the *almajirai* had discussed that most mothers would not want their sons to leave. Yet, to them, this was a sign of compassion and concern rather than of weakness. Also, some exceptions notwithstanding, most *almajirai* spoke in respectful tones about their *malam*'s wife or wives. Meanwhile, the youths contributed numerous stories to the script about mean and stingy female employers, which account for the film's highly critical portrayal of these women.

Difficult structural conditions weighing down on both the *almajirai* and their female employers can help explain the many tensions between them. Older *almajirai* may feel humiliated when being ordered around by female employers (some of whom are barely their senior), yet they struggle to find other income opportunities. Moreover, many households live on a tight budget, which creates pressure to make ends meet. Men usually hand money for daily purchases to their wives who then buy from young hawkers peddling their wares from house to house, or they send children, including *almajirai*, to do the shopping. In this context, *almajirai* may be accused of not brokering a good enough deal from sellers, or of pocketing the money they are sent with. During scriptwriting, the participating *almajirai* drafted a scene exemplifying this:

Uwar gida [female employer]: Please give me the change. Whenever one sends you, you dawdle . . . [short hesitation] These vegetables – how much did you buy them?
Aminu: I bought them as you told me. I'll go to school now, it's time.
Uwar gida: Aminu, by God, you won't go anywhere until you replaced these vegetables. You bought me too little. You claim to have bought these for the money I sent you with. Go back, I don't want vegetables like this.

While male family heads usually keep a distance from the petty details of managing daily reproductive tasks, women find themselves haggling over money and work contributions, which adds to their image as pettyminded and cantankerous. Other tensions present in the lives of women in Hausa society are also likely to be transferred onto the *almajirai*. Fights between co-wives are frequent, I learned, and these are likely to make themselves felt in the *almajirai*'s daily routines. One of the boys participating in the film project, for instance, described that the *uwar gida* (senior wife) of the house for which he fetched water would pay him only when he poured water into the bucket in her room, and not when he brought water to her co-wives' rooms.

Relationships among *almajirai*

There were occasions when I felt that the boys and youths I was close to were reluctant to identify as *almajirai*. We may, for instance, recall the situation described in Chapter 6 when Balado concealed his *almajiri* identity from the girls visiting my compound. On many other occasions, the boys and young men I got to know well embraced the concept of '*almajiri*' willingly. Many of the 'radio speeches' they playfully recorded with my tape recorder as well as their statements for the end credits of our film began or ended with a forceful self-identification as an *almajiri* (for example, Shu'aibu: 'This is my answer. From Muhammadu Shu'aibu, Dambatta, the *almajiri*, alhamdulillah [praise be to God]'). The young people also had quite precise ideas of who else counted as an *almajiri*. For example, the students of my English classes in the rural town of Albasu, which I had set up explicitly for *almajirai*, had a clear opinion on who had sufficient '*almajiri* credentials' to be allowed to attend. Some former *almajirai* were 'approved'. But Ya'u – whom the District Head's family had presented to me as an *almajiri* – did not qualify as a 'proper' *almajiri* in the eyes of the other boys, even though he lived away from home and was enrolled 'full-time' in a Qur'anic school. He did not beg for his food but ate at the District Head's house, where he also worked. Two youths with whom I discussed his case concluded that he was too much the protégé of the District Head's house, and not sufficiently under the authority of his *malam*, to study seriously.

For an *almajiri*'s standing among his peers and the privileges he can therefore enjoy, his Qur'anic learning and his 'seniority' matter: that is, how long a boy has spent studying the Qur'an, and how intimately he knows the challenges of *almajiri* life – and how to surmount them. Youths bragged about having become 'toughened up' and about having survived *kolo*, or young *almajiri*-ship. 'Seasoned' *almajirai* tease newcomers, I learned, for example for not wanting to study and for thinking only about food. Being used to village life where food is limited in variety, available only at mealtimes, and seasonally scarce, newly enrolled boys would get overly excited by the culinary offers of the city, I was told. They would spend much of their time eating, and much of their money buying food (depleting the little money their relatives have given them), and would end up going to the toilet excessively. Beyond a boy's Qur'anic learning and 'longevity' as an *almajiri*, having acquired 'modern' secular and 'modern' Islamic (*Islamiyya*) knowledge before joining the *almajiri* system, and being able to display and share it, also adds to a boy's standing among his peers.

Relationships between young *almajirai* and their older fellow students play an important role in how students experience their daily lives. Older students (singular: *gardi*; plural: *gardawa*) are to a large extent responsible for teaching and supervising younger students on a day-to-day basis, and thus shape the character of a particular school. Two of the youths participating in the film project discussed the lack of older students who would take care of the younger *almajirai* and their studies as a potential reason for changing to another school. Their absence is not the only thing that risks making the lives of young *almajirai* difficult though: *gardawa* were also pointed out as a potentially major source of abuse. In our film, an older student constantly bullies Aminu, the protagonist, to the point at which the latter runs away from school. The *malam*'s wife at my urban field site of Sabuwar Ƙofa, pondering the messages of the film after we had watched it together, told me that her husband had once expelled a tyrannical *gardi* from school after he had injured a younger boy.

Young *almajirai* (*kolo*) are very much at the 'bottom of the social pile' (Walker et al. 2013: 229) in their schools, and older students (*titibiri*, *gardawa*) often take advantage. For instance, younger students may be sent by older students to beg for food for them. I heard of students who write Qur'anic verses on the right hand of the boys they send to beg: if the ink has come off when the boy comes back (licked off together with the food eaten 'clandestinely' rather than being handed in), he will be in trouble. In my English classes at the CAESI, an NGO in Kano offering food and secular schooling to *almajirai*, I used to lend out my pens for the duration of the lesson if I noticed a student who did not have one. Yet, unless I had enough pens to equip everybody who was missing one, I could be sure that as soon as I turned my back on the class, pens were snatched from the younger boys and 'redistributed' among the older students.[5] Young *almajirai* also struggle to find acceptable places to sleep (places that are protected from the rain and do not smell of urine), as older students claim the good spots for themselves.

Yet, while young *almajirai* are clearly at the receiving end of much abuse and exploitation, *gardawa* are held to account to some extent through certain mechanisms. Young *almajirai* study under one *gardi*'s supervision, and from what I understood, they have some freedom to choose 'their' *gardi*. The relationship between Muhammadu and Rabi'u, two of the older *almajirai* I got to know well at Sabuwar Ƙofa, cooled down significantly after Tasi'u, Rabi'u's cousin, who had studied under

---

[5] When I enquired why the students were so reluctant to tell me if they were without a pen, I learned that their other teacher beat students who arrived without pens.

Muhammadu's supervision for some time (Muhammadu was renowned for his learning and strictness), returned to Rabi'u's oversight. When I asked Rabi'u about the incident, he explained that Muhammadu was unhappy about losing Tasi'u and that he probably suspected him, Rabi'u, of bad-mouthing him in front of Tasi'u.

Aspiring scholars are distinguished by whether or not they have and maintain the trust and allegiance of the young *almajirai* for whose Qur'anic studies and moral education (*tarbiyya*) they are responsible. Senior teachers may entrust some of their young *almajirai* to promising young teachers graduating from their school as a kind of human 'start-up capital'. Moreover, if one recognises Qur'anic teaching as ultimately a form of worship (which God will reward), it is easy to see why older and more advanced students are expected to take an active part in the instruction of the younger ones and often embrace this role willingly. Both Naziru and Sadisu advocated for the young *almajirai* in their charge: for example, they helped them find a place to sleep (in our entrance room), and provided them with leftover food from our household. Older *almajirai* would also chide younger boys for being dirty and would remind them to wash themselves. Many of the rules guiding everyday conduct in Qur'anic schools are made and enforced by older students – with the passive consent of teachers higher up in the school hierarchy, who, however, may keep a distance from the everyday banalities of managing young students.

In sum, I gained the impression that relationships between older and younger *almajirai* are to some extent symbiotic: while young students need a teacher and advocate, older students need a testing ground to practise their teaching and 'human resource management' skills, and someone who begs for them when they have no other way of accessing food. This should not obscure the weak position and vulnerability of the young students, though, which the youths participating in the film project also acknowledged. The fact that they had survived *kolo*, or young *almajiri*-ship, was an experience that bound them together and that could be looked back on with a sense of accomplishment. Yet, the youths still insisted that very young boys should not be enrolled. Such boys were too weak to do physical work, and, reduced to what they could get from begging, would inevitably suffer, they argued. One boy explained that, because they begged on the street and in car parks, chanting '*Allah ya kiyaye, Allah ya kare*' ('May God protect/look after you'), they got on people's nerves and were insulted and chased away, bringing the entire *almajiri* system into disrepute. In their messages in the end credits of the film, the *almajirai* recommended that parents should not enrol small boys, and that if they did enrol them they should visit them regularly.

The *almajirai* also had misgivings about boys who spend long hours on the street begging (some of whom are 'street boys' and are not – or no longer – affiliated to any Qur'anic school). These boys have attracted much negative attention, which may explain why the *almajirai* sought to distance themselves from them. During our discussions of the photographs the *almajirai* at Sabuwar Ƙofa had taken with disposable cameras in 2009, the *almajirai* drew a strong dividing line between boys begging for money on the street and boys begging for food at houses. While they considered 'begging at houses' acceptable and safe, they deemed 'begging on the street' corrupting and dangerous. There was some disagreement as to why *almajirai* take to the street to beg – whether it was because of 'profligacy' (*iskanci*) or because of a need for cash (which may be particularly pressing among boys too small to earn cash by working). The boys concurred, however, that begging on the street was physically dangerous, as boys risked being hit by a car, and that it went hand in hand with truancy. One boy went so far as to claim that begging on the street was not even 'proper begging', as begging (*bara*) was 'house by house' (as opposed to *maula*, which is usually for money). As mentioned earlier, the boys agreed that in order to earn cash income, working in a house was preferable to begging for money on the street – even though the latter was considered financially more rewarding. One of the *almajirai* at Sabuwar Ƙofa explained in a 'radio interview' he recorded in 2009:

It is better to work in a house than to beg on the street; you earn more respect when you work in houses to get money than if you beg on the street. Your parent may see you on the street begging and think you are not studying well.

Conclusion: looking beyond the classroom

This chapter has discussed how the *almajirai* pursue a respectable position within society by casting themselves as particularly moral and pious. It has also described how the *almajirai* relate to others in weak positions in society, and that these relations are frequently fraught with tensions. While the *almajirai* emphasise their moral and religious credentials in order to position themselves favourably vis-à-vis the better-off in society, who often frown upon the Qur'anic students, they simultaneously assert their own moral and social worth against the backdrop of others whose social standing is low.

Neat notions of agency as coterminous with resistance to structures of oppression do not allow us to capture the behaviours of the *almajirai* described here. There are, of course, instances when the *almajirai* are not complicit with the powers that be, for example when they claim the moral and religious high ground, criticising those who disregard and despise them. However, there are also instances when the *almajirai* reproduce discourses that malign poor and socially powerless people, even though they, too, are victims of such discourses. The behaviours of the *almajirai* described in this chapter thus corroborate Mahmood's (2001) finding that people's 'capacity for action' reflects their position within relations of subordination – and that these relations aren't easily challenged from the inside.

That the *almajirai* vie for the recognition of others in society shows how deeply they are affected by widespread rejection, and how misplaced are depictions of them as 'loose molecules' (Kaplan 1994: 46) detached from dominant notions of morality. Of course, this does not mean that they are docile recipients of the condescending treatment they receive. On the contrary, the boys and youths in my research did not withhold their criticism of the rich in society. Yet, neither did they envisage taking justice into their own hands, as accounts of them as 'monsters in the breeding'[6] would have it. Instead, they pinned their hope on God, who, they were convinced, would eventually ensure justice, and punish stinginess and malice.

Finally, the observations in this chapter on the *almajirai*'s moral and religious identities and on their relationships with other members of society – both the better-off and the worse-off – emphasise how crucial it is to look beyond the classroom if we want to understand what the *almajirai* learn. As has been argued by a range of authors, schools are merely one among many settings within which 'education' takes place (e.g. Levinson and Holland 1996; Starrett 1998: 89ff.; Katz 2004). We cannot understand such complicated issues as the notions of morality that the *almajirai* develop, the religious identities they embrace, or the position they assume vis-à-vis other members of society unless we scrutinise their place within wider social relationships that shape their experiences. While it would be rash to assume any straightforward, linear relationship between experiences of abuse or denigration and particular convictions and dispositions, it would be equally rash to ignore such wider, potentially problematic experiences (see also Chapter 5).

The next chapter explores questions of religious beliefs and practices in more depth, taking stock of the religious skills as well as the knowledge the *almajirai* acquire. The next chapter also evaluates the status of this knowledge and these skills in society today, and analyses the opportunities they open up for the *almajirai* within northern Nigeria's 'prayer economy'.

---

[6] 'Rehabilitating our almajiris' (2011).

8 Spiritual security services in an insecure setting
Kano's 'prayer economy'

> *Muhammadu (aged 15)*: If they brought the *hadith* teachers now, would your teachers [*malamai*] agree to them staying and teaching [the students]?
>
> *Saidu (aged 11)*: We are not of the same opinion as our teachers, but we want the *hadith* teachers. ('Radio interview')

The last decades have seen important transformations in the religious educational landscape in Islamic West Africa. Educational reformers of various orientations have sought to bring religious learning arrangements 'up to date' by opening and supporting 'modern' Islamic schools (*Islamiyya* schools in Nigeria; *écoles franco-arabes* or *médersas* in many parts of francophone West Africa), whose curriculum and teaching methods diverge substantially from those of classical Qur'anic schools. Also, educational reformers, especially those of a 'reformist' or pro-Salafi bent, have promoted novel approaches to handling religious knowledge. They have pushed for its 'democratisation' and release from the monopoly of the classically trained religious scholars (*'ulama*). These trends have profoundly affected the position of these *'ulama*, and by extension the position and future prospects of the *almajirai* studying under their guidance. This chapter explores these changes from the latter's point of view.

Several studies contribute to our understanding of religious educational change in Muslim West Africa by exposing the ideologies, epistemologies, and agendas of 'reformist' Islamic movements in the region, which have been important protagonists of educational reform (e.g. Umar 1993; 2001; Loimeier 1997; 2005; Kane 2003; Brigaglia 2005; 2009; 2012; Gomez-Perez 2005; Brenner 2007; Thurston 2015). Other studies have highlighted that educational reform has not been the preserve of Salafi-oriented Muslims, but has been championed by Muslims across the religious spectrum (e.g. Brigaglia 2007; Thurston 2016a on Nigeria; Kane 2016: 138ff. on Sufi educational reformers in Senegal). While the motivations underpinning educational reform are thus fairly well documented, surprisingly little is known about the impact it has had

181

on those who stood to lose most from it: the classically trained 'ulama and, by extension, the young almajirai studying with them.

Rudolph Ware's (2014) book on classical Qur'anic schooling in Senegal constitutes an important exception to this trend and offers some useful clues to understanding the impact of religious educational reform on the Qur'anic education system. While not being oblivious to Sufi reform initiatives (ibid.: 223ff.), he argues that vehement critique from 'reformist' or Salafi-oriented Muslims has marginalised the classical tradition of Islamic learning and promoted 'modern', 'depersonalised', and presumably 'disembodied'[1] forms of knowledge instead. Unfortunately, Ware barely explores what the students in classical Qur'anic schools make of such 'modern' forms of religious knowledge. This is unfortunate because their views and potential sympathies for 'modern' Islamic education could reveal internal critiques of the classical system. Saidu, the young almajiri quoted at the beginning of this chapter, for example, voices clear disagreement with his teacher, as well as a desire to access knowledge (of the ahadith, the traditions of the Prophet Muhammad) that Islamiyya schools routinely impart and that Qur'anic schools usually withhold from students who have not yet mastered the entire Qur'an (that is, they know how to read, write, and recite it correctly).

Listening closely to the young students in classical Qur'anic schools can also reveal that, paradoxically, the rise of 'modern' Islamic knowledge has occasioned new experiences of exclusion, even though a 'democratising' thrust had underpinned its spread. While many almajirai have come to regard 'modern' Islamic education, which is both common and popular in their urban places of study, as desirable, the same is not necessarily true of their rural parents. Some arguably (still) perceive Islamiyya schools as a spearhead of Izala reformism, and thus oppose them. Others want to make sure that their sons master and memorise the Qur'an, something to which 'modern' Islamic schools pay only limited attention. Finally, some hope to instil into their sons a particular 'habitus' for which they consider it necessary to undergo the privations of a life as an almajiri.

Beyond ideological and epistemological divides, social and economic pressures also matter for school enrolments. Family break-ups and poverty make it difficult for boys to stay at 'home'. Unlike Islamiyya schools, classical Qur'anic schools offer a way forward in such circumstances. Finally, 'modern' religious education implies not only opportunity costs – for example in the form of lost revenue from children's work – but also direct costs: for textbooks, writing materials, and uniforms (cf. Brenner 2007 on madrasas in Mali). Admittedly, many Islamiyya schools cater to poor children and are likely to be lenient with children who

---

[1] See my critique in Chapter 1.

simply do not have the means to pay. Yet, most of them depend on the financial contributions of their students towards their running costs, and some are indeed set up as economic enterprises, thus participating in the 'commodification' of religious education, described, for example, by Dilger and Schulz (2013: 370).

This chapter takes up the themes set out here. The first section outlines the very real appeal that classical Qur'anic learning still holds today for many Muslims in northern Nigeria. I shed light on the logics behind the strong focus on Qur'anic memorisation, countering characterisations of it as dull rote learning stifling children's creativity and numbing critical minds (e.g. Friedman 2001; Looney 2003). I also explore the economic and political significance of the Qur'anic knowledge imparted in classical Qur'anic schools, illuminating their historical utility in the 'prayer economy'. The chapter then explores how religious reform and fragmentation have affected the *almajirai* and their future prospects. The market in 'spiritual security services' has become increasingly crowded, diminishing the livelihood prospects of those with only limited access to the requisite knowledge and skills. In this context, the *almajirai* aspire to and seek to access knowledge commonly withheld from them. What are the chances that they will one day derive a viable livelihood from their sacred knowledge – if this is their ambition? I argue that for someone formed exclusively within the classical Qur'anic education system, these chances are declining, given the growing competition from 'modern' educated religious scholars. Finally, wider trends towards an increasing commodification of social relationships in northern Nigeria, whose problematic consequences have been highlighted in previous chapters, also render livelihoods in the 'prayer economy' precarious and unpredictable.

Embodying the Qur'an

Among Muslims in northern Nigeria, it is widely accepted that it is a religious duty to acquire knowledge, and that the Qur'an constitutes the necessary first step (Last 2000b: 375). Religious learning and facilitating the acquisition of religious knowledge, either directly through teaching or indirectly by enrolling a child in school, are seen as meritorious deeds that will be rewarded by God (cf. Fortier 1997 on Mauritania; Hefner 2007). The boys and youths living as *almajirai* interpreted their parents' decision to enrol them as a response to a religious duty which they would be held accountable for if they failed to fulfil it. This is exemplified by Anas's (aged 15) statement:

People bring their children to Qur'anic school . . . because they want them to have the knowledge . . . Allah said if you didn't take your child to school, what will you tell the child on judgement day?

Lacking the necessary knowledge to practise their religion 'correctly' does not exculpate believers who practise it 'wrongly'. For example, I told the youths participating in the film project that, according to my Ugandan flatmate at Sabuwar Kofa, no Muslim in his home country knew, let alone carried out, the extensive ablutions the *almajirai* performed before the Friday midday prayer. One of the youths replied that a lack of knowledge was not an excuse before God, since God had enjoined all believers to search for knowledge.

The memorisation of the Qur'an takes a central position in this quest for knowledge. Historically, it helped preserve the Qur'an in the absence of affordable books, and, through recitation, made it accessible even to people who could neither read nor write (see Last 1993; Boyle 2004). Memorisation has maintained its importance as the Qur'an is considered to be the actual word of God. As such, its 'formal features' share the 'sacredness of its meaning' (Brigaglia 2005: 424). Given its heavenly origin, the Qur'an is considered 'unique in certitude' and 'fundamentally beneficial' in nature (Bin Omar 1993: 29, as cited in Boyle 2004: 14–5).

The belief that the Qur'an represents revealed and therefore necessarily true knowledge accounts for the common lack of explicit explanation of the memorised verses during the early stages of Qur'anic learning (see Eickelman 1978). Knowledge in this context is a more nuanced concept than the ability to understand and explain. It also encompasses notions of 'mnemonic possession', such as the ability to recite from memory (Eickelman 1985: 64). As the Qur'an becomes embodied through memorisation, it comes to serve as 'a source of ongoing knowledge and protection' (Boyle 2004: 83) and as a kind of compass engraved in the body that can provide direction later in life (ibid.; see also Fortier 1998). Memorisation is a necessary 'first step in understanding (not a substitute for it) as it ensures that sacred knowledge is passed on in proper form so that it can be understood later' (Boyle 2004: 84). Ware's descriptions of Qur'anic school pupils as 'walking Qur'ans' and 'vessels for God's verbatim speech' (Ware 2014: 1) provide productive images for this 'incarnation' (ibid.: 8) of the Qur'an. Memorising the Qur'an, Ware argues, helps 'to inculcate Islamic sensibilities in human beings, to instil the character of the Qur'an within living agents' (ibid.: 14).

Corroborating these conceptual approaches to Qur'anic learning, many of the *almajirai* I spoke to asserted that learning the Qur'an earned them rewards in the afterlife and was also useful in this life as a protective shield against mischief. Ibrahim (aged 24), for instance, said that 'whoever has Qur'anic studies in this life, if he really studied because of Allah, I don't think he will suffer in this life'. One *malam* declared to me that studying the Qur'an would improve one's character (*hali*) and temper (*zuciya*) and that Nigerian politicians behaved the way they did –

that is, they stole money from poor people – because they had stopped studying the Qur'an.

The meaning of Qur'anic knowledge was clearest in the *almajirai*'s comparisons between Qur'anic and secular knowledge. They reasoned that Qur'anic knowledge, by virtue of having been acquired, earned them direct benefits in the sight of God in this life and the next, whereas secular knowledge would have to be translated into facts that please God first (by way of doing pious deeds). Several older *almajirai* (particularly those who had begun their Qur'anic studies only recently) told me that it is preferable for a child to learn the Qur'an early on, as 'when you are very little, that is when you understand better'. Western conceptions of education assume for most domains of knowledge that a child's ability to understand improves as she or he grows older. Language learning is a notable exception and a productive analogy to Qur'anic learning. Here, the assumption is that the young mind, still malleable, can better grasp new knowledge.

Recitation of the Qur'an is at the heart of Muslim religious practice. The first word revealed to the Prophet Muhammad is said to have been '*iqra*': 'recite!' (e.g. Fortier 1997: 103). The word 'Qur'an' derives from this, and one of its meanings is 'recitation' (e.g. Wagner 1991: 265). Prayer is usually taken to mean reciting the Qur'an. Therefore, learning to recite, by way of memorising, takes a central place within Islamic education. To perform the five daily prayers, one needs to know at least some surahs by heart.[2] As recitation is crucial to religious collective enterprises such as praying, training in recitation also prepares people for participation in social life (Boyle 2004: 96). In Hausa, the standard way of enquiring whether somebody is Muslim is to ask whether she or he prays (*tana/yana sallah?*). Whoever prays is usually considered part of the Muslim community (Paden 1973: 37).[3] This expression highlights how crucial learning to pray (and to recite the appropriate verses) is to being part of this community.

When men pray together, the one considered most knowledgeable religiously is usually invited to lead the prayer, which honours him. During filmmaking, the participating *almajirai* bantered over who should lead their midday prayer. Those who were put forward acted coyly but were visibly honoured by the proposal. The social implications of acquiring (or failing to acquire) Qur'anic knowledge figured centrally in the students' accounts of why they deemed Qur'anic knowledge important.

---

[2] The *malam* with whom I was studying the Qur'an in my rural field site, Albasu, brought this point home to me by demonstrating how he would have to interrupt his prayer if he was to dig out his booklet and look up his verses in the middle of it.

[3] The frequent recourse of Boko Haram to *takfir*, or the 'excommunication' of other Muslims, which Brigaglia (2015: 181) traces back to Wahhabi ideology, breaks with this inclusive definition.

Inusa (aged 15), for instance, claimed that 'if someone grows up without knowing what to recite during *sallah* [prayer] . . . it's a problem'. In a similar vein, Dahiru (aged about 20) asserted that he would be ashamed hearing his friends recite the *sallah* verses and not being able to recite them himself: 'If they know the Qur'an and I don't know the Qur'an – I only know *boko* ['modern' secular knowledge] – it is a shameful thing for me.'

Children and learners (including myself) are routinely encouraged to showcase what they have learned: I was told 'Let's hear!' (*Bari mu ji!*) whenever I mentioned that I had also memorised some verses of the Qur'an. Learning is thus publicly monitored and success is rewarded with appreciative remarks. Many boys develop considerable ambition for their studies. Abdullahi, one of the film youths, for example, recounted his early years as an *almajiri*, claiming that he even preferred at times to stay in school rather than return home for a holiday so that he would not forget what he had memorised.

Brigaglia (2009: 343–4) writes that historical forms of Islamic education in West Africa are characterised by a 'deep fracture' between the elementary stages of learning, focused on the '*passive* memorization of the Qur'an and . . . practical embodiment of the essential markers of a Muslim life', and the advanced stages, when students are encouraged to *actively* search for knowledge of various disciplines.[4] My informants consistently perceived the Qur'an as a necessary first step for acquiring more knowledge throughout their life course, and not as the final stage. Time and resource constraints may, however, make it difficult for poor young men to devote as much time to their studies as they would wish.

The students conceived of mastering the Qur'an as a kind of 'entry ticket' they had to earn first before they would be allowed to move on to other fields of knowledge to which they aspired. The fathers I interviewed argued that a proper focus on the Qur'an is only possible if a student has no access to other materials that may confuse or distract him. Due to the great importance attached to the Qur'an, no one wanted to incur the risk that his sons would not learn it properly. One *almajiri* claimed that students who are offered a translation before having properly memorised the Qur'an risk citing it incorrectly.

Murray Last (1993: 122) states, in relation to northern Nigeria, that 'knowledge of texts and the ability to quote *in extenso* is a mark of learning'. Alas, only those who know the translation can demonstrate their degree of mastery – and thus reap prestige – by making appropriate practical reference to the memorised text (see, e.g., Eickelman 1978).

---

[4] The curriculum of advanced studies usually draws on standard classical Maghrebian sources covering Maliki law, Arabic literature and grammar, and Ash'ari theology (Brigaglia 2009: 343–4). Many students are also introduced to Sufi practices and to the knowledge relevant for the 'prayer economy'.

For example, they can choose a verse that is particularly appropriate to a given situation when leading a prayer or making supplications (*addu'a*). Translation and interpretation (*tafsīr*) are the preserve of advanced learners, at least among people following the logic of the classical system of religious learning (see Brigaglia 2009). Usually students must have done their first *sauka* before they get access to other subjects that will reveal the meaning of the Qur'an to them. Equally, students are introduced only gradually to situation-specific supplications (*addu'a*) and to the hidden 'medicinal repertoire' that the Qur'an is believed to contain: knowledge relevant for the 'prayer economy', to which I now turn.

The political and economic significance of Qur'anic knowledge

For many Muslims in Kano, as elsewhere in Muslim West Africa (e.g. Bledsoe and Robey 1986; Soares 1996), scholarship of the Qur'an is a form of worship and a way of becoming a socially viable member of society, capable of participating in such religious collective enterprises as praying. What is more, it is also a way to pursue both power and a livelihood. Last (1988: 187) writes about Islamic scholars in Kano that they 'have access ... to the knowledge of how to use the powers that Allah has locked into his creations (plants, minerals, and animals; men, spirits, or simply words)'. They can manipulate this power, for instance by writing certain Qur'anic verses – whose secret meaning is known only to a few initiates – on a wooden board (*allo*) to be washed off and drunk (as *rubutun sha*; literally, writing for drinking) or rubbed on the body (see Ware 2014 on similar practices in Senegal). Qur'anic scholars or *malamai* also manufacture charms (*laya*), tightly folded pieces of paper with Qur'anic verses written on them and covered with animal hide, which are worn on the body. Purposive prayers or supplications (*addu'a*) form another part of the classical repertoire of spiritual power. Finally, *almajirai* who have learned to read the entire Qur'an are often 'employed' to recite it. Clients requesting such help to achieve desired ends usually approach the *almajirai*'s teachers, who then organise group readings (*takara*) among their students.

Such spiritual interventions or 'remedies' (*magani*) are aimed first and foremost at social problems (cf. Hassane 2005: 375 on Niger). For example, *rubutun sha* was commended to me as a means to protect oneself against evil-wishers or to achieve popularity (*farin jini*). I also saw women seeking a *malam*'s help to win back a husband's love and sexual desire from an unwelcome new co-wife, to find a new (and better!) husband, and to alleviate melancholy (*yawwacin tunani, bacin rai*). *Almajirai* drink *rubutun sha* so that they learn better and do not feel homesick. I was offered *rubutun sha* that would prevent me from getting tired while teaching English, and was 'threatened' that *magani* (medicine) would be mixed into my food to make me want to stay in Nigeria for ever. Particular verses of the Qur'an can help one overcome indecisiveness and give the necessary confidence to take a difficult decision – for example, which of several suitors to marry – or to thrive in business or politics.

Last explains that spiritual medicine is efficacious in that it bolsters people's confidence. Stories about the supernatural powers some *mala-mai* wield can have very real consequences if 'they are treated as true. They... contribute to an individual's charisma, and create the reputations, generate the fears, and instil the confidence on the basis of which people make decisions and act' (Last 1988: 198). While Qur'anic cures are believed to work primarily in the realm of interpersonal relationships, people may also resort to them against physical illnesses. Taking recourse to Qur'anic medicines does not preclude the use of 'modern' medicines, and I have seen people reciting a specific Qur'anic verse to fight off a migraine while taking a paracetamol at the same time. The expectation is for spiritual medicine to take effect slowly, 'not like European medicine that works within minutes'.[5] Such remedies would not work if the finite term God had given to one's life had come to its end (*ajali*). Spiritual medicine thus works within its divinely ordained limits: it aims to restore and preserve order, not to change it (Last 1988: 202). However, spiritual remedies and power have political and economic significance well beyond individual ailments and close personal relationships.

First of all, spiritual remedies matter in business. Masquelier (2009: 18–9) remarks that, in neighbouring Niger, in a context of economic crisis 'where relations between production and value, work and wealth, are increasingly mystified', the spiritual economy prospers as people look for religious recipes for success. Since the oil boom of the 1970s, work and wealth, as well as production and value, have increasingly been decoupled in Nigeria, arguably also boosting the spiritual economy there. Kano, as an important commercial hub in the region, has long been a preferred destination for Qur'anic scholars, and especially since the oil boom (see Last 1988 and Abba 1983: 197–8). 'It is the rich who are looking for *magani* [medicine],' said Ibrahim, a *gardi* or assistant teacher in his early twenties whom I befriended in the village of Daho, explaining to me why he went to Kano to earn money rather than staying in Daho.

Spiritual services also matter in politics. According to Last (1988), demand for them surged in post-independence Nigeria, when political careers became increasingly jeopardous: 'The possibility of coups and

---

[5] The standard 'remedy' for various ailments sold over the counter in pharmacies is a mixture of paracetamol and caffeine – which admittedly relieves pain quickly, even though it leaves its root causes unaddressed.

similar political reversals of fortune, far from calling into question the efficacy of the techniques offered by scholars, has accentuated their importance' (ibid.: 196). The return to competitive politics in 1999, and the violence related to Boko Haram, may well have increased the risks and pressures involved in a political career. People in Kano told me that, in times of political crisis, the spiritual business thrives as these are moments when people seek protection. Some *malamai* reputedly have medicine on offer that makes people immune to bullets. Others can let people disappear or make them lose their senses.[6] In view of the indiscriminate violence of the Boko Haram crisis, it is easy to understand the appeal of such promises of protection. While demand is high, however, the offer of spiritual assurances has diversified, and spiritual services, which historically implied a long-term reciprocal relationship between service providers and clients, have become increasingly commodified. The next sections discuss the increasing competition that Qur'anic scholars face today, and the *almajirai*'s reactions to this competition.

A crowded 'prayer economy'

Since the 1970s and 1980s, northern Nigeria's religious scene has become increasingly fragmented, relegating the inter-Sufi tensions of earlier decades to the background. Importantly, northern Nigeria has seen the emergence – and subsequent fragmentation (see Brigaglia 2015; Thurston 2015) – of mass anti-Sufi and pro-Salafi 'reformist' movements (e.g. Loimeier 1997; Kane 2003). These have had important repercussions on the 'prayer economy', where the monopoly of classically trained *'ulama* offering spiritual services and 'insurance' for risky projects or lifestyles has increasingly come under attack. First of all, Salafi-oriented reformers have accused these *'ulama* of unlawful innovation (*bid'a*), condemning, for example, practices such as the use and production of charms and 'potions' as rooted in 'culture' rather than religion (Lubeck et al. 2003; Hassane 2005: 38–5). The *almajirai*'s practice of begging has also increasingly attracted criticism as un-Islamic; arguably, Islam permits begging only in acute emergencies.

A central endeavour of the 'reformist' thrust, furthermore, has been to 'democratise' access to sacred knowledge in order to ensure a more 'enlightened' religious practice. By encouraging 'the independent effort of the believer to directly interpret, rigorously filter and literally apply the foundational texts of Muslim sacred scripture (Qur'an and Hadith)' (Brigaglia 2015: 181), reformers indirectly attacked the power of the

---

[6] If *malamai* are not seen doing this more often, it is because God disapproves of such 'interferences'.

classically trained *'ulama*: if believers could independently access religious meanings, religious knowledge brokers would be made redundant.

A crucial element of reformers' attempts to 'democratise' access to religious knowledge was the provision of written translations of the Qur'an. Since the late 1970s, several such translations into the vernacular Hausa language have been published, prominent among them that of *Izala* leader Abubakar Gumi (1922–92), which was published in 1979 (see Brigaglia 2005). If every believer could read and even interpret the Qur'an herself or himself, there was no need for the intervention of religious 'experts' (Loimeier 2005: 410ff.; see also Brenner and Last 1985: 439).

Finally, reformers sought to put their 'democratising' mission into practice by extending modernised religious education to wider parts of the population. 'Modern'-educated Muslims had inherited power from the British at independence in 1960. In 1976, Nigeria launched its first Universal Primary Education (UPE) campaign. In this context, the position of the classically trained religious and intellectual elite was in the process of being dismantled. While some members of this elite tried to keep step with these processes by opening and promoting 'modern' Islamic schools (Brigaglia 2007: 180–1; see also Umar 2001: 131), 'reformist' Muslims soon overtook their more 'tradition'-oriented competitors, pushing for the massive establishment of 'modern' Islamic schools or *Islamiyya* schools (see Chapter 3). Today, *Islamiyya* schools are widespread, especially in the urban areas of northern Nigeria. They are operated by Muslims of various religious orientations, and are also popular among people, notably urban dwellers, who do not otherwise have much regard for 'reformist' ideas.

Memorising the Qur'an plays a much smaller role in these 'modern' schools than in the classical Qur'anic schools of the *almajiri* system; instead, they emphasise explicating the meaning of the Qur'anic verses they teach, and knowledge of Arabic. Many *Islamiyya* schools teach their students to recite the Qur'an in the *qirā'a* of Hafs, resembling in sound the Arabic spoken on the Arabian Peninsula, thereby staking claims to 'high culture' Islam while distinguishing themselves from the classical Qur'anic schools that use the 'folk' Warsh version (see Brenner and Last 1985: 443; cf. Launay 1992: 81ff.).[7] *Islamiyya* schools also have a reputation for teaching *addini*, or practical knowledge about religious practice associated with the *ahadith*. They familiarise students with the intricacies of performing ablutions and prayers, and teach them the appropriate supplications for specific situations. This makes them

---

[7] That most Qur'anic schools neglect or treat as secondary the teaching of *tajwīd* (the rules of pronunciation and recitation of the Qur'an) has been part of the criticisms reformers have levelled at them (Brigaglia 2012: 5; see also Sani 2015).

an attractive option – not only for boys but also for girls, for whom the imperative is to learn the basics of Islamic practice in a timely manner before marriage.

Taken together, the developments described here have considerably diminished the standing of people educated exclusively within the *almajiri* system. Additionally, *almajiri* graduates now face competition from a range of more 'modern' religious entrepreneurs.[8] The 'modern' Islamic (*Islamiyya*) schools established in Nigeria from the second half of the twentieth century onwards have produced numerous religious scholars, many of whom have achieved a university education in Nigeria or abroad, and who are of a very different mould from the classically trained *'ulama* (Anonymous 2012: 122; see also Thurston 2016c: 92ff.). Some of them also espouse somewhat unorthodox doctrines. The quick rise to fame of preachers or religious entrepreneurs such as Ja'far Adam and Boko Haram leader Muhammad Yusuf has been attributed to their choosing an 'attractive short-cut' instead of a slow rise through the ranks of established religious hierarchies: they decided 'to start a new religious discourse that would be distinctively different from the established doctrines' (ibid.: 122; see also Masquelier 2009 on 'self-authorised' preachers in Niger).

Such unconventional, 'entrepreneurial' (Sounaye 2013) careers are significantly aided by the ubiquity of 'small media' – videocassettes and audiotapes, CDs and DVDs, and more recently sermon podcasts and video clips that can be shared via smartphone and digital social media. They make it possible for messages to spread widely without being filtered through the religious establishment. The use of 'small media' – which disseminate 'knowledge' to everyone who bothers to listen – follows a logic diametrically opposed to that of the classical system of knowledge transmission, where disciples 'earn' access to secret knowledge through personal bonds of loyalty and submission (see Larkin 2009; Gomez-Perez et al. 2009; Sounaye 2014).

Seeking withheld wisdom

The *almajirai* are well aware of sectarian divides, and of the contempt in which some 'reformist' Muslims hold the Qur'anic education system. *'Yan Izala* (a term used broadly to refer to Salafi-oriented Muslims) would not only refuse to give food to begging *almajirai* but may even beat them, the *almajirai* told me. They were aware of doctrinal

---

[8] Tellingly, the *malam* whom the District Head of Albasu invited to give a sermon during Ramadan on religiously appropriate behaviour to the women attending our evening classes had pursued a 'modern' secular education, and studied for a university degree in Arabic studies afterwards.

differences, for example about the legitimacy of prayer beads (which some 'reformists' reject, but *almajirai* use),[9] about the sighting of the moon at the end of Ramadan ('reformist' Muslims and formal sector workers in northern Nigeria mostly follow the Sultan of Sokoto, whereas many other Muslims insist on sighting the moon 'themselves'),[10] or about the different *qirā'a* styles.

Unsurprisingly, given the animosities between 'reformists' and classically trained *'ulama*, I did not meet anyone who confessed to being a supporter of the *Izala* or any other Salafi-inspired group among the students and teachers of the *almajiri* system. However, not all necessarily belong to one of the Sufi orders (*Tijaniyya* or *Qadiriyya*). One youth suggested that many *almajirai* eschew *tariqa* membership because they feel that it implies 'taking sides' in religious questions, which they prefer not to do. But stickers with the bust of *Tijaniyya* shaykh Ibrahim Niasse decorate many *almajirai*'s phones and begging bowls. Which *tariqa* one identifies with is not a divisive issue, however, and I met *almajirai* who did not share their *malam*'s *tariqa* affiliation. The *almajirai* also espoused rather tolerant attitudes towards the *Izala*, arguing that, after all, the different groups (*Izala* included) were all Muslims. *'Yan Izala* would, however, sometimes go astray, and 'just say the Prophet said this or that, whereas truly he didn't say that'.[11] *Izala* and *tariqa* members would not follow each other's prayers, Muhammadu (aged 17) explained, but, to him, this didn't matter. He would prefer to pray in a *tariqa* mosque, but if none was close, he would pray anywhere. Overall, I gained the impression that the *almajirai*, like the youths with whom Masquelier (2009: 63–4) conducted research in southern Niger, 'want[ed] nothing to do with the sectarian disputes that absorbed their elders' attention in the last decade of the twentieth century'.

Beyond particular doctrinal disputes, many of the ideas and practices initially associated with 'reformist' Islam have become widely popular today, at least among urban populations in northern Nigeria, and prestige and status increasingly derive from mastering the 'modern' forms of knowledge it promotes (cf. Launay 1992: 81ff. on comparable trends in Côte d'Ivoire). 'Modern' Islamic schools imparting such knowledge are widespread today, especially in urban areas.

---

[9] Abdullahi (aged about 20) argued that even though the Prophet did not use prayer beads himself, given the *almajirai*'s hardships, they could legitimately use them: tired from getting up at dawn, and from working in addition to studying, it would be difficult for them to keep track of the 3×33 prayers they were supposed to say without an aide-memoire.

[10] Some people did not think that the Emir was honest, I was told, and would therefore prefer not to trust his verdict.

[11] The youths claimed, for example, that some *Izala* preachers (in their view) falsely proclaimed that it was acceptable to eat horsemeat.

The *almajirai*, largely excluded from the knowledge and 'symbolic capital' *Islamiyya* schools impart, are at the receiving end of these developments. As mastery of the Qur'an is largely the only explicitly taught content of the *almajiri* system, its students are frequently reproached with failing to acquire the necessary knowledge to practise their religion, a criticism that teachers and students of the system are aware of. For instance, a *malam* whom I was close to in my rural field site, Albasu, commented to me that many people say about *almajirai* that they 'know how to read [the Qur'an] [*karatu*] but not how to worship [*ibada*]'. Muhammadu, an *almajiri* at Sabuwar Kofa, explained to me in a 'radio interview' he recorded with my tape recorder why it was important to achieve knowledge other than the Qur'an, to my surprise taking up many of the 'reformist' critiques of classical Qur'anic learning:

It's possible that you know the Qur'an, and you don't know the translation, or you know the verses to recite when praying, but you don't know the rules, and the rules are inside the *ahadith*. Sometimes some things are not good when you do them during prayer, and it's written in the *ahadith*, not inside the Qur'an . . . I want to study the *ahadith* after I finish my [Qur'anic] studies. By the grace of Allah.

Given the spread of *Islamiyya* schools that readily give access to both translations of the Qur'an and other Islamic subjects, it is hardly surprising that the *almajirai* want to achieve Islamic knowledge beyond the Qur'an. The boys and youths I got to know well during my research expressed this wish repeatedly, for example in the 'radio interview' I cited at the opening of this chapter, where Saidu declares that: 'We are not of the same opinion as our teachers, but we want the *hadith* teachers.'

The *almajirai* I was close to with whom I discussed the issue felt that in certain aspects of religious practice the students of *Islamiyya* schools had advantages over them. There was a consensus among them that the recitation practised by *Islamiyya* schools (*qirā'a* of Hafs) was more aesthetic (*ya fi kyau, ya fi dadi*) than theirs (*qirā'a* of Warsh). Several of the *almajirai* participating in the film project, when practising with my tape recorder for their statements in the end credits, began with Arabic-accented salutations ('*Salām 'alaykum wa rahmatullahi wa barakātuhu*'), as if to lay claim to the prestige associated with the 'high culture' Islam evoked by such a pronunciation.

At the same time, the *almajirai* also put forward arguments in favour of their own education system. Their own way of reciting was easier to learn (*ya fi sauki*) than the *Islamiyya* way, they contended. Kabiru argued the case for Qur'anic schools with reference to the greater diligence he thought they enforced. Whereas *Islamiyya* school students could get away with mistakes, students of Qur'anic schools risked being beaten for lapses. They would therefore master the text better.

Contrasting their own education system with the *Islamiyya* schools, the *almajirai* emphasised the non-commercial nature of Qur'anic schools, arguing that parents could

bring students to the Qur'anic teachers without giving the Qur'anic teacher anything. It's only God who pays them...you don't have to go and give them money...that is why the Qur'anic schools are different from the others. (Naziru, 'radio interview')

People do not view the relationship between *almajirai* and their *malam* simply as the provision and consumption of educational services. Instead, their relationship is often equated to that of a father and son. A teacher who has been entrusted (*amana*) a boy incurs responsibility not only towards his parents but also towards God, as, ultimately, it is to God that he renders his service. Dan'Ala, an *almajiri* in his late teens, put it in the following way: 'If you give other people's children knowledge, you will get blessing in the sight of God. And when you get to heaven, God will cross you over [the narrow bridge over hell].' Since a teacher assumes responsibility beyond plain service provision, he cannot simply be paid off with money. Incidentally, many of the *almajirai* are also from families too poor to regularly pay school fees for all their children.

Thus, while *almajirai* still find ways of justifying their education to themselves, their environment, especially in their urban places of study, nevertheless pushes them to develop aspirations reaching beyond the knowledge to which they are given access. The young *almajirai* I got to know actively sought to acquire religious knowledge excluded from their curriculum. Some students secretly enrolled in an *Islamiyya* school in the neighbourhood, but had to drop out after their teacher found out. The *almajirai* learned the meaning of the text that they memorised from the Qur'anic exegesis at the Friday mosque, from books they owned, which contained both Arabic verses and Hausa translations (which the boys who had received some secular education could decipher), from the radio, from preachers on the street or in the market, and by guessing from similarities between Arabic and Hausa. Finally, podcasts of sermons circulate widely among *almajirai* owning mobile phones, and those who do not have a phone of their own may listen to such sermons on a friend's phone.

From the way in which some boys frequently invoked God's presumed position on certain contentious issues to make their point,[12] I gained the impression that they claimed to possess some degree of specialised knowledge – an ability to interpret and thus turn religious knowledge

---

[12] For example, 'Even Allah says you should know him first before you worship him' ('radio interview'); 'Allah will also punish them for giving him bad food' ('radio interview'); 'Allah said what you cannot eat, don't give it to someone to eat, even if he's a mad man' ('radio interview').

to their own purposes – even though they were formally not entitled to such knowledge. Several officials at the Kano Ministry of Education to whom I presented some of the boys' statements frowned upon their presumption to make their own interpretations.[13]

A student's progress in his Qur'anic studies as well as his financial means determine whether Islamic subjects other than the Qur'an are accessible to him. Muhammadu's case illustrates this well. When I first met him in summer 2009, he was still in the intermediate stages of Qur'anic learning (thirtieth *izu* (Arabic: *hizb*; plural: *ahzab*), i.e. 'halfway' through the Qur'an's 60 equal-sized portions or *izufai*). In a mock 'radio interview' he lamented that some teachers expelled students if they found that they had enrolled in an *Islamiyya* school behind their back. He explained that such teachers believed that 'if you were brought to study the Qur'an, and you enrol in an *Islamiyya* school, you become a *dan gari* [literally, a 'son of the town']; if you get exposed to urban ways [*waye*], you move away from your original focus, and you become like the people from town'.[14]

Muhammadu also brought up financial constraints in his 'radio interview': unlike *Islamiyya* school teachers, Qur'anic *malamai* would teach for God's rewards alone. If a Qur'anic school wanted to employ an *Islamiyya* teacher, who would pay for it? The students, far from their parents, would not be able to afford it. His perspective was shaped by his experience of exclusion from knowledge he cherished. Two years later, having achieved his *sauka*, which earned him his teacher's permission to broaden his Islamic studies, he explained to me that today many Qur'anic schools would either teach *litattafai* (literally 'books', connoting subjects other than the Qur'an), have someone come in to teach them, or let their students go somewhere else to learn them. While older and more advanced *almajirai* thus manage to 'catch up' on knowledge that did not initially form part of their curriculum, we have to keep in mind that studying implies opportunity costs that not all poor young men are able to afford.

As if to compound the *almajirai's* difficulties regarding access to 'modern' knowledge, many Qur'anic teachers are not exactly forthcoming when it comes to the potentially profitable aspects of their own knowledge, such as the secrets relevant to the 'prayer economy' discussed in

---

[13] One of my PowerPoint slides included, for example, the statement of one *almajiri* that: 'If your parents took you to Qur'anic school, and you refuse to study and say you only prefer *boko*, what will you tell Allah in heaven? . . . I have to obey them, because it is said that "whoever obeys his parents, obeys Allah".'

[14] Muhammadu's Qur'anic teacher did not object to *Islamiyya* education and indeed enrolled his own children in it. Teachers forbidding their students from attending *Islamiyya* schools may be acting at the behest of the students' rural parents, who are arguably more reserved towards 'modern' Islamic schooling, presupposing their association with *Izala* reformism.

this chapter. As in any competitive market, market power is secured by distinguishing oneself from others and by securing one's advantage over competitors.

Ware (2014: 53), writing about the relationship between students and teachers in Qur'anic schools in Senegal, states that '[l]ove, service, and gifts were understood as the keys to unlocking the benefits of knowledge. Indeed, it is still widely held that without receiving a teacher's gratitude... and blessing... one cannot profit from one's learning'. But there is a more profane dimension to the relationship between teacher and disciple as well: unless a student shows sufficient *biyayya*– that is, loyalty and obedience – his *malam* may refuse to share his secret knowledge with him. Bledsoe and Robey (1986) note for Sierra Leone that such a concentration of power risks giving rise to exploitative relationships, where students with ambitions in the 'prayer economy' vie for their teacher's goodwill without any assurance that their efforts will pay off. In extreme cases, students are forced to work for their teachers in slave-like conditions. But, on the other hand, entrepreneurs within the spiritual economy abound, and students who find their desire for knowledge frustrated in the long term may well decide to 'vote with their feet' and move on.

Most *almajirai*, including young ones, are highly mobile, and may move from one school to another if their studies do not progress according to expectations, if they encounter difficulties (in terms of finding food, cash, or hygiene facilities, for instance), or if they desire a change of routine and insights into a new *malam*'s knowledge. The teachers I interviewed, who had successfully completed their Qur'anic education, had each attended up to 14 different schools. Almost all older students who had lived as *almajirai* since they were young boys had changed schools at least once.

Reichmuth (1989: 51) argues that, while a *malam*'s ability to provide spiritual guidance and help for adult clients is most important for his economic success, it is through his teaching activities that he 'gains respect and reverence' (see also Paden 1973: 58). In addition to being 'living proof' of a teacher's aptitude and thus a means to attract donations, students make financial contributions – albeit small ones – to their teachers' livelihoods (especially on Wednesdays, before the weekend starts), and, upon enrolment and graduation, parents are expected to give gifts (especially grain).[15] A *malam* may also call upon his students' labour for other works around his compound (for example to fix crumbling mud walls or

---

[15] I gained the impression that the sums given on Wednesdays (*kudin laraba*) were little more than symbolic. At Sabuwar Kofa, students paid 5 Naira (approximately US$0.03) each. The gifts given upon enrolment and graduation are more substantial, and the donations made by the people attending a graduation ceremony also go to the *malam*.

leaking roofs), and for daily household tasks such as fetching water, running errands, or doing laundry. In rural areas, *almajirai* are also expected to contribute agricultural labour to their teachers' livelihoods. Younger students collect firewood (during the dry season when they do not risk trampling down crops) and fodder (during the rainy season when weeds spring up). Older students work the fields: make ridges, plant, weed, hoe, and harvest.[16]

In brief, a *malam* can draw on his *almajirai*'s labour for a plethora of activities, and while there is a rough understanding about what demands are legitimate, the details of the arrangement are up for negotiation and the subject of potential conflicts. One of the *malamai* I got to know in Albasu, for example, not only made his students work on his fields but also demanded his share from what they scavenged, be it a couple of Naira they earned for an errand or as *sadaka*, or mangoes picked from a 'public' mango tree. From what I could gauge, most other senior *malamai*, knowing their students' incomes to be meagre, demand neither a share nor the disclosure of their students' finances. Rather, in the rare case of a windfall profit, students would inform their *malam* of their own volition, and offer him a share, paralleling the way money is distributed within households.[17]

Through the grapevine, I heard that the *almajirai* of the rather meticulous *malam* described above held critical views of him. Nevertheless, the *rubutun sha* he made them drink convinced discontented students to stay on. To the youth who recounted the incident, the fact that some students had indeed spent long years at his school proved the efficacy of his 'medicine' (and thus his skill as a scholar). In brief, successful *malamai* not only furnish proof of their abilities – which will convince students to stay – they also steer a middle ground in terms of how large a labour contribution they demand from their students and how generously they share their secrets with them.

Viable livelihoods? Commodification of spiritual services

Given the difficulties the *almajirai* face when it comes to accessing now prestigious 'modern' Islamic knowledge on the one hand and their *malam*'s secrets on the other, to what extent does the spiritual economy still offer livelihood opportunities for those formed within the classical

---

[16] A common arrangement is that students are given food from the teacher's house or some cash (50–200 Naira, or approximately US$0.30–1.20) on the days they work for him. On Thursdays and Fridays, *almajirai* are free to work on their own account (by selling fodder or firewood or by hiring themselves out as farmhands).

[17] More problematic are the relationships between young *almajirai* and the assistant teachers or *gardawa* supervising their studies. Arguably, the latter often rely quite heavily on the contributions they levy from the former (see Chapter 7).

Qur'anic education system? Kabiru (aged about 20), a former *almajiri* whom I interviewed in Albasu, told me that 'you waste time' if you want to go far enough in your Qur'anic studies for them to become a proper source of income. Young aspiring teachers from poor peasant households may not be able to devote quite as much time to their studies as they would like because they must help their fathers with farm work. Only solving 'big problems' fetches big money, and only the 'big *malamai*' are capable of that (Ibrahim, in his early twenties). Most of the *almajirai* I spoke to hoped to become involved in a well-paying business activity of some sort (perhaps as shop owners or wholesalers), and – maybe as a consequence of the difficulties those trying to make a living as Qur'anic scholars face – only a minority aspired to becoming Qur'anic teachers or preachers (see Chapter 9).

Even established *malamai* with an appointment as an imam and a considerable student body may live rather precarious lives, despite the alms they receive for administering life event ceremonies (naming ceremonies, weddings, funerals) and on the occasion of the two Eid celebrations. The *malam* at Sabuwar Kofa feared eviction by his landlord in whose mosque he had been teaching for almost 20 years. The landlord declared several times to me that he had grown tired of the *almajirai* and their at times unruly behaviour, and considered establishing an *Islamiyya* school on the mosque premises instead. The *malam*'s wife was exploring options to earn some extra money through tailoring and selling home-made pasta. If her husband lost his post as imam and did not find another mosque to teach in, they would be in financial difficulties, since he 'did not have any other craft [*sana'a*]'. The senior *malam* in Daho, one of the smaller villages I visited frequently during my time in Albasu, had an additional job as caretaker at the health centre of the village.

Malamai with connections to politics or business may share in their clients' potential windfalls, but they also share in the professional hazards afflicting politicians and entrepreneurs in a high-risk environment such as Nigeria. If a venture is unsuccessful, *malamai* lose their source of income and support. The *malam* at Sabuwar Kofa had pinned his hopes on a friend and client involved in politics who had promised to build a house and mosque for him, but apparently he did not succeed with his political venture. A *malam* I knew well in Albasu declared to me that the Shekarau supporters among the *'ulama* had forfeited their influence after Rabi'u Kwankwaso was elected governor of Kano State in April 2011, ousting the incumbent Ibrahim Shekarau.

Soares (1996: 748) argues in the Malian context that the 'prayer economy' amplifies the unequal distribution of power:

The giving of gifts of greater value, which political and economic power allows, serves ultimately to confer additional power on these elite followers. In a sense, they are able to convert one form of capital (political, economic) into another (spiritual/symbolic). And in turn there is usually the hope that this spiritual capital will be transformed into additional political and economic power or resources.

Similar processes may be at work in northern Nigeria. But even if ventures are successful, *malamai* may not necessarily share in the gains. One *malam* I visited frequently in Albasu lamented that 'a mere 20 per cent of clients' would continue supporting their *malam* after achieving what they had commissioned his support for. His complaint ties in with a wider trend towards the commodification of social relationships. The *almajirai* I was close to lamented that their provision of spiritual services was turned into a one-off exchange of services for cash in which the affluent shun any longer-term responsibility for their well-being. One of the youths participating in the filmmaking project said during the scriptwriting process:

There are people that won't stop to help you until they have some problem themselves. That's when they'll call upon you. When [someone] is well, he doesn't care about you, but when he's unwell, you'll see him gather 70 or 50 *almajirai*, and give them 1,500 or 2,000 Naira [to say prayers for him].

Insiders in the *almajiri* system held on to the idea that the provision of spiritual services should be based on long-term reciprocity within the community. On various occasions, people told me that Qur'anic scholarship was not a *sana'a* (an occupation or means of gaining a living), but a religious service. The implication of this is that the upkeep of *malamai* ought to be taken care of by the religious community for the sake of its long-term spiritual health. Yet, today, the 'prayer market' relies more and more on one-off financial transactions. On two occasions, women from the household of the District Head in Albasu engaged me to commission spiritual services for them from the *malamai* I visited frequently. For example, I was sent to find out how many alms (*sadaka*) a *malam* would want for prayers for a difficult son. On both occasions, the *malamai* stated a sum only at my insistence. Their first reaction was to say that they would not charge anything: they wanted their leaders to be well. Malam Nasiru explained that his medicine was not a one-off remedy: one would have to take it repeatedly, and, God willing, it would work eventually. Yet, as I did not give up easily, I was eventually told a precise sum to be given as alms for the requested services.

Those in the lower echelons of the 'prayer economy' whose repertoire of Qur'anic cures is limited are unlikely to make much money from their provision of spiritual services: people with purchasing power are likely to consult 'big' *malamai*. This leaves mostly the market segment of the poor to the 'small' *malamai*. In addition to seeking relief from the myriad stresses of living in poverty, with public healthcare in disarray, poor people also resort to spiritual remedies to avoid the costs of 'modern' medicine. Yet, their purchasing power is low.

Finally, 'spiritual skills' may be used to foster social relationships. The supply of *rubutun sha*, for instance, may be rewarded with meals or a place to sleep or with a patron's goodwill. I also saw it being used (by *almajirai* themselves, and by parents instructing boys to produce it) as a gift to be taken on a visit or offered to a guest by people who would have been hard-pressed to give material presents. In these cases, it came close in its meaning to an 'energy drink' aimed at boosting the bodily defences of the recipient. Some women mentioned *rubutun sha* to explain why they wanted their sons to acquire Qur'anic knowledge. Given that there are few alternative opportunities to learn economically and socially useful skills, it makes sense for families to ensure that some of their sons learn spiritual skills. However, the fact remains that access to prestigious forms of knowledge – including 'modern' Islamic knowledge – that allow some to thrive within the spiritual economy is stratified and well beyond the reach of most *almajirai*.

Conclusion: 'adverse incorporation' into the 'prayer economy'

Classical Qur'anic learning – and especially the memorisation of the Qur'an – has often been dismissed as backward, stultifying, and without any apparent economic use. This chapter has outlined the logics under-pinning Qur'anic memorisation in northern Nigeria, and has shown the religious and social, as well as the economic and political, implications of such learning. Qur'anic memorisation helps young people embody God's word, which thereby becomes an ingrained source of continual protection and guidance. Memorisation is also crucial to prepare boys for participation in adult communal endeavours such as worship. This buttresses the argument made in Chapter 4 that Qur'anic education is crucial to prepare boys for the transition to male adulthood in northern Nigeria. Finally, Qur'anic learning has economic and political signifi-cance, as the services of Qur'anic scholars are solicited by many, includ-ing by such 'modern' figures as businessmen and politicians seeking to ensure the success of risky enterprises in an increasingly volatile eco-nomic and political environment. The fact that this is the case suggests that it would be rash to dismiss Qur'anic scholarship as obsolete and out of sync with present-day realities.

In addition to being gendered, access to prestigious religious knowl-edge has always been somewhat stratified in northern Nigeria. What has changed over the past decades are the logics regulating access to such knowledge. As Butler argues about Niger: 'Madrasas, Franco-Arabe schools, and secular schools bill outright . . . By contrast, the families of the Qur'anic students are frequently enmeshed in gift economies, offering ongoing and fluid recompense to the marabout in addition to any labour that the student might provide' (Butler 2016: 298). Occasional gifts and 'the capacity to provide labor' (ibid.: 298) are sufficient to obtain access to classical Qur'anic education. The *almajiri* system can thus accommodate poor families and the temporary barren spells these are likely to experience, even though, with work obligations sapping their free time, boys and young men from such families are unlikely to go far in their studies.

Access to 'modern' Islamic education, on the other hand, depends more explicitly on one's ability to pay (on time), thus contributing to the commodification of religious knowledge. We must recognise, though, that many *Islamiyya* schools accommodate poor students, and that its commodification is not the only factor making it difficult for boys from poor rural families to access 'modern' Islamic knowledge. Rural parents' reservations about *Islamiyya* schools as presumed tools in the 'reformist' and anti-Sufi struggle of the *Izala* also play a role. Yet, the *almajirai*, seeing how popular *Islamiyya* schools are in the urban environments of their schools, do not necessarily share their parents' attitudes, and feel excluded from knowledge they aspire to. This illustrates once more how stays in urban areas encourage the *almajirai* to distance themselves from the rural 'habitus' their education system seeks to instil in them.

Given their difficulties in securing prestigious knowledge, what are the *almajirai*'s prospects for securing a livelihood within the spiritual services economy? First of all, they have to contend with a new class of 'modern' religious scholars to which the expansion of 'modern' religious education has given rise, and who challenge the classically trained '*ulama* for their positions in the 'prayer economy'. Compounding the problems posed by increasing competition, trends towards an increasing commodification of social relations have encompassed the spiritual services economy. Once based on long-term reciprocity within the community, akin to a stable patron–client structure, today spiritual service provision has turned into a one-off exchange of cures for cash in which the affluent shun any longer-term responsibility for the well-being of the Qur'anic students and teachers they engage. Qur'anic scholars may be employed to 'insure' politically or economically risky projects (through prayers and other spiritual services). Yet, they are not guaranteed a stake should a venture succeed.

Butler (2006) considers the decline of long-term patronage for 'marabouts' in Niger and the manoeuvring of clients to avoid paying in full the results of the increasing impoverishment of the population. Yet, he also argues that 'marabouts' may be increasingly dissatisfied with the compensation they receive in a context where 'the reaches of a cash economy hav[e] become not only more visible but more instrumental in life', including in the lives of the 'marabouts' (ibid.: 319). Both observations are pertinent for the Nigerian context. Many *malamai* lament that their students' parents and other clients lack the means to compensate them adequately. What is more, as Chapter 6 has shown, many *almajirai* and *gardawa* aspire to urban 'cosmopolitan' lifestyles and an escape from poverty, both of which heighten their need for cash. Yet, given that it is not only poor people who commission spiritual services and that most frustration among *gardawa* and *malamai* is directed at better-off members of society who shun payment and long-term commitments, even though they could presumably afford it, we should also consider alternative explanations, notably the rise of a new individualistic and acquisitive economic spirit in northern Nigeria.

This ties in with more general arguments I make in this book about the 'adverse incorporation' of the *almajirai* into the institutions of mainstream society. Hickey and du Toit (2007) propose this notion to capture how, among other things, the workings of capitalist markets contribute to keeping people poor. In a similar way, we may conceive of the *almajirai*'s role within the 'prayer economy' as a form of 'adverse spiritual incorporation'. Their struggles within the 'prayer economy' are intimately linked to wider trends within the political economy, and notably to the commodification of social relationships. Those with political and economic power can purchase spiritual services from the *almajirai* that will presumably help them sustain and augment their power without necessarily making their assistants part of their success. The spiritual economy relegates the *almajirai* to contributory roles in fabricating other people's good fortune, without giving them much of a share in the outcome. The next and final chapter explores the *almajirai*'s future prospects beyond the spiritual economy.

9 Roles, risks, and reproduction
What *almajiri* education implies for society and for the future

In a global context of widespread anxieties about Islamic radicalisation and militancy, institutions of Islamic learning have attracted overwhelmingly negative attention. Among policymakers, they ring alarm bells as supposed stumbling blocks on the way to universal basic education, preventing children from learning economically useful skills (Adetayo and Alechenu 2012). Their teaching pedagogy has been likened to rote learning and indoctrination, presumably turning children into gullible recipients of hate-filled messages (e.g. Looney 2003). The fact that many of the young people enrolled in Islamic educational institutions are both male and poor has inflated anxieties about them yet further. In the Nigerian context, many people – including many academics – have asserted that the combination of poverty, Islamic education, and young males is inherently problematic, and that this combination could explain, for example, the current Boko Haram Islamist insurgency, even though the existing evidence suggests a more complicated picture. As discussed in Chapter 2, both the educational and the socio-economic profiles of Boko Haram supporters are indeed quite diverse.

Negative perceptions fuel suspicious and hostile attitudes as well as policies that aim to control and contain groups considered threatening. On the other hand, empirically informed explorations of the ways in which poor young Muslims studying in Islamic schools engage with and make sense of the constraints they face in their lives are scarce. This is unfortunate, as such investigations can help us understand what experiences are particularly problematic, and what factors moderate and mediate these.

Tracing the trajectories of boys and young men through northern Nigeria's Qur'anic education system, this book has sought to dispel some of the widely circulating myths about Islamic educational institutions. The Qur'anic education or *almajiri* system has sparked controversies in the context of growing concerns about child welfare, attempts to universalise basic education, and fears of Islamic radicalisation and militancy. Many consider the *almajiri* system unable to equip its students with the necessary skills to become functional members of society. The *almajirai* are depicted in media headlines as a 'ticking time bomb'[1] and their schools as 'breeding grounds'[2] for thugs and terrorists. Given how much controversy and suspicion the system sparks, an empirically informed exploration of the experiences of the young people enrolled in it is long overdue.

Drawing on insights from education studies, poverty research, childhood and youth studies, and the anthropology of Islam, the preceding chapters have explored the discourses circulating about Qur'anic students in Nigeria and beyond, and have argued that we should take them with a pinch of salt. Often such discourses lack empirical nuance and thus stand in the way of a more accurate evaluation of the *almajirai*'s conditions and concerns. This book offers a picture of the *almajiri* system informed by ethnographic and 'participatory' fieldwork with *almajirai* and the communities they come from, exploring the conditions under which families decide to enrol boys as *almajirai* despite the increasingly negative image of this education system and the low prospects that *almajiri* education will lead to profitable and sustainable livelihoods. Finally, light is shed on the experiences young people have as *almajirai* by exploring their work roles as domestic helpers, by scrutinising their efforts to cope with poverty and aspirations that they struggle to achieve, and by tracing their pursuit of a respectable position within society through moral and pious self-conceptions.

By expanding the analysis started in the previous chapter with regard to the 'prayer economy', and by exploring what happens – or is likely to happen – to *almajirai* once they leave the Qur'anic education system, this conclusion adds an additional piece to the picture. We can then return to the question of what role the education system plays in social reproduction and the (re)production of poverty. To what extent do the *almajirai* succeed in acquiring the skills, knowledge, and means necessary to launch successful adult lives? And what do their difficulties reveal about the workings of education in the lives of poor young people, and about the processes underpinning protracted poverty more widely? How do the *almajirai* engage with difficult circumstances? And what does this teach us about the options for action open to poor boys and young men in general?

Any evaluation of the future roles the *almajirai* will play within society, and thus of the overall role that the *almajiri* system plays in social reproduction and the entrenchment of poverty, is necessarily tentative. We cannot know for sure what the future holds for young men graduating from the *almajiri* system today. We can only extrapolate from the experiences of 'current' ex-*almajirai* (i.e. men who have already

---

[1] 'Almajiris: Nigeria's ticking time bomb' (n.d.).
[2] 'Rehabilitating our almajiris' (2011).

graduated from the *almajiri* system), and from an assessment of current conditions in Kano and Nigeria. In the context of ongoing social, economic, and political transformations, what looks likely today may look less likely tomorrow.

Bearing this limitation in mind, the next sections reconnect the *almajirai* to the larger Nigerian socio-economic, cultural-religious, and political context, exploring what their experiences and future prospects imply for the way in which they engage with the state and the rest of society, and what place they are likely to occupy within these. I also reflect on the wider questions that this book has pursued: namely, what role education plays for social reproduction, what mechanisms – beyond education – matter for (re)producing poverty, and how young people negatively affected by such processes deal with difficult circumstances, not least through recourse to religion. I conclude with thoughts on how a politics of poverty and dignity could be integrated.

Skills and knowledge

Almajirai first attracted particular scholarly attention in the 1980s when researchers discussed their role in the Maitatsine crisis. Then, a number of authors suggested that the *almajiri* system not only attracted scores of unskilled idle youths into the cities, but also served to initiate its students into urban life and the spheres of trade, craft, and labour (Winters 1987: 179; Reichmuth 1989: 49). When conducting my fieldwork some 20 years later, the *almajirai*'s informal initiation into the urban economy was never pointed out to me as an active reason for opting for *almajiri* enrolment. But parents and older students are keenly aware that *almajiri* enrolment in metropolitan Kano opens up new economic activities for young people that are absent in rural areas, especially during the dry season. Older *almajirai* in Daho told me several times that they preferred studying in urban areas as there was no money to be made in rural areas.

The older students I met during my research all had impressive track records of casual employment and small trading into which the younger students are gradually socialised by undertaking minor tasks, such as running errands. The *almajirai* wash and iron clothes, are involved in the sale of tea, juice, food colourings, vegetables, Hausa novels, drinking water, phone recharging cards, and clothes, wash cars, water flowers, carry loads, and work as motorbike taxi drivers (*'yan acaba*), shop assistants, and dishwashers. In Malam Gali's school, one of the Qur'anic schools I visited regularly in urban Kano, most of the older and some of the younger students were involved in the yoghurt trade, which they managed in all its stages from purchase at a factory in adjacent Kaduna State through to street peddling. A few students learn a craft systematically from relatives or friends. Some manufacture caps. One student was learning to sew, while one trained as a mechanic and another as a carpenter.

Through their involvement in various activities, passing from petty job to petty job with great ease, constantly keeping their eyes open for new and better opportunities, acquiring trading skills and enlarging their network of informants, collaborators, and potential employers, the students become experts in eking out a living in Kano's urban economy (cf. Clough 1981: 277, who also finds that migration as an *almajiri* enlarges the network a young man can rely on in trade). Developing close ties with employer-patrons may open up access to loaned trading capital (ibid.).

Those *almajirai* who had never attended 'modern' schools often surprised me with the literacy and numeracy skills they had acquired. Through their frequent exchange and close cooperation with 'modern' educated people (either in the houses where they worked or in the marketplace), they had learned to write Hausa in Latin script quite well. 'Nobody who really wants to learn the *boko* alphabet today will fail to learn it,' the *almajirai* in Albasu told me once when I praised their knowledge of Latin letters after an English class, and having mastered the Arabic alphabet previously makes the task less daunting. However, most *almajirai* acquire neither enough literacy nor enough 'social capital' to be eligible for formal sector employment, which is accessible only to a very small percentage of the population.

Aspirations, expectations, and opportunities

It is useful to distinguish between 'aspirations' and 'expectations', as MacLeod (1987) suggests. While the former express personal hopes and desires with little consideration of limitations arising from a lack of opportunities, personal skills, knowledge, mobility, and so on, the latter take such constraints into account (ibid.: 60; see also Crivello 2009). To enquire into the *almajirai*'s future aspirations (as distinct from their realistic expectations) reveals the ideals they are pursuing. Their – reality-adjusted – expectations, on the other hand, tell us about their perspectives on where they stand in society, and how much control they think they have over their lives.

It has been argued that the *almajirai*, thanks to their modest and down-to-earth education, do not have the inflated expectations for formal sector jobs common among high-school and university students, which, according to proponents of the 'youth bulge hypothesis', lead the latter to turn to crime and violence once their high hopes are shattered (cf. Urdal 2004). The *almajiri* system, some people claim, actually safeguards against the production of additional, unemployable, 'modern'-educated school leavers who 'believe they can't do the petty things the *almajirai* do' and who therefore become *'yan daba*, or hoodlums.[3] Abdalla Uba Adamu, a professor at Bayero University Kano, told me that 'you rarely find an unemployed *almajiri*', as the *almajirai* learn to fend for themselves early on (see also Iguda n.d.: 14; Okoye and Yau 1999: 41).

However, neither *almajirai* nor 'modern'-educated youths are homogeneous groups with predetermined futures and there are no grounds to assume that *almajirai* are immune from high-flown aspirations. When Abbas, a student at Bayero University Kano who supported our film project for a brief period, asked the participating *almajirai* what they wanted to become in life, the majority of youths present declared that they aspired to a formal sector job (such as soldier, customs officer, or simply 'government worker', *ma'aikatan gwamnati*). The circumstances of the conversation may have influenced the *almajirai*'s answers: in the eyes of the *almajirai*, studying at university made Abbas a likely candidate for future formal sector employment, I think, and therefore an appropriate audience for such aspirations.[4] But aspirations for formal sector employment came up far too often in my interviews to dismiss them as merely a passing fancy. Several students in Malam Gali's school in urban Kano, for example, expressed the wish to become a judge, soldier, primary school teacher, or government official, which reflects the respect society accords these professions.

Yet, I also encountered several youths who, humble in their future aspirations, declared that they would willingly accept whichever fate God had planned for them. A number of *almajirai* aspired to becoming Qur'anic teachers or preachers (*mai wa'azi*). Most students hoped to get involved in a well-paying business activity of some sort (perhaps as shop owners or wholesalers). This chimes with Abba's finding as early as 1983 that '*almajiranci* is now adopted by many as a stepping stone to other occupations like trading' rather than to a scholarly career (1983: 197).

Few *almajirai* talked about becoming farmers in the future. This may be because few rural dwellers have farming as their only livelihood activity and so respondents may have taken participation in agricultural work for granted. It may also relate to the low regard some *almajirai* have for *kauyanci* or 'village habits' and their perception that agricultural work is both arduous and unprofitable. Abba (1983) suggests that the quick money available in urban areas during the oil boom years has changed perceptions of the relative worth of different professions. In the city, even

---

[3] Interview with Professor Abdalla Uba Adamu, Bayero University Kano, 26 July 2009.
[4] How privileged the *almajirai* considered Abbas to be became apparent when they laughed at his proclamation that the government ignored not merely the rights (*'yanci*) of the *almajirai* but also the rights of university students like him. 'It's your parents who gives you [the financial support needed]!' one of the youths retorted.

'illiterates' could become wealthy 'while the "fools" who remain in the village doing useful things like studying and growing food remain poor' (ibid.: 203). It seems that this changed perception also holds sway among *almajirai*.

Interestingly, learning a craft (beyond becoming a bus driver) figured in the imagination of very few young people. My sense is that the *almajirai*'s preference for trade over crafts originates in their horizon of experience (most people around them are traders) and their understanding that most of the rich in Kano acquired their wealth through 'business'. What is more, historically, many crafts were casted. That the Prophet Mohammed was a trader adds to the prestige of that profession. Finally, learning a craft requires the sympathy and support of someone who can teach it.

While some *almajirai* have high hopes for their economic futures, what can they realistically expect to be doing in their future lives? Are there likely to be social and economic opportunities for them to seize? The experiences of adult life of the former *almajirai* I met throughout my research were quite varied depending on the people they met (for example at work), the opportunities they encountered (in terms of furthering their education, for instance), and the demands their own families made on them. Several older generation government officials, university lecturers, and successful businessmen in Kano have gone through the Qur'anic education system.[5] These are, however, a tiny fraction of the millions who have passed through the *almajiri* system over the decades. Furthermore, secular education today has become more widespread, and 'modern' Islamic education increasingly encroaches upon the former monopoly on religious knowledge of the classically trained *'ulama*. Most *almajirai* are likely to be limited to the lower reaches of the 'prayer economy'. Kano's population has grown and the number of available formal sector jobs reduced. Poor infrastructure and a notoriously erratic electricity supply have taken their toll on industry (Tiffen 2001: 32). The insecurity surrounding the Boko Haram crisis has arguably discouraged investment in northern Nigeria, and has led some entrepreneurs to relocate their businesses to parts of Nigeria considered safer.[6] Since oil prices plunged in late 2014, Nigeria as a whole has slid into recession, which has gravely exacerbated already difficult conditions in the north.[7]

[5] A prominent example is Alhaji Isyaka Rabi'u, founder of the airline IRS and one of the richest men in Kano.
[6] For example, 'Why northerners feel done down' (2013).
[7] All the *almajirai* whom Sadisu, one of the film youth with whom I have stayed in close touch since leaving Kano, consulted for me in 2017 on their current conditions emphasised that they struggled more than before to secure their daily needs. Prices have gone up drastically for food and basic items such as soap and clothes. In addition, as many households are hardpressed themselves, they give less charity and perform tasks themselves for which previously they would have subcontracted an *almajiri*.

All these factors suggest that past 'success stories' become less and less imitable for the students currently enrolled in the *almajiri* system.

Tiffen (2001: 14) writes that *almajiri* education 'was a common first step to an urban life for many Kano residents'. In urban Kano, I met ex-*almajirai* who, through their former employers, had found work (such as factory work) that paid enough to sustain a family in an urban area. I met others who, incrementally, had expanded the business they had engaged in already as *almajirai* (tailoring, cap-making, retail sale) to the extent that it could just about sustain a family. Predictably, all the *malamai* of the schools I interacted with were former *almajirai*.

Are opportunities to settle in urban Kano still readily available? Meagher (2001: 47), who studied rural–urban linkages in Nasarawan Doya village in northern Kaduna State, observes that over half of the returnees to the village 'were Koranic students with virtually no Western education and no money' who 'retreat[ed] from collapsed opportunities outside the village'. Those who remained in urban areas were better educated and better skilled, and came from the better-off village households.

In Albasu, I met numerous young men who had spent at least part of their boyhood and youth as *almajirai*. They had returned to their home village to launch adult careers: that is, to build a house, or at least a room, often inside or bordering their father's compound, to accommodate their wife or wives and children. Some returned to their rural home to support ageing parents, others because they failed to find ways of setting themselves up as married men in the city. It was taken for granted that they would help their fathers with the farm work.

Almajiri enrolment may also provide an avenue 'to life in a new rural area', as Tiffen (2001: 14) suggests. Malam Ahmed in Albasu, in his late thirties, exemplifies such a trajectory: originally from Garko LGA, he came to Albasu as a *gardi* (an older *almajiri*), where he then married and stayed. He had farmland, on which his *almajirai* worked, although it was over an hour's walk from the village.

In brief, farmland is still available, though it may not be conveniently located. Yet, while high crop prices have created some new opportunities for farmers, many cannot seize them because they lack capital to buy inputs (Meagher 2001: 51). Non-farm activities – a small shop, some retail sale, a service such as barbering – provide limited opportunities to earn cash, but are bedevilled by the rural population's declining purchasing power, high transport costs, and lack of capital (ibid.). Several young men in Albasu continued to enrol in Qur'anic schools in urban Kano as dry season migrants (*'yan ci rani*) to earn some cash while there was little work to do at home. Even men in their thirties, with wives and children, would engage in such migrations, and sometimes take young boys with them whom they would teach.

Several of the former *almajirai* I got to know had either pursued or were currently pursuing a secular education, which some had already started when young and then interrupted to enrol as *almajirai*. The feasibility of such endeavours depended on whether they had money and time (depending on family obligations and the nature of their income-generating activities), as well as on personal determination. While there are various types of adult education in the form of evening classes on offer in urban Kano, ranging from primary to diploma or degree level, there were few such opportunities in the rural town of Albasu. Aspirants had either to commute (which was costly) or to set themselves up in more urban locales with a *malam* or relatives. I also met a number of former *almajirai* furthering their Islamic education in a formal setting. Two attended the Aminu Kano College of Islamic Legal Studies, which admits students who have memorised the Qur'an in its entirety (*hafiz*) irrespective of whether they hold a secular school certificate. While pursuing 'modern' education gave young men an opportunity to access knowledge they had so far been excluded from, we must keep in mind that, as discussed before, even those with 'modern' degrees struggle to find employment in the formal economy.

The *almajirai*, especially the older ones, were aware that, given the current state of affairs in Kano, it would be difficult for them to realise their aspirations. For instance, after I had interviewed him and other students at Malam Gali's school about their future aspirations (among them working for the government and in government schools), Jamilu (aged 19) queried what the purpose of voicing such high aspirations was, if the government was not going to make capital available. As *almajirai* without *boko* education, there was no way they would be able to accomplish what they had set out for themselves. The *almajirai* at Sabuwar Kofa, who approached me for support for their business ideas, were acutely aware of the difficulties involved in gathering the necessary start-up capital.

Roles and belonging within Nigeria and the Muslim *umma*

Do the *almajirai* become 'loose molecules' (Kaplan 1994) without attachments and beyond social control? Where do they belong when they grow up? What communities do they identify with, and what is their standing within these communities? To what extent can they live up to the expectations of these communities towards them?

Last (2009: 7) writes that 'Muslim northerners have dual citizenship: one in Nigeria, the other in the wider Islamic *umma*'. Within the wider Islamic *umma*, the *almajirai* are struggling to find their feet, given the onslaught on their religious credentials by 'reformist' Muslims. While classical learning still enjoys respect, especially among the rural population, prestige and status increasingly derive from mastering the 'modern' forms of knowledge associated with 'modern' Islamic school-ing. The spiritual services offered by *almajirai* and their *malamai* have attracted harsh criticism as unlawful cultural accretions to Islam. As dis-cussed in Chapter 8, many *almajirai* who have acquired only Qur'anic knowledge aspire to other forms of knowledge (cf. Clough 2009: 602).

What is the *almajirai*'s relationship to the Nigerian state? Many Nige-rians conceive of the *almajirai* as one of the quintessential challenges to a peaceful united Nigeria. What does the situation look like from the *almajirai*'s point of view? How does 'Nigeria' figure in their imagination? To what extent can it mobilise their loyalty?

While there are notable exceptions,[8] most *almajirai* do not get a chance to travel beyond the north of Nigeria, and they have a rather sketchy idea of what life in the south of the country – or beyond – is like. At the risk of stating the obvious, the *almajirai* have few opportunities to engage with avowedly non-Islamic modes of thinking and acting. From a positive point of view, this meant that I was met with overwhelming curiosity and never-ending questions about Christians and Christianity, of which I was taken to be a representative. But Christian-socialised, Hausa-mangling researchers do not often pass by. From a negative point of view, the fact that opportunities to meet the 'other' are rare could mean that *almajirai* (and others) have few, if any, opportunities to experience people of dif-ferent faiths as potentially likeable human beings with similar concerns to their own.

The geographical distance between 'Muslim north' and 'Christian south' explains this only in part. When I discussed interfaith relations with one of the *malamai* in Albasu, for example, he referred to the 'cor-pers' living in Albasu as an example of the way in which Christians resented Muslims in Nigeria. As public health workers, some would deliberately give Muslim children 'bad' injections to harm them, he declared, and they would dart black looks at his school when walking past, disapproving of their studies. His statement is indicative of how the absence of a common language, differences in 'habitus', and badly managed encounters may impede fruitful exchange even when geograph-ical or religious distance is not an issue: most 'corpers' in Albasu were Yoruba Muslims. But as they hardly spoke Hausa, mostly disregarded the local dress code, and lived on the very edge of town, they were poorly integrated into the community, and neither side experienced their pres-ence as particularly desirable or enriching.

---

[8] One of the former *almajirai* I interviewed in Albasu had lived in Lagos with his family when small. Ibrahim, a young aspiring *malam* in Daho, had travelled to Lagos during the previous dry season with other young men from his village. The elderly wives of the *malam* in Daho had been on *hajj* with previous husbands. Malam Ahmadu and his wife had lived in Saudi Arabia for several years.

The statement of one of the youths participating in the film project about a Christian Nigerian who drew public criticism during one of our film shooting sessions is indicative of how the boundaries of the polity or community are drawn. Despite our implorations, the woman had refused to take a break from operating her – very noisy – grinding machine during the moments when we hoped to operate our – very noise-sensitive – camera. When I pointed out to the youth with whom I was discussing the incident afterwards that she also had a right to go about her business undisturbed, he concurred: everyone, even if they were not an *'yar kasa* (a citizen; literally a 'daughter of the soil'), had a right to operate their business. While he pleaded tolerance for the woman, he did not consider her an equal citizen in Kano.

How do *almajirai* experience the Nigerian state in their daily lives? Last (2009: 5) argues that '[t]oday, with no rural taxation, the presence of the Nigerian government isn't so obtrusive' (compared with colonial rule, when taxes were levied more forcefully). By the 1990s, when it had become easier to get rich from oil than from taxing people, 'Nigerian farmers were almost free of "Nigeria"' (ibid.: 5). But since suspicions towards Qur'anic schools have escalated in the context of the current Boko Haram crisis, the state has begun monitoring *almajirai* more closely. Bans on begging have been passed in some states, including Kano, where members of the *Hisbah* religious police have been arresting *almajirai* they find begging. Amnesty International (2015a: 39ff.) has documented indiscriminate raids on Qur'anic schools by security forces in northern Cameroon, and we have reason to suspect that Qur'anic schools in north-eastern Nigeria have not fared any better. The justification Boko Haram leaders put forward for their attacks on primary schools in Borno State was alleged raids of religious schools by security forces (Mohammed 2014: 28).

Are there opportunities for poor youths in general, and *almajirai* in particular, to achieve personal goals through avenues offered by the Nigerian state and to feel politically efficacious? The youths I got to know well did not perceive this to be the case. During the scriptwriting for our film, for example, the participating youths asked why the political leaders of Nigeria did not accord *almajirai* their rights (*'yancinsu*) in the same way that they accorded *boko* school students their rights. '*Almajirai* are citizens [*'yan kasa*] but they are loathed as if they were of no use within the country,' one boy lamented.

'[O]rdinary people can scarcely influence, let alone control, "Nigeria", not even through periodic elections,' Last writes (2009: 3). The *almajirai* did not feel that they had much voice politically. Almost all older *almajirai* I got to know went to vote in the presidential election of 2011, which took place during my fieldwork, but few of them believed that by casting their vote they could make a difference. This feeling became even more pronounced after it became clear that General Muhammadu Buhari, whom most of them had supported, had not been victorious.[9] One of the *almajirai* I was close to, for example, did not go to vote in the gubernatorial election that took place ten days after the presidential election on 16 April 2011 because he was 'angry': since the *manya* (the rich and powerful) had not listened to their will during the presidential election, what was the point of casting his vote again? While my informants greeted Buhari's eventual victory in 2015 with excitement, given his repeated absences from office for medical reasons, and the general deterioration of the economic situation in the north in the wake of the recession, the high hopes placed in his ascent to power have likely been disappointed.

When I expressed surprise about the fact that *almajirai* did not take more frequently to the streets to protest about their poor living conditions,[10] two former *almajirai* in Albasu told me that:

there [referring to Europe], if they make an uproar [*rigima*], they will be given what they want. But here when they protest, it's the poor, some get killed on top ... Uproar is of no use ... You know, the government, they have what they need; they are the rich. If there's protest, they won't come. They won't protest, and their children neither. Necessarily it's the poor and their children who will protest.

Unfortunately, the deaths during the national strike against the fuel subsidy removal in January 2012 did little to reassure ordinary Nigerians that it is possible to register dissent safely. In sum, the *almajirai* (like many others in northern Nigeria) rarely pin their hopes for positive change in their lives on the Nigerian state.

Roles and belonging within the local Hausa community

If we look at the *almajirai's* sense of belonging and ability to meet the expectations of their social environment (or their ability to be at least on a par with their peers), the conclusions are less daunting. Overall, in terms of economic opportunities, little distinguishes young men with an *almajiri* background from other poor young men who have attended, but not necessarily continued in, secular education. Admittedly, the latter

---

[9] General Muhammadu Buhari, who had briefly been in power during military rule from 1983 to 1985 (before being overthrown by General Ibrahim Babangida), ran – unsuccessfully – as a presidential candidate for the CPC (Congress for Progressive Change) in 2011 and – successfully – for the APC (All Progressives Congress) in 2015. In Kano, many people perceived him as a champion of the northern poor.

[10] No data exists about *almajirai's* protest behaviour but popular opinion has it that they have participated in wider popular uprisings, including, for example, the post-election violence in 2011 and the nationwide protests against the removal of the fuel subsidy in January 2012.

will not have such a long road before them if they want to upgrade their secular education to a diploma or degree. A secondary school certificate alone, however, is not an entry ticket to a formal sector job, and makes little difference in the street economy. The brother of Ibrahim (a *gardi* I befriended in Daho), who was a secondary school leaver, worked as an odd-job man at Daho's motor park. His mother lamented that he would not even find the 'cooking money' (*kudin girki*) to feed his wife and children, and depended on his parents' support to survive. Many of the motorbike taxi drivers (*'yan acaba*) who drove me around over the course of my stay in Kano, and to whom I chatted, had high school certificates and even university degrees, but failed to find better-paying jobs.

What do we know about *almajirai* severing ties to their rural homes? I argued in Chapter 6 that, despite opportunities to plunge to some extent into the anonymity offered by a big city, few *almajirai* lose touch completely with their communities of origin. Many authors have shed light on the complexities of rural–urban connections in contemporary Africa and the role such connections play in helping people cope with the adverse effects of economic restructuring (Potts 1995; Geschiere and Gugler 1998; Ferguson 1999). 'Belonging' in this context is not a simple matter of where one resides. Combining sojourns in both rural and urban areas helps the *almajirai* to meet some of the expectations of the local Muslim Hausa community towards them.

Adult members of Muslim Hausa society are expected to marry, and to be married (although their spouses may change) for the rest of their adult lives. The *almajirai* are aware of this expectation. When I explained to Naziru, one of the youths participating in the film project, that I was not planning to get married any time soon and that in Europe people in general tend to marry late, he told me that 'if you are a Muslim, people will insult you if you don't get married'. I did not gain the impression that the *almajirai* considered the expenses associated with the wedding itself particularly daunting: yes, one could spend much money on the handbags, shoes, cosmetics, and cloths given as bride price, but that was *al'ada*, 'custom' or 'culture', and not required from a religious point of view. But to get (and stay!) married, one must have a house, or at least a room, to accommodate a wife (or wives) and children, and if a man cannot provide for his dependants, his marriage is unlikely to last long (cf. Masquelier 2005b on the difficulties young men face in southern Niger).

Interestingly, *almajiri* enrolment – and migration more generally – may offer an opportunity to postpone marriage and the associated obligations. Abba (1983: 198), who interviewed *almajirai* in Kano, cites one respondent as saying that he enrolled as an *almajiri* because 'he wanted to escape early marriage'. The parents of Ibrahim, a young *gardi* I befriended in Daho, wanted their son to marry soon to ensure his good reputation, but he preferred to earn money first so that he could build a decent house. 'Once you are married, trouble has started,' he declared. During his trips to Kano and Lagos, he was safe from parental pressure.

Young men use *almajiri* enrolment not only to set themselves up in urban areas where they are more likely to scrape together the necessary resources to prepare for marriage, but also to sustain families they have already founded. One of the *gardawa* in Malam Ahmadu's school at Sabuwar Ƙofa, who enrolled there during the dry season, for example, approached me asking whether I had any work for him (such as washing and ironing clothes – jobs that could be done outside my compound): he was in urgent need of money to support his wife and child at home. Enrolment as an *almajiri*, by offering at least marginally more opportunities to earn cash than remaining in a rural area, helps young men fulfil their social and religious marriage obligations to some extent.

None of the *gardawa* and graduated *almajirai* I interviewed said that finding a spouse was any easier or more difficult for young men with *almajiri* education than for those without. It is quite common for *malamai* to give their daughters to one of their students in marriage, but as most teachers have far more students than daughters, this is not what happens in most cases. There are also 'alms marriages' (*auren sadaka*), where fathers offer their daughters to a *malam* as a gift (see M. F. Smith 1954; Clough 2009). No marriage payments (*sadaki*) are made in this case, but as only a fraction of former *almajirai* become established scholars, for most *almajirai* an 'alms marriage' is not a likely prospect, and they marry the same way as other rural young men. Women in Albasu mentioned their husbands' educational backgrounds only in passing,[11] and specified whether they had been an *almajiri* only after I enquired. Having an '*almajiri* past' did not seem to mark a man's adult identity in any decisive way.

Almajiri enrolment may help young men live up to the expectations of their rural communities, but how about the *almajirai*'s own expectations? I argued in Chapter 6 that many *almajirai* develop aspirations for urban and cosmopolitan lifestyles that do not fit with what their rural homes can offer. Their proximity to urban lifestyles makes some *almajirai* want to distance themselves from *ƙauyanci*, the rural lifestyle and lack of 'exposure' (*wayo*) of their parents – even though many will have little choice but to return to a rural livelihood themselves. At the same time, the *almajirai*'s relationships with the people in the urban neighbourhoods of their schools also involve tensions. The torrents of abuse that many *almajirai* are exposed to in urban areas may make it difficult for them to feel that they really belong.

<hr />

[11] For example, 'my ex-husband was a student of my father' (who is a *malam*); 'my husband struggles with the ABC'.

A risk or 'at risk'?

What are the implications of their experiences and limited future prospects for the ways in which the *almajirai* engage with the state and the rest of society? I have lamented in various places in this book that the *almajirai* are construed as passive victims, easy to manipulate, and invariably susceptible to 'risk'. Such assumptions find expression, for instance, when people warn that *almajiri* education can 'render [children] pliant, obedient to only one line of command, ready to be unleashed at the rest of society' (Soyinka 2012) or when *almajirai* are described as young people whose 'future . . . is permanently ruined' (Okoye and Yau 1999: 3).

We do have reason to worry about the *almajirai*'s frustration with 'Nigeria', especially in a context where the state's approach towards them is becoming increasingly hostile and aggressive. We also need to be concerned about the extent to which they acquire skills that will allow them to live decent adult lives. The difficulties the *almajirai* face in terms of their daily subsistence, their precarious health situation, and safety concerns related to their presence on the streets and in heavy traffic have been highlighted.

Despite these difficulties, we cannot take it for granted that the *almajirai* succumb to adversity. Young people may prove surprisingly resourceful in navigating risks, and they may thrive even in difficult circumstances. Rather than accepting negative outcomes as inevitable, we should investigate what factors bolster resilience. Moreover, assumptions about the vulnerability of boys and young men growing up in poverty often build on particular conceptions of what constitute risks for them, leaving little room for their own perspectives and experiences (see Boyden 1997 [1990]). A focus on young people's own perceptions, however, can bring to the fore aspects of their lives that are either uncomfortable to outsiders or difficult to spot.

Few people, for example, acknowledge the abuse and denigration the *almajirai* experience in urban areas and in their work roles as domestic helpers. The difficulties in terms of accessing food and cash that the *almajirai* face in rural areas, where they are beyond the gaze of the media and policymakers, go largely unnoticed. Few people are aware of the dynamics that compound the *almajirai*'s low status: the *almajirai* feel that they are held accountable for deeds that, in their view, other urban youths are responsible for. People can offload complaints about the unruly behaviour and petty offences of youths in the neighbourhood on the doorstep of Qur'anic schools without having to enquire any further. Without protectors or guardians close by, the *almajirai* have little chance of standing their ground against accusations they perceive as unfair. As they often lack the power to refute unjustified accusations, these feed negative stereotypes, which may give rise to fresh accusations.

Can the *almajiri* system in its current form ensure sufficient care and supervision for all students? Certain mechanisms ensure a modicum of accountability, such as students' ability to 'vote with their feet' and to change schools. Many *almajirai* own mobile phones today and regularly speak with their parents, though admittedly this is especially the case for older students who are generally less vulnerable than younger ones. Teachers make a strong commitment, not only towards parents but also towards God, to care for the boys entrusted to them (*amana*). Parents choose teachers whom they trust, and often enrol sons alongside older siblings and relatives or other boys from the same village. But there are significant gaps in the system. Parents, for instance, do not necessarily know the *gardawa* or young *malamai* who take their sons on their dry season migratory tours.

The *almajirai* themselves recognise several risks inherent in the setup of their school system, such as the limits to a teacher's accountability where there are large numbers of students or long periods elapsing between direct contact of parents and sons. However, they also locate threats for their moral upbringing in the urban neighbourhoods of their schools, and argue that pitiless employers antagonise *almajirai*, that *'yan daba* lure young *almajirai* into their orbit, or that neighbourhood children distract *almajirai* from their studies by drawing them into their play. These factors rarely figure in outsiders' accounts of what constitute 'risks' for *almajirai*.

This book has argued that we should take seriously young people's own views on their lives and the challenges they face. But we also need to pay due attention to the broader structural inequalities that produce risks and determine their uneven distribution. Structural inequalities make some boys more likely 'candidates' for *almajiri* enrolment than others. A range of cultural and religious considerations motivate parents to enrol sons as *almajirai*. But many poor rural households also opt for the *almajiri* system because they cannot afford to put all their children through 'modern' education, or because 'modern' education occupies children during times when their agricultural labour is needed. When households dissolve due to divorce or parental death, *almajiri* enrolment offers a way out of constrained circumstances.

'Social exclusion', 'adverse incorporation', and young people's 'capacity for action'

Throughout this book, I have shown how ongoing processes of social and economic change in Nigeria do not merely bypass the *almajirai*, but incorporate them in adverse ways. Being confronted with 'modern' models of boyhood and youth (as epitomised by 'modern' schooling), without being able to emulate them, can trigger feelings of inadequacy and exclusion. That 'modern' education (secular and Islamic) has become the privileged route to power and status today makes it difficult for the *almajirai* to conceive of themselves positively. Being close to urban middle classes, moreover, fuels material ambitions and hopes for urban lifestyles. These, however, are difficult to achieve. Population growth and the overall neglect of the agricultural sector have impoverished large parts of the rural population and have increased competition in the urban petty economy. Under these conditions, the *almajirai* struggle to make ends meet. In their work roles as domestic helpers, the *almajirai* are incorporated into the domestic economies of better-off urban households on largely disadvantageous terms. The spiritual economy relegates them to contributory roles in producing other people's better fortunes without giving them much of a share of the outcome. Their low status means that they can easily be used as scapegoats and 'screens' for negative projections. The experiences of the *almajirai* underline the fact that we cannot understand poverty and the processes (re)producing it unless we acknowledge their inherently social nature. As I have argued throughout this book, the *almajirai*'s experiences of exclusion on the one hand, and, on the other, their weak position, for example in domestic economies, in the symbolic realm, and within the spiritual domain, are products of 'the active dynamics of social interaction' (Kabeer 2000: 84).

In the preceding pages, I have shown that the *almajirai* are unlikely to escape poverty as they come of age. This is a consequence not least of the adverse ways in which they are incorporated into society throughout their schooling careers. Close contact with better-off households only rarely translates into opportunities for social mobility; their provision of spiritual services is commodified and hardly rewarded with longer-term patronage. Yet, more positively, we may note that some of the exclusions the *almajirai* experience are temporary, and end once they graduate. Domestic employment is a limited phase. Their chances of marrying and launching adult careers are no worse than those of other poor young men from rural communities. Furthermore, their perseverance through the hardships of an *almajiri* education and acquisition of sacred knowledge may gain them respect in their home communities, even if this is less than would be accorded to a man with extensive 'modern' Islamic knowledge (cf. Clough 2009: 602). Those who have little religious knowledge, whether classical or 'modern' – as is the case for most women – are certainly worse off. These observations highlight the importance of paying close attention to the different degrees and temporalities of disadvantage when using broad concepts such as 'social exclusion' and 'adverse incorporation' to capture experiences of poverty.

What can we learn from looking at the *almajirai* about how poor boys and young men who experience adverse incorporation into society navigate difficult circumstances? What can we learn about how they respond to the risks intrinsic to contexts fraught with inequality, such as experiences of exclusion, and difficult- or impossible-to-achieve aspirations? The *almajirai* reinterpret their deprivation as a voluntary exercise in asceticism that steels their character and trains them to endure hardship. They also conceal the fact that they are poor as much as possible in a context where poverty has unfavourable connotations, a phenomenon I proposed to understand through the Bourdieusian notion of 'symbolic violence'.

The *almajirai*'s ways of engaging with their situation show the dilemmas of young people growing up in poverty and incorporated into mainstream society on adverse terms. As a consequence of adverse 'terms of trade' between recognition and redistribution, the *almajirai*'s concerns with recognition displace demands for redistribution to some extent. In certain circumstances, the *almajirai* reinterpret their deprived circumstances as intentional and educative, or try to hide them altogether, instead of demanding relief.

Paradoxically, by focusing on recognition demands, the *almajirai* risk strengthening 'othering' logics. As the *almajirai* declare themselves to be devoted searchers of sacred knowledge who deliberately forego the presumed comforts of home, they supply the material from which culturalist explanations of the *almajiri* system are constructed. The tale about faithful seekers of knowledge can easily be turned into a tale about parental and religious blockheadedness. This second tale stigmatises the *almajirai* and their parents, and obliterates the economic basis of the *almajiri* system.

Notions of agency as synonymous with resistance to structures of oppression, which have been popular within childhood and youth studies, do not fit the *almajirai*. Undoubtedly, there are instances when the *almajirai* refuse to be reduced to the position of compliant subject, for example when they mobilise religious and moral arguments in their struggles to maintain a positive outlook on themselves and their lives, and they fight to win at least a moral victory over those who denigrate them. Yet, in other instances they comply with power structures that affect them (and others) negatively, for example when they conceal their poverty and reproduce discourses that disparage poor people. These behaviours of the *almajirai* confirm Mahmood's (2001) finding that people's 'capacity for action' is profoundly influenced by their position within relations of domination – and that these relations are difficult to transform from the inside.

Bearing these observations in mind, what can we learn from the *almajirai* about the role of religion in the lives of poor boys and young men? On the occasions when the *almajirai* used religious discourses to justify their destitute circumstances, religion moderated feelings of inadequacy and shame triggered by experiences of exclusion. Former *almajirai* focused on religious achievements rather than economic failure. Simultaneously, however, the *almajirai* aspired to lifestyles not necessarily consistent with such discourses. Rather than striving for dogmatic coherence or consistency, I would argue, the *almajirai* make spontaneous and creative use of the discourses available to them to keep a positive outlook on themselves and their lives in a context where many people despise them. This confirms Masquelier's (2007: 249) observation about youths in Niger that they approach Islam in a pragmatic way that prioritises everyday survival over religious dogmatism. It also buttresses the argument I made in the introduction to this book that studies of Muslims' everyday lives should acknowledge the context-dependent and fragmented nature of pious conduct.

The *almajirai* I got to know well were caught midway between urban, cosmopolitan aspirations, which, however, were difficult or impossible for them to achieve, and discourses that emphasised religious devotion and asceticism, which no longer earned them the same respect or social standing as in the past. Arguably, the *almajirai*'s belief in the promise of an urban, cosmopolitan lifestyle stalls a more thoroughgoing critique both of consumerism and of the terms on which wealthier members of society relate to them. In Chapter 5, I argued that the *almajirai* pin their hopes for social and economic advancement and the realisation of their 'cosmopolitan' dreams on 'good patrons'. Some employers indeed help 'their' *almajirai* achieve social and economic mobility. Knowing of this possibility keeps the *almajirai*'s hopes for a similar opportunity alive, and makes it possible to some extent to treat '[t]he bad boss . . . as an aberration' (Scheper-Hughes 1992: 126). Arguably, this precludes more radical critiques of the highly problematic relationships in which the *almajirai* often find themselves.

Social reproduction, intergenerational change, and the workings of education

How does the *almajirai*'s education system fit into processes of social reproduction? How is it affected by social changes such as large-scale impoverishment and growing disparities in opportunities and wealth, and how does it in turn contribute to such processes? How are the experiences *almajirai* have today different from those of previous generations? Finally, what can we learn from the *almajiri* system about the workings of education in the lives of poor boys and young men more widely?

Historically, the *almajiri* system allowed rural peasant households to raise boys in ways that conformed to norms about their gender-appropriate upbringing and ensured social reproduction. It taught boys agricultural skills during the rainy season, and life and survival skills during the agriculturally idle dry season. Boys learned to subsist on their own in urban areas, and built up connections to draw on when returning to urban areas as dry season migrants later in life. The experiences *almajirai* had while enrolled were sufficiently positive and consistent with the motivations underpinning enrolment that they allowed the educational system to reproduce itself. Most of the fathers of *almajirai* I spoke to had gone through the system themselves. Their experiences as *almajirai* had not discouraged them from enrolling their own sons.

To what extent can enrolment in the *almajiri* system still ensure good outcomes now and in the future for the boys and young men enrolled in it and for society more broadly? What becomes of *almajirai* once they leave the Qur'anic education system? Prognoses are necessarily tentative: the situation in which current *almajirai* will find themselves once they come of age and graduate may well be different from the conditions under which former *almajirai* currently live. But some general conclusions can nevertheless be made.

The spiritual knowledge and skills the *almajirai* acquire are likely to diminish in value as competition from *Islamiyya* school students for prestige and social standing increases. The services in which graduates of the *almajiri* system specialise – the production of spiritual medicines – are becoming increasingly commodified, which means that long-term reciprocal exchange relationships are giving way to one-off transactions that do not provide the *almajirai* with the same livelihood security. In terms of secular skills, many *almajirai* become proficient petty traders, skilled in the art of eking out a living in Kano's urban street economy. While there are exceptions and success stories, competition is tough, and a successful career in trading is difficult for those without access to capital. For most, returning home to rural areas is an option (if not foreclosed by parental death, divorce, or estrangement), but again, without capital to purchase inputs, it is difficult to farm profitably, and rural opportunities to earn non-farm income have, on the whole, declined.

With inequalities on the rise, sojourns in urban areas expose *almajirai* to experiences today that may well be inconsistent with a reproduction of their education system. *Kauyanci* or 'village manners' are looked down upon. Most *almajirai* are well aware that many people equate the *almajiri* system with such rural 'backwardness' and it seems improbable that they would deliberately expose their own sons to such denigration. Being confronted with consumerist attitudes and urban and cosmopolitan lifestyles strains the *almajirai*'s commitment to values such as asceticism and endurance that underpin the *almajiri* system. Finally, living close to children with 'modern' childhoods, who are spared the trouble of earning their own livelihood and who have access to 'modern' education, is likely to affect the *almajirai*. They are aware how crucial 'modern' forms of knowledge – be they religious or secular – are to achieve status today, and many of them aspire to such knowledge themselves.

To use Pierre Bourdieu's terms, as the *almajirai*'s rural 'habitus' encounters a field in which it does not have currency and within which it is looked down upon, it stops being 'like "a fish in water"' (Bourdieu and Wacquant 1992: 127) and change becomes not merely possible but likely. This highlights once more how important it is to look beyond curricula and classrooms to the wider social environments of religious schools if we want to understand what their students learn and what kinds of dispositions they acquire.

In the wake of the socio-economic, religious, and cultural changes described here, the experiences of current *almajirai* are likely to be quite different from the experiences of their fathers' generation. What does this imply for the future of this educational institution, and for the composition of future student generations? I do not think any parent would intentionally exclude his son from knowledge he himself deems essential to succeed in life. However, 'modern' forms of knowledge are inaccessible to many poor children, and it is uncertain whether this will improve in the near future. If it does not, poverty more than anything else will likely determine who enrols their sons as *almajirai*.

The *almajiri* system is often described as a relic from the past that will disappear once the resistance of 'backward' parents against 'modern' developments has been overcome. However, such thinking overlooks the role that current conditions and ongoing social changes play in keeping the system alive and in fuelling demand. As I described in Chapter 4, *almajiri* enrolment provides a solution to some of the challenges of daily subsistence. It helps families cope with seasonal food shortages that are indicative of wider processes of rural impoverishment, and offers a way forward, at least for boys, when households break up as a result of parental death or divorce. Finally, it helps youths and young men earn the cash needed to start or maintain a family. As inequalities in education and wealth are growing on a global scale, it is important to acknowledge that recourse to educational institutions inherited from the past does not necessarily signal a rejection of 'modern' institutions, as often the latter are difficult to access, especially for the poor.

In addition, 'education' is conventionally understood as a preparatory phase whose fruits – in the form of gainful employment – are to be reaped in the future. That *almajiri* education promises few such fruits reinforces the perception that parents enrolling their sons in the system are backward in their aspirations and lack concern for their sons' futures. Such a view, however, fails to acknowledge that 'meritocratic' discourses about 'modern' education as a springboard for social mobility ring hollow in the ears of many poor people. Structural inequalities not only bar many poor children and youths in northern Nigeria, as elsewhere, from accessing meaningful and relevant 'modern' education, but also influence who can translate such an education into gainful opportunities in the future. Furthermore, assessing the *almajiri* system merely with its implications for students' economic futures in mind ignores the fact that the goals pursued through education do not limit themselves to the economic realm, and that people may hold religious education – as well as the pedagogical practices that go with it – in genuine esteem.

While this is an important insight, it leaves us with the question of why high esteem for educational systems that emphasise the acquisition of religious and social rather than economically profitable knowledge and skills often seems to coincide with structural conditions that bar people from accessing alternative options. The Bourdieusian notion of 'habitus' as a repository of societal power relations can offer a fruitful way of approaching this question. Yet, while Bourdieu uses 'habitus' mainly to understand how dominated people participate in reproducing their own subordination by limiting their aspirations, I argue here that if people can be seen to 'make a virtue of necessity' when justifying their educational choices, this does not necessarily imply that their aspirations are limited, nor does it necessarily preclude an awareness of the structural forces creating this necessity in the first place. Finally, if people portray educational choices made in very constraining circumstances as positive decisions taken to honour religious and social commitments rather than dwelling on their material constraints, we have to understand this not least in light of their wider struggles to save face in a context where poor people are frequently looked down upon.

To sum up, while the *almajiri* system is able to ensure good outcomes in the long term only to a limited extent, it helps families deal with the challenges of daily subsistence. It is important to acknowledge not only motivations geared towards the future but also pressing present-day needs when trying to understand child-rearing and educational choices that appear to reproduce disadvantage. I have pursued a similar argument with respect to the *almajirai*'s struggles to maintain a positive sense of self and purpose: ad hoc attempts to fend off assaults on their dignity often take precedence over longer-term strategies to mobilise resources to alleviate their poverty. This may, of course, also result from a realistic assessment of the chances of a politics of poverty succeeding.

Ways forward? Integrating the politics of poverty and of dignity

According to Fraser (1996: 67), the tension between the politics of poverty and the politics of dignity can be resolved if we seek transformative rather than affirmative approaches to redistribution, and if we pursue universalist or deconstructive approaches to recognition rather than differentialist ones. Affirmative distribution risks 'creating stigmatized classes of vulnerable people perceived as beneficiaries of special largesse', singled out not merely 'for material aid but also for public hostility' (ibid.: 46–8). Transformative redistribution, on the other hand, aims to restructure the relations of production so as to address the underlying causes of inequality and injustice. Differentialist recognition can exacerbate cleavages by focusing on what distinguishes certain groups of people from others. Universalist or deconstructive recognition, on the other hand, 'seeks to deconstruct the very terms in which attributed differences are currently elaborated. This type of claim... tends to promote the dedifferentiation of existing social groups, although without necessarily seeking homogeneity' (ibid.: 46–7).

Integrating the politics of poverty and the politics of dignity is not impossible if we are mindful of the imbrication of economy and culture, and of the ways in which redistribution affects recognition and vice versa. Fraser argues that:

> To build broad support for economic transformation today may require first challenging cultural attitudes that demean poor and working people... Likewise, poor and working people may need a counter-'identity politics' to support their struggles for economic justice... a politics of class recognition may be needed both in itself and to get a politics of redistribution off the ground. (ibid.: 19–20)

What do Fraser's considerations imply for how we should best approach the *almajirai*? As long as poverty has such unfavourable connotations in northern Nigeria, the *almajirai* will likely hesitate to emphasise the material reasons for their enrolment in the system. Instead, they are likely to project an image of themselves as zealous seekers of sacred knowledge. Rather than emphasising similarities, such an image foregrounds the differences between *almajirai* and other poor boys and young men. It portrays *almajiri* enrolment as a consequence of particularly strict religious observance and zeal, which presumably sets *almajirai* apart from others. Religious zeal certainly matters for *almajiri* enrolments. But so do poverty and the difficulties poor families face when they seek to ensure their children's 'modern' education.

The boundaries between *almajirai* and other poor boys and youths, then, are less clear-cut than it may seem at first sight. Boys move back and forth between different educational options depending on personal and family circumstances. Few boys are 'pure' products of the *almajiri* system. In a way, the *almajirai* epitomise larger problematic trends that affect most poor boys and young men in northern Nigeria, whether or not they currently live as *almajirai*. In addition, many of the trends affecting the *almajirai* negatively take an even heavier toll on girls, whose education is likely to be of lower priority to families than that of boys, and whose status is generally lower than that of their male counterparts. The escalating costs and deteriorating quality of 'modern' education are likely to influence the schooling trajectories and future prospects of most children in northern Nigeria. High divorce and maternal mortality rates affect not only *almajirai*, and the same is true of precarious livelihoods and a largely deteriorating rural economy.

What does this imply? Portraying the *almajirai* as a distinct social category suggests that the 'problem' they pose can be solved through specially tailored interventions: a ban on the system, or the construction of '*Almajiri* Model Schools'. Yet, such an approach neither acknowledges nor addresses the broader problematic trends in northern Nigeria that affect all poor young people, even though these trends underpin the enrolment of boys and youths as *almajirai*. It is important to address the difficulties faced by boys and young men currently enrolled as *almajirai*. But it is also important to think about the factors that cause enrolment.

Reiterating Fraser (1996: 46), affirmative approaches to redistribution carry the risk of singling out their beneficiaries not merely 'for material aid but also for public hostility'. President Goodluck Jonathan's announcement that '*Almajiri* Model Schools' would be built sparked considerable resentment in some online forums (see Chapter 2). There is a constant tension between recognising the *almajirai* as a group in need of support, and exposing them to people's resentment as 'undeserving' scroungers. It will only be possible to escape this tension through a deconstruction of discourses that stigmatise poor people, including the *almajirai*. To date, however, given their weak social position, the *almajirai*'s demands for recognition aim lower than that.

In a context where recognition is accorded on the basis of the social structure one belongs to, *almajirai* demand that their belonging be recognised. They want to be recognised as *'yan ƙasa*, as citizens (literally, 'sons of the soil') who deserve the same rights (*'yanci*) as 'modern' school students (*'yan boko*). They aim to counter assaults on their dignity by asserting that they have supporters and protectors just like others. The *almajirai*'s claims are based on social logics that primarily entitle respect to those who can produce evidence of belonging and support or protection. Rather than challenging the grounds on which status categories are currently elaborated, the *almajirai* claim to fall within the category accorded status and respect. Yet, status categories built on people's ability to produce evidence of belonging and support disregard those who fail to produce such evidence. To really improve the situation of *almajirai*, and that of others who are socially excluded, it is thus necessary to fight the stigma attached to poverty, and to promote respect on the basis of one's worth as a human being rather than as a function of one's position within social hierarchies.

Annex
Synopsis of '*Duniya Juyi Juyi* – How Life Goes'

Docudrama by and about *almajirai*
69 minutes, Hausa with English subtitles

The Hausa term *almajiri* derives from the Arabic *al-muhajir*, which means 'migrant'. Some people also say the syllable 'Al' stands for Allah, while 'Ma' stands for the Prophet Muhammad (S.A.W.), and 'Jiri' for the archangel Jibril. The *almajirai* are boys and young men from primary school age to their early twenties who have come to the cities and villages in northern Nigeria to study the Qur'an. The *almajirai* do not stay with their parents, most of whom reside in rural areas, but live with their Qur'anic teacher (*malam*).

'Modern' subjects do not form part of their curriculum. Instead, the *almajirai* learn to read, write, and recite the Qur'an. During the lesson-free time, they earn their livelihood: older students (*gardawa*) do menial jobs and engage in petty trade or handicrafts. Younger students work as household helps, or beg for food and money on the streets, which makes them a highly visible feature of the urban landscape.

While many people hold strong views about the *almajiri* system, sadly, the *almajirai* themselves are rarely listened to. This film hopes to offer an insight into their perspectives and concerns. Nine young people from three different Qur'anic schools in Kano State have been trained to write the script for this film, to do most of the acting, to handle the camera, and to give the stage directions. This film shows their views and experiences they had while living as *almajirai* in Kano.

Main cast and credits

Crew

Director	Abdullahi Yahaya Sa'ad
Assistant Director	Buhari Murtala
Cameraman	Sadisu Salisu
Assistant Cameraman	Muhammad Naziru Usman
Lighting	Kabiru Idris
Location Manager	Auwalu Mahamud
Welfare Officer	Isma'il Abdullahi
Continuity Officer	Anas Ali
Script Consultant	Nasiru Bappah Muhammad
Editor	Auwal K Indabawa
Producer, Subtitles	Hannah Hoechner
Executive Producer	Frank Roger
Music	Nura Nash
Sound	Rabi'u Dalle

Cast

Aminu	*Aminu*	Ikiramatu Mukhtar
Baban Aminu	*Aminu's father*	Sani Garba SK
Babar Aminu	*Aminu's mother*	Zuwaira Abdulsalam
Malam	*Qur'anic teacher*	Husaini Sule Koki
Shafi'u	*Shafi'u*	Muhammad Naziru Usman
Ibrahim	*Ibrahim*	Auwalu Mahamud
Uwar dakin Aminu	*Aminu's employer*	Lubabatu Madaki
Matar kwamishina	*Commissioner's wife*	Maryam Sulaiman
Kanin baban Aminu	*Aminu's uncle*	Auwal K Indabawa
Mai shago	*Shop owner*	Mustapha Musty
Yara na rijiya	*Children at the well*	Salisu Iliyasu, Inusa Ali
Tsohuwa	*Old woman*	Abu Dan Shamaki
Kananan almajirai na karatu	*Small almajirai reading*	Kabiru Yahaya, Husaini Yahaya, Adamu Dahiru, Yunusa Dahiru, Dahiru Abubakar, Yakubu Husaini, Hamza Yahaya, Shafi'u Sa'idu, Gazzali Adamu, Sadiq Adamu, Aliyu Musa, Musubahu Sulaiman, Inusa Muhammad
Gardawa biyu	*Two older almajirai*	Buhari Murtala, Abdullahi Yahaya Sa'ad
Mai gadi	*Guard*	Sadisu Salisu
Yaron shago	*Shop assistant*	Anas Ali
Gardawa na nasiha	*Older almajirai being given advice*	Yahaya Abdullahi, Muhammad Abba, Isma'il Abdullahi, Auwalu Mahamud, Naziru Usman, Kabiru Idris

Yaro na shago	*Boy in the shop*	Aminu Shu'aibu
'Ya 'yan uwar ɗakin Aminu	*Children of Aminu's employer*	Sulaiman Usman, Ruƙayya Matawalle
Yaro mai wulaƙanta almajiri	*Boy insulting almajirai*	Nura Yusuf
Yayar yaron mai wulaƙanta almajiri	*Sister of boy insulting almajirai*	Maimuna Yusuf
Almajirai na gurin kwana	*Almajirai at sleeping place*	Hamisu Yahaya, Shu'aibu Aliyu, Isma'il Abdullahi, Naziru Usman, Auwalu Mahamud
Almajirai na langa	*Almajirai playing jumping game*	Yakubu Tasi'u, Kamisu Sani, Bashir Adamu, Gazali Adamu, Kabiru Idris
Ma'tafiyan kan hanya	*People passing by*	Bashir Al'asan, Sani Usman
Yaro mai karyayyen Allo	*Boy with broken slate*	Gambo Sulaiman
Almajirai na nasiha	*Almajirai being given advice*	Muhammad Aminu, Shafi'u Musa, Fahad Saminu, Yakubu Husaini, Auwalu Mahamud, Naziru Usman, Iƙira Mukhtar, Yahaya Abdullahi, Aliyu Umar

A project of Goethe-Institut Kano in collaboration with Child *Almajiri* Empowerment and Support Initiative (CAESI), Kano/Nigeria
© **Goethe-Institut 2011**

Glossary and abbreviations

Glossary

addini	religion in an applied sense (Hausa)
addu'a	purposive prayer/supplication (Hausa)
allo	wooden board on which the Qur'an is written (Hausa)
almajirci or *almajiranci*	discipleship, practice of living as an *almajiri* (Hausa)
almajiri, pl.: *almajirai*	full time male Qur'anic student (Hausa)
bara	begging for alms (Hausa)
bid'a	unlawful innovation in religious practices (Arabic)
boko	'modern' secular education; can also mean sham/pseudo (Hausa)
Boko Haram	name commonly used to refer to the militant Islamists battling the Nigerian state since 2009, translated by most commentators as 'Western education is forbidden'
ci rani	dry season migration; literally 'to eat away the dry season' (Hausa)
corper	member of the National Youth Service Corps
Eid al-Fitr	major Muslim holiday, feast at the end of Ramadan (Arabic)
Eid al-Kabir / Eid al-Adha	major Muslim holiday, feast of the sacrifice (Arabic)
gardi, pl: *gardawa*	older student of Qur'anic school/assistant teacher (Hausa)
gata	guardian/protector; someone you can legitimately expect to stand up for you and provide financially for you (Hausa)
hadith, pl.: *ahadith*	traditions of the Prophet Muhammad (Arabic)
Hakimi	District Head, traditional title (Hausa)
hakuri	patience, endurance (Hausa)
Hausa	lingua franca of northern Nigeria

Hausaland	area of northern Nigeria and south-eastern Niger inhabited by people for whom Hausa is a first language
hijrah	migration of the Prophet Mohammed and his followers from Mecca to Medina (Arabic)
Islamiyya school	'modern' Islamic school; school using 'modern' teaching technologies, including classrooms, desks, chairs, books, age grading, and certification
Izala	short for *Jama'at Izalat al-Bid'a wa-Iqamat al-Sunna* (Arabic, 'Society for Removing Heretical Innovation and Establishing the Sunna')
jama'a	community, congregation (Hausa, Arabic loanword)
karatu	reading, studies, often used to refer to Qur'anic studies (Hausa)
kunya	shame in the sense of modesty, self-restraint or shyness, referring to behaviour considered appropriate to one's age, gender, and social status (Hausa)
kolo	young *almajiri*-ship, term used to refer to the experiences particularly of young *almajirai* (Hausa)
magani	medicine, remedy (Hausa)
makarantar allo, pl.: *makarantun allo*	classical Qur'anic school (literally 'wooden board school') (Hausa)
malam, pl.: *malamai*	Qur'anic teacher, honorific form of address (Hausa)
maula	begging, especially by small children on the roads, at traffic junctions, petrol stations or motor parks (Hausa)
miya	stew (made, for example, of Baobab tree leaves, okra, or pumpkin and spinach) to be eaten with cereal porridge (*tuwo*) (Hausa)
Naira	Nigerian currency, US\$1 ≈ 165 Naira (in 2011)
purdah	female seclusion
Qadiriyya	one of the two strongest Sufi orders in northern Nigeria
qirā'a	Qur'anic recitation style (Arabic)
rubutun sha	spiritual medicine produced by writing certain Qur'anic verses on a wooden board to be washed off and drunk (Hausa)

Sabuwar Ƙofa	New Gate (one of the gates in the city wall surrounding the Old City of Kano)
sadaka	alms, charity (Hausa)
Sallah	prayer (referring to the five daily prayers); term also used for either of the two major Muslim holidays *Eid al-Fitr* and *Eid al-Kabir* (Hausa)
sauka	graduation, usually referring to a student's 'first' graduation (when he has mastered reading, writing, and reciting the entire Qur'an; at this stage most students will have memorised at least some of the surahs of the Qur'an); a student does his 'second' *sauka* (rare) after he has learned to recite the entire Qur'an from memory, and his 'third' *sauka* (even rarer) when he can write the entire Qur'an from memory (Hausa)
shari'a	religious legal, civic, and social code in Islam based on the Qur'an, sayings of the Prophet Mohammed, and judgements of Islamic scholars
soro	entrance room to a house/compound, especially a concrete building (Hausa)
tafsīr	Qur'anic exegesis (Arabic)
Tahfeez school	'modernised' Qur'anic school, which uses 'modern' teaching technologies but has largely retained the heavy emphasis on Qur'anic memorisation common in classical Qur'anic schools
tajwīd	rules of pronunciation and recitation of the Qur'an (Arabic)
takfīr	excommunication (Arabic)
talaka, pl.: *talakawa*	poor person, commoner (Hausa)
talibé	full-time male Qur'anic student (Wolof)
tarbiyya	character training, 'good upbringing', moral education (Hausa, Arabic loanword)
tariqa	a Sufi order (Arabic)
Tijaniyya	one of the two strongest Sufi orders in northern Nigeria
tsangaya, pl.: *tsangayu*	classical Qur'anic school located in a remote area (literally 'a hamlet') (Hausa)
tuwo	cereal porridge, usually eaten with a vegetable stew (*miya*) (Hausa)
'ulama, sg.: 'alim	class of religious scholars (Arabic)

umma	Muslim community/community of believers (Arabic)
zakat	obligatory alms, 2.5 per cent of a person's net worth annually (Arabic)

Abbreviations

APC	All Progressives Congress
CAESI	Child *Almajiri* Empowerment and Support Initiative (a Kano-based NGO aiming to extend support to *almajirai*)
CPC	Congress for Progressive Change
DfID	Department for International Development (UK Government Department)
ESSPIN	Education Sector Support Programme in Nigeria (DfID-funded)
JSS	junior secondary school
LGA	Local Government Area (administrative unit below the state level)
NAPTIP	National Agency for the Prohibition of Trafficking in Persons
NYSC	National Youth Service Corps (community service performed by recent university graduates)
SSS	senior secondary school
UBE	Universal Basic Education
UPE	Universal Primary Education
VSO	Voluntary Service Overseas (international development charity)

Bibliography

Abba, I. A. 1983. 'Bara by some almajirai in Kano City in the twentieth century: a critical assessment' in B. M. Barkindo (ed.), *Studies in the History of Kano*. Ibadan: Heinemann, pp. 193–206.

Abbink, J. and van Kessel, I. 2005. *Vanguard or Vandals: youth, politics, and conflict in Africa*. Leiden: Brill.

Abdu, L., Withers, J., Habib, A. G., Mijinyawa, M. S. and Yusef, S. M. 2013. 'Disease pattern and social needs of street people in the Race Course area of Kano, Nigeria', *Journal of Health Care for the Poor and Underserved* 24 (1): 97–105.

Abdurrahman, A. M. and Canham, P. 1978. *The Ink of the Scholar: the Islamic tradition of education in Nigeria*. Lagos: Macmillan Nigeria.

Abubakar, A. 2009. 'Nigeria struggles to curb rise in child beggars', *Telegraph*, 18 November.

Adams, K. M. and Dickey, S. 2000. *Home and Hegemony: domestic service and identity politics in South and Southeast Asia*. Ann Arbor: University of Michigan Press.

Adedibu, A. A. and Jelili, M. O. 2011. 'Characteristics and types of beggars in Nigerian cities: implications for public policy', *Centrepoint Journal (Humanities Edition)* 14 (1): 144–67.

Aderinoye, R. 2007. *Nigeria Non-formal Education. Country profile prepared for the Education for All Global Monitoring Report 2008. Education for All by 2015: will we make it?* Paris: UNESCO.

Adetayo, O. and Alechenu, J. 2012. 'Growing almajiri population dangerous to national devt – Jonathan', *Punch*, 11 April.

Admassie, A. 2003. 'Child labour and schooling in the context of a subsistence rural economy: can they be compatible?', *International Journal of Educational Development* 23 (2): 167–85.

Aghedo, I. and Eke, S. J. 2013. 'From alms to arms: the almajiri phenomenon and internal security in Nigeria', *Korean Journal of Policy Studies* 28 (3): 97–123.

Ajeigbe, H. A., Mohammed, S. G., Adeosun, J. O. and Ihedioha, D. 2010. *Farmers' Guide to Increased Productivity of Improved Legume: cereal cropping systems in the savannas of Nigeria*. Ibadan, Nigeria: International Institute of Tropical Agriculture.

Al-Qaradawi, Y. 1994. *The Problem of Poverty and How it was Treated by Islam*, 10th edn. Beirut: Al-Rissala Foundation.

235

Alabo-George, R. 2012. 'Derivation and deprivation: why the north is poor', *Vanguard*, 4 March.

Alderson, P. 2001. 'Research by children', *International Journal of Social Research Methodology* 4 (2): 139–53.

Aliyu, S. 2011. 'Kwankwaso cancels five-day Sallah festivity', *Daily Trust*, 31 August.

Allen, C. 1995. 'Understanding African politics', *Review of African Political Economy* 65: 301–20.

Alonso, W. and Starr, P. 1987. *The Politics of Numbers*. New York: Russell Sage Foundation.

Aluaigba, M. T. 2009. 'Circumventing or superimposing poverty on the African child? The almajiri syndrome in Northern Nigeria', *Childhood in Africa* 1 (1): 1–37.

Amnesty International. 2015a. *Human Rights under Fire: attacks and violations in Cameroon's struggle with Boko Haram*. London: Amnesty International.

Amnesty International. 2015b. *'Our Job Is To Shoot, Slaughter and Kill.' Boko Haram's reign of terror in north-east Nigeria*. London: Amnesty International.

Amzat, J. 2008. 'Lumpen childhood in Nigeria: a case of the almajirai in Northern Nigeria', *Hemispheres* 23: 55–66.

Anonymous. 2012. 'The popular discourses of Salafi radicalism and Salafi counter-radicalism in Nigeria: a case study of Boko Haram', *Journal of Religion in Africa* 42: 118–44.

Anti-Slavery International 2003. *Projet Sous-Régional de Lutte contre le Travail et le Trafic des Enfants Domestiques*. London: Anti-Slavery International.

Antoninis, M. 2012. 'Tackling the largest global education challenge? Secular and religious education in northern Nigeria'. CSAE Working Paper No. 17. Oxford: Centre for the Study of African Economies, University of Oxford.

Appadurai, A. 2004. 'The capacity to aspire: culture and the terms of recognition' in V. Rao and M. Walton (eds), *Culture and Publication*. Stanford, CA: Stanford University Press, pp. 59–84.

Archer, L. and Francis, B. 2006. 'Challenging classes? Exploring the role of social class within the identities and achievement of British Chinese pupils', *Sociology* 40 (1): 29–49.

Arewa House. 2000. *Towards the Improvement of Education in the Northern States of Nigeria. Agenda for action*. Northern Education Research Project. Kaduna, Nigeria: Arewa House.

Asad, T. 2000. 'Agency and pain: an exploration', *Culture and Religion* 1 (1): 29–60.

Awofeso, N., Ritchie, J. and Degeling, P. 2003. 'The almajiri heritage and the threat of non-state terrorism in Northern Nigeria: lessons from Central Asia and Pakistan', *Studies in Conflict and Terrorism* 26 (4): 311–25.

Ayuba, A. 2012. 'Almajiri: a national emergency (1). Opinion', *Leadership*, 9 April.

Baba, N. M. 2011. 'Islamic schools, the ulama, and the state in the educational development of Northern Nigeria', *Bulletin de L'APAD* 33: 39–59.

Bambale, A. J. 2007. 'Almajiranchi and the problem of begging in Kano State: the role of Shekarau Administration (2003–2007)'. Paper presented at the 7th BEN Africa Annual Conference, Addis Ababa, Ethiopia, 1–3 August.

Bano, M. 2012. *The Rational Believer: choices and decisions in the madrassas of Pakistan*. Ithaca: Cornell University Press.

Bano, M., Antonisis, M. and Ross, J. 2011. *Islamiyya, Qur'anic and Tsangaya Education Institutions Census in Kano State. Final draft report.* Kano, Nigeria: Education Sector Support Programme in Nigeria.

Barker, J. and Weller, S. 2003. '"Is it fun?" Developing children-centered research methods', *International Journal of Sociology and Social Policy* 23 (1/2): 33–58.

Bauman, Z. 1990. 'Modernity and ambivalence', *Theory, Culture and Society* 7 (2): 143–69.

Bayat, A. and Herrera, L. 2010. *Being Young and Muslim: new cultural politics in the global south and north.* Oxford: Oxford University Press.

Becker, G. 1993 [1964]. *Human Capital: a theoretical and empirical analysis, with special reference to education.* London: University of Chicago Press.

Behrend, H. 2000. '"Feeling global": the Likoni Ferry photographers of Mombasa, Kenya', *African Arts* 33 (3): 70–7.

Bell, D. 2015. 'Choosing *medersa*: discourses on secular versus Islamic education in Mali, West Africa', *Africa Today* 61 (3): 45–63.

Berger, P. 1967. *The Sacred Canopy: elements of a sociological theory of religion.* Garden City, NY: Doubleday.

Bilkisu, H. 2011. 'UBEC's almajiri education agenda', *Daily Trust*, 13 January.

Bin Omar, A. 1993. 'In Quest of an Islamic Ideal of Education: A study of the role of the traditional Pondok institution in Malaysia'. PhD thesis, Temple University, Philadelphia.

Bledsoe, C. H. 1990. '"No success without struggle": social mobility and hardship for foster children in Sierra Leone', *Man* 25 (1): 70–88.

Bledsoe, C. H. and Robey, K. M. 1986. 'Arabic literacy and secrecy among the Mende of Sierra Leone', *Man (New Series)* 21 (2): 202–26.

Bonner, M. 2005. 'Poverty and economics in the Qur'an', *Journal of Interdisciplinary History* 35 (3): 391–406.

Bordonaro, L. I. 2012. 'Agency does not mean freedom: Cape Verdean street children and the politics of children's agency', *Children's Geographies* 10 (4): 413–26.

Bordonaro, L. I. and Payne, R. 2012. 'Ambiguous agency: critical perspectives on social interventions with children and youth in Africa', *Children's Geographies* 10 (4): 365–72.

Bourdieu, P. 1971. 'Genèse et structure du champ religieux', *Revue française de sociologie* 12 (3): 295–334.

Bourdieu, P. 1984. *Distinction: a social critique of the judgement of taste.* London: Routledge.

Bourdieu, P. 1988. 'Vive la crise! For heterodoxy in social science', *Theory and Society* 19 (5): 773–88.

Bourdieu, P. 1990a. *The Logic of Practice.* Cambridge: Polity Press.

Bourdieu, P. 1990b. *In Other Words: essays towards a reflexive sociology.* Cambridge: Polity Press.

Bourdieu, P. and Passeron, J.-C. 1990 [1977]. *Reproduction in Education, Society and Culture.* London: Sage.

Bourdieu, P. and Wacquant, L. 1992. *An Invitation to Reflexive Sociology.* Oxford: Polity Press and Blackwell.

Bourdieu, P. and Wacquant, L. 2004. 'Symbolic violence' in N. Scheper-Hughes and P. Bourgois (eds), *Violence in War and Peace.* Malden, MA: Blackwell, pp. 272–4.

Bourdillon, M. 2009. 'Children as domestic employees: problems and promises', *Journal of Children and Poverty* 15 (1): 1–18.

Bourgois, P. I. 1995. *In Search of Respect: selling crack in El Barrio. Structural analysis in the social sciences.* Cambridge: Cambridge University Press.

Boyd, J. and Last, M. 1985. 'The role of women as "agents religieux" in Sokoto', *Canadian Journal of African Studies* 19 (2): 283–300.

Boyden, J. 1997 [1990]. 'Childhood and the policy makers: a comparative perspective on the globalization of childhood' in A. James and A. Prout (eds), *Constructing and Reconstructing Childhood: contemporary issues in the sociological study of childhood*, 2nd edn. London: Falmer Press, pp. 190–229.

Boyden, J. and Cooper, E. 2007. 'Questioning the power of resilience: are children up to the task of disrupting the transmission of poverty?' CPRC Working Paper No. 73. Oxford: Chronic Poverty Research Centre/Young Lives, Oxford Department of International Development.

Boyden, J. and Ennew, J. 1997. *Children in Focus: a manual for participatory research with children.* Stockholm: Rädda Barnen.

Boyden, J., Ling, B. and Myers, W. E. 1998. *What Works for Working Children.* Stockholm: Rädda Barnen.

Boyle, H. N. 2004. *Quranic Schools: agents of preservation and change.* London: Routledge Falmer.

Bracking, S. 2003. 'The political economy of chronic poverty'. CPRC Working Paper No. 23. Manchester: Chronic Poverty Research Centre, University of Manchester.

Bray, M. 1981. *Universal Primary Education in Nigeria: a study of Kano State.* London: Routledge and Kegan Paul.

Bray, R. 2003. 'Predicting the social consequences of orphanhood in South Africa'. CSSR Working Paper No. 29. Cape Town: Centre for Social Science Research, University of Cape Town.

Brenner, L. 2000. *Controlling Knowledge: religion, power and schooling in a West African Muslim society.* London: Hurst and Co.

Brenner, L. 2007. 'The transformation of Muslim schooling in Mali: the madrasa as an institution of social and religious mediation' in R. W. Hefner and M. Q. Zaman (eds), *Schooling Islam: the culture and politics of modern Muslim education.* Princeton, NJ: Princeton University Press, pp. 199–223.

Brenner, L. and Last, M. 1985. 'The role of language in West African Islam', *Africa* 55 (4): 432–46.

Brigaglia, A. 2005. 'Two published Hausa translations of the Qur'an and their doctrinal background', *Journal of Religion in Africa* 35 (4): 424–49.

Brigaglia, A. 2007. 'The Radio Kaduna Tafsir (1978–1992) and the construction of public images of Muslim scholars in the Nigerian media', *Journal for Islamic Studies* 27: 173–210.

Brigaglia, A. 2008. '"We ain't coming to take people away": a Sufi praise-song and the representation of police forces in Northern Nigeria', *Annual Review of Islam in Africa* 10: 50–7.

Brigaglia, A. 2009. 'Learning, gnosis and exegesis: public tafsīr and Sufi revival in the city of Kano (Northern Nigeria), 1950–1970', *Die Welt des Islams* 49: 334–66.

Brigaglia, A. 2012. 'A contribution to the history of the Wahhabi da'wa in West Africa: the career and the murder of Shaykh Ja'far Mahmoud Adam (Daura, ca. 1961/1962–Kano 2007)', *Islamic Africa* 3 (1): 1–23.

Brigaglia, A. 2015. 'The volatility of Salafi political theology, the war on terror and the genesis of Boko Haram', *Diritto e Questioni Pubbliche* 15 (2):
175–201.
British Council and Harvard School of Public Health 2010. 'Nigeria: the next
generation report'. PGDA Working Paper No. 62. Boston, MA: Program on
the Global Demography of Aging, University of Harvard.
Butler, N. 2006. 'Costs of knowledge: some economic underpinnings of spiritual relations in Islam in Niger' in N. Dannhaeuser and C. Werner (eds),
Markets and Market Liberalization: ethnographic reflections. Oxford: Elsevier,
pp. 309–28.
Butler, N. 2016. 'Collapsed pluralities: Islamic education, learning, and creativity in Niger' in R. Launay (ed.), *Islamic Education in Africa: writing boards and blackboards*. Bloomington, IN: University of Indiana Press,
pp. 285–306.
Callaway, B. J. 1987. *Muslim Hausa Women in Nigeria: tradition and change*. New
York: Syracuse University Press.
Casey, C. 2007. '"Policing" through violence: fear, vigilantism, and the politics
of Islam in northern Nigeria' in D. Pratten and A. Sen (eds), *Global Vigi-
lantes*. London: Hurst, pp. 93–124.
Casey, C. 2008. '"Marginal Muslims": politics and the perceptual bounds
of Islamic authenticity in Northern Nigeria', *Africa Today* 54 (3): 67–
92.
Chabal, P. and Daloz, J.-P. 1999. *Africa Works: disorder as political instrument*.
Oxford: James Currey.
Chambers, R. 1983. *Rural Development: putting the last first*. Harlow: Longman
Scientific and Technical.
Chambers, R. 1997. *Whose Reality Counts?: putting the first last*. London: Inter-
mediate Technology Publications.
Chase, E. and Walker, R. 2013. 'The co-construction of shame in the context of
poverty: beyond a threat to the social bond', *Sociology* 47: 739–54.
Cheeseman, N. 2006. 'The Rise and Fall of Civil-authoritarianism in Africa:
patronage, participation, and political parties in Kenya and Zambia'. PhD
thesis, Department of Politics and International Relations, University of
Oxford.
Christiansen, C., Utas, M. and Vigh, H. E. (eds). 2006. *Navigating Youth, Gen-
erating Adulthood: social becoming in an African context*. Uppsala: Nordiska
Afrikainstitutet.
Clough, P. 1981. 'Farmers and traders in Hausaland', *Development and Change*
12: 273–92.
Clough, P. 2009. 'The impact of rural political economy on gender relations in
Islamizing Hausaland, Nigeria', *Africa* 79 (4): 595–613.
COCFOCAN. n.d. 'The child-almajiri'. Kano, Nigeria: Coalition of Commu-
nity Based Organizations Focused on Child Almajiri in Nigeria.
Cohen, S. 2002 [1972]. *Folk Devils and Moral Panics: the creation of the mods and
rockers*. London: Routledge.
Cole, J. 2004. 'Fresh contact in Tamatave, Madagascar: sex, money, and intergenerational transformation', *American Ethnologist* 31 (4): 573–88.
Comaroff, J. and Comaroff, J. L. 1999. 'Occult economies and the violence of
abstraction: notes from the South African postcolony', *American Ethnologist*
26 (2): 279–303.

Comaroff, J. and Comaroff, J. L. 2006. 'Reflections on youth, from the past to the postcolony' in M. S. Fisher and G. Downey (eds), *Frontiers of Capital: ethnographic reflections on the new economy*. Durham, NC: Duke University Press, pp. 267–81.

Connell, R. W. and Messerschmidt, J. W. 2005. 'Hegemonic masculinity: rethinking the concept', *Gender and Society* 19 (6): 829–59.

Connolly, P. 1998. *Racism, Gender Identities and Young Children: social relations in a multi-ethnic, inner-city primary school*. London: Routledge.

Cooke, B. and Kothari, U. 2001. *Participation: the new tyranny?* London: Zed Books.

Cornwall, A. and Lindisfarne, N. 1994. 'Dislocating masculinity: gender, power and anthropology' in A. Cornwall and N. Lindisfarne (eds), *Dislocating Masculinity: comparative ethnographies*. London and New York: Routledge, pp. 11–47.

Crick, M. 1992. 'Ali and me: an essay in street-corner anthropology' in J. Okely and H. Callaway (eds), *Anthropology and Autobiography*. London: Routledge, pp. 175–92.

Crivello, G. 2009. '"Becoming somebody": youth transitions through education and migration – evidence from Young Lives, Peru'. Working Paper No. 43. Oxford: Young Lives, Department of International Development, University of Oxford.

Cruise O'Brien, D. B. 1971. *The Mourides of Senegal: the political and economic organisation of an Islamic brotherhood*. Oxford: Clarendon Press.

Csapo, M. 1983. 'Universal primary education in Nigeria: its problems and implications', *African Studies Review* 26 (1): 91–106.

Damen, J. G., Luka, J., Biwan, E. I. and Lugos, M. 2011. 'Prevalence of intestinal parasites among pupils in rural North Eastern Nigeria', *Nigerian Medical Journal* 52 (1): 4–6.

Dan-Asabe, A. U. 1991. 'Yandaba: the "terrorists" of Kano Metropolitan?' in M. Last (ed.), *Kano Studies: youth and health in Kano today*. Kano, Nigeria: Bayero University, pp. 85–111.

De Boeck, F. and Honwana, A. 2005. 'Children and youth in Africa: agency, identity, and place' in A. Honwana and F. De Boeck (eds), *Makers and Breakers: children and youth in postcolonial Africa*. Oxford, Trenton, NJ and Dakar: James Currey, Africa World Press and CODESRIA, pp. 1–19.

de Haan, A. 1998. '"Social exclusion": an alternative concept for the study of deprivation?', *IDS Bulletin* 29 (1): 10–19.

de Haan, A. 2011. 'Social exclusion and the road not taken: an insider account of conceptual travel within development practice'. CPRC Working Paper No. 218. Manchester: Chronic Poverty Research Centre, University of Manchester.

Deakin, N., Davis, A. and Thomas, N. 1995. *Public Welfare Services and Social Exclusion: the development of consumer-oriented initiatives in the European Union*. Dublin: European Foundation for the Improvement of Living and Working Conditions.

Demerath, P. 1999. 'The cultural production of educational utility in Pere Village, Papua New Guinea', *Comparative Education Review* 43 (2): 162–92.

Demerath, P. 2000. 'The social cost of acting "extra": students' moral judgments of self, social relations, and academic success in Papua New Guinea', *American Journal of Education* 108 (3): 196–235.

Department of State. 2009. *Trafficking in Persons Report*. Washington, DC: US Department of State.

Dickey, S. 2000. 'Permeable homes: domestic service, household space, and the vulnerability of class boundaries in urban India', *American Ethnologist* 27 (2): 462–89.

Dilger, H. and Schulz, D. 2013. 'Politics of religious schooling: Christian and Muslim engagements with education in Africa. Introduction', *Journal of Religion in Africa* 43: 365–78.

Diouf, M. 1996. 'Urban youth and Senegalese politics: Dakar 1988–1994', *Public Culture* 8: 225–49.

Dobronravine, N. and Philips, J. E. 2004. 'Hausa Ajami literature and script: colonial innovations and post-colonial myths in Northern Nigeria', *Sudanic Africa* 15: 85–110.

Dore, R. 1976. *The Diploma Disease: education, qualification and development*. Berkeley: University of California Press.

Dos Santos, T. 1970. 'The structure of dependence', *American Economic Review* 60 (2): 231–6.

Douglas, M. 2001 [1966]. *Purity and Danger: an analysis of the concepts of pollution and taboo*. London: Routledge.

du Toit, A. 2005. 'Forgotten by the highway: globalisation, adverse incorporation and chronic poverty in a commercial farming district'. CPRC Working Paper No. 49. Manchester: Chronic Poverty Research Centre, University of Manchester.

Durham, D. 2004. 'Disappearing youth: youth as a social shifter in Botswana', *American Ethnologist* 31 (4): 589–605.

Durham, D. 2008. 'Apathy and agency: the romance of agency and youth in Botswana' in J. Cole and D. Durham (eds), *Figuring the Future: globalization and the temporalities of children and youth*. Santa Fe: School for Advanced Research Press, pp. 151–78.

Eickelman, D. F. 1978. 'The art of memory: Islamic education and its social reproduction', *Comparative Studies in Society and History* 20 (4): 485–516.

Eickelman, D. F. 1985. *Knowledge and Power in Morocco: the education of a twentieth-century notable*. Princeton, NJ: Princeton University Press.

Elazeh, M. 2016. 'Kano deports 3,000 almajiri to Katsina', *Leadership*, 17 February.

Esposito, J. L. and Mogahed, D. 2007. *Who Speaks for Islam? What a billion Muslims really think*. New York: Gallup Press.

ESSPIN. n.d. *Integrating the Old with the New: Islamic education responds to the demands of modern society*. ESSPIN Experiences. Abuja, Nigeria: Education Sector Support Programme in Nigeria.

Everatt, D. 2000. 'From urban warrior to market segment? Youth in South Africa 1990–2000', *Quarterly Journal of the South African National NGO Coalition and Interfund* 3 (2): 4–37.

Fabiyi, M. E. 2008. 'Misconceptions in analyzing Northern Nigeria and the implications for Nigerian unity: contextualizing & adressing the almajirai challenge', *Nigeria World*, 19 December.

Fada, A. A. 2005. 'Factors Perpetuating the Almajiri System of Education in Northern Nigeria: a case study of Zaria and environs, Kaduna State'. MSc thesis, Department of Sociology, Ahmadu Bello University, Zaria.

Fafunwa, A. B. 1974. *History of Education in Nigeria*. London: George Allen and Unwin.

Fair, C. C. 2007. 'Militant recruitment in Pakistan: a new look at the militancy–madrasah connection', *Asia Policy* 4 (1): 107–34.

Fawole, O. A., Ogunkan, D. V. and Omoruan, A. 2011. 'The menace of begging in Nigerian cities: a sociological analysis', *International Journal of Sociology and Anthropology* 3 (1): 9–14.

Federal Ministry of Health. 2011. *Saving Newborn Lives in Nigeria: newborn health in the context of the Integrated Maternal, Newborn and Child Health Strategy*, revised 2nd edn. Abuja, Nigeria: Federal Ministry of Health.

Ferguson, J. 1999. *Expectations of Modernity: myths and meanings of urban life on the Zambian Copperbelt*. Berkeley: University of California Press.

Fonseca, I. 1995. *Bury Me Standing: the gypsies and their journey*. New York: Vintage Books.

Fortier, C. 1997. 'Mémorisation et audition: l'enseignement coranique chez les Maures de Mauretanie', *Islam et sociétés au sud du Sahara* 11: 85–105.

Fortier, C. 1998. 'Le corps comme mémoire: du giron maternel à la férule du maître coranique', *Journal des Africanistes* 68 (1–2): 197–224.

Fourchard, L. 2005. 'Introduction. Nigeria: a missionary nation?' in L. Fourchard, A. Mary and R. Otayek (eds), *Entreprises religieuses transnationales en Afrique de l'Ouest*. Ibadan and Paris: IFRA and Karthala, pp. 341–7.

Fourchard, L. 2006. 'Lagos and the invention of juvenile delinquency in Nigeria', *Journal of African History* 47 (1): 115–37.

Frankel, S. 2007. 'Researching children's morality: developing research methods that allow children's involvement in discourses relevant to their everyday lives', *Childhoods Today* 1 (1): 1–25.

Fraser, N. 1996. 'Social Justice in the Age of Identity Politics: redistribution, recognition, and participation'. Tanner Lectures on Human Values, University of Stanford, 30 April–2 May.

Fraser, N. and Honneth, A. 2003. *Redistribution or Recognition? A political-philosophical discourse*. London: Verso.

Freidus, A. 2010. 'Raising Malawi's children: unanticipated outcomes associated with institutionalised care', *Children and Society* 24: 293–303.

Friedman, T. L. 2001. 'In Pakistan, it's jihad 101', *New York Times*, 13 November.

Froerer, P. 2011. 'Education, inequality and social mobility in central India', *European Journal of Development Research* 23 (5): 695–711.

Froerer, P. and Portisch, A. 2011. 'Introduction to the Special Issue: learning, livelihoods, and social mobility', *Anthropology and Education Quarterly* 43 (4): 332–43.

Gabhainn, S. N. and Sixsmith, J. 2006. 'Children photographing well-being: facilitating participation in research', *Children and Society* 20: 249–59.

Galadanci, H. S., Idris, S. A., Sadauki, H. M. and Yakasai, I. A. 2010. 'Programs and policies for reducing maternal mortality in Kano State, Nigeria: a review', *African Journal of Reproductive Health* 14 (3): 31–7.

Garba, A. 2015. 'Buhari presidency and Northern Nigeria', *Vanguard*, 19 May.

Gaudio, R. P. 2009. *Allah Made Us: sexual outlaws in an Islamic African city*. Malden, MA: Wiley-Blackwell.

Gérard, É. 1999. 'Logiques sociales et enjeux de scolarisation en Afrique. Réflexions sur des cas d'écoles maliens et burkinabè', *Politique Africaine* 76: 153–63.

Geschiere, P. and Gugler, J. 1998. 'The urban–rural connection: changing issues of belonging and identification', *Africa* 68 (3): 309–19.

Gewirtz, S. and Cribb, A. 2003. 'Recent readings of social reproduction: four fundamental problematics', *International Studies in Sociology of Education* 13 (3): 243–60.

Gifford, P. 2004. *Ghana's New Christianity: Pentecostalism in a globalizing African economy*. London: Hurst and Co.

Goffman, E. 1963. *Stigma: notes on the management of spoiled identity*. Englewood Cliffs, NJ: Prentice-Hall.

Goffman, E. 1975. *Frame Analysis: an essay on the organization of experience*. Harmondsworth: Penguin.

Goldberg, J. 2000. 'Inside Jihad U.; the education of a Holy Warrior', *New York Times*, 25 June.

Gomez-Perez, M. 2005. 'Généalogie de l'islam réformiste au Sénégal des années 50 à nos jours. Figures, savoirs et réseaux' in L. Fourchard, A. Mary and R. Otayek (eds), *Entreprises religieuses transnationales en Afrique de l'Ouest*. Ibadan and Paris: IFRA and Karthala, pp. 193–222.

Gomez-Perez, M. and LeBlanc, M. N. 2012. 'Introduction. De la jeunesse à l'intergénérationnel' in M. Gomez-Perez and M. N. LeBlanc (eds), *L'Afrique des générations. Entre tensions et négociations*. Paris: Karthala, pp. 11–34.

Gomez-Perez, M., LeBlanc, M. N. and Savadogo, M. 2009. 'Young men and Islam in the 1990s: rethinking an intergenerational perspective', *Journal of Religion in Africa* 39 (2): 186–218.

Gondola, C. D. 1999. 'Dream and drama: the search for elegance among Congolese youth', *African Studies Review* 42 (1): 23–48.

Goody, E. N. 1982. *Parenthood and Social Reproduction: fostering and occupational roles in West Africa*. Cambridge: Cambridge University Press.

Griswold, E. 2014. 'Why fear Boko Haram', *Slate*, 28 April.

Gunder Frank, A. 1966. 'The development of underdevelopment', *Monthly Review* 18 (4): 17–31.

Hall, S., Critcher, C., Jefferson, T., Clarke, J. and Roberts, B. 1978. *Policing the Crisis: mugging, the state, and law and order*. London: Macmillan.

Hampshire, K., Porter, G., Agblorti, S., Robson, E., Munthali, A. and Abane, A. 2015. 'Context matters: fostering, orphanhood and schooling in sub-Saharan Africa', *Journal of Biosocial Sciences* 47 (2): 141–64.

Hansen, K. T. 2000. 'Ambiguous hegemonies: identity politics and domestic service' in K. M. Adams and S. Dickey (eds), *Home and Hegemony: domestic service and identity politics in South and Southeast Asia*. Ann Arbor: University of Michigan Press, pp. 283–92.

Haqqani, H. 2002. 'Islam's medieval outposts', *Foreign Policy* 133 (November/December): 59–64.

Hart, J. 2008a. 'Business as usual? The global political economy of childhood poverty'. Technical Notes No. 13. Oxford: Young Lives, Oxford Department of International Development.

Hart, J. 2008b. 'Children's participation and international development: attending to the political', *International Journal of Children's Rights* 16 (3): 407–18.

Haruna, M. and Abdullahi, S. A. 1991. 'The "soccer craze" and club formation among Hausa youth in Kano, Nigeria' in M. Last (ed.), *Kano Studies: youth and health in Kano today*. Kano, Nigeria: Bayero University, pp. 113–24.

Hashim, I. M. 2005. 'Exploring the linkages between children's independent migration and education: evidence from Ghana'. Working Paper T12. Brighton: Development Research Centre on Migration, Globalisation and Poverty, University of Sussex.

Hashim, Y. and Walker, J.-A. 2012. 'Muslim others: criss-crossing ethno-religious identities and conflict in Kano'. Paper presented at the conference 'Interfaith Relations in Northern Nigeria: from Research to Policy and Practice', Abuja, Nigeria, 1–2 August.

Hassane, S. 2005. 'Les nouvelles élites islamiques du Niger et du Nigeria du Nord. Itinéraires et prédications fondatrices (1950–2003)' in L. Fourchard, A. Mary and R. Otayek (eds), *Entreprises religieuses transnationales en Afrique de l'Ouest*. Ibadan and Paris: IFRA and Karthala, pp. 373–94.

Haug Fjone, H. and Ytterhus, B. 2009. 'How children with parents suffering from mental health distress search for "normality" and avoid stigma. To be or not to be ... is not the questin', *Childhood* 16 (4): 461–77.

Hefner, R. W. 2007. 'The culture, politics and future of Muslim education' in R. W. Hefner and M. Q. Zaman (eds), *Schooling Islam: the culture and politics of modern Muslim education*. Princeton, NJ and Woodstock: Princeton University Press, pp. 1–39.

Hefner, R. W. and Zaman, M. Q. 2007. *Schooling Islam: the culture and politics of modern Muslim education*. Princeton, NJ and Woodstock: Princeton University Press.

Hemming, P. J. and Madge, N. 2011. 'Researching children, youth and religion: identity, complexity and agency', *Childhood* 19 (1): 38–51.

Hickey, S. and du Toit, A. 2007. 'Adverse incorporation, social exclusion and chronic poverty'. CPRC Working Paper No. 81. Manchester: Chronic Poverty Research Centre, University of Manchester.

Higazi, A. 2015. 'Mobilisation into and against Boko Haram in North-East Nigeria' in M. Cahen, M.-E. Pommerolle and K. Tall (eds), *Collective Mobilisations in Africa: contestation, resistance, revolt*. Leiden: Brill, pp. 305–58.

Hill, P. 1969. 'Hidden trade in Hausaland', *Man (New Series)* 4 (3): 392–409.

Hill, P. 1972. *Rural Hausa: a village and a setting*. Cambridge: Cambridge University Press.

Hill, P. 1977. *Population, Prosperity and Poverty: rural Kano 1900 and 1970*. Cambridge: Cambridge University Press.

Hirschkind, C. 2001. 'The ethics of listening: cassette-sermon audition in contemporary Egypt', *American Ethnologist* 28 (3): 623–49.

Hiskett, M. 1987. 'The Maitatsine riots in Kano, 1980: an assessment', *Journal of Religion in Africa* 17 (3): 209–23.

Hoechner, H. 2011. 'Striving for knowledge and dignity: how Qur'anic students in Kano, Nigeria, learn to live with rejection and educational disadvantage', *European Journal of Development Research* 23 (5): 712–28.

Hoechner, H. 2014a. 'Experiencing inequality at close range: almajiri students and Qur'anic schools in Kano' in A. R. Mustapha (ed.), *Sects and Social Disorder: Muslim identities and conflict in Northern Nigeria*. Woodbridge: James Currey, pp. 98–125.

Hoechner, H. 2014b. 'Traditional Qur'anic students (almajirai) in Nigeria: fair game for unfair accusations?' in M.-A. Pérouse de Montclos (ed.), *Boko Haram: Islamism, politics, security and the state in Nigeria*. Leiden: African Studies Centre, pp. 63–84.

Hoechner, H. 2015a. 'Participatory filmmaking with Qur'anic students in Kano, Nigeria: "speak good about us or keep quiet!"', *International Journal of Social Research Methodology*,18 (6): 635–49.

Hoechner, H. 2015b. 'Porridge, piety and patience: young Qur'anic students' experiences of poverty in Kano, Nigeria', *Africa* 85 (2): 269–88.

Hoechner, H. 2016. 'Growing close where inequalities grow large? A patron for Qur'anic students in Nigeria' in C. Allerton (ed.), *Children: ethnographic encounters*. Oxford: Bloomsbury, pp. 127–30.

Hoechner, H. 2017. 'Accomplice, patron, go-between? A role to play with poor migrant Qur'anic students in northern Nigeria', *Qualitative Research*.

Honwana, A. 2005. 'Innocent and guilty: child-soldiers as interstitial and tactical agents' in A. Honwana and F. De Boeck (eds), *Makers and Breakers: children and youth in postcolonial Africa*. Oxford, Trenton, NJ and Dakar: James Currey, Africa World Press and CODESRIA, pp. 31–52.

Honwana, A. 2009. 'Children in war: reintegrating child soldiers', *IDS Bulletin* 40 (1): 63–8.

Honwana, A. and De Boeck, F. 2005. *Makers and Breakers: children and youth in postcolonial Africa*. Oxford, Trenton, NJ and Dakar: James Currey, Africa World Press and CODESRIA.

Hubbard, J. P. 1975. 'Government and education in Northern Nigeria 1900–1940' in G. N. Brown and M. Hiskett (eds), *Conflict and Harmony in Education in Tropical Africa*. London: Allen and Unwin, pp. 152–67.

Hubbard, J. P. 2000. *Education under Colonial Rule: a history of Katsina College: 1921–1942*. Lanham, MD: University Press of America.

Human Rights Watch. 2003. *Borderline Slavery: child trafficking in Togo*. New York: Human Rights Watch.

Human Rights Watch. 2010. *'Sur le dos des enfants': Mendicité forcée et autres mauvais traitements à l'encontre des talibés au Sénégal*. New York: Human Rights Watch.

Hutson, A. S. 1999. 'The development of women's authority in the Kano Tijaniyya 1894–1963', *Africa Today* 46 (3/4): 43–64.

Iguda, S. n.d. *Tsangaya Education in Focus: conceptual approaches and policies of Malam Ibrahim Shekarau towards a better Qur'anic education*. Kano, Nigeria: Office of the Special Advisor on Education and Information Technology, Kano State.

Iliffe, J. 1987. *The African Poor: a history*. Cambridge: Cambridge University Press.

ILO-IPEC. 2004. *Helping Hands or Shackled Lives? Understanding child domestic labour and responses to it*. Geneva: International Labour Organization.

International Crisis Group. 2014. *Curbing Violence in Nigeria (II): the Boko Haram insurgency*. Brussels: International Crisis Group.

International Crisis Group. 2002. *Pakistan: madrasas, extremism and the military*. Islamabad and Brussels: International Crisis Group.

Jacquemin, M. Y. 2004. 'Children's domestic work in Abidjan, Côte d'Ivoire: the petites bonnes have the floor', *Childhood* 11 (3): 383–97.

Jacquemin, M. Y. 2009. '(In)visible young female migrant workers: "little domestics" in West Africa. Comparative perspectives on girls and young women's work'. Paper presented at the conference 'Child and Youth Migration in West Africa: Research Progress and Implications for Policy', Accra, Ghana, 9–10 June.

Jahoda, A., Wilson, A., Stalker, K. and Cairney, A. 2010. 'Living with stigma and the self-perceptions of people with mild intellectual disabilities', *Journal of Social Issues* 66 (3): 521–34.

James, A. and Prout, A. 1997 [1990]. *Constructing and Reconstructing Childhood: contemporary issues in the sociolical study of childhood*, 2nd edn. London: Falmer.

Janson, M. 2014. *Islam, Youth, and Modernity in the Gambia: the Tablighi Jama'at*. Cambridge: Cambridge University Press.

Jeffrey, C. 2009. 'Geographies of children and youth I: eroding maps of life', *Progress in Human Geography* 34 (4): 496–505.

Jeffrey, C. 2011. 'Geographies of children and youth II: global youth agency', *Progress in Human Geography* 36 (2): 245–53.

Jeffrey, C., Jeffery, P. and Jeffery, R. 2004. '"A useless thing!" or "Nectar of the gods?" The cultural production of education and young men's struggles for respect in liberalizing north India', *Annals of the Association of American Geographers* 94 (4): 961–81.

Jeffrey, C., Jeffery, P. and Jeffery, R. 2008. *Degrees without Freedom? Education, masculinities and unemployment in North India*. Stanford, CA: Stanford University Press.

Jenks, C. 1996. *Childhood*. London: Routledge.

Johnson, D. 2008. *An Assessment of the Development Needs of Teachers in Nigeria: Kwara State case study*. Abuja, Nigeria: Education Sector Support Programme in Nigeria.

Jonckers, D. 1997. 'Les enfants confiés' in M. Pilon, T. Locoh, E. Vignikin and P. Vimard (eds), *Ménages et familles en Afrique*. Paris: CEPED, pp. 193–208.

Jumare, F. I. 2012. 'Almajiri: the invisible child', *Politico*, 22 August.

Kabeer, N. 2000. 'Exclusion, poverty and discrimination. towards an analytical framework', *IDS Bulletin* 31 (4): 83–97.

Kabir, M., Iliyasu, Z., Abubakar, I. S. and Ahmad, D. Z. 2005. 'Medico-social problems of itinerant Qur'anic scholars in Kano', *Nigerian Journal of Paediatrics* 31: 15–18.

Kandiyoti, D. 1994. 'The paradoxes of masculinity: some thoughts on segregated societies' in A. Cornwall and N. Lindisfarne (eds), *Dislocating Masculinity: comparative ethnographies*. London and New York: Routledge, pp. 197–213.

Kane, O. 2003. *Muslim Modernity in Postcolonial Nigeria: a study of the Society for the Removal of Innovation and Reinstatement of Tradition*. Boston, MA: Brill.

Kane, O. 2016. *Beyond Timbuktu: an intellectual history of Muslim West Africa*. Cambridge, MA: Harvard University Press.

Kano State Government. 2012. *Report of the Committee on Almajiri System of Education*. Kano, Nigeria: Kano State Government.

Kaplan, R. D. 1994. 'The coming anarchy: how scarcity, crime, overpopulation, tribalism, and disease are rapidly destroying the social fabric of our planet', *Atlantic Monthly* 273 (2): 44–76.

Katz, C. 2004. *Growing Up Global: economic restructuring and children's everyday lives*. Minneapolis, MN: University of Minnesota Press.

Khalid, S. 1997. 'A Socio-economic Study of the Transformation of Migrant Qur'anic Schools System (Almajiranci) in Sokoto Metropolis, 1970–1995'. PhD thesis, Department of Sociology, Bayero University Kano.

Kirk-Greene, A. H. M. 1975. *The Genesis of the Nigerian Civil War and the Theory of Fear.* Uppsala: Scandinavian Institute of African Studies.

Klocker, N. 2007. 'An example of "thin" agency: child domestic workers in Tanzania' in R. Panelli, S. Punch and E. Robson (eds), *Global Perspectives on Rural Childhood and Youth: young rural lives.* London: Routledge, pp. 83–94.

Klocker, N. 2011. 'Negotiating change: working with children and their employers to transform child domestic work in Iringa, Tanzania', *Children's Geographies* 9 (2): 205–20.

Kumolu, C. 2012. 'Almajiri education: modern gang up against ancient tradition?', *Vanguard,* 26 April.

Lamont, M. and Mizrachi, N. 2013. *Responses to Stigmatisation in Comparative Perspective.* London: Routledge.

Lancy, D. F. 2012. 'Unmasking children's agency', *AnthropoChildren* 2: 1–20.

Langevang, T. and Gough, K. V. 2009. 'Surviving through movement: the mobility of urban youth in Ghana', *Social and Cultural Geography* 10 (7): 741–56.

Larkin, B. 2009. 'Islamic renewal, radio and the surface of things' in B. Meyer (ed.), *Aesthetic Formations: media, religion and the senses.* New York: Palgrave, pp. 117–36.

Last, M. 1967. *The Sokoto Caliphate.* London: Longmans.

Last, M. 1970. 'Aspects of administration and dissent in Hausaland, 1800–1968', *Africa* 40 (4): 345–57.

Last, M. 1988. 'Charisma and medicine in Northern Nigeria' in D. B. Cruise O'Brien and C. Coulon (eds), *Charisma and Brotherhood in African Islam.* Harlow: Longman, pp. 116–31.

Last, M. 1993. 'The traditional Muslim intellectual in Hausaland: the background' in T. Falola (ed.), *African Historiography.* Harlow: Longman, pp. 116–31.

Last, M. 2000a. 'Social exclusion in northern Nigeria' in J. Hubert (ed.), *Madness, Disability and Social Exclusion: the archaeology and anthropology of 'difference'.* London: Routledge, pp. 217–39.

Last, M. 2000b. 'Children and the experience of violence: contrasting cultures of punishment in Northern Nigeria', *Africa* 70 (3): 359–93.

Last, M. 2000c. 'Reconciliation and memory in postwar Nigeria' in V. Das (ed.), *Violence and Subjectivity.* London: University of California Press, pp. 315–32.

Last, M. 2004. 'Towards a political history of youth in Muslim Northern Nigeria 1750–2000' In J. Abbink and I. van Kessel (eds), *Vanguard or Vandals: youth, politics and conflict in Africa.* Leiden: Brill, pp. 37–54.

Last, M. 2007. 'Muslims and Christians in Nigeria: an economy of political panic', *Round Table,* 96 (392): 605–16.

Last, M. 2008a. 'The pattern of dissent: Boko Haram in Nigeria 2009', *Annual Review of Islam in Africa* 10: 7–11.

Last, M. 2008b. 'The search for security in Muslim Northern Nigeria', *Africa* 78 (1): 41–63.

Last, M. 2009. 'Nation-breaking and not-belonging in Nigeria: withdrawal, resistance, riot?' Paper presented at the 3rd European Conference on African Studies, Leipzig, Germany, 4–7 June.

Launay, R. 1992. *Beyond the Stream: Islam and society in a West African town.* Berkeley: University of California Press.

Launay, R. 2016a. 'Introduction: writing boards and blackboards' in R. Launay (ed.), *Islamic Education in Africa: writing boards and blackboards.* Bloomington, IN: University of Indiana Press, pp. 1–26.

Launay, R. 2016b. *Islamic Education in Africa: writing boards and blackboards.* Bloomington, IN: University of Indiana Press.

Levinson, B. A. and Holland, D. 1996. 'The cultural production of the educated person: an introduction' in B. A. Levinson, D. E. Foley and D. C. Holland (eds), *The Cultural Production of the Educated Person: critical ethnographies of schooling and local practice.* Albany: State University of New York, pp. 1–54.

Levinson, B. A., Foley, D. E. and Holland, D. C. 1996. *The Cultural Production of the Educated Person: critical ethnographies of schooling and local practice.* Albany: State University of New York.

Lewis, O. 1959. *Five Families: Mexican case studies in the culture of poverty.* New York: Basic Books.

Loimeier, R. 1997. 'Islamic reform and political change: the example of Abubakar Gumi and the 'yan Izala movement in Nigeria' in D. Westerlund and E. E. Rosander (eds), *African Islam and Islam in Africa: encounters between Sufis and Islamists.* Athens, OH: Ohio University Press, pp. 286–307.

Loimeier, R. 2003. 'Patterns and peculiarities of Islamic reform in Africa', *Journal of Religion in Africa* 33 (3): 237–62.

Loimeier, R. 2005. 'Translating the Qur'an in sub-Saharan Africa: dynamics and disputes', *Journal of Religion in Africa* 35 (4): 403–23.

Looney, R. 2003. 'Reforming Pakistan's educational system: the challenge of the madrassas', *Journal of Social, Political, and Economic Studies* 28 (3): 257–74.

Lovejoy, P. E. and Hogendorn, J. S. 1993. *Slow Death for Slavery: the course of abolition in Northern Nigeria, 1897–1936.* Cambridge: Cambridge University Press.

Lubeck, P. 1981. 'Islamic networks and urban capitalism: an instance of articulation from Northern Nigeria', *Cahiers d'Études Africaines* 21 (81/83): 67–78.

Lubeck, P. 1985. 'Islamic protest under semi-industrial capitalism: 'Yan Tatsine explained', *Africa* 55 (4): 369–89.

Lubeck, P., Lipschutz, R. and Weeks, E. 2003. 'The globality of Islam: Sharia as a Nigerian "self-determination" movement'. QEH Working Paper Series No. 106. Oxford: Oxford Department of International Development.

MacLeod, J. 1987. *Ain't No Makin' It: leveled aspirations in a low-income neighbourhood.* Boulder, CO: Westview Press.

Mahmood, S. 2001. 'Feminist theory, embodiment, and the docile agent: some reflections on the Egyptian Islamic revival', *Cultural Anthropology* 16 (2): 202–36.

Mahmood, S. 2005. *Politics of Piety.* Princeton, NJ: Princeton University Press.

Mains, D. 2007. 'Neoliberal times: progress, boredom, and shame among young men in urban Ethiopia', *American Ethnologist* 34 (4): 659–73.

Malkki, L. H. 1996. 'Speechless emissaries: refugees, humanitarianism, and dehistoricization', *Cultural Anthropology* 11 (3): 377–404.

Mamdani, M. 1996. *Citizen and Subject: contemporary Africa and the legacy of late colonialism.* Princeton, NJ: Princeton University Press.

Mann, G. 2012. 'On being despised: growing up a Congolese refugee in Dar es
    Salaam' in J. Boyden and M. Bourdillon (eds), *Childhood Poverty: multidisci-
    plinary approaches*. Basingstoke: Palgrave Macmillan, pp. 185–99.
Marsden, 2005. *Living Islam: Muslim religious experience in Pakistan's North-West
    frontier*. Cambridge: Cambridge University Press.
Marshall, R. 1991. 'Power in the name of Jesus', *Review of African Political Econ-
    omy* 18 (52): 21–37.
Masquelier, A. 2005a. 'Dirt, undress, and difference: an introduction'
    in A. Masquelier (ed.), *Dirt, Undress, and Difference: critical perspectives on
    the body's surface*. Bloomington, IN: Indiana University Press, pp. 1–33.
Masquelier, A. 2005b. 'The scorpion's sting: youth, marriage and the struggle
    for social maturity in Niger', *Journal of the Royal Anthropological Institute* 11:
    59–83.
Masquelier, A. 2007. 'Negotiating futures: Islam, youth and the state in Niger',
    in B. F. Soares and R. Otayek (eds), *Islam and Muslim Politics in Africa*. New
    York: Palgrave Macmillan, pp. 243–62.
Masquelier, A. 2009. *Women and Islamic Revival in a West African Town*. Bloom-
    ington, IN: Indiana University Press.
Masquelier, A. 2015. 'Qur'an schooling and the production of mindful bodies in
    West Africa', *Journal of Africana Religions* 3 (2): 184–92.
McCain, C. 2013. 'Nollywood, Kannywood, and a decade of Hausa film cen-
    sorship in Nigeria' in D. Biltereyst and R. Winkel (eds), *Silencing Cin-
    ema: film censorship around the world*. New York: Palgrave Macmillan,
    pp. 223–40.
McNay, L. 1999. 'Gender, habitus and the field: Pierre Bourdieu and the limits
    of reflexivity', *Theory, Culture and Society* 16: 95–117.
Mead, M. 1928. *Coming of Age in Samoa: a psychological study of primitive youth
    for Western civilisation*. New York: William Morrow and Co.
Meagher, K. 2001. 'The invasion of the opportunity snatchers: the rural–urban
    interface in Northern Nigeria', *Journal of Contemporary African Studies*
    19 (1): 39–54.
Meintjes, H. and Giese, S. 2006. 'Spinning the epidemic: the making of mytholo-
    gies of orphanhood in the context of AIDS', *Childhood* 13 (3): 407–30.
Mercy Corps. 2016. *'Motivations and Empty Promises': Voices of former Boko
    Haram combatants and Nigerian youth*. Portland, OR and Edinburgh: Mercy
    Corps.
Meyer, B. 1999. *Translating the Devil: religion and modernity among the Ewe in
    Ghana*. Edinburgh: Edinburgh University Press.
Mills, G. Y. 1997. 'Is it is or is it ain't: the impact of selective perception on the
    image making of traditional African dance', *Journal of Black Studies* 28 (2):
    139–56.
Ministry of Education. 2008. *Educational Sector Analysis*. Kano, Nigeria: Min-
    istry of Education, Kano State.
Ministry of Education. 2010. *Annual Education Sector Performance Report 2010*.
    Kano, Nigeria: Ministry of Education, Kano State.
Ministry of Education. 2011. *Annual Education Sector Performance Report 2011*.
    Kano, Nigeria: Ministry of Education, Kano State.
Mohammed, H. 2001. 'The transformation of almajiranci in Kano under the
    structural adjustment programme'. *FAIS Journal of Humanities* 1 (3).

Mohammed, K. 2014. 'The message and methods of Boko Haram' in M.-A. Pérouse de Montclos (ed.), *Boko Haram: Islamism, politics, security and the state in Nigeria*. Leiden: African Studies Centre, pp. 9–32.

Moncrieffe, J. and Eyben, R. 2007. *The Power of Labelling: how people are categorized and why it matters*. London: Sterling.

Morgan, S. L., Mohammed, I. Z. and Abdullahi, S. 2010. 'Patron–client relationships and low education among youth in Kano, Nigeria', *African Studies Review* 53 (1): 79–103.

Morrow, V. 2001. 'Using qualitative methods to elicit young people's perspectives on their environments: some ideas for community health initiatives', *Health Education Research* 16 (3): 255–68.

Mortimore, M. 1998. *Roots in the African Dust*. Cambridge: Cambridge University Press.

Mortimore, M. 2003. 'Long-term change in African drylands: can recent history point towards development pathways?', *Oxford Development Studies* 31 (4): 503–18.

Mösch, T. 2014. 'Opinion: "Fateful day for human rights in Nigeria"', *Deutsche Welle*, 15 January.

Moyer, E. 2004. 'Popular cartographies: youthful imaginings of the global in the streets of Dar es Salaam, Tanzania', *City and Society* 16 (2): 117–43.

Mustapha, A. R. 2006. *Ethnic Structure, Inequality and Governance of the Public Sector in Nigeria*. Democracy, Governance and Human Rights Programme Paper No. 24. Geneva: United Nations Research Institute for Social Development.

Mustapha, A. R. 2014. 'Understanding Boko Haram' in A. R. Mustapha (ed.), *Sects and Social Disorder: Muslim identities and conflict in northern Nigeria*. Somerset, James Currey, pp. 147–98.

Mustapha, A. R. and Bunza, M. U. 2014. Contemporary Islamic sects & groups in northern Nigeria. In A. R. Mustapha, ed, *Sects and Social Disorder. Muslim identities and conflict in northern Nigeria*. Woodbridge: James Currey, pp. 54–97.

Mustapha, A. R. and Meagher, K. 1992. 'Stress, adaptation, and resilience in rural Kano', *Capitalism, Nature, Socialism* 5 (2): 107–17.

Mustapha, A. R. and Meagher, K. 2000. 'Agrarian production, public policy and the state in Kano Region, 1900–2000'. Working Paper No. 35. Crewkerne: Drylands Research.

Mustapha, A. R. and Whitfield, L. 2009. 'African democratisation: the journey so far' in A. R. Mustapha and L. Whitfield (eds), *Turning Points in African Democracy*. Woodbridge: Boydell and Brewer, pp. 1–12.

Nast, H. 1998. 'The body as "place": reflexivity and fieldwork in Kano, Nigeria' in H. Nast and S. Pile (eds), *Places Through the Body*. London: Routledge, pp. 69–86.

National Bureau of Statistics. 2012. *Nigeria Poverty Profile 2010*. Abuja, Nigeria: National Bureau of Statistics.

National Bureau of Statistics. 2016. *Statistical Report on Women and Men in Nigeria 2015*. Abuja, Nigeria: National Bureau of Statistics.

National Population Commission. 2009. *Nigeria Demographic and Health Survey 2008*. Abuja, Nigeria: National Population Commission.

National Population Commission. 2011a. *Nigeria Demographic and Health Survey (DHS) EdData Profile 1990, 2003, and 2008: education data for decision-making*. Abuja, Nigeria: National Population Commission.

National Population Commission. 2011b. *Nigeria Demographic and Health Survey (DHS) EdData 2010*. Abuja, Nigeria: National Population Commission.

National Population Commission. 2014. *Nigeria Demographic and Health Survey 2013*. Abuja, Nigeria, and Rockville, MD: National Population Commission and ICF International.

National Population Commission. 2016. *Statistical Report of Men and Women in Nigeria 2015*. Abuja, Nigeria: National Population Commission.

NCWD. 2001. *Almajiri and Qur'anic Education*. Kaduna, Nigeria: National Council for the Welfare of the Destitute, Almajirci Directorate.

Ndagi, M. U. 2012. 'Plaiting louse-infested hair', *Weekly Trust*, 5 May.

Newman, A. 2016. 'Faith, Identity, Status and Schooling: an ethnography of educational decision-making in northern Senegal'. PhD thesis, Department of Social Anthropology, University of Sussex.

Nickerson, R. S. 1998. 'Confirmation bias: a ubiquitous phenomenon in many guises', *Review of General Psychology* 2 (2): 175–220.

Notermans, C. 2008. 'The emotional world of kinship: children's experiences of fosterage in East Cameroon', *Childhood* 15 (3): 355–77.

NSRP. n.d. 'The response of the Kano State Government to violent conflict since 2009: lessons learned and policy implications'. NSRP Policy Brief No. 1. Abuja, Nigeria: Nigeria Stability and Reconciliation Programme.

O'Brien, S. 2007. 'La charia contestée: démocratie, débat et diversité musulmane dans les "étas charia" du Nigeria', *Politique Africaine* 106: 46–68.

Office of the Special Advisor. 2005. *Census of Islamiyya, Qur'anic/Tsangaya and Ilmi Schools in Kano State, 2003*. Kano, Nigeria: Office of the Special Advisor on Education and Information Technology, Kano State.

Ogunkan, D. V. 2011. 'Begging and almsgiving in Nigeria: the Islamic perspective', *International Journal of Sociology and Anthropology* 3 (4): 127–31.

Ojuah, M. U. and Arikpo, A. B. 2011. 'Role of non-formal education (NFE) under universal basic education (UBE) law in Nigeria', *Journal of Educational and Social Research* 1 (3): 61–70.

Okoye, F. and Yau, Y. Z. 1999. *The Condition of Almajirai in the North West Zone of Nigeria*. Kaduna, Nigeria: Human Rights Monitor and UNICEF.

Olagunju, L. 2012. 'Almajirai, street kids and a nation's future', *Nigerian Tribune*, 20 April.

Olatunji, B. 2010. 'FG inaugurates Almajiri Education Committee', *This Day*, 19 October.

Olujuwon, T. 2008. 'Combating trafficking in person: a case study of Nigeria', *European Journal of Scientific Research* 24 (1): 23–32.

Onuoha, F. C. 2011. 'The audacity of the Boko Haram: background, analysis and emerging trend', *Security Journal* 25 (2): 134–51.

Ostien, P. 2012. 'Percentages by religion of the 1952 and 1963 populations of Nigeria's present 36 states'. NRN Background Paper No. 1. Oxford: Nigeria Research Network.

Ostien, P. n.d. 'Sharia in Nigeria', *Oxford Islamic Studies Online*.

Otayek, R. and Soares, B. F. 2007. 'Introduction: Islam and Muslim politics in Africa' in B. F. Soares and R. Otayek (eds), *Islam and Muslim Politics in Africa*. London: Palgrave Macmillan, pp. 1–24.

Ouzgane, L. (ed.) 2006. *Islamic Masculinities*. London and New York: Zed Books.

Owasanoye, B. 2005. 'The regulation of child custody and access in Nigeria', *Family Law Quarterly* 39 (2): 405–28.

Owuamanam, J., Aborisade, S., Ubabukoh, O. and Attah, D. 2012. 'Almajiri schools: civil rights group disagrees with Afenifere, ACF', *Punch*, 13 April.

Oxford Poverty and Human Development Initiative. 2013. *Country Briefing: Nigeria. Multidimensional poverty index data bank*. Oxford: Oxford Poverty and Human Development Initiative, University of Oxford.

Paden, J. N. 1973. *Religion and Political Culture in Kano*. Berkeley: University of California Press.

Panelli, R., Punch, S. and Robson, E. 2007. *Global Perspectives on Rural Childhood and Youth*. London: Routledge.

Perry, D. L. 2004. 'Muslim child disciples, global civil society, and children's rights in Senegal: the discourses of strategic structuralism', *Anthropological Quarterly* 77 (1): 47–86.

Pew Forum. 2010. *Tolerance and Tension: Islam and Christianity in sub-Saharan Africa*. Washington, DC: Pew Forum on Religion and Public Life.

Philips, J. E. 2004. 'Hausa in the twentieth century: an overview', *Sudan Africa* 15: 55–84.

Pittin, R. 1986. 'The control of reproduction: principle and practice in Nigeria', *Review of African Political Economy* 35: 40–53.

Pittin, R. 1991. 'Women, work and ideology in Nigeria', *Review of African Political Economy* 18 (52): 38–52.

Porter, C. 2009. 'After 2015: promoting pro-poor policy after the MDGs'. Background paper for High-level Policy Forum, Department for International Development, Brussels, 23 June.

Potts, D. 1995. 'Shall we go home? Increasing urban poverty in African cities and migration processes', *Geographical Journal* 161 (3): 245–64.

Punch, S. 2002. 'Research with children: the same or different from research with adults?', *Childhood* 9 (3): 321–41.

Purefoy, C. 2010. 'Nigeria's almajiri children learning a life of poverty and violence', CNN World, 8 January.

Rahnema, M. 1992. 'Participation' in W. Sachs (ed.), *The Development Dictionary: a guide to knowledge as power*. London: Zed Books, pp. 116–31.

Rao, N. and Hossain, M. I. 2011. 'Confronting poverty and educational inequalities: madrasas as a strategy for contesting dominant literacy in rural Bangladesh', *International Journal of Educational Development* 31: 623–33.

Rao, N. and Hossain, M. I. 2012. '"I want to be respected": migration, mobility, and the construction of alternate educational discourses in rural Bangladesh', *Anthropology and Education Quarterly* 43 (4): 415–28.

Reay, D. 2004. '"It's all becoming a habitus": beyond the habitual use of habitus in educational research', *British Journal of Sociology of Education* 25 (4): 431–44.

Redfield, P. and Bornstein, E. 2011. 'An introduction to the anthropology of humanitarianism' in E. Bornstein and P. Redfield (eds), *Forces of Compassion: humanitarianism between ethics and politics*. Santa Fe: SAR Press, pp. 3–30.

Reichmuth, S. 1989. 'New trends in Islamic education in Nigeria: a preliminary account', *Die Welt des Islams* XXIX: 41–60.

Reid, M. 2013. *Law and Piety in Medieval Islam*. Cambridge: Cambridge University Press.

Ridge, T. 2002. *Childhood Poverty and Social Exclusion: from a child's perspective*. Bristol: Policy Press.

Rival, L. 1996. 'Formal schooling and the production of modern citizens in the Ecuadorian Amazon' in B. A. Levinson, D. E. Foley and D. C. Holland (eds), *The Cultural Production of the Educated Person: critical ethnographies of schooling and local practice*. Albany: State University of New York, pp. 153–68.

Robertson, R. W. E. 2012. *Pre-emptive Threat Mitigation: neutralizing the Boko Haram threat to U.S. interests*. Newport, RI: Naval War College.

Robson, E. 2000. 'Wife seclusion and the spatial praxis of gender ideology in Nigerian Hausaland', *Gender, Place and Culture* 7 (2): 179–99.

Robson, E. 2004. 'Children at work in rural northern Nigeria: patterns of age, space and gender', *Journal of Rural Studies* 20 (2): 193–210.

Robson, E. 2006. 'The "kitchen" as women's space in rural Hausaland, Northern Nigeria', *Gender, Place and Culture* 13 (6): 669–76.

Robson, E., Bell, S. and Klocker, N. 2007. 'Conceptualising agency in the lives of rural young people' in R. Panelli, S. Punch and E. Robson (eds), *Global Perspectives on Rural Childhood and Youth: young rural lives*. London: Routledge, pp. 135–48.

Robson, E., Porter, G., Hampshire, K. and Bourdillon, M. 2009. '"Doing it right?": working with young researchers in Malawi to investigate children, transport and mobility', *Children's Geographies* 7 (4): 467–80.

Rosemberg, F. and Andrade, L. F. 1999. 'Ruthless rhetoric: child and youth prostitution in Brazil', *Childhood* 6 (1): 113–31.

Ross, W. 2014. 'Boko Haram Kano attack: loss of life at a staggering scale', BBC, 30 November.

Ruddick, S. 2003. 'The politics of aging: globalization and the restructuring of youth and childhood', *Antipode* 35 (2): 334–62.

Ruggeri Laderchi, C., Saith, R. and Steward, F. 2003. 'Does it matter that we don't agree on the definition of poverty? A comparison of four approaches'. QEH Working Paper Series No. 107. Oxford: Oxford Department of International Development.

Saidu, K. 2010. 'Dislodging almajiris' bowls with skills', *Nation*, 11 January.

Salaam, A. O. 2011. 'Yandaba on the streets of Kano: social conditions and criminality', *Vulnerable Children and Youth Studies: An International Interdisciplinary Journal for Research, Policy and Care* 6 (1): 68–77.

Salih, S. A. 1999. *The Challenges of Poverty Alleviation in IDB Member Countries*. Jeddah: The Islamic Development Bank.

Sanankoua, D. B. 1985. 'Les écoles "Coraniques" au Mali: problèmes actuels', *Canadian Journal of African Studies* 19 (2): 359–67.

Sani, N. 2015. 'Recitation and memorization of the Qur'an in Nigeria: a comparison of traditional and modern Qur'anic schools'. Paper presented at the

2nd International Conference on Arabic Studies and Islamic Civilization, Kuala Lumpur, Malaysia, 9–10 March.

Sanneh, L. O. 1975. 'The Islamic education of an African child: stresses and tensions' in G. N. Brown and M. Hiskett (eds), *Conflict and Harmony in Education in Tropical Africa*. London: Allen and Unwin, pp. 168–86.

Saul, M. 1984. 'The Quranic farm and child labour in Upper Volta'. *Africa* 54 (2): 71–87.

Sawa, B. A. and Adebayo, A. A. 2011. 'The impact of climate change on precipitation effectiveness indices in Northern Nigeria', *Research Journal of Environmental and Earth Sciences* 3 (5): 481–6.

Sayer, A. 2005. *The Moral Significance of Class*. Cambridge: Cambridge University Press.

Scheper-Hughes, N. 1992. *Death Without Weeping: the violence of everyday life in Brazil*. London: University of California Press.

Schielke, S. 2009. 'Being good in Ramadan: ambivalence, fragmentation, and the moral self in the lives of young Egyptians', *Journal of the Royal Anthropological Institute* 15: S24–S40.

Schildkrout, E. 1982. 'Dependence and autonomy: the economic activities of secluded women in Kano, Nigeria' in E. Bay (ed.), *Women and Work in Africa*. Boulder, CO: Westview Press, pp. 55–82.

Schildkrout, E. 2002 [1978]. 'Age and gender in Hausa society: socio-economic roles of children in urban Kano', *Childhood* 9 (3): 342–68.

Scott, J. C. 1985. *Weapons of the Weak: everyday forms of peasant resistance*. London: Yale University Press.

Seesemann, R. 1999. '"Where East meets West": the development of Qur'anic education in Darfur', *Islam et Sociétés au Sud du Sahara* 13: 41–61.

Seesemann, R. 2007. 'Kenyan Muslims, the aftermath of 9/11, and the "War on Terror"' in B. F. Soares and R. Otayek (eds), *Islam and Muslim Politics in Africa*. New York: Palgrave Macmillan, pp. 157–76.

Seesemann, R. 2011. *The Divine Flood: Ibrahim Niasse and the roots of a twentieth-century Sufi revival*. Oxford: Oxford University Press.

Sen, A. 1983. 'Poor, relatively speaking', *Oxford Economic Papers* 35: 153–69.

Sen, A. 1999. *Development as Freedom*. Oxford: Oxford University Press.

Shah, S. 2000. 'Service or servitude? The domestication of household labor in Nepal' in K. M. Adams and S. Dickey (eds), *Home and Hegemony: domestic service and identity politics in South and Southeast Asia*. Ann Arbor: University of Michigan Press, pp. 87–117.

Sigona, N. 2005. 'Locating "the gypsy problem". The Roma in Italy: stereotyping, labelling and "nomad camps"', *Journal of Ethnic and Migration Studies* 31 (4): 741–56.

Silver, H. 1994. 'Social exclusion and social solidarity: three paradigms', *International Labour Review* 133 (5–6): 531–78.

Singer, P. W. 2001. 'Pakistan's madrassahs: ensuring a system of education not jihad'. Analysis Paper No. 14. Washington, DC: Brookings Institution.

Smith, D. J. 2007. *A Culture of Corruption: everyday deception and popular discontent in Nigeria*. Princeton, NJ: Princeton University Press.

Smith, M. F. 1954. *Baba of Karo: a woman of the Muslim Hausa*. London: Faber and Faber.

Smith, M. G. 1954. 'Introduction' in M. F. Smith, *Baba of Karo: a woman of the Muslim Hausa*. London: Faber and Faber, pp. 11–34.

Smith, M. G. 1957. 'Cooperation in Hausa society', *Information* 11: 1–20.

Smith, M. G. 1959. 'The Hausa system of social status', *Africa* 29 (3): 239–52.

Soares, B. F. 1996. 'The prayer economy in a Malian town', *Cahiers d'Études Africaines* 36 (4): 739–53.

Soares, B. F. and Osella, F. 2009. 'Islam, politics, anthropology', *Journal of the Royal Anthropological Institute* 15: S1–S23.

Solivetti, L. M. 1994. 'Family, marriage and divorce in a Hausa community: a sociological model', *Africa* 64 (2): 252–71.

Sommers, M. 2010. 'Urban youth in Africa', *Environment and Urbanization* 22 (2): 317–32.

Sounaye, A. 2013. 'Alarama is all at once: preacher, media "savvy", and religious entrepreneur in Niamey', *Journal of African Cultural Studies* 25 (1): 88–102.

Sounaye, A. 2014. 'Mobile Sunna: Islam, small media and community in Niger', *Social Compass* 61 (1): 21–9.

Soyinka, W. 2012. 'The butchers of Nigeria', *Newsweek Magazine*, 16 January.

Stambach, A. 2000. *Schooling, Community and Gender in East Africa.* London: Routledge.

Starrett, G. 1998. *Putting Islam to Work: education, politics, and religious transformation in Egypt.* Berkeley: University of California Press.

Starrett, G. 2006. 'The American interest in Islamic schooling: a misplaced emphasis?', *Middle East Policy* XIII (1): 120–31.

Stephens, S. 1995. 'Introduction: children and the politics of culture in "late capitalism"' in S. Stephens (ed.), *Children and the Politics of Culture*. Princeton, NJ: Princeton University Press, pp. 3–48.

Sule-Kano, A. 2008. 'Poverty and the traditional Qur'anic school system in Northern Nigeria: the politics of the almajiri-phenomenon'. Paper presented at 'Conference on Nigerian Youth and National Development', Centre for Democratic Research and Training, Mambayya House, Bayero University, Kano, Nigeria, 5–6 August.

Suleiman, S. 2009. 'Iliya, the Almajiri', *234NEXT*, 22 July.

Sutton, L. 2009) '"They'd only call you a scally if you are poor": the impact of socio-economic status on children's identities', *Children's Geographies* 7 (3): 277–90.

Tahir, G. 2001. 'Federal government intervention in universal basic education', *UBE Forum: A Journal of Basic Education in Nigeria* 1 (1): 1–12.

Tamari, T. and Bondarev, D. 2013. 'Introduction and annotated bibliography', *Journal of Qur'anic Studies* 15 (3): 1–55.

Terre des Hommes. 2003. *Les filles domestiques au Burkina Faso: traite ou migration? Analyse de la migration laborieuse des enfants de la province du Sourou.* Paris: Fédération Internationale Terre des Hommes.

Thorsen, D. 2006. 'Child migrants in transit: strategies to assert new identities in rural Burkina Faso' in C. Christiansen, M. Utas and H. E. Vigh (eds), *Navigating Youth, Generating Adulthood: social becoming in an African context.* Uppsala: Nordic Africa Institute, pp. 88–114.

Thorsen, D. 2012. *Child Domestic Workers: evidence from West and Central Africa.* Dakar: UNICEF.

Thurston, A. 2015. 'Muslim politics and shari'a in Kano State, Northern Nigeria', *African Affairs* 114 (454): 28–51.

Thurston, A. 2016a. 'Colonial control, Nigerian agency, Arab outreach, and Islamic education in Northern Nigeria, 1900–1966' in R. Launay (ed.),

Islamic Education in Africa: writing boards and blackboards. Bloomington, IN: University of Indiana Press, pp. 119–36.

Thurston, A. 2016b. '"The disease is unbelief": Boko Haram's religious and political worldview'. *Brookings Project on US Relations with the Islamic World No. 22*. Washington, DC: Centre for Middle Eastern Policy, Brookings Institution.

Thurston, A. 2016c. *Salafism in Nigeria: Islam, preaching, and politics*. Cambridge: Cambridge University Press.

Tibenderana, P. K. 1983. 'The emirs and the spread of Western education in Northern Nigeria, 1910–1946', *Journal of African History* 24 (4): 517–34.

Tiffen, M. 2001. 'Profile of demographic change in the Kano-Maradi region, 1960–2000'. Drylands Working Paper No. 24. Crewkerne: Drylands Research.

Tomasevski, K. 2005. 'Not education for all, only for those who can pay: the World Bank's model for financing primary education', *Law, Social Justice and Global Development Journal* 9 (1): 1–19.

Tukur, M. 2016. *British Colonisation of Northern Nigeria, 1897–1914: a reinterpretation of colonial sources*. Dakar: Amalion Publishing.

Tukur, S. 2017. 'Shocking revelation: 100,000 killed, two million displaced by Boko Haram insurgency, Borno governor says', *Premium Times*, 13 February.

UBE. 2003. *Universal Basic Education Programme. Annual Report 2002*. Abuja, Nigeria: Universal Basic Education Programme.

UBEC. 2010. *National Framework for the Development and Integration of Almajiri Education into UBE Programme*. Abuja, Nigeria: Universal Basic Education Commission.

UBEC. 2015. *Update on Almajiri Education Programme*. Abuja, Nigeria: Almajiri Education Programme Unit, Universal Basic Education Commission.

Umar, M. S. 1993. 'Changing Islamic identity in Nigeria from the 1960s to the 1980s: from Sufism to anti-Sufism' in L. Brenner (ed.), *Muslim Identity and Social Change in Sub-Saharan Africa*. Bloomington, IN: Indiana University Press, pp. 154–78.

Umar, M. S. 2001. 'Education and Islamic trends in Northern Nigeria: 1970s-1990s', *Africa Today* 48 (2): 127–50.

Umar, M. S. 2003. 'Profiles of new Islamic schools in Northern Nigeria', *Maghreb Review* 28 (2–3): 146–69.

Umar, M. S. 2006. *Islam and Colonialism: intellectual responses of Muslims of Northern Nigeria to British Colonial Rule*. Leiden: Brill.

UNFPA. 2014. *The Power of 1.8 Billion: adolescents, youth, and the transformation of the future. The State of World Population 2014*. New York: United Nations Populations Fund.

UNICEF. 1999. 'Child domestic work'. Innocenti Digest No. 5. Florence: Innocenti Research Centre and UNICEF.

United Nations. 2009. 'World population prospects: the 2008 revision, highlights'. Working Paper No. ESA/P/WP.210. New York: United Nations, Department of Economic and Social Affairs, Population Division.

Urdal, H. 2004. 'The devil in the demographics: the effect of youth bulges on domestic armed conflict, 1950–2000'. Social Development Papers

No. 14. Washington, DC: Conflict Prevention and Reconstruction Unit, World Bank.

Usman, L. M. 2008. 'Assessing the universal basic education primary and Koranic schools' synergy for Almajiri street boys in Nigeria', *International Journal of Educational Management* 22 (1): 62–73.

Utas, M. 2005. 'Agency of victims: young women in the Liberian civil war' in A. Honwana and F. De Boeck (eds), *Makers and Breakers: children and youth in postcolonial Africa*. Oxford, Trenton, NJ and Dakar: James Currey, Africa World Press and CODESRIA, pp. 53–80.

Uwais, M., Mansfield, D., Bamali, T. I. and Manuel, C. 2009. 'Improving the legal investment climate for women in Africa: Nigeria'. Draft report prepared for the World Bank.

Valentine, G. 1996. 'Angels and devils: moral landscapes of childhood', *Environment and Planning D: Society and Space* 14: 581–99.

van Santen, J. C. M. 2001. 'Not just any "street" child: universals and particulars of childhood in North-Cameroonian society', *International Journal of Anthropology* 16 (2/3): 113–25.

Vigh, H. E. 2010. 'Youth mobilisation as social navigation. Reflections on the concept of dubriagem', *Cadernos de Estudos Africanos* 18/19: 140–64.

Wacquant, L. 2003. 'Toward a dictatorship over the poor? Notes on the penalization of poverty in Brazil', *Punishment and Society* 5 (2): 197–205.

Wagner, D. A. 1991. 'Islamic education' in A. Lewy (ed.), *The International Encyclopedia of Curriculum*. Elmsford, NY: Pergamon Press, pp. 265–7.

Walker, A. 2016. *'Eat the Heart of the Infidel': the harrowing of Nigeria and the rise of Boko Haram*. London: Hurst.

Walker, R., Kyomuhendo, G. B., Chase, E., Choudhry, S., Gubrium, E. K., Nicola, J. Y., Lødemel, I., Mathew, L., Mwiine, A., Pellissery, S. and Ming, Y. 2013. 'Poverty in global perspective: is shame a common denominator?', *Journal of Social Policy* 42 (2): 215–33.

Ware, R. 2014. *The Walking Qur'an: Islamic education, embodied knowledge, and history in West Africa*. Chapel Hill: University of North Carolina University Press.

Wasiuzzaman, S. and Wells, K. 2010. 'Assembling webs of support: child domestic workers in India', *Children and Society* 24 (4): 282–92.

Weiss, B. 2002. 'Thug realism: inhabiting fantasy in urban Tanzania', *Cultural Anthropology* 17 (1): 93–124.

Werthmann, K. 1997. *Nachbarinnen. Die Alltagswelt muslimischer Frauen in einer nigerianischen Großstadt*. Frankfurt: Brandes and Apsel.

Werthmann, K. 2002. *'Matan Bariki*, "women of the barracks" Muslim Hausa women in an urban neighbourhood in Northern Nigeria', *Africa* 72 (1): 112–30.

Werthmann, K. 2004. 'A field full of researchers: fieldwork as a collective experience'. Working Paper No. 33. Mainz: Department of Anthropology and African Studies, Johannes Gutenberg University of Mainz.

West Africa Insight. 2010. 'Almajiris "street children" and sectarian conflicts in Northern Nigeria', *West Africa Insight: Destitution and Homelessness* 1 (3): 7–9.

Whitehead, S. M. and Barrett, F. J. 2001. *The Masculinities Reader*. Cambridge: Polity.

Whitfield, L. and Mustapha, A. R. 2009. 'Conclusion: the politics of African states in the era of democratisation' in A. R. Mustapha and L. Whitfield (eds), *Turning Points in African Democracy*. Woodbridge: Boydell and Brewer, pp. 202–27.

Wilks, I. 1968. 'The transmission of Islamic learning in the Western Sudan' in J. Goody (ed.), *Literacy in Traditional Societies*. New York: Cambridge University Press, pp. 162–97.

Willis, P. 1977. *Learning to Labour: how working class kids get working class jobs*. Farnborough: Saxon House.

Willis, P. 1981. 'Cultural production is different from cultural reproduction is different from social reproduction is different from reproduction', *Interchange* 12 (2–3): 48–67.

Winters, C. A. 1987. 'Koranic education and militant Islam in Nigeria', *International Review of Education* 33 (2): 171–85.

Winthrop, R. and Graff, C. 2010. 'Beyond madrasas: assessing the links between education and militancy in Pakistan'. Working Paper No. 2. Washington, DC: Center for Universal Education, Brookings Institution.

World Bank. 2006. *Development and the Next Generation: world development report 2007*. Washington, DC: World Bank.

World Health Organization. 2015. *Trends in Maternal Mortality: 1990 to 2015*. Geneva: World Health Organization.

Ya'u, Y. Z. 2000. 'The youth, economic crisis and identity transformation: the case of the *yandaba* in Kano' in A. Jega (ed.), *Identity Transformation and Identity Politics under Structural Adjustment in Nigeria*. Uppsala: Nordiska Afrikainstitutet, in collaboration with The Centre for Research and Documentation, Kano, pp. 161–80.

Yahya, M. 2006. 'Polio vaccines: "no thank you!" Barriers to polio eradication in northern Nigeria', *African Affairs* 106 (423): 185–204.

Young, L. and Barrett, H. 2001. 'Adapting visual methods: action research with Kampala street children', *Area* 33 (2): 141–52.

Yusha'u, M. A., Tsafe, A. K., Babangida, S. I. and Lawal, N. I. 2013. 'Problems and prospects of integrated almajiri education in Northern Nigeria', *Scientific Journal of Pure and Applied Sciences* 2 (3): 125–34.

NEWSPAPER ARTICLES

'A nation of 167m in a world of 7bn'. 2011. Editorial. *Leadership*, 10 November.

'Almajiri integrated model school: where pupils want to be doctors, engineers'. 2013. *This Day*, 16 November.

'Almajiris: towards creating brighter future for the street kids'. 2012. *This Day*, 22 April.

'Another 1,000 divorcees, widows up for wedding in Kano'. 2013. *Premium Times*, 23 May.

'FG missteps on almajiri school scheme'. 2012. *The Punch*, 23 April.

'Mixing the modern and the traditional. Trying to teach children not to be extremists'. 2014. *The Economist*, 26 July.

'Nigeria's 10mn child beggars'. 2009. *Nigerian Curiosity*, 23 December.

'Plateau govt bans street begging'. 2009. *Vanguard*, 24 August.
'Rehabilitating our almajiris'. 2011. Editorial. *234NEXT*, 22 June.
'Why northerners feel done down'. 2013. *The Economist*, 30 November.

WEBSITES AND BLOGS

Almajiri Education Foundation n.d. 'CONSS, Coalition of NGOs (non-governmental organisations) in Sokoto State'. www.conss.net/almajiri.htm (accessed 3 January 2012).
'Almajiris: Nigeria's ticking time bomb'. n.d. *Nairaland*. www.nairaland.com/nigeria/topic-653197.0.html (accessed 14 January 2012).
Beehner, L. 2007. 'The effects of "youth bulge" on civil conflicts'. The Council on Foreign Relations, 27 April. www.cfr.org/world/effects-youth-bulge-civil-conflicts/p13093 (accessed 25 July 2016).
'Child beggars of Nigeria's Koranic schools'. 2008. *BBC*, 23 December. http://news.bbc.co.uk/1/hi/world/africa/7796109.stm
'Classroom shortages threaten primary education targets'. 2008. *IRIN Africa*. www.irinnews.org/printreport.aspx?reportid=76243 (accessed 5 October 2013).
Comolli, V. 2013. 'The lost boys of Kano'. International Institute for Strategic Studies, 24 April. www.iiss.org/en/iiss%20voices/blogsections/iiss-voices-2013-1e35/april-2013-982b/lost-boys-of-kano-3fe2
Gusau, A. M. n.d. 'Almajiri bill: the masochism of integration'. *Gamji*. www.gamji.com/article8000/NEWS8925.htm (accessed 5 October 2013).
International Telecommunication Union. n.d. 'Statistics'. www.itu.int/en/ITU-D/Statistics/Pages/stat/default.aspx (accessed 29 September 2012).
IOM Displacement Tracking Matrix. http://nigeria.iom.int/dtm (accessed 9 June 2017).
Kano State Government. n.d. 'Kano to revolutionize Almajiri system – Kwankwaso'. Kano State Government. http://kano.gov.ng/new/index.php/12-news/268-almajiri (accessed 17 October 2013).
'Osama baby craze hits Nigeria'. 2002. *BBC*, 3 January. http://news.bbc.co.uk/1/hi/world/africa/1741171.stm
Right to Education. 2015. 'African Committee of Experts on the Rights and Welfare of the Child finds Senegal in violation of right to education in Talibés children case'. www.right-to-education.org/news/african-committee-experts-rights-and-welfare-child-finds-senegal-violation-right-education (accessed 24 June 2017).
Shehu, M. n.d. 'Almajiri bill: the masochism of integration'. *Gamji*. www.gamji.com/article8000/NEWS8955.htm (accessed 4 October 2013).
Tilde, A. U. 2009. 'The future of the almajiri (2)'. *Gamji*. www.gamji.com/tilde/tilde106.htm (accessed 26 September 2012).
Tilde, A. U. n.d. 'The future of the almajiri (3)'. *Gamji*. www.gamji.com/tilde/tilde107.htm (accessed 26 September 2012).
UNAIDS. 2015. 'HIV and AIDS estimates (2015)'. www.unaids.org/en/regionscountries/countries/nigeria/ (accessed 8 July 2017).
UNICEF. 2017. 'On Nigerian Children's Day, UNICEF calls for an end to violence against children and adoption of Child Rights Acts in all states'. UNICEF. www.unicef.org/nigeria/media_11542.html

United Nations Office for the Coordination of Humanitarian Affairs (UNOCHA). www.unocha.org/nigeria (accessed 9 June 2017).

Usman, Z. 2011. 'Debenhams' adverts signs in Hausa: worth celebrating or shameful?' *Zainab's Musings*. http://zainabusman.wordpress.com/2012/05/12/debenhams-adverts-signs-in-hausa-worth-celebrating-or-shameful/ (accessed 25 October 2012).

World Bank. n.d. 'Fertility rate, total (births per woman)'. http://data.worldbank.org/indicator/SP.DYN.TFRT.IN?view=map&year_high_desc=true (accessed 28 June 2017).

World Factbook. n.d. Central Intelligence Agency. www.cia.gov/library/publications/the-world-factbook/geos/ni.html (accessed 27 September 2012).

Index

Titles in the series